MW01633111

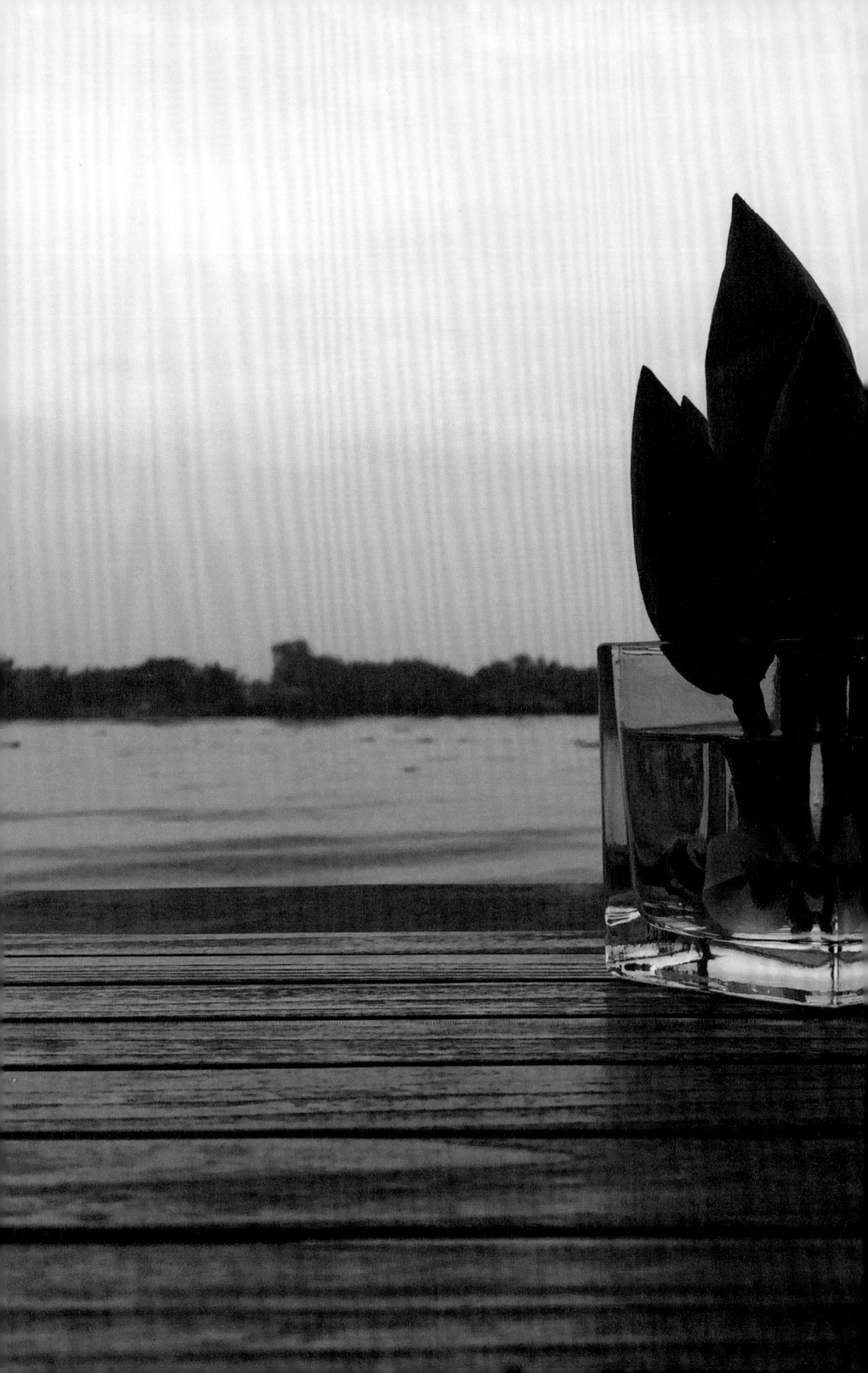

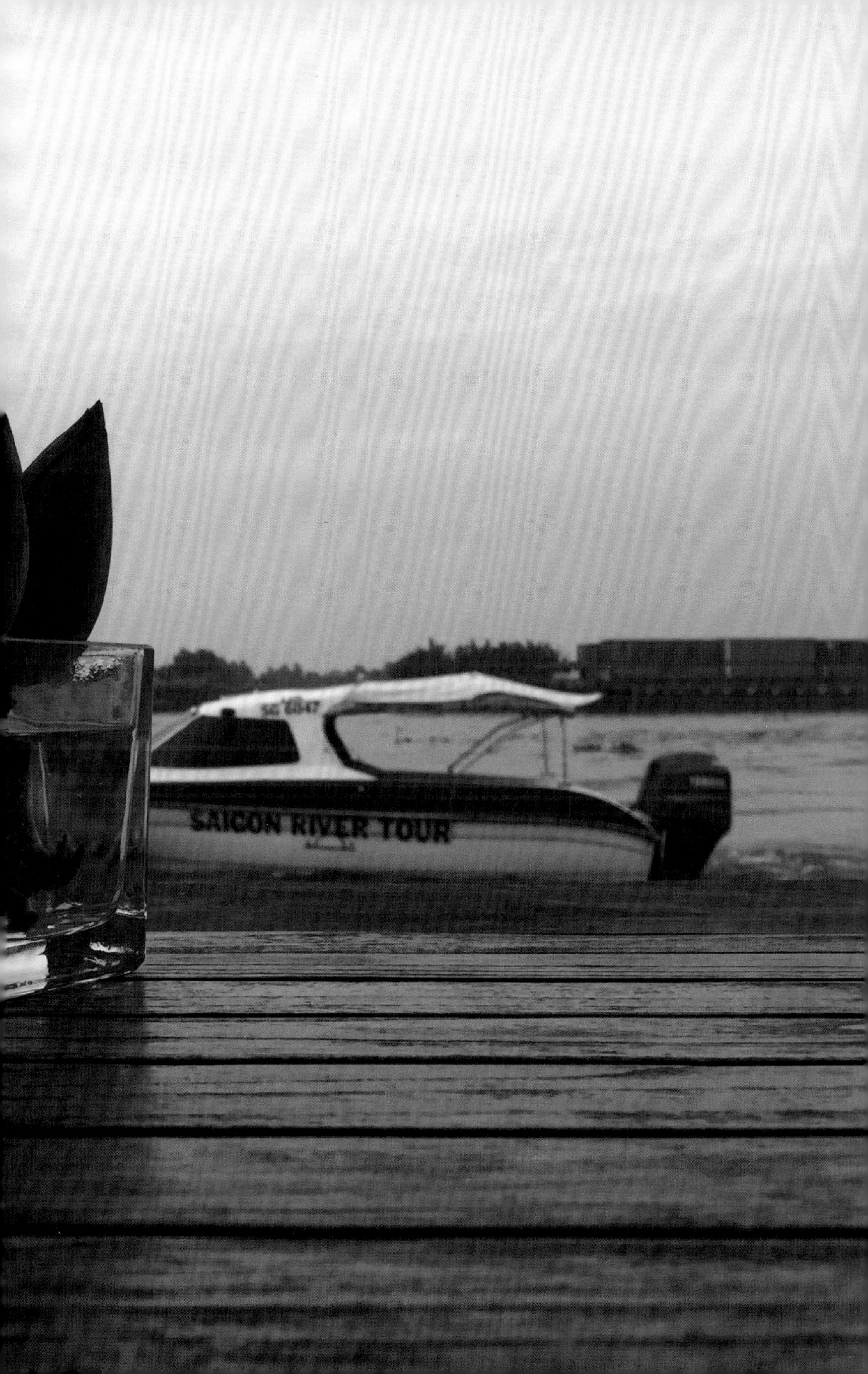
SAIGON RIVER TOUR

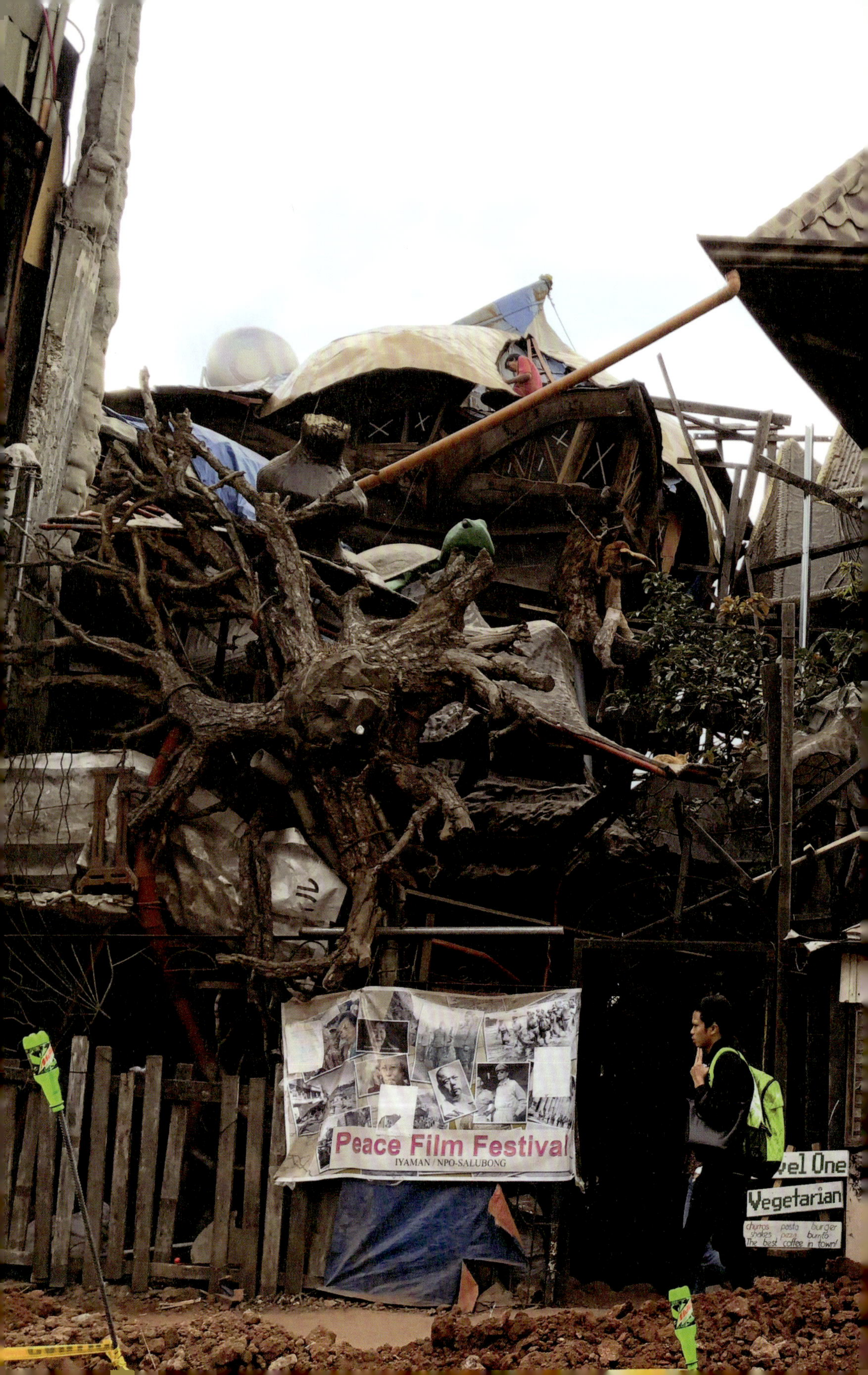
Peace Film Festival
IYAMAN / NPO-SALUBONG
vel One
Vegetarian
churros pasta burger
shakes pizza burrito
The best coffee in town!

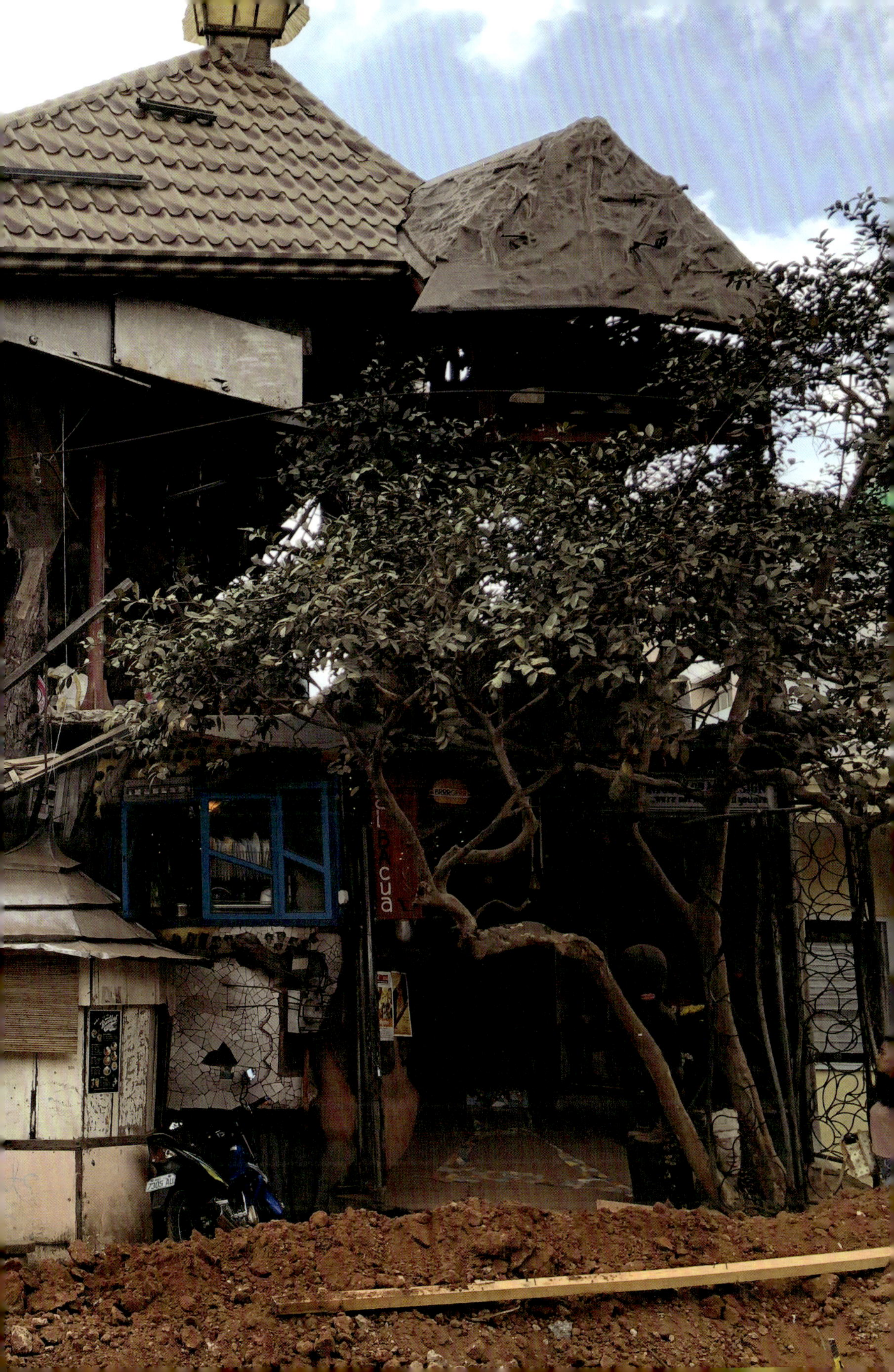

SHARJAH BIENNIAL 14

J o u r n e y B e y o n d t h
e A r r o w J o u r n e y B e
y o n d t h e A r r o w J o u
r n e y B e y o n d t h e A r
r o w J o u r n e y B e y o n
d t h e A r r o w J o u r n e
y B e y o n d t h e A r r o w
J o u r n e y B e y o n d t h
e A r r o w J o u r n e y B e
y o n d t h e A r r o w J o u
r n e y B e y o n d t h e A r
r o w J o u r n e y B e y o n
d t h e A r r o w J o u r n e

Edited by Zoe Butt

Journey Beyond the Arrow

Sharjah Biennial 14: Leaving the Echo Chamber
Curated By Zoe Butt, Omar Kholeif and Claire Tancons

Published by:

Sharjah Art Foundation
PO Box 19989, Sharjah
United Arab Emirates
www.sharjahart.org

DelMonico Books,
an imprint of Prestel,
a member of Verlagsgruppe
Random House GmbH

Prestel Verlag
Neumarkter Strasse 28
81673 Munich

Prestel Publishing Ltd.
14-17 Wells Street
London W1T 3PD

Prestel Publishing
900 Broadway, Suite 603
New York, NY 10003

www.prestel.com

ISBN 978-9948-38-744-2
(Sharjah Art Foundation)

ISBN 978-3-7913-5850-5
(Prestel)

Library of Congress Control Number: 2019931319

This book was published for
Sharjah Biennial 14: Leaving the Echo Chamber
March 7–June 10, 2019

Sharjah Art Foundation,
President and Director
Hoor Al Qasimi

Editor
Zoe Butt

Assistant Editor
Lee Weng Choy

Publication Coordinators
Reem Shadid
Saira Ansari

Copy editor
Eti Bonn-Muller

Designer
Kemistry Design

Printed in the
United Arab Emirates

Sharjah Art Foundation Staff and Sharjah Biennial 14
. Sheikha Hoor Al Qasimi, Director and President
. Reem Shadid, Deputy Director

Curatorial and Programmes
. Momen Al Ajouz
. Mariam Al Askari
. Anahita Harding
. Carmen Hassan
. Ryan Inouye
. Zeina Al Kattan
. Amal Al Khaja
. Noora Al Mualla
. May Alqaydi
. Ambika Rajgopal
. Mahmoud El-Safadi
. Raneem Turjman
. Ayman Zedani
. Mohammad Asadullah (Intern)
. Amy-Clare McCarthy (Intern)

Exhibition Design and Production
. Eng. Hassan Ali Mahmood
. Mona El Mousfy
. Eng. Younus Suliman
. Aia Azad
. Mona Al Chaar
. Maria Kalaiji
. Tigran Kostandyan
. Hinjal Kumar
. Farah Al Qedra
. Lana El Samman
. Sirine El Samman (Intern)

Logistics
. Mohammed Fawwaz
. Mahmoud Al Jaddah
. Syed Kashif Syed Sibt
. Ali Tawfiq

Publications and Research
. Saira Ansari
. Sheherbano Iqbal
. Areej Kaoud
. Wasan Yousif

Education
. Sana Haroon Abdulmajeed
. Madiha Adel
. Hessa Al Ajmani
. Tahani Y K AlAshqar
. Jinan Coulter
. Shefa Al Hammadi
. Maryam Ali AlHammadi
. Mouza Al Hamrani
. Heba Hosny
. Hussein Al Khayyat
. Sherine Mohammed
. Hamad Ghanim Mughawer
. Manal Al Muttawa
. Nasir Ahmed Nasrallah
. Arwa Nasreldin
. Mahmood Bin Shamsan

Marketing and Communication
. Yusra Abdelhakam
. Ragaa Amin
. Huda Amini
. Lojain Ismail

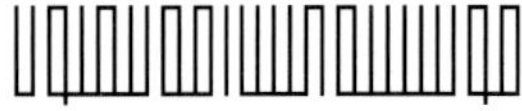

SHARJAH ART FOUNDATION

. Nawale Lacroix
. Naveed Majeed
. Ali Mrad
. Alyazeyah Al Reyaysa
. Carine Rizk
. Tracy Jad Sawan
. Tuba Tortob

Design, Image and Archives
. Hind Al Ali
. Alia Al Amri
. Dima Bittard
. Mohammed Al Hmadi
. Shanavas Jamaluddin
. Ghaya Bin Mesmar
. Unnikrishnan Suresh
. Louie Aloc De la Torre
. Magdi Emad (Intern)
. Rahaf Jumran (Intern)

Editing and Translation
. Ismail AlRifaie
. Ziad Abdullah
. Kathleen Butti
. Abdullah Hussein
. Sezar Ibrahem

International Programmes and Development
. Judith Greer
. Nawar Al Qassimi
. Alaeldin Ahmed
. Ali Al Hadidi
. Eshtar Hussain
. Ruqaia Ibrahim
. Sara Imad Eldin
. Maryam AlQassimi
. Suraya El Amin

IT
. Mahesh Kumar
. Nitin Alden Mathias
. Noaf Yousif

Finance and Administration
. Fatma Al Jasmi
. Dalia Al Shehhi
. Abdulhamed Abdulghfor
. Humam Ahmad
. Mansour Ahmed
. Amina Al Ali
. Amjeth Khan Muhamed Ali
. Huda Al Ali
. Khaula Al Ameri
. Sara AlBloushi
. Maitha Buti Bin Ashoor
. Babylyn Tacos Deliva
. Mark Gillbert
. Aisha Al Hammadi
. Amal Al Hammadi
. Nouria Al Hammadi
. Aisha Al Hashmi
. Alyaa Al Hosani
. Sufiyan Iqbal
. Saifuddin Klzhakkedath
. Ann Tharwat Milad
. Alyazyah Ahmed Al Raeesi
. Nafeesa Umma
. Abdul Rahman Al Yafeai

Hospitality
. Najeeba Aslam
. Abdelhamid Ayesh Abo Ebeiid
. Shaima Hussain (Intern)

Visitor Services
. Ali Ahmad
. Ibrahim Ahmed
. Ahmed Ali
. Saeed Ali
. Ayoub Arbaoui
. Hajer Boulahbel
. Zahra Al Hassan
. Mahmoud Hatem
. Ahmed Hussain
. Hassan Madhlom
. Khalid Mohammed
. Abdul Haseeb Moidunni
. Abdullah Al Shamsi
. Saleh Al Soufi
. Khalifa Sultan
. Omar Al Obaidly
. Faisal Ali (Intern)
. Fatima Amjath (Intern)
. Abderrahmane Ammar (Intern)
. Yousif Hussein (Intern)
. Mahmoud Kandeel (Intern)
. Mustafa Kandeel (Intern)

Installation Technicians
. Salil AbdulSalam
. Suhaib Ali Abdul Shakoor
. Masroof Ahmed
. Habib Akhtar
. Javed Ali
. Hamed Allah
. Mark Anthony
. Mohamed Atif
. Minhad Azeem
. Hussain Baloch
. Sameer Chalil
. Sameer Cuto
. Ali Suliman Darweesh
. Hassan Darwish
. Sunil Devasia
. Mahesh Dharmmarjan
. Muhammad Farooq
. Muhammed Fazal
. Abdul Ghaffar
. Mohamed Ghalib
. Ameen Ul Haq
. Irfan Iqbal
. Syed Jalaluddin
. Arshad Khalil
. Abid Amir Khan
. Asad Ullah Khan
. Atlas Amir Dawar Khan
. Ayoub Khan
. Ibrahim Khan
. Mohamed Khan Mira Khan
. Muslim Khan
. Nadeem Khan
. Savdar Khan
. Wasseem Khan
. Sudheersha Mohamed Khani
. Mustafa Kinagat
. Shabeer Kizhakkedath
. Noufal Koya
. Shrinidhi Madival
. Sunil Mathew
. AbdulRahman Mavella
. Satheesh Mundeerath
. Aswani Kummar Raveendran Nair
. Andre Perez
. Tahir Pervez
. Shihabudheen Poonthala
. Shuaib Poonthala
. Joy Pulikkottil
. Fazel Rahman
. Raqib Said
. Moidu Koroth Saidalu
. Alaa Sami
. Khalid Sami
. Manu Scaria
. Abdul Khaliq Shan
. Aboobacker Siddeque
. Sreerenj Sudhakaran
. Shajahan Kannokaran Sulaiman
. Zathbit Ullah Welayat Ullah

Van Cleef & Arpels

VCA

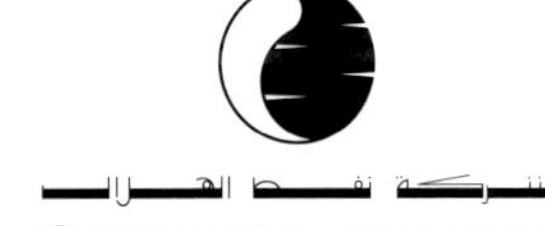

Contents

J o u r n e y B e y o n d t h

e A r r o w J o u r n e y B e

y o n d t h e A r r o w J o u

r n e y B e y o n d t h e A r

r o w J o u r n e y B e y o n

d t h e A r r o w J o u r n e

y B e y o n d t h e A r r o w

J o u r n e y B e y o n d t h

e A r r o w J o u r n e y B e

y o n d t h e A r r o w J o u

r n e y B e y o n d t h e A r

r o w J o u r n e y B e y o n

d t h e A r r o w J o u r n e

y B e y o n d t h e A r r o w

J o u r n e y B e y o n d t h

e A r r o w J o u r n e y B e

y o n d t h e A r r o w J o u

r n e y B e y o n d t h e A r

r o w J o u r n e y B e y o n

d t h e A r r o w J o u r n e

y B e y o n d t h e A r r o w

J o u r n e y B e y o n d t h

e A r r o w F o r e w o r d J

o u r n e y B e y o n d t h e

A r r o w J o u r n e y B e y

o n d t h e A r r o w J o u r

n e y B e y o n d t h e A r r

o w J o u r n e y B e y o n d

t h e A r r o w J o u r n e y

B e y o n d t h e A r r o w J

Extending Sharjah Biennial's engagement with artists from different countries and generations, Sharjah Biennial 14: *Leaving the Echo Chamber* continues its history of support for art and culture in the region and beyond. The fourteenth edition of the biennial, established in 1993, provides an international platform for artists to present work that engages with their local environments but also resonates more broadly with a global audience.

Invited for their substantial work and research, curators Zoe Butt, Omar Kholeif and Claire Tancons collectively conceived of 'leaving the echo chamber' as the framework for Sharjah Biennial 14. In the context of the biennial, the 'echo chamber' encompasses the noise of mainstream media coverage, conspiracy theories, sensationalised storytelling and social media feeds that reverberates within closed systems and networks that prevent people from engaging with each other in complex ways. Although the biennial does not propose answers or solutions, it does offer opportunities to closely examine how stories are told and from what perspectives they are communicated and historicised. In distinct and interrelated platforms, each curator endeavours to amplify the development of new and ongoing ideas through artistic and cultural production that moves beyond existing models of thought and relationships.

Together, the three platforms encourage thinking about interconnectedness across time, culture and geography as new horizons of thought and experience emerge. In *Journey Beyond the Arrow*, Butt takes a long look at the movement of humanity and the tools that have enabled its survival. Artists grapple with practices that have facilitated the transference of knowledge across land and sea as well as the profound intergenerational impact of colonialism, economic exploitation and ideology, which requires nuanced insight and response. Kholeif's *Making New Time* examines today's experience of accelerating time in the midst of seismic technological, social and political change. Artists in this platform encourage consideration of how both new technology and histories of material culture augment the limits of perception and belief that inevitably shape an understanding of reality. Tancons' *Look for Me All Around You* underscores displacement as a foundational experience of modernity, drawing on pan-African thinker and activist Marcus Mosiah Garvey Jr's (1887–1940) call to 'Look for me in the whirlwind or a storm, look for me all around you...' (1925). She has assembled a group of artists who predominantly work in performance to acknowledge the presence of people and histories that often only register in fleeting or immaterial forms.

At March Meeting 2019, during the opening week of the biennial, three days of talks, readings and performances by local, regional and international speakers expand on the dynamic presentations of the more than 80 artists in the biennial. The invited speakers broaden the dialogue beyond the biennial by mobilising related discussions in art, architecture, education, philosophy and more. In so doing, Butt, Kholeif and Tancons prompt a reassessment of our moment and contribute to the development of Sharjah as an important meeting place for artists and the public.

J o u r n e y B e y o n d t h
e A r r o w J o u r n e y B e
y o n d t h e A r r o w J o u
r n e y B e y o n d t h e A r
r o w J o u r n e y B e y o n
d t h e A r r o w J o u r n e
y B e y o n d t h e A r r o w
J o u r n e y B e y o n d t h
e A r r o w J o u r n e y B e
y o n d t h e A r r o w J o u
r n e y B e y o n d t h e A r
r o w J o u r n e y B e y o n
d t h e A r r o w J o u r n e
y B e y o n d t h e A r r o w
J o u r n e y B e y o n d t h

e A r r o w J o u r n e y B e

y o n d t h e A r r o w J o u

r n e y B e y o n d t h e A r

r o w J o u r n e y B e y o n

d t h e A r r o w J o u r n e

y B e y o n d t h e A r r o w

J o u r n e y A c k n o w l e

d g e m e n t s B e y o n d t

h e A r r o w J o u r n e y B

e y o n d t h e A r r o w J o

u r n e y B e y o n d t h e A

r r o w J o u r n e y B e y o

n d t h e A r r o w J o u r n

e y B e y o n d t h e A r r o

w J o u r n e y B e y o n d t

The seed of *Journey Beyond the Arrow* begins in 2013 with N'Gone Fall generously introducing me to Sylvaine Diop in Dakar, Senegal. On the eve of my arrival I met Sylviane's brother, Christian, who shared his experiences as a French-Senegalese soldier posted to Vietnam and Cambodia in the 1970s. His eyewitness accounts of the fall of Saigon and the evacuation of Phnom Penh, stories not shared (or known) in my Saigon community today, made me realise how much work there is to do in deepening knowledge of colonial experience—across its burdened 'subjects'. The growth of this seed appeared with my participation in an International Institute of Asian Studies conference in Accra, Ghana in 2015 titled 'Africa-Asia: A New Axis of Knowledge'. While in Ghana, I visited El Mina Fort with Françoise Vergès, and she detailed the atrocities of slavery and colonial shame within its bounds. I am forever grateful to her for also taking me to the Java Museum during that same trip, which revealed to me why Indonesian *batik* and *wayang* have a presence in Ghana (Dutch colonial interests). These stories spurred the introductory text to this catalogue, a tome whose design is inspired by the artistic practice of Shubigi Rao, particularly her self-published 'PULP' series of books with their evocative excavation of knowledge demolished, burnt, fragmented, erased, tortured and made invisible. Their colophons and citations are a treasure trove for the adventure traveller seeking a different kind of bibliographic memory.

Journey Beyond the Arrow gives visuality to thinking that has been in process—consciously and subconsciously, mostly out of public eye and with trusted networks—for much longer than the two-year biennial research period. Thus these acknowledgements deserve much more mention than can be permitted here—my thanks to the countless beyond the scope of this page. A nod and hug must go towards San Art and all the hard work and laughs in realising *Conscious Realities* (2013–2016), a project that arguably gave ground as a 'think-tank' towards my co-curation of SB14.

For the exhibition Sharjah Biennial 14: *Leaving the Echo Chamber – Journey Beyond the Arrow*, and this associated catalogue, I must thank the steadfast ear, mind and strategies of Lee Weng Choy, who listened to me and edited my work, always without much prior notice; Rushdi Anwar for his artistic rigour, humour, patience and caressed guidance of my doubts and questions; Suhanya Raffel, who was the first to counsel me about my proposal and give me confidence that what I was seeing and feeling was critical and worthy and needed; my family for their proud understanding of my absence; and particular dear friends and colleagues who went to great lengths to share their knowledge, networks, expertise and support in the navigating of the necessary artistic production: Agung Hujatnikajennong, Sharmini Periera, Merv Espina, Gridthiya Gaeweewong, Roger Nelson, Erin Gleeson, Ben Valentine, Joselina Cruz, David Teh, N'Gone Fall, Kate Fowle, Pauline J. Yao, Maud Page, Koyo Kouoh, Pooja Sood, Reha Sodhi, Lu Jie, Joshua Lim, Youdon Chazotsang, Lena Bui and Long (Bill) Nguyen.

This entire endeavour would not have been possible for me to mentally and emotionally complete without the commitment and understanding of Thuy Nguyen, Founder and Director, and all the staff of The Factory Contemporary Arts Centre in Ho Chi Minh City (where I remain Artistic Director). I thank them all from the bottom of my heart for enduring my necessary comings and goings.

To be able to make visual the conversations in my head, conversations I never dreamt I could make happen—that gratitude goes firstly to Sheikha Hoor Al Qasimi for believing in me (without a mandatory proposal!) and to Reem Shadid for her trust. Both these leading minds of the Sharjah Art Foundation are what I have admired from afar, and I feel utterly blessed to have had the chance to work with and alongside their staff, which, to me, are unrivalled.

Finally (and most critically!), to the artists and writers. My work (life) sings because of you. I am eternally grateful for your intellect, your commitment to your work, but most of all, your friendship. I have learnt so much.

Cảm ơn bạn rất nhiều

J o u r n e y B e y o n d t h
e A r r o w J o u r n e y B e
y o n d t h e A r r o w J o u
r n e y B e y o n d t h e A r
r o w J o u r n e y B e y o n
d t h e A r r o w J o u r n e
y B e y o n d t h e A r r o w
J o u r n e y B e y o n d t h
e A r r o w J o u r n e y B e
y o n d t h e A r r o w J o u
r n e y B e y o n d t h e A r
r o w J o u r n e y B e y o n
d t h e A r r o w J o u r n e
y B e y o n d t h e A r r o w
J o u r n e y B e y o n d t h

e A r r o w J o u r n e y B e
y o n d t h e A r r o w J o u
r n e y B e y o n d t h e A r
r o w J o u r n e y B e y o n
d t h e A r r o w J o u r n e
y B e y o n d t h e A r r o w
J o u r n e y B e y o n d t h
e A r r o w J o u r n e y B e
y o n d t h e A r r o w J o u
r n e y B e y o n d t h e A r
r o w J o u r n e y B e y o n
d t h e A r r o w J o u r n e
y B e y o n d t h e A r r o w
J o u r n e y B e y o n d t h
e J o u r n e y A r r o w B e

The journey is a lonely one. It does not end on the top of the mountain. Those who, by relentless effort and the guidance of the stars (the cosmos or their ancestors), eventually reach the peak and are obliged to return to their countrymen with a map of the terrain. That is where the plight of a messenger begins. Lack of appreciation of the prophets by their peers is written all over history. It is so much easier to sleep or run with the pack. Unaffected by the inertia of crowds, the calling for the seers among artists endures. Calling for what? To fan the fire of awareness, to document and witness their time, to keep the ember of conscience burning' <Katrin de Guia. 'Kapwa: The Self In the Other: Worldviews and Lifestyles of Filipino Culture-Bearers', Anvil Publishing, Pasig City, The Phillippines, 2005, pg. 82>

Two particular experiences have been in constant recall in this *Journey Beyond the Arrow*. The first took place in 2013. I had just arrived into late-afternoon Dakar, Senegal, having travelled nearly forty-eight hours in economy mode from Ho Chi Minh City, Vietnam. A stooped and wiry man greeted me with his 'taxi', its boot held up by a wooden trunk, the base of his car splintered, revealing the bare earth beneath. He cajoled the engine, and we teetered around the coastline; my fears almost confirmed when the car abruptly jerked to a stop, steam rising from its bonnet. I looked up to my right: there, in the magnificent coastline jutting out in front of me, loomed an utterly gigantic sculpture, the *Monument to the African Renaissance* (2010), built by Mansudae Overseas Projects from Pyongyang, North Korea. Here was a most uncanny introduction to West Africa, via another member of the communist bloc, reminding me of my part of the world. Later that evening, I shared a meal with a French-Senegalese soldier who related his eye-witness account of the fall of Saigon, and when Pol Pot ordered the evacuation of Phnom Penh. Time and space felt collapsed. My own context/geography from so far unexpectedly echoing so near...

To read more about communities from Vietnam in Senegal see the work of Tuan Andrew Nguyen p.g. 94

Two years later, and I was in Elmina Fort, off the coast of Accra, Ghana. My conscience and heart were in a violent state of helplessness, as I felt at once repulsed and incredulous about the conditions suffered by the thousands who had been 'processed' as slaves in this Dutch-created hell. As I walked through the 'church' on the central grounds of this once-prison, I felt scornful of the remnants of colonialism attempting to make a reconciliatory gesture to their previous 'subjects' by turning this building into a museum. I exited the fort and walked down the main street of this fishing village known as Elmina, past the Posuban shrines,[1] only to find the Java Museum, with its batiks and *wayang kulit*, or shadow puppetry, amongst the mildewing photographs of a Ghanaian prince and his Indonesian wives. Here the Belanda Hitam, or 'Black Dutchmen', are given memorial, the story of their trade as trophies to the Dutch East Indies recorded in this little-

To read more about the Belanda Hitam in Indonesia, see the project of Jompet Kuswidananto, pg. 112

1 Posuban shrines are a part of Akan culture (centred in today's southern Ghana); the Asafo are their warriors.

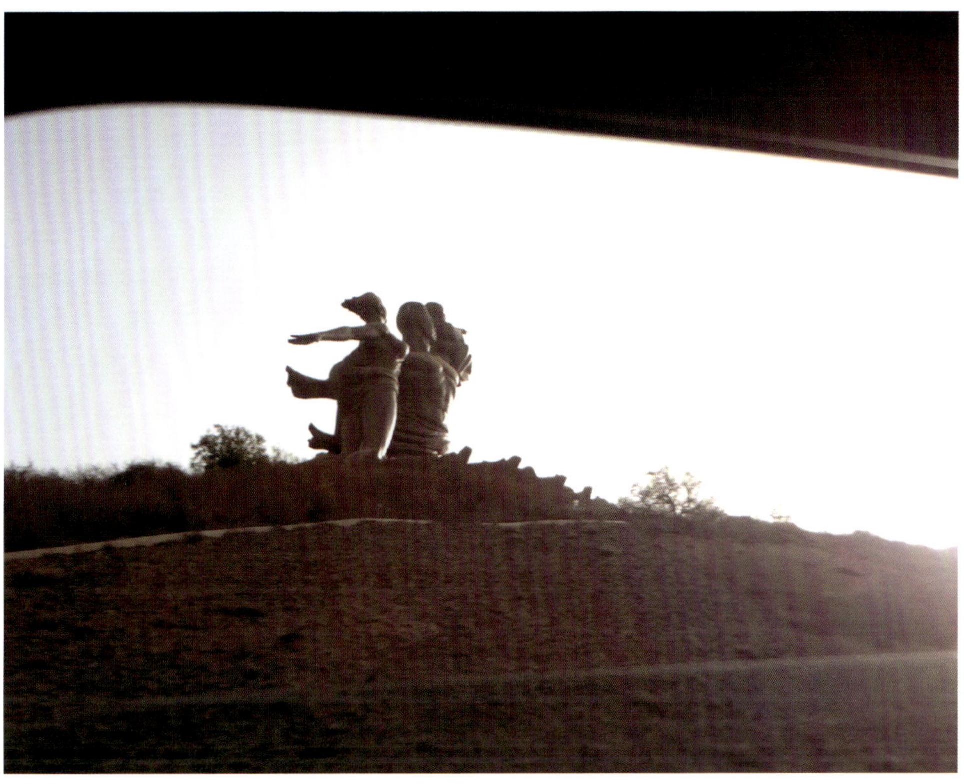

African Renaissance Monument, Dakar, Senegal

known house on a hill. Again, time and space felt collapsed – my context/geography unexpectedly echoing...but what, exactly, is *my* context/geography?

These experiences have been indelibly imprinted upon me. Indeed, they have seeded a continuing intrigue for the wondrous and calamitous length, breadth and depth of human movement across this globe; for the myriad of human consciousness that *continues* to move across land and sea in voluntary and involuntary patterns of discovery, conquest, witness and exile. In these particular recollections, I realise how my own understandings of Africa's connections to South East Asia have been grossly limited to an arrow of historicity, politically determined as 'colonialism'.

Yet the human journey surrounding such history – its cause and effects; its feedback, its 'echo' – are little known in the memory

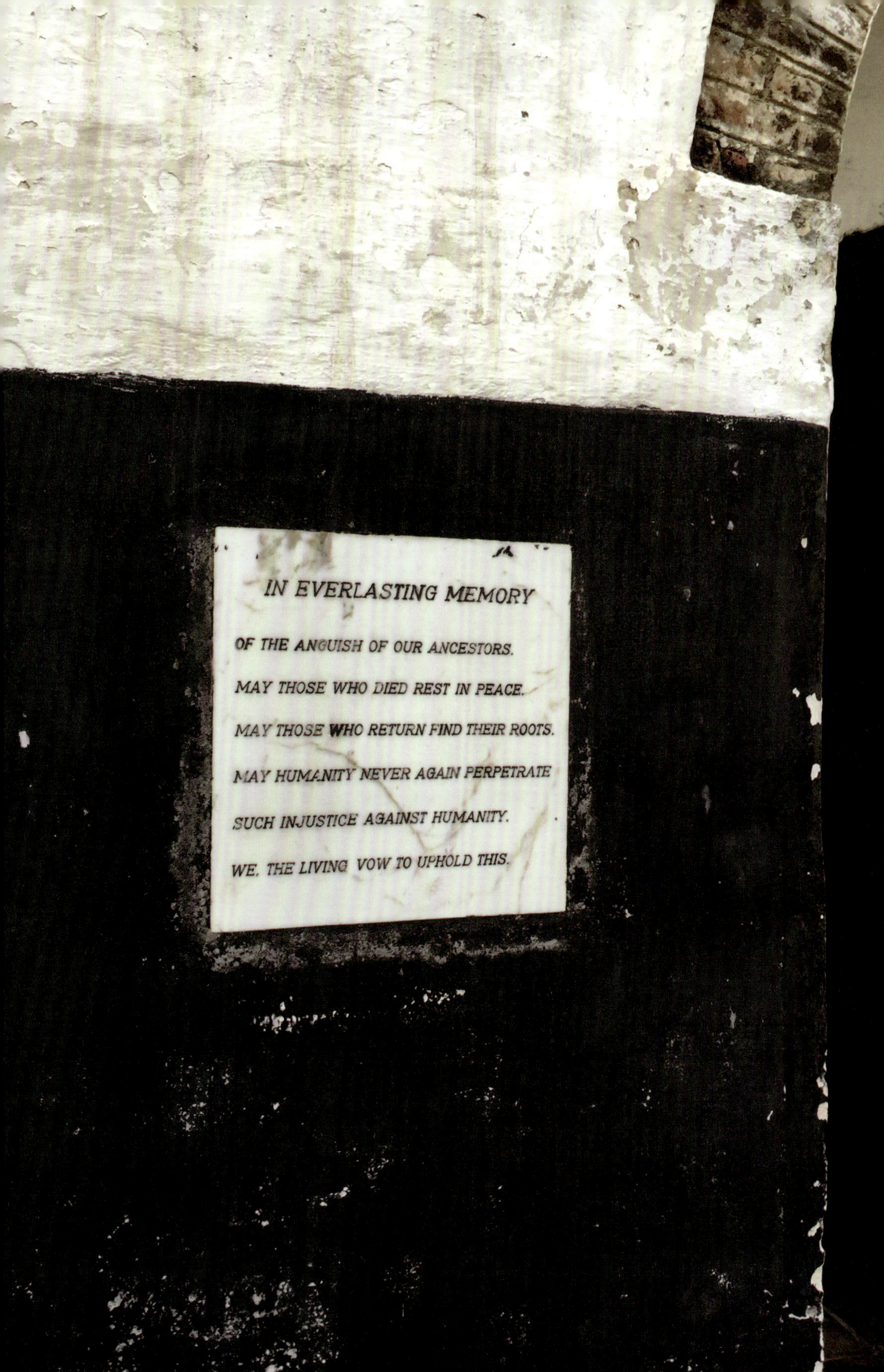
IN EVERLASTING MEMORY
OF THE ANGUISH OF OUR ANCESTORS.
MAY THOSE WHO DIED REST IN PEACE.
MAY THOSE WHO RETURN FIND THEIR ROOTS.
MAY HUMANITY NEVER AGAIN PERPETRATE
SUCH INJUSTICE AGAINST HUMANITY.
WE, THE LIVING VOW TO UPHOLD THIS.

of my own lived community. Today, the collective recall of the past clamours for sense; instead, we have textbooks of little historical truth, online archives that have been questionably fabricated, and governmentally surveilled bureaucracies that oversee academic systems of research and rigour, which struggles to keep up with the pace of change surrounding their assumed 'D'isciplines'. With this struggle for a long-term collective conscience, it is thus, perhaps, no wonder that our 'experience economy' is driven by a focus on the arrival – the destination. Today, our desires seek satiation by whatever means necessary, an arrow of time oblivious to its context of disastrous entropy (think: environmental degradation due to our reliance on fossil fuels; rising suicide rates as a consequence of online social alienation; water shortages and air pollution resulting from overconsumption, to name but a few).

The above-mentioned experiences – motivated by the curatorial curiosity to research and witness, but a labour I make no conceit as immune from the tinge of touristic delight – doubly reiterate for me that, despite the advantages of flight and virtuality in our globalising world, the limits of geography *inherently* matter, that technology can *exacerbate* what is desired and familiar, that history will *never* be History. Crucially, such encounters recall my own context/geography of a 'South East Asia', in addition to my own diasporic errantry[2] as a Hong Kong/British Australian – reminding me of the utter privilege of being able to *choose* the community I call 'home', and reminding me to remember my place as 'invited guest' in a culture and community for which I feel awe, respect and responsibility.

My personal *Journey Beyond the Arrow*, over nearly the past two decades, has involved investigating the 'toolkits' of artists. I have thus examined the historical context of the bow (the artistic practice) that lets fly the arrow of the human echo – an echo rife with the diversity of human production in all its *relation* to language, memory, belief, ritual and cultural practice. Through sites of artistic production, I have learned

Elmina Fort, Elmina, Senegal

Verb, noun, subject, object, are not fixed in their places because, in the words of Glissant, 'in Relation every subject is an object and every object is a subject' (Translator notes by Betsy Wing, for Edouard Glissant 'Poetics of Relation', pg. xx

2 'Errance for Glissant, while not aimed like an arrow's trajectory, nor circular and repetitive like the nomad's, is not idle roaming, but includes a sense of sacred motivation'. (Translator's notes by Betsy Wing for Édouard Glissant. Edouard Glissant, *Poetics of Relation* [Michigan: University of Michigan Press, 2010], 211.)

from the grass roots, conscionable actions of artists living predominantly in zones of political poverty. Their imaginative retelling of humanity (via their artworks, their voices, their actions) has opened my mind to the restrictions placed on the capacity and visibility of our echo due to the chamber in which it predominantly resides. For this chamber – within a global-political, economically intertwined, yet governmentally divisive framework – is often culturally stymied by traditional customs, insidiously lined with authoritarianism, popularly motivated by a culture of 'like' and blindly participating in an algorithmic world that determines quantity as meaning.

Inside such a chamber – which bolsters the notion of 'profit' with few ethical parameters for Planet Earth's diverse animate and inanimate forms; which is predicated on a human fear of mortality and the inability to trust and be held accountable; which is thus obsessed with short-term gain – it is sadly predictable that the luminosity of human production and its movement across this Earth has been siphoned or overlooked, rationalised or deleted, redefined and controlled, and, ultimately, 'archived' by a 'colonial matrix of power'.[3] This continued policing of a 'sanitised history' in the twenty-first century is what motivates and complicates the artistic endeavours of *Journey Beyond the Arrow*. The artists participating in the exhibition examine the deeper historical cause and effect of the intermingling of official and unofficial histories, while focusing predominantly on our globalising Souths.[4]

What follows is a curatorial honouring, a narration of the relationships between the artworks in this exhibition that have shaped this journey. (It is not lost on me that, in narrating, I am thus naming and categorising – *again*; although here, I make no claim of authority in subject or form.) This detailing is in

Modernization, mostly along capitalist lines, became the universalist creed that glorified the autonomous rights-bearing individual and hailed his rational choice-making capacity as freedom. Economic growth was posited as the end-all of political life and the chief marker of progress worldwide, not to mention the gateway to happiness. Communism was totalitarian. Ergo its ideological opponent, American liberalism, represented freedom, which in turn was best advanced by moneymaking.... One evitable result of cutting the 'cord of consciousness' linking the past to the present was sanitized history. The centuries of civil war, imperial conquest, genocide and slavery in Europe and America were downplayed in accounts that showed how the Atlantic West privileged with reason and individual autonomy made the modern world, and became with its liberal democracies a vision of the superior people everyone else ought to catch up with. (Loc 596. Pankaj Mishra 'Age of Anger: A History of the Present'

3 'Delinking from coloniality [shorthand for the Colonial Matrix of Power] means delinking from the enunciation in which knowledge is fabricated and managed (languages, institutions, actors) to legitimize dispossession and control in all the domains of the instituted (politics, economy, knowledge, racism and sexism, and the ontologisation of *nature*, all of which impinges on land dispossession)'. 'Thinking and Engaging with the Decolonial: A Conversation Between Walter D. Mignolo and Wanda Nanibush', *Afterall*, Vol. 45, Spring/Summer 2018, p. 25.

4 The phrase 'globalising Souths' refers to communities from the southern part of the world and their 'decolonial' desire to create alliances on their own terms, in response to their own needs, whereas 'Global South' is a phrase that replaced 'developing countries' in response to a hierarchy imposed by First World economies. To use 'globalising Souths' is to acknowledge that the once-considered 'developing' worlds are now in a position to initiate and maintain their own levers of strategy and resistance without necessarily relying on a presumed neo-liberal order.

gratitude to the artists represented here, whose exploration of cultural legacy and philosophical connection, across multiple flows of human movement, has fundamentally anchored this on-going *Journey Beyond the Arrow*.

interruptions to pattern – annotations, anecdotes, addendums

In 1511, Malacca was laid siege by the Portuguese. A Malay man by the name of Enrique de Malacca (though he is also known by many other titles) became an indentured servant of Ferdinand Magellan, the Portuguese explorer credited by History as the first to circumnavigate the globe. However, Magellan died from a bamboo arrow wound in Mactan in the Philippines, and it is therefore contested that it was actually Enrique de Malacca – a slave – who was the first to travel around the world. The essay-films and carved wooden dioramas of KIDLAT TAHIMIK metaphorically give wind to the sails of Enrique (and other Goddesses of Winds) as collector of loot. The artist's broader oeuvre unpacks the role of *bahala na*[5] in the social tales of the historical underdog, illustrating how a myriad of contemporary maladies could be empowered by believing in the interconnectivity of *kapwa*.[6] AHMAD FUAD OSMAN is similarly inspired by Enrique, eulogising the journey of this slave (or was he a royal guide?) in the presentation of a memorial as a fictional archive of his life and journey, a critical testament to the Malay Archipelago as a once-cosmopolitan entrepôt – a meeting point between Persia, Arabia, China, Siam and Europe. This criss-crossing of the Indian Ocean wrought much trade, wealth and intermarriage, all somewhat aided by the relationships between members of the Arab World, as 'chronoLOGICalised' in the object-driven mapping of ROSLISHAM (ISE) ISMAIL.

"I'm known by various names, some call me Daeng Malik Silnak, and others called me Nakhoda Ismail, Makiung, Datuk Laut Dalam, Datuk Laut Hitam, Trengganu, Panglima Awang, Henry the Black, Enrique el Negro, Enrique de Cebu, Enrique Maluku and Enrique de Malacca.... I'm a son of the Malay Archipelago" – excerpt from Ahmad Fuad Osman's film 'Imago Mundi'. See pg. 202

5 *Bahala na* ('*bahala*' referring to care and being responsible) is an indigenous Filipino value that places trust and determination in the face of uncertainty. Filipino psychologist Alfredo Lagmay traced 'the roots of this value to a social structure that challenges people to use their inherent abilities to cope with constant change...*"Bahala na"* is a mirror of Filipino people in their process of dealing with nature, [as] opposed to the Western ways which are more like a conquest. *Bahala na* is a kind of accepting the very nature of things'. Katrin de Guia, *Kapwa: The Self in the Other: Worldviews and Lifestyles of Filipino Culture-Bearers* (Pasig City, The Philippines: Anvil Publishing, 2005), 85–86.

6 '*Kapwa* is a Tagalog term widely used when addressing another with the intention of establishing a connection....*Kapwa* at the core of the Filipino personality identifies personhood as an ecology-friendly, systemic orientation. It signals that "I am one with humanity, and I am connected with creation. I experience myself as a part of the world and acknowledge that the life-space on earth is but one for all. As a person, I am willing to integrate myself into this global family"'. Ibid, 8–9.

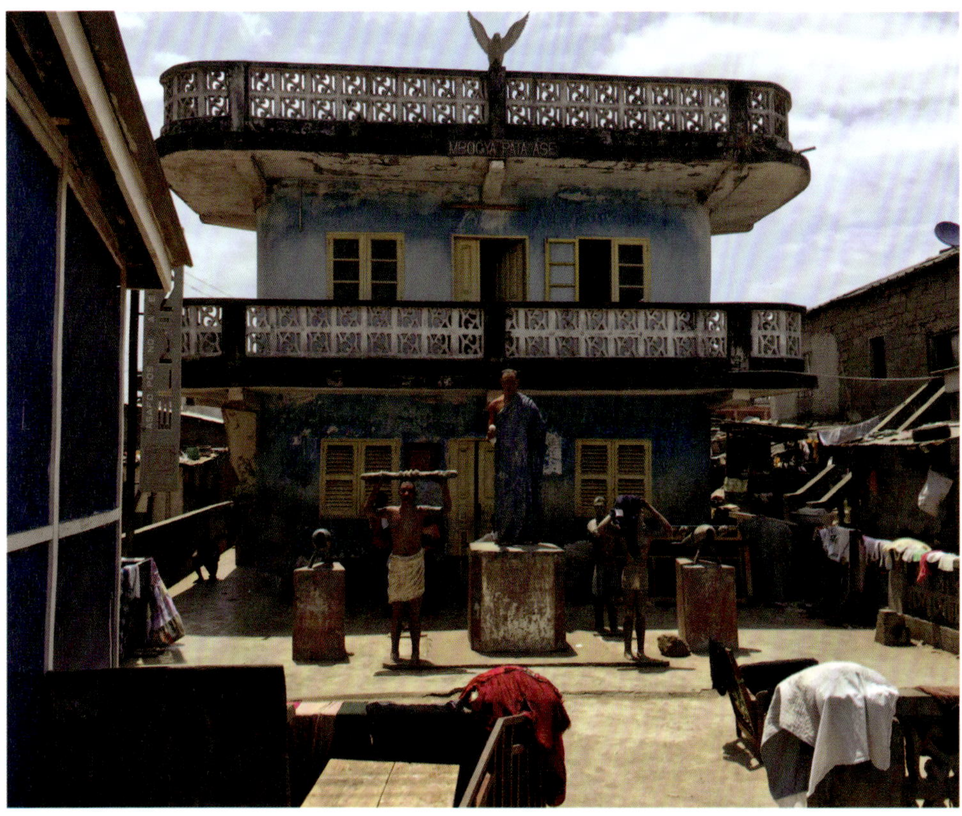

Posuban Shrines, Elmina, Senegal

These seafaring explorations by the Dutch, British, Spanish and French, as well as the Portuguese from Vichy, monopolised the trade customs of a networked commerce in spice, soon shifting rulers' eyes to colonial control of these lands and the transport of their prize (spice) – and thus forever altering the synergy between its peoples. Ho Tzu Nyen recalls, with his project *Critical Dictionary of South East Asia* (2017–ongoing) that this geographical region (historically once referred as the 'Spice Islands') was termed as such in 1941 in *Progress and Welfare in Southeast Asia* by John Sydenham Furnivall, a British-born colonial public servant and writer. Ho chooses to counter the term and its political divisions through the sounds, symbols and shared rituals of these underlying cultures – taking us into a virtual reality where the resonance between these differing communities marks cultural allegiance and synergies of divine authority. *Intriguingly*, despite Western colonial powers eventually dividing and conquering the region, it was the Japanese who were the first to violently claim these communities under one rule during World War II (1939–45).

Phan Thảo Nguyên creates magical historical-fiction for the ageing witnesses of the millions who died from starvation along the Red River Delta in North Vietnam, in part due to occupying Japanese forces following orders to 'uproot rice, plant jute' – each a much-needed resource in the economy for arms. This physical 'planting' of reserves (both human and agricultural) in the fight for control of resources is given an alternate intrigue in the comparative archives of Antariksa. Working with artists (Tsuyoshi Ozawa, Makoto Murata, Surya Wirawan, Saseo Ono), who revive the accounts of the delinquent, the defector, the activist, Antariksa exposes the Japanese artist dispatched as a colonial (propagandist) soldier to Indonesia and their little-known impact on the birthing (and interpretation) of a 'modern' Indonesian art. (The art produced during this era, which ended with the nuclear annihilation of Hiroshima and mass military defeat, remains to this day hidden in shame and is not publicly discussed in Japan). Exploring this inheritance of national shame, Meiro Koizumi filmically records a proposal for ritualising guilt by inviting a group of Japanese youth to repeat incessantly the graphic verbal confessions of a war veteran who lives in silent anguish, struggling with his recall of his role in perpetuating violence in China during the Second Sino-Japanese War (1937–1945).

Today, the militarisation of memory and the effects of indoctrinating obedience insidiously slither with terror and ingenuity as symptoms and divisive strategies in communities still yearning for sovereignty. T. Shanaathanan investigates the methods of state and non-state actors in the generation of identity papers in post–civil war Sri Lanka, where tension between Hindus and Buddhists continues to map human movement, revealing the imitation of power and the prejudiced embodiment of legality as a means of control. Ampannee Satoh provides insight into an unmarked monument as witness to two rebellions of the twentieth century in Pattani,

Southern Thailand, where rumour of ancient ritual violently arose to remind a militarised Buddhist ideology that its 'truth' management[7] could never erase its adherent's Islamic *and* Thai Malay roots. KHADIM ALI takes the phenomenon of militarising the ideology of faith one step further by revealing present-day Afghanistan's landscape of 'charity', where Rustam, the legendary hero of the *Shahnameh*,[8] is a symbol co-opted by the Taliban, whose 'aid' and 'education' of the poor and illiterate serve to normalise (i.e., make beautiful and fashionable) the presence and meaning of violence in everyday life. This pathologisation of the weapon as symbol and essential mechanism of defence enables and, ultimately, empowers a desire for control of progress; such thinking is also analogous to the historical creation of physical trade links (rail, road and sea) across political borders.

China's monumentally ambitious One Belt, One Road initiative is one such project,[9] with arguable precedent in the country's socialist 'gifting' of the TAZARA Railway,[10] which was built between 1968 and 1975 (during the Cultural Revolution), to Zambia. ANAWANA HALOBA journeys across this line, examining the motivation behind, and impact of, China's largesse to a landlocked country desperate to avoid the then-apartheid grip of neighbouring South Africa. In contrast to this little-known 'friendship in solidarity', XU ZHEN cycles the perspective of China forward to its 'capitalism with communist characteristics'. It is 2008, and Xu performatively re-enacts, in a freezing Beijing gallery, the 1994 Pulitzer Prize–winning

7 See Chaiwat Satha-Anand, The silence of the bullet monument: Violence and "Truth" management, Dusun-nyor 1948 (2006) and Kru-Ze, *Critical Asian Studies*, 38: 1, 11–37 (2004).

8 The *Shahnemah*, or the *Book of Kings* is an epic Persian poem written by Ferdowsi (ca. 977–1010 CE). This folktale chronicles the period from the beginnings of the world to the Islamic conquest of Persia. Rustam is this tale's most celebrated hero and the mightiest of its warriors; he is known for his strength, bravery and loyalty, and for defending the weak against their enemies.

9 'One Belt, One Road', or, officially, 'The Silk Road Economic Belt and the 21st-Century Maritime Silk Road', is a development strategy of the People's Republic of China. Unveiled in 2013, it encompasses cooperation with approximately sixty countries in Asia, Europe, Oceania and East Africa. The Asian Infrastructure Investment Bank and the Silk Road Fund, both Chinese financial institutions, fund this major infrastructure project. See https://www.mckinsey.com/featured-insights/china/chinas-one-belt-one-road-will-it-reshape-global-trade (accessed 19 August 2018).

10 The TAZARA (or Uhuru) Railway links Dar es Salaam in eastern Tanzania with Kapiri Mposhi in Zambia. Funded by the Chinese – at a time when China sought diplomatic support against the United States and the Soviet Union – the railway was jointly built by the governments of Tanzania, Zambia and China. The goal was to free landlocked Zambia from its economic dependence on the white-minority governments of neighbouring Rhodesia and South Africa. The TAZARA Railway remains one of China's largest foreign aid projects. 'It is often argued that Tanzania is a strategically important partner for China given its location as an Indian Ocean gateway to mineral-rich southern Africa'. See Muslim Ullah Khan, 'China-Africa Economic Relations: A Brief Analysis', The Africa Economic Forum, 2015.

photograph of an emaciated Sudanese child being eyed by a hungry vulture. This deliberate indulgence in photographic sensationalism (with a Chinese audience predominantly ignorant of the repercussions of the original photograph, which caused an international outcry and the photographer's eventual suicide) reveals not only Xu's capacity to expose China's social prejudices and historical amnesia, but also the influence of the gendering of history – for it was, indeed, the outcry of women in Beijing's artist community that ultimately resulted in the early closure of this performance.

NEO MUYANGA follows the trail of pioneering South African singer, songwriter and civil rights activist Miriam Makeba, whose popular embrace by the West in the 1960s provided a unique platform from which to voice abhorrence for the rise of apartheid – an opinion deemed politically inflammatory at home. Muyanga rejoices in the activist's exile through song, journeying with her through a celebration of the diversity of an 'Africa' that remembers Makeba as an international icon and a symbol of refuge for those both culturally and spiritually displaced. LISA REIHANA similarly acknowledges the complexity of race relations and womanhood in her historically fictionalised tale of Charlotte Badger, the first Pakeha white woman who not only lived under Maori protection, but also gave birth to Aotearoa's first mixed-race child. Reihana animates Badger's tale of eighteenth-century New Zealand, where Maori women were measured for their value against the procurement of muskets and trade, and disenfranchised from their matriarchal right to inherit land. (Yet it was this indigenous moral principle that arguably fuelled the Electoral Act of 1893, which marked New Zealand as the first self-governing country in the world to give women the right to vote.)

Muyanga's and Reihana's empowering stories of individual diasporic experiences as political embodiments of social agency – a diaspora of undeniable residual colonial consequence – are also collective occurrences that identify not only the exodus of cultural communities, but also those who adopt political alliances. JOMPET KUSWIDANDANTO'S light installation explores the decadent rise (and Dutch celebration) of Keroncong in Indonesia, a folk music of local mixed-blood tradition, popularized at 'Sociëteit Concordia'[11], where guests were ironically racially segregated upon entry (natives, Chinese descent, Indo-African and Indo-Dutch KNIL royal soldiers), their alliances here filmically captured, laced in melodic memory. TUẤN ANDREW NGUYỄN emotionally excavates Dakar and its *tirailleurs Sénégalais* (French Senegalese) soldiers who returned home with their Vietnamese wives, their counter memory to colonial aftermath resting untold in graves whose ghosts command the dreams (and longing) of their descendants.

Such stories of military honour, trophies and traitors may not always figure at the forefront of the textual building of 'new worlds', though the creative trails of music, film and literature remain full of the complexity of 'home' and nostalgia. MARK SALVATUS presents his father's 1970s vintage vinyl records, a culturally eclectic collection built as the Philippine-American War (1899–1902) raged. The artist discovers the 1901 Philippine Constabulary Band (the first non-American band to entertain, in 1909, at the inauguration of an American President) and thus, fascinated by the migratory dispersal of Filipina entertainment, explores Dubai's network of unsung Filipina bar heroes. KAWAYAN DE GUIA's sculptures are transformed spools of film, composed of melted negatives of Filipino drama; this circulation of memory and desire ironically merge as several oil spills, an image of equal lust (and expiry). Such dispersed and reconstructed cultural drama is similarly bootlegged in the myriad photocopy centres of Dubai. Here, romance novellas in Urdu, Hindi, Arabic and Tagalog are carted in and out by migrant workers in their zillion suitcases, which LANTIAN XIE collects, presents and intervenes with (in a Tagalog version) in homage to this extra-national labour force.

11 Sociëteit Concordia was the dance hall, entertainment and social gathering venue for the wealthy in the early 1900s in Bandung. In 1955, this building was also chosen as the site for the Bandung Conference – a critical first step towards the beginning of the Non-Aligned Movement.

under(upper)standing of the world

While I am enamoured by how artists and their toolkits give image to the aforementioned human trajectories – from boats to railways; from performing guilt to photographic sensationalism; from carpets to identity papers; from gongs to muskets; from songs to vinyl records and more – I also find it essential to question how their purpose in the world is determined. Those with the power to use guns, grant identity papers and give permission to sail are often empowered – instrumentalised – by an elite minority whose perspective pervades and controls the idea of a 'universal humanity'. The irony of such systematisation, along with its physical and psychological technology, lies in its *affect*. The enigma of human emotion, what I refer as 'the under(upper)standing of the world (its *essential* tangible intangibilities)' is where artistic intent can be most pointed, providing a space where time is paused, where beauty is found in the omnipresent; where spiritual reprieve is granted – a place of catharsis earned or a monument to the invisible is made visible.

Such vision is found in the private sanctuaries of LEE MINGWEI, who invites us to write letters of gratitude, forgiveness or apology to those we value, but have yet to acknowledge. It is found in the evocative *durée* of SHIRAZ BAYJOO, whose interior and exterior landscapes of Mauritius are mirror-marked by the Arab, French and British colonial slave trade, his roving lens begging to give presence to the remnants of its repetitive occurrence. NALINI MALANI's figurative paintings pulse in reverse glow with the pain of love endured in absentia due to political lines of terror that forbid its union, casting a forlorn gaze upon the plight of contested Kashmir, questioning to whom it belongs. This personification of land is further explored in the playfully cynical mappings of human history, which usurp a presumed West to East, in the monumental psychogeography of QIU ZHIJIE, or the comparative differences in historical peaks and flows as told by men and then women in the figuratively sketched charts of ADRIANA BUSTOS. These macrovisions of human intellect, however, could not be so easily shared, were it not for the gift of language. The opacity of the vast human lexicon is the most illustrative of our echo, and its legacies (for far too many languages are irrevocably at death's door) are extolled in the performative installation of LÉULI ESHRĀGHI. Speaking in various tongues, he recalls his ancestors from Pars, Samoa and Guangdong, questioning the global commodification of their cultural symbols.

In our topsy-turvy world, where appearance is privileged, where what is private is surveilled, where what operates as public is privately owned, where informality is the guise for critical community action, where brand logos are considered more important than the functionality of the product itself, CARLOS GARAICOA proposed to reconfigure a highway underpass in downtown Sharjah, turning this public thoroughfare into living architecture that welcomes all classes, genders and ethnicities into a surrealistic domestic hallway replete with household lamps, artificial grass and hanging natural fernery[12]. This creation of the familiar as unfamiliar – the 'strangeing' of human experience – is also canvased in the hybrid drawing/video installation of ROHINI DEVASHER. Inspired by Jules Verne's *Voyages Extraordinaires* (1864), here there are worlds within worlds, with volcanic shafts for access, surrounded internally and externally by a continuous Oceanus, returning a perspective of our globe as a gift treasured with wondrous awe.

Ensuring under(upper)standing is with presence in the world requires human facilitation and guidance. Here, I also wish to pay homage to the agency of artists in their transmission of cultural knowledge – as provocative educators, cultural infrastructure builders, writers and archivists – as *critical elements of their overall artistic practice.*[13] Such 'culture as resistance' (what Kidlat Tahimik might call '*bathala na*')

12 It was with deep disappointment that this commission of Carlos Garacoia was not realized for SB14, due to financial and time constraints.

13 The artists in *Journey Beyond the Arrow* whose creative practice and educational structure extend beyond participating in exhibitions and marking artwork include: Qiu Zhijie, founder of Total Art Studio at the Hangzhou Academy of Fine Arts in Hangzhou, China; T. Shanaathanan, co-founder of the Department of Art History at the University of Jaffna in Sri Lanka; Khadim Ali, co-founder of Bamiyan Art Space in Bamiyan, Afghanistan; Carlos Garaicoa, founder of Artista x Artista in Havana, Cuba; Tuấn Andrew Nguyễn, co-founder of Sàn Art in Ho Chi Minh City, Vietnam; Kidlat Tahimik, founder of Ili-Likha Watering Hole in Baguio, Philippines; Mark Salvatus, co-founder of 98B COLLABoratory in Manila, Philippines; Antariksa, co-founder of KUNCI Cultural Studies Center in Yogyakarta, Indonesia; and Jompet Kuswidananto, co-founder of Teater Garasi in Yogyakarta, Indonesia. Their innovative thinking deserves so much more detail here.

is the creation of differing methods and processes for the collaborative and interdependent generation of historical consciousnesses, each contextually specific to their time and locale. For this *Journey Beyond the Arrow*, two particular artistic initiatives were invited to devise specific 'toolkits'[14] for Sharjah audiences, with propositions that challenge the practice (and product) of art. The 31st Century Museum of Contemporary Spirit, a collaborative study of human intention, manifested as a workshop for the collection of observing and enacting empathy as a grounding principle of human action. Gudskul challenged the hierarchies of knowledge dissemination and transference by asking for 'speculative collectivism' in devising 'how-to' manuals for human survival in the twenty-first century, thus engaging (and recording) all walks of life as both teacher *and* student.

Epilogue

The city of Sharjah plays host to the entire undertaking of the Sharjah Biennial. The Sharjah Art Foundation's denizen of courtyards, repurposed traditional dwellings and newly fashioned 'white-cube' galleries offer a unique interplay of spaces in which these human echoes can resonate. Biennial exhibition formats have historically wrought expectations of site-specificity to space, and there have thus been critical responses to the limits of the institutionalisation of exhibition-making in the West. Yet rather than seeking to respond to physical architecture, per se, *Leaving the Echo Chamber – Journey Beyond the Arrow* looks to the history of the 'site' as a *conceptual* reference point. Reflecting on the population of the United Arab Emirates – which is pervaded, and dare I say economically reliant, on the movement of migrant workers and foreign expats, its cultural community inherently diasporic in belief and ritual – I became intrigued by the reverse impact of this Arab World on my own context/geography, an inverse contemplation that I found neatly dovetails with my personal preoccupations with the impact of exchange and experience

14 A 'toolkit', in this context, is a set of artistic propositions that instructs an alternate methodology in the determination of art. It critically engages the nature of 'intent' as a set of socially engaged motivations that have collective value and meaning.

between colonial subjects (as opposed to the myriad of cultural projects by the likes of the French Institute Alliance Française or the Goethe-Institut, which continue only to support dialogue in my region between its once-'subject' and its once-'occupier'). Specifically, this *Journey Beyond the Arrow* asks members of the audience to contemplate the impact of their own cultural privilege and history on locales and communities that have often been overlooked as a part of their collective consciousness (thus, the exhibition's small focus on the history of the Arab World in South East Asia, for example).

An Islamic community, Sharjah is one of the most religiously traditional *in practice* in the United Arab Emirates. The tension between traditional values and progressive ones has been remarkably embraced and, indeed, celebrated in the myriad artistic and broader cultural programs of the Sharjah Art Foundation. This notable characteristic (though a form of respect fraught with its own ethical and practical dilemmas) somewhat mirrors my own context of capitalist-with-communist-characteristics in Vietnam. In Sharjah, the processes of working *in between* official and experimental zones of 'culture' (showcasing in outdoor venues versus indoor areas, for example) presents unique opportunities to interrogate the sanctioning of aesthetics according to a culture's customs and rituals.

Journey Beyond the Arrow considers wonder in an interlinked and diverse human echo. It is therefore ultimately necessary to respect the differences between cultures as well as the various perspectives on how social conduct is allowed to be visible. For it is in this *difference* that the plurality in human endeavour creates a juxtaposition, and thus innovation – a plurality that ironically equally sustains our touristic (i.e., economic) participation in exotifying cultures (a fundamental need in today's overly market-driven mentality).

My desire to provide a deeper sense of time to reflect on – and thus complicate – shared experience between cultures is, perhaps, the ultimate goal here: to remind ourselves of the inherent temporality of man-made borders and their definitions, and to broaden our understanding of culture and its origins. For if, indeed, there is one celebrated constant in this *Journey Beyond the Arrow*, it is that our objects, rituals and languages in this world are not fixed in interpretation; that such variance is essential to the expansion of human exchange; and that the difference in usage, the difference in contexts – the metaphorical bow that lets loose tools in new and wondrous ways – is critical to the survival of the human race, to our inhabiting a planet of equal diversity in wide-ranging climes.

J o u r n e y B e y o n d t h
e A r r o w J o u r n e y B e
y o n d t h e A r r o w J o u
r n e y B e y o n d t h e A r
r o w J o u r n e y B e y o n
d t h e A r r o w J o u r n e
y B e y o n d t h e A r r o w
J o u r n e y B e y o n d t h
e A r r o w J o u r n e y B e
y o n d t h e A r r o w J o u
r n e y B e y o n d t h e A r
r o w J o u r n e y B e y o n
d t h e A r r o w J o u r n e
y B e y o n d t h e A r r o w
J o u r n e y B e y o n d t h

e A r r o w S o l i i t a i ,

J o u r n e y s o l i u t a !

B e y o n d t h e A r r o w J

o u r n e y B e y o n d t h e

A r r o w J o u r n e y B e y

o n d t h e A r r o w J o u r

n e y B e y o n d t h e A r r

o w T r e a d S e a w a r d ,

J o u r n e y I n l a n d ! B

e y o n d t h e A r r o w J o

u r n e y B e y o n d t h e A

r r o w A N o t e t o S e l f

J o u r n e y B e y o n d t h

e A r r o w J o u r n e y B e

y o n d t h e A r r o w J o u

I have lived and thrived as a grateful visitor to the great bay Narrm and the surrounding waterways, forests and plains of Kulin Nation territory for almost ten years. Amongst the many blessings I have received in this place is the notion of belonging in diaspora through close kinship with the diverse peoples who presently live in Birrarung-ga, place of the Birrarung river, flowing out into Narrm, often called Melbourne. The smell of manna gum leaves crushed tenderly in your hands for the release of healing they hold and sight of the first raindrops that fall to hug the sweltering land in the middle of the summer are two often-remembered moments that are determined not by humans, but by our tree and sky kin, in a language that is homely and tender.

I often wonder how to grow more deeply – in my body and in my chosen kin and bloodlines – in the warm knowledge of what diaspora brings. The privilege of folauga, voyaging to be with kin, friends and peers, in short-burst intensive residencies, is one such mode of organising that quickens my mind and heart, and through which I have met many relatives from distant and nearby archipelagos. Indigenous peoples from every coast, mountain, plain and forest of the Great Ocean, its furthest reaches and beyond, in the arid places of home often called deserts, too. Both of my parents come from avid genealogy-keeping traditions, as a matter of intergenerational memory on my Pārs plateau side, where my father and some of his siblings survived the Iranian state-sponsored murder of my grandparents, aunt and others, but with the deep wound and trauma of surviving without language, familial wealth and wisdom, if not for a few belongings and stories. Even without the Persian language flowing from my vocal chords, I have found friends with whom to share meals and music, stories and traditions, spanning Iran, Afghanistan, Lebanon, Turkey, India and Bangladesh, mostly in Birrarung-ga/Narrm, but also in Dhaka, Kolkata and Berlin. I have found the Rajput miniature painting style imprinted on Mughal architecture, Bangla histories before the British, and Irānzamin, Greater Iran, legacies spanning the region well before the current geopolitical framework. It's like going to South Asia is one long step homewards, because in each place, I am already becoming-home, fa'afale; becoming-village, fa'anu'u. When I am in Guangdong, will I hear the names of my ancestors' villages in dream states, and find them when I've awoken? Was the gulf between Hong Kong and China what held me back from hearing the calls at night when I visited last year, becoming the first one in five generations to seek out our ancestors' places? Will Tudi Gong hear my prayers, or is there another god to whom I should pray that I don't yet know?

In a car navigating through the traffic of Kolkata, I am shaken; I feel at home in this place, where I have been for under a week. Yet temporality is distinct here. The constant intermingling of visual signs of Bangla, Hindi and English testify to a multilingual world that is home to me, one that has always been home to me, that is a territory of the spoken and the meaningful, and that is spatialised, but also borderless. What does it mean to introduce myself in Sāmoan in this place, and also to recognise Santali and other Indigenous languages that have been assailed not only by English, but also by larger group languages? The warmth of the monsoonal humidity, that peak tropical thunder, is also a home that my body can never forget, because it is where I viscerally belong, despite living and thriving in cooler climates for much of my life. The initial rush of warm knowing when I leave the plane, along with the sharp yearning my body experiences when I later re-enter the plane, is a place of melancholic folauga that I am privileged to experience; it links me to warm, home places across the planet, where fruits and vegetables, crops and colonisations, have been shared in varying measures for the past 500 years.

Often when I feel homesick, I wonder where this territory of the heart is; specifically, what I am missing and, whether it is the Sāmoan archipelago that I first think of, or another mostly invisible Indigenous territory, where the spirit-, sex-, mind- and body-shaming we have known since the missionaries, planters and colonisers arrived centuries ago, no longer hurts, pains, aggrieves, maims us. On my mother's side, I call on multiple villages in the Sāmoan archipelago whose genealogy-keeping traditions are speculative narratives directly linking us to the Ancestors and the estates they have bequeathed to us. I aspire to live in a time before and after Euro-American time, when tau gafa marks circular genealogical time that roots us in kinship with all other beings; when tala and taeao narrate important and personalised histories in orature that transcend our present binds; when our sensual, visual and spoken languages once more fulfil responsibilities to the Ancestors and to the Futures. When I know my relatives in territories often called Alaska, Okinawa, California, Taiwan, New Britain, Tierra del Fuego and Tasmania. In all these places, Indigenous and non-European cultural resurgence brings a newness to the speaking of names and singing of chants that the lands, waters and skies know best, know deepest.

Often, when I feel homesick, I listen to songs in ʻōlelo Hawaiʻi, reo Māori, Mexican Spanish, Yolŋu Matha, Persian and gagana Sāmoa. I live in my emotions as a queer person whose Ancestors loved and cared in ways that seem so hard to enact in our communities, today. So much toxicity on online platforms renders us enemies of each other. The internalised structural, epistemic and embodied colonisations cover our senses from recognising and undoing the sicknesses and losses that burden us. Our primary Ancestor, the Great Ocean, the splendour of our poetry, ceremony, landed-living and ways of knowing. The ways home are through all our relations; repeating cycles to breathe deeper and dream lucidly once more. Our caves cleaned of trash, our temples uncovered in the forest, free from under the sea of hotels and military bases and nuclear plants and plantations; our hearts warmed to the embrace of genealogical time and Indigenous future-focused ways of being. We are the people we have been waiting for; we have been waiting so long for this. We must heed the smartest of them all, our manava, our belly-knowing. Today, manava indicates where I will next be healed in the tattooed literature of the shared Great Ocean. Tomorrow, we will love and care anew.

J o u r n e y B e y o n d t h
e A r r o w J o u r n e y B e
y o n d t h e A r r o w J o u
r n e y B e y o n d t h e A r
r o w J o u r n e y B e y o n
d t h e A r r o w J o u r n e
y B e y o n d t h e A r r o w
J o u r n e y B e y o n d t h
e A r r o w J o u r n e y B e
y o n d t h e A r r o w J o u
r n e y B e y o n d t h e A r
r o w J o u r n e y B e y o n
d t h e A r r o w J o u r n e
y B e y o n d t h e A r r o w
J o u r n e y B e y o n d t h

e A r r o w J o u r n e y B e

y o n d O c e a n s t h e A r

r o w a n d S e a s : J o u r

n e y T e a r i n g U s B e y

o n d f r o m A l l t h e A r

r o w T h a t W e H a v e J o

u r n e y B e y o n d t h e A

r r o w J o u r n e y s B e y

o n d t h e A r r o w J o u r

n e y B e y o n d t h e A r r

o w J o u r n e y B e y o n d

t h e A r r o w J o u r n e y

B e y o n d t h e A r r o w J

o u r n e y B e y o n d t h e

A r r o w J o u r n e y B e y

The sea tore away from me all that I had. In doing so, it gave me an interior life far sooner than I would have had otherwise, but at great cost.[1]

—Meena Alexander

I want to start with this sentence from the Kerala poet Meena Alexander and explore how the sea – in this case, the Indian Ocean – has been tearing us away from 'all that we have', and suggest that the sea tears us away from an anticolonial and postcolonial land-grounded thought, that it leads us to rethink the connection between land and water and to conceive a land/water continuum rather than two antagonistic territories. The land/water continuum transforms our views on the past, present and future; questions continent or nation as the only space upon which history and culture are written. Continuum does not mean uniformity or the same space, but it indicates another cartography in which the forces of nature are integrated into history. There is thus no natural history on one side (in which seas are included) and human history on the other. As historian of the oceans Eelco J. Rohling has written, '...life on Earth, including humanity, is closely intertwined with changes in the oceans and climate, no matter whether these result from natural variability or human impacts'.[2] He adds that oceans started to experience changes due to human actions only in the 1800s. The history of the oceans and of their role in the possibility of human life on Earth challenges Western conceptions of temporality, spatiality and residency. Rivers, lakes, land, oceans and the seas are not simply roads of communication, but inseparable from our lives as humans and the world in which we live. As sea-level rise seems inevitable, and as the populations that will first experience its consequences live in greater numbers in the Indian Ocean, is it not time to imagine a decolonial theory of land/water? It must be imagined with a multiplicity of actors in mind: seas, rivers, women and men of different status, lands, cities, winds, technocrats, sailors, merchants, pilgrims...

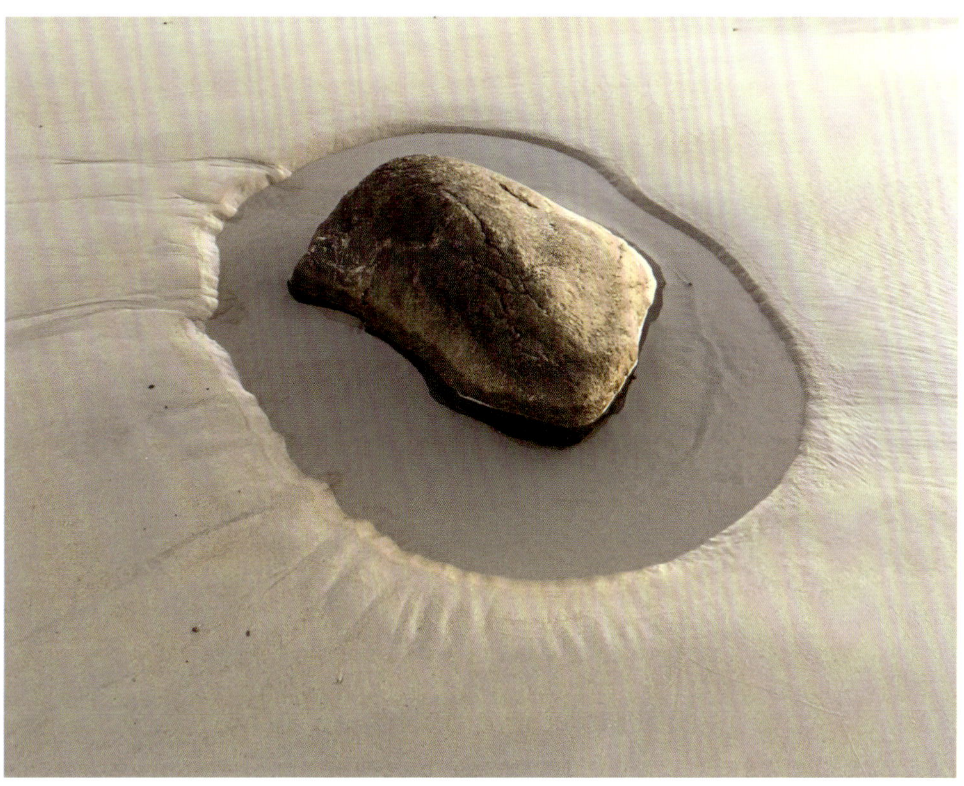

See the work of Shiraz Bayjoo for a similar history within the Indian Ocean concerning Mauritius on pg 222

I grew up in the Indian Ocean, on Reunion Island. There was no escaping the ocean. It had brought French ships carrying colonisers who took possession of the uninhabited island in the name of the king, as these things were done in the seventeenth century – Europeans could claim possession by the mere act of proclaiming it. Though the ocean had a long history as a site of exchanges and encounters, of trade, conflicts and negotiations, it made an entrance into the European narrative as a space without history and for wars over trade and possessions. It was a space from which slave ships and ships full of indentured workers and Asian migrants had arrived and gone back to Europe full of sugar and coffee.

Yet the ocean also had its own life and its own rhythms; it brought destructive hurricanes and pleasurable winds. It had been a millenary cultural space between Africa and Asia. None

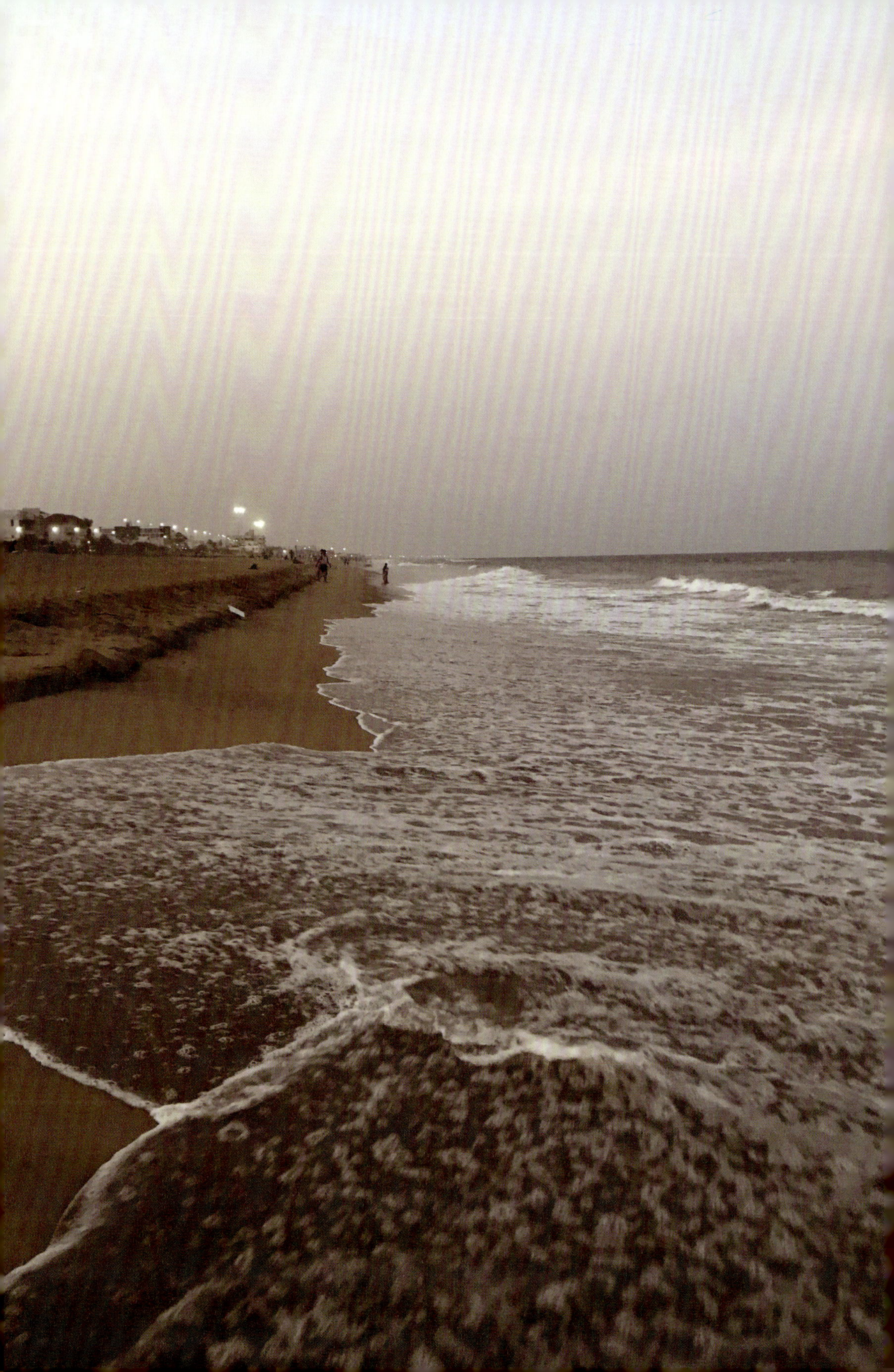

of this was taught at school. With imperialism, maritime history and culture had become the domain of white men, of captains, admirals and explorers, of naval battles and military ships, but not the domain of African and Arab navigators, pilgrims, merchants, sailors, the enslaved and travellers. The ocean, though, does not belong to Western navies and admirals, but to the pearl divers of Qatar; to the people who have been forced to cross it or those who have chosen to cross it; to the ones who have built communities on its fringes; to fishing people; to Indian women and men who were forced to the Kala Pani, to go over the 'black waters'; to the Chinese, Sri Lankans, Malaysians, Comorians, Ethiopians, Indians, Indonesians, Mozambicans who died in its waters or survived and settled on another rim of the ocean. From this long history, of people criss-crossing the Indian Ocean, another temporality emerges that denationalises maritime history and traces multiple cartographies. Today, the ocean needs to be reappropriated from increased privatisation and militarisation; as more military bases are being built, new bodies are being thrown over the sides of boats to die, and communities living on its shores are being dispossessed for the construction of resorts.

Is it possible to maintain the marginalisation of the seas in decolonial theory when they have become, as they used to be, sites where destructive powers seek to establish their hegemony? Anticolonial struggle was, for understandable reasons, based on land: it involved taking back the territory from the colonial settlers, renaming it, resetting its borders and writing the history that supported a national project. In doing so, the seas and the oceans in the making and unmaking of the colonial world were forgotten. Forgotten the role of rivers in the making of cultures and imagination; forgotten the role of the seas in connecting people; forgotten the role of oceans as sites that political prisoners, colonial soldiers, migrants and exiles had to cross, as routes for forging solidarity, for the circulation of ideas and people, for the making of bridges. The seas and oceans have been captured by the slave traders, the admirals, the oil diggers, the military and the scientists. *They* are now the ones who are telling its history.

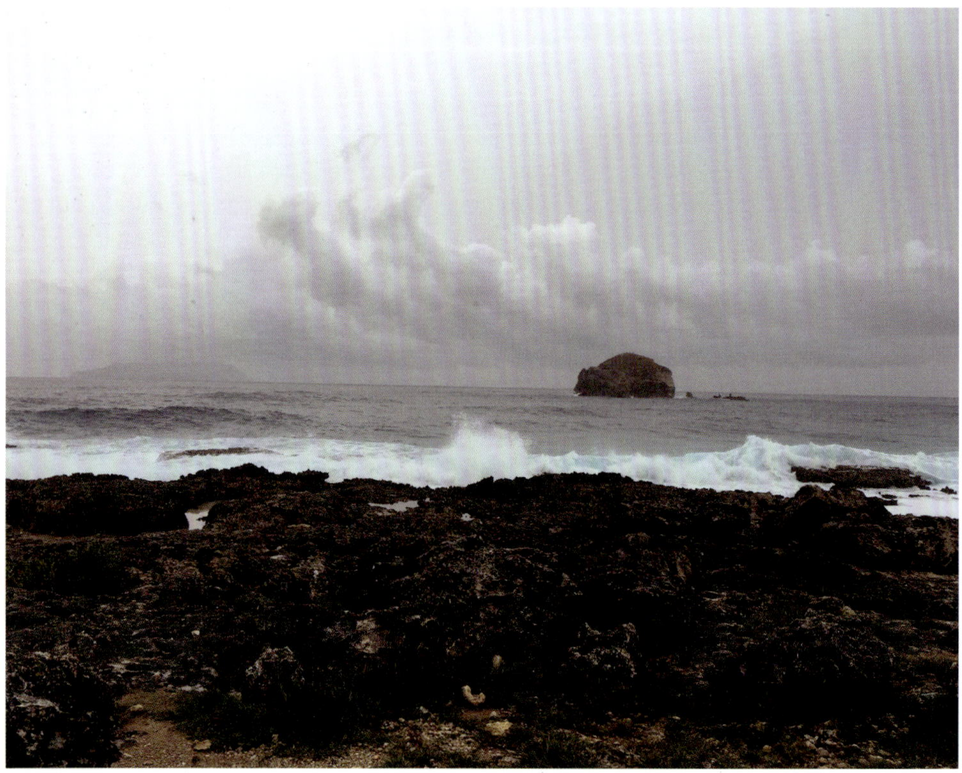

However, though the majority of the wretched of the Earth live and depend on land, need housing and must fight for access to clean water, education and healthcare, as well as to land rights around the world, we may be reminded that 90 percent of trade is currently transported by sea,[3] that cables for all kinds of communication that have become essential are submarine, that the source of energy that is the most largely spent (oil) is brought by oil tankers. The Indian Ocean has offered decolonial methodologies different from those developed in South America or Europe, because of its long history of connections between Africa and Asia, and with Europe. Yet, rather than trying to elaborate a site-based theory (strictly Indian Ocean), we must not forget the Indian Ocean's connections with the Pacific, the Mediterranean and the Atlantic, and to all the seas and rivers that constitute our vast liquid world.

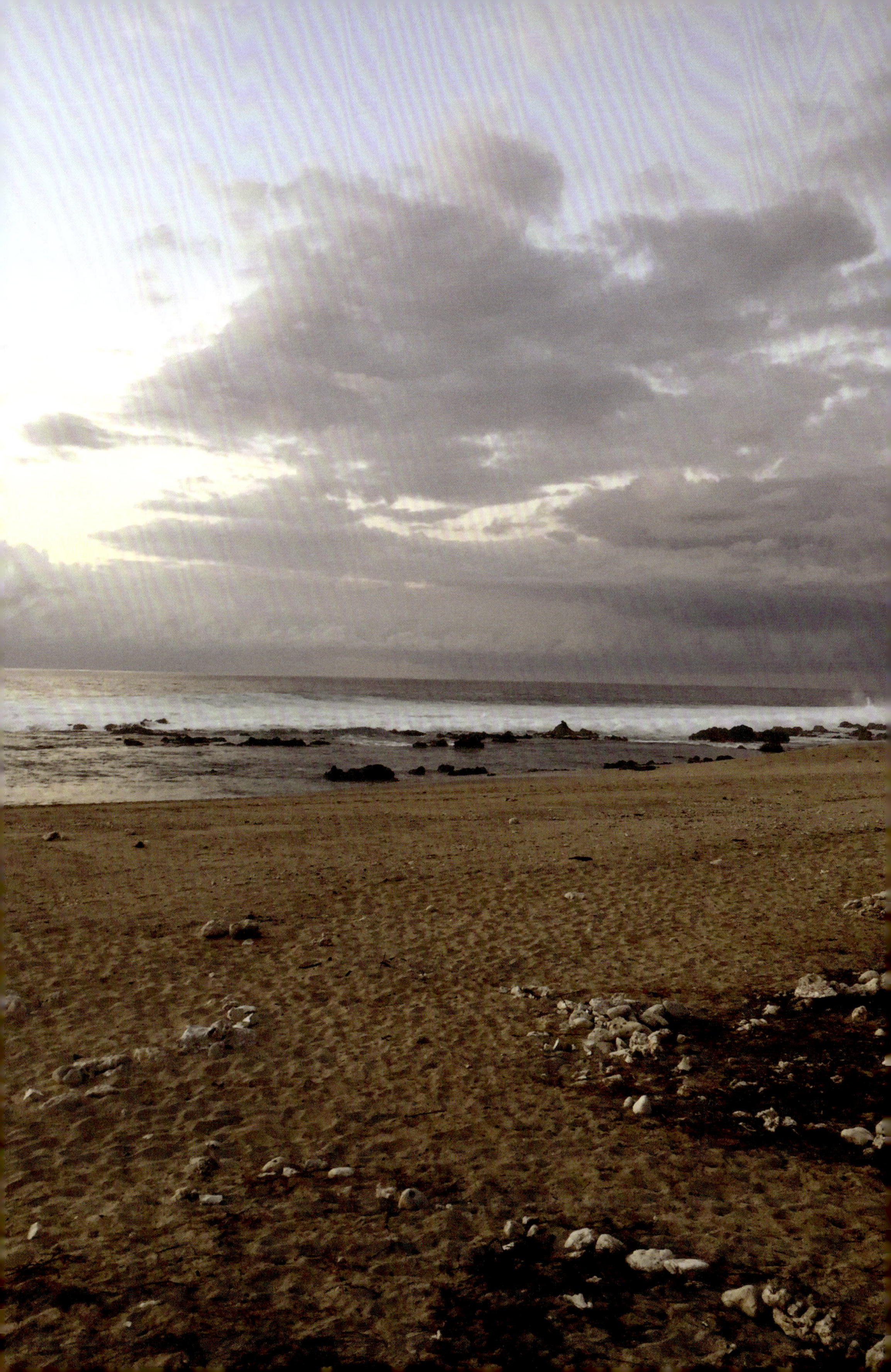

Through the Straits of Hormuz and Malacca, where ships once brought tonnes of textiles, peppers, china and spices, now 32.2 million barrels of crude oil and petroleum are transported every day. Where port cities – Sofala, Kilwa, Mombasa, Mogadishu, Hormuz, Kozhikode, Canton – once traded with each other, the Portuguese, Dutch, French and British sought to establish their monopolies. It is also good to remember that India had once 'clothed the world'; that in 1500, cotton textiles 'spread from India via land and sea to as far as Indonesia, Japan, east and Saudi Arabia, Ethiopia, Egypt and West Africa', that 'considerable quantities of Asian textiles also arrived in Congo as luxury cloths designed in rich and colourful ways'.[4] Now, women are burnt alive in Bangladesh textile factories for the pleasure of Western brands. Now, submarines explore the bottom of the oceans in search of mineral deposits for future extractivist economy. Where once the shores of the Island of Mozambique as well as Zanzibar witnessed groups of captives being taken to slavery, they are now being used for resorts, where tourists are offered the fantasy of 'the Orient'. New borderlines are being drawn on the oceans and the seas, delimitating spaces for state control, where migrants are hunted, thrown overboard by smugglers and left to die of thirst, hunger and drowning. The seas have always been mass graves, from the time of slave trades to imperialistic wars to contemporary routes of migration. In the Indian Ocean, where 40 percent of the world's offshore petroleum is produced, nearly 100,000 ships transit annually[5] and thirteen of the world's busiest ports are located in Asia.[6] On its surface, ships almost emptied of crews, carrying containers as high as ten-storey buildings, float like phantom vessels, bringing goods from one continent to another. Where European powers once fought to transform a multilingual, multicultural and highly mixed land/water continuum into a space carefully divided between them, now regional and global powers are vying for its control. In the Indian Ocean, women, children and men die fleeing war and genocide, poverty induced by neo-liberal capitalism and its local cronies. We learned the names of the islands that have become prisons of the twenty-first century, such as Manus Island, or whose lagoons are now cemeteries, such as Mayotte, and the dead of the Red Sea, of the Bay of

Bengal... The masculinist and military desire to master the seas seeks to extend its reach over the ocean's surface, shores and seabed, as well as over its islands. In other words, though we conceive of our world as being a place where we can walk, we should pay attention to the ways in which the seas are privatised and militarised. It is not that far-fetched to imagine continents locked in by superior powers and islands whose access to the high seas would be heavily regulated by these powers. Is it not what is happening to the African continent, where Europe has given to some African states the role of policing migrants, turning a blind eye to the politics of rape, torture, trafficking and enslavement, and thus heavily reducing the freedom of Africans to travel, locking them onto a continent to protect Fortress Europe? Military control of the seas could reduce military control on land. The rallying cry of racists – 'Lock them up!' – is slowly expanding to the entire African continent, with states bordering its coasts playing auxiliary armies; and if the latter choose to let mercenary groups enforce the order, then none of these states would protest. The objective would be to build walls everywhere, on land and on water.

Reappropriating the oceans means questioning the borders that states are drawing on the water, imagining how to represent the land/water continuum, elaborating a politics of maritime hospitality.

Who Said It Was Simple to Remember?

It was at the end of the 1990s, I cannot remember exactly when, but as I was travelling for the first time to Zanzibar, I bought *Empires of the Monsoon: A history of the Indian Ocean and its invaders* by Richard Hall.[7] The book was not written by a subaltern of the global South, but by a white man who had grown up in Australia, been educated in the British system and presented himself as an historical writer and journalist who sought to capture the European reader's imagination by stating that '[a]lmost nothing was know[n] in the West of the exotic cultures and wealth of the Indian Ocean and its peoples', and told readers that they could expect a history of 'brutality, betrayal and colonial ambition...told with an eye for the exotic'.[8]

Yet, as I was reading it, I could not stop telling myself, *this is it*! This is what I had known all along: that the Indian Ocean had been, for centuries, a site of cultural exchange; a space of encounters, of circulation of migrants, pilgrims, the enslaved, merchants, sailors and ideas, tastes, beliefs, sounds, languages. This was what I had learned growing up on Reunion Island – that although it was a French territory, it did not belong to the French world, but to the African/Asian one; hence, to a more complex cartography and temporality than what the colonial or even the postcolonial national narratives suggested. It gave me great pride to belong to an ocean that had not been culturally defined by Europe, one that could not be identified with *one* world, *one* culture. What I enjoyed in Hall's book was not the narration of great events, but the bits of information here and there that spoke of a multifarious world, a world that could not easily be summarised. For instance, 'by the early thirteenth century a senior trade official, Zhao Rugua, had been able to put together a fairly detailed account of East Africa's imports' with ships carrying 'white and red cotton cloth, porcelain and copper', or that the architects of the 'Great Zimbabwe', which 'had been the most powerful capital in southern Africa' between the twelfth and the fifteenth century, knew sophisticated techniques of building. My interest in crafts, textiles, techniques and the aesthetics of the mundane had found its focus: a world of waters full of wonder and surprise.

Austronesians were the first great navigators of the Indian Ocean, charting its immensity by following the stars, the currents and the colour of the water. Yet once the mystery of the monsoons had been cracked (around the first century CE) and people understood that from May to September, winds go from the northern tip of Madagascar to India, and from September to May, the other way around, they loaded boats with goods and navigated from port to port around the ocean's rim. Besides the mastery of the pendular movement of the monsoons, which led to the creation and development of commercial routes along the Indian Ocean Rim, two inventions helped to create a maritime and cultural world. The first entailed the development of three boats that would dominate the seas for centuries: the *dhow*, the Austronesian raft and the

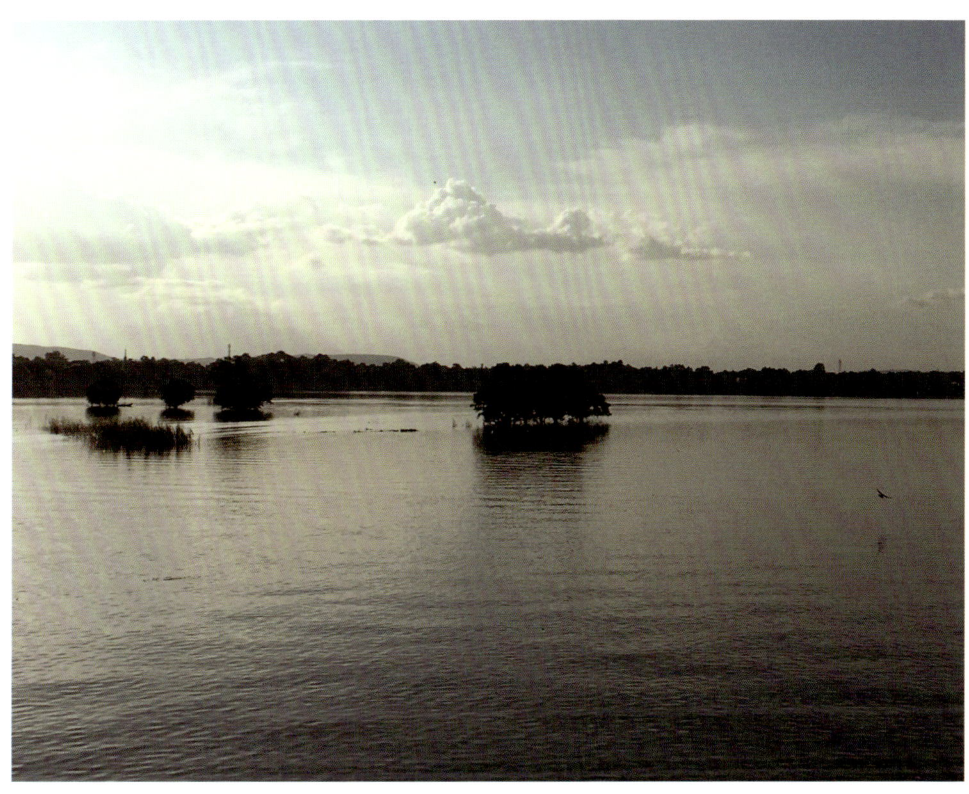

junk. The second involved the amelioration and diffusion of two instruments: the astrolabe, which has been used widely by the Arab maritime world since the ninth century, and the Chinese compass, which has been widely used since the eleventh century. Muslim navigators and merchants soon dominated the Indian Ocean trade. The seventh century saw the creation of the first Swahili cities. In the tenth century, Al-Istakhrî published an atlas with twenty maps of land and three maps of the surrounding waters: the Caspian Sea, the Mediterranean and the Indian Ocean. In the twelfth century, Al-Idrîsî edited a quite complete atlas with a famous map of the Indian Ocean, which showed Africa on the upper part and a comparatively small Europe at the bottom. Archives have recorded the names of famous merchants known to trade with China, such as Abul Qasim Ramisht, a very prosperous one from Siraf who lived in the twelfth century.

see the work of Ahmad Fuad Osman whose inclusion of the 'astrolabe' reveals the 'journey of a slave' on page 202

In 1341, Ibn Battûta described Kozhikode, which he called 'Kâlikoûth', in these terms: 'We went to Kâlikoûth, one of the greatest ports of the coast of Malabar. People from China, Java, Ceylon, Maldives, Yemen, and Fars meet there, as well as people from a diversity of regions. The great merchant Mithkâl lives in the city...he owns ships that go to China, Yemen and Fars'.[9] The voyages of the Chinese Admiral Zheng in the fifteenth century have added to a south-south world. Africans could be found in India and China, living as sailors, enslaved individuals, merchants or soldiers. Indians settled in African port cities; Jewish and Christian communities established settlements in India; pilgrims came from Japan and China to visit the sites where the Buddha meditated in India and Sri Lanka.

Mombasa, Malindi, Kilwa, Sofala and Mogadishu in Africa; Jeddah, Aden and Hormuz in the Persian Gulf; Surat, Cambay, Quilon, Kozhikode (Calicut), Chittagong, Kanchipura, Machilipatnam and Srinijaya in India; Pegou in Burma, then Aceh; and Canton in China (the oldest still-existing port in the world) can trace historical routes of exchange and encounter. Pearls, perfumes, Persian faience and china, cotton, silk, gold, silver, camels, cinnamon, pepper (the Chinese, who consume a lot of pepper, bought 75 percent of the Indonesian production), enslaved children, women and men were moved from one continent to another. In 1521, Piri Ré'is, a Turkish poet, thus described Indian Ocean port cities: 'Of these cities on its shores, ô my friend / I will tell you everything and what you can find / The country is called, let you know, Sefâla / Its metal is gold, ô thy who has a good reputation / One is called Mombasa, the other Malindi / Another is Mosambique and also Kilwa / Another famous one is Mongtiche / It is the biggest city of this country / Each year the Portuguese ships / Come to take all the gold'.[10]

The destruction of cities by Europeans, the creation of new cities, the forced migrations and the displacement of populations induced by European colonial and imperial policies charted migrations from the fifteenth century onwards. European powers organised the deportation of captives into servitude and the transportation of thousands of indentured workers – from India and China; and in lesser numbers, from Mozambique; and further away, from Yemen, New Caledonia, Vietnam – to their colonised territories on the Indian Ocean Rim and beyond. Gujaratis migrated to the southwest islands of the Indian Ocean; Hindus and Chinese to East Africa and the southwest islands.

Yet for someone also interested in the mundane, the unexpected, as well as in those who barely appear in the narratives or the representations – women – I have collected bits of accounts along the way. The story of nineteenth-century Indian women sewing the seeds of spices into the hems of their dresses, planting them upon arrival in the yard of the quarantine barracks where they were held on Reunion Island. The story of the young Tanzanian female film-maker who told me in 2000 that her favourite dish was borscht, because her mother, who was from Romania, had married a young man from Dar es Salaam (her father), who had been sent amongst many others to study in eastern socialist countries. The story of the young Chinese woman who was the owner of a restaurant in Dar es Salaam and cooked patrons' meals only after having examined their tongues and breath, so that her dishes would contribute to their well-being. Her mother had been a Chinese/Swahili interpreter during the building of the TAZARA (the Tanzania/Zambia railway) in the 1960s; upon her return to China, she never stopped thinking about going back to Tanzania. She had named her daughter Feizhou ('Africa' in Chinese) to honour a place that she had made hers; she spoke so often of Tanzania that her daughter had decided to settle there. The story of Malagasy nannies that I saw in Beirut taking care of middle-class children. The story of women who work as cleaners or sex workers, or in the textile industry in the Indian Ocean Rim to feed the insatiable appetite for cheap and new clothes. The story of Sri Lankan women seeking work in the Middle East, forced by recruiters to take injections of the contraceptive Depo-Provera. And the story of the old man in Gujarat who had five big clocks on the wall of his living room indicating the time of the places to which his sons had migrated. Is it possible to ignore these stories? How does one imagine a decolonial theory of the land/sea continuum when

see the work of Anawana Haloba on pg.182 for her own reflection on the legacy of the TAZARA Railway land and the seas have been marked by the slave trade, slavery, imperialism, capitalism? We have to listen not only to the words uttered in the holds of ships, but also to the words of the songs of the seas, of the women who perform the rituals to purify the water. It has to be a decolonial feminist theory, which does not mean a theory that includes women, but a theory that starts from the role given to the black woman's womb in the making of modernity as well as the fundamental role that Asian and African women are playing today in the global industries of care and cleaning.

In her magnificent book *In the Wake: On Blackness and Being*, Christina Sharpe does not 'seek to explain or resolve the question of this exclusion (of Blackness in modernity) in terms of assimilation, inclusion or civil or human rights, but rather depict aesthetically the impossibility of such resolution by representing the paradoxes of blackness within and after the legacies of slavery's denial of Black humanity'.[11] Following her analysis of what comes in the wake of ships crossing the Indian Ocean, multiple histories emerge that need to be translated aesthetically.

> *The sea has no custom, no ceremony. It allows a theater for poetry, for a voice that cries out, that splits into one, two, three or more, chanting the figurations of the soul, marking a migrant memory.*
>
> —Meena Alexander

The sea may have no custom, no ceremony, but people have rituals, customs, poems, ceremonies dedicated to bodies of water. Water brings life and death, blessings and threats; it relieves thirst, but can be poisoned or bloody.[12] To the Senegalese professor of aesthetics, Iba Ndiaye Diadji, water is intrinsic to African ontology, but we could say the same of Asian ontology and descendants of the enslaved and the indentured. The enslaved thought that their souls would cross the ocean to return to their homeland. According to tradition in Mauritius, Ganga Talao, a lake in the middle of the island, is considered to be either one source of the sacred Ganges or a source of its resurgence, connecting the island in the southwest of the Indian Ocean to the large river of India. Another explanation is that Shiva, along with his spouse, Parvati, was so taken by the beauty of the island that he shed a tear that *became* Ganga Talao.

What will happen if we forget the traditional techniques and ways to navigate? If we surrender control of the seas to militarised states? If we become locked on land, forced to go through increased tools of electronic surveillance and facial recognition, because states and their armies augment their privatisation of the seas for their wars and trade, and the shores for the pleasure of the powerful? If continents become prison-islands? What will happen if we lose the seas? This is why we need to recover bodies of water from the hold of nationalistic and imperialistic politics. It means moving from the concept of the seas as a space of structural violence, where saving someone from drowning; offering a glass of water to the thirsty; protecting the shores, mangroves, fish and corals are criminalised. It means siding with the communities of the seas and their shores, and continuing to write alternative narratives; to sing songs of the oceans, to read poetry, to perform rituals to all bodies of water in their intimate connections with the land.

The Small Island

In June 2018, I travelled to Reunion Island for a few days to attend a conference and to check if the work on my parents' graves had been properly done. It was early morning when I arrived at the cemetery, which is not far from the ocean and has been built as a garden. Graves in Reunion are always very well maintained, covered with flowers and mementoes. They can become shrines, like the revered grave of Sitarane, the name that Simicoudza Simicourba – who terrorised the colonial society with his crimes and was condemned to death in 1911 – gave to himself. His tomb is now painted in bright red and black, colours that are usually forbidden in Catholic cemeteries, and has become a place of worship, where lit cigarettes and glasses of rum are offered, so that Sitarane can continue to enjoy the pleasures of life.

Women and men were cleaning their family graves, carrying watering cans to freshen plants and trees. I did the same. I congratulated the workers on a job well done and took the old plates. That night, I consulted a wise man to know what to do with these plates; they were not pieces of garbage that I could throw away. He told me how to 'clean' them, which entailed passing half a lime over the surface. I could then give them to him, and he would erase the names, break the plates and discharge the pieces into the ocean. I had gone to his house with a friend who was seeking advice for a forthcoming *samblani* (the Creole word given to the ceremony done forty days after a death). We arrived around 6:00 p.m. at his mother-in-law's house, where a dozen people were waiting; we went around giving three kisses to each of them, as it is the custom. Women gathered to talk on one side, men on another. Again, we were not far from the ocean. This presence of the ocean throughout my stay was a reminder of its importance to understanding the personal cartography I had constructed during childhood and since. My intimate cartography is a land/water continuum. My parents, who met in Paris at a time when the city was a meeting point for future anticolonial leaders in the French empire, had come by boat to the island through the Suez Canal. I was a baby, but I want to think that I understood it to be a baptism in the waters, which would become my space of decolonial feminist consciousness.

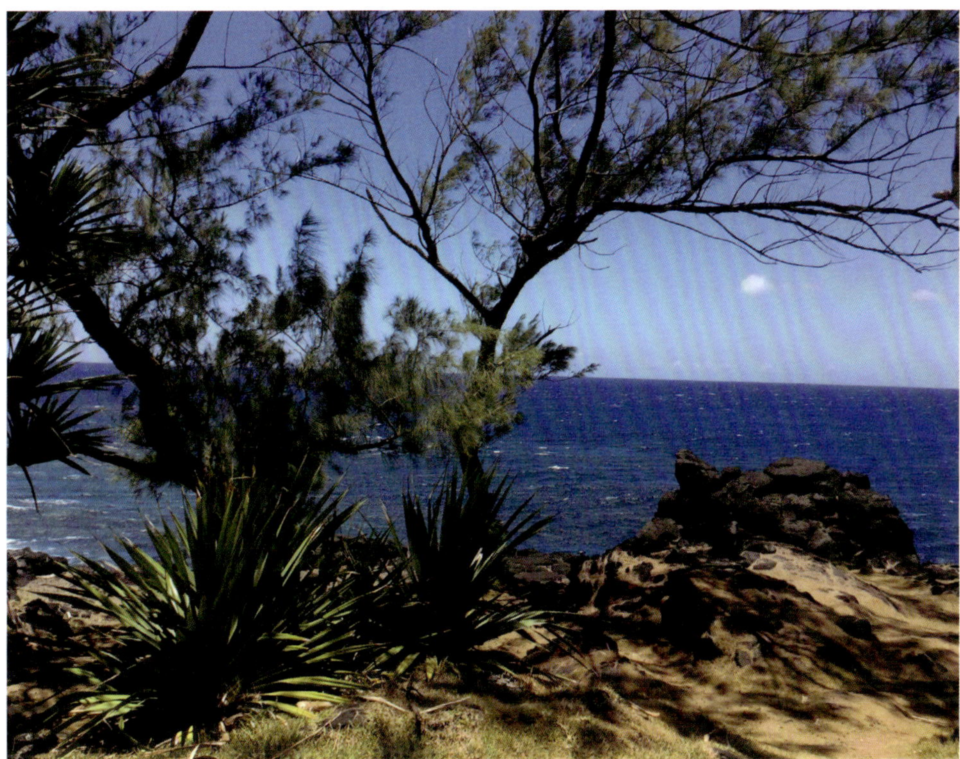

1 Meena Alexander, *Poetics of Dislocation* (Ann Arbor: University of Michigan Press, 2009), 178.

2 Eelco J. Rohling, *The Oceans: A Deep History* (Princeton: Princeton University Press, 2017), 2.

3 Sea trade has increased by more than 35 percent between 1998 and 2008. See Tim Sweijs, Willem Cleven, Mira Levi, Joelle Tabak, Zinzi Speear and Jeroen de Jonge, 'The Maritime Future of the Indian Ocean: Putting the G back into Great Power Politics', *The Hague Centre for Strategic Studies* (HCSS), no. 13 (October 2010): 17, https://hcss.nl/sites/default/files/files/reports/HCSS_FI-13_09_10_Indian_Ocean.pdf.

4 Giorgio Riello and Tirthankar Roy, 'The World of South Asian Textiles, 1500–1850', in *How India Clothed the World: The World of South Asian Textiles 1500–1850*, eds. Giorgio Riello and Tirthankar Roy (Leiden: Brill, 2009), 3–4.

5 'Competition in the Indian Ocean', Council on Foreign Relations, accessed 12 April 2018, https://www.cfr.org/backgrounder/competition-indian-ocean.

6 https://business.un.org/en/entities/13 International Maritime Organization (IMO) accessed 12/APRIL/2018 Ibid., 16.

7 Richard Hall, *Empires of the Monsoon: A history of the Indian Ocean and its invaders* (London: Harpers Collins, 1996).

8 Ibid., back cover.

9 Tim Mackintosh-Smith, ed., *The Travels of Ibn Buttutah* (Sydney: Pan Macmillan Australia, 2003), 206–07.

10 Zhao Ruga, *Description of the Barbarous Peoples*, published in 1225, as quoted in Lauren Arnold, *Princely Gifts and Papal Treasures: The Franciscan Mission to China* (San Francisco: Desiderata Press, 1999), p.15

11 Christina Sharpe, *In the Wake: On Blackness and Being* (Durham: Duke University Press, 2016), 14.

12 For an analysis of water in Swahili poetry and langage, see Katriina Ranne, 'Heavenly Drops: The Image of Water in Traditional Swahili Poetry', Universität Leipzig – Institut für Afrikanistik, *Swahili Forum*, no. 17 (2010): 58–81.

J o u r n e y B e y o n d t h
e A r r o w J o u r n e y B e
y o n d t h e A r r o w J o u
r n e y B e y o n d t h e A r
r o w J o u r n e y B e y o n
d t h e A r r o w J o u r n e
y B e y o n d t h e A r r o w
J o u r n e y B e y o n d t h
e A r r o w J o u r n e y B e
y o n d t h e A r r o w J o u
r n e y B e y o n d t h e A r
r o w J o u r n e y B e y o n
d t h e A r r o w J o u r n e
y B e y o n d t h e A r r o w
J o u r n e y B e y o n d t h

e A r r o w J o u r n e y B e
y o n d t h e A r r o w J o u
r n e y B e y o n d t h e A r
r o w S h i f t i n g t h e J
o u r n e y G e o g r a p h y
B e y o n d o f D o i n g , t
h e S e n s i n g a n d A r r
o w T h i n k i n g J o u n e
y o f B e y o n d t h e A r r
o w J o u r n e y B e y o n d
t h e A r r o w g J o u r n e
y B e y o n d t h e A r r o w
J o u r n e y B e y o n d t h
e A r r o w J o u r n e y B e
y o n d t h e A r r o w J o u

I. Geopolitical Aesthesis and Visionary Delinking

The descriptor for the overall vision of Sharjah Biennial 14: *Leaving the Echo Chamber*, as well as the statement for the segment curated by Zoe Butt, *Journey Beyond the Arrow*, both resonate with issues and concerns that I have been exploring, thinking about, writing on and engaging with, through workshops and public speeches, for a number of years now.[1] I perceive in the overall design of SB14 an invitation to delink from the *universal* effect of North Atlantic fictions.[2]

The conception of any art biennial today involves words of global currency, such as 'art' and 'aesthetics', not to mention other words, like 'democracy', 'progress', 'development' and 'modernisation'. One can recognise these terms as populating our echo chambers, creating a sense of referential 'reality'. However, the fact is that these terms have been invented by certain actors at certain times to serve certain purposes. The biennial descriptor faces this predicament head-on; the aim of SB14 is to question the possibilities and purposes of producing art '...when history is increasingly fictionalized, when ideas of "society" are invariably displaced, when borders and beliefs are under constant renegotiation, and our material culture is under the constant threat of human destruction and climate degradation'.[3]

Highlighted in this passage is a sense of the loss of balance or equilibrium that the world population is experiencing today. This is a situation, I would contend, in which art and biennials are complicit; so instead of simply asking for 'the possibilities and purposes of producing art', I would suggest turning the question of 'possibilities and purposes' onto itself: When, where and under what conditions can 'art' and 'biennials' emerge to frame and orient cultural practices that can, indeed, leave the 'echo chamber'?

The frame for a certain limited and Euro-centred kind of making, called 'art', and a certain temporal sequence of events, called the 'biennial', was inscribed in Venice in 1895. Not in Zimbabwe or China, Bolivia or Indonesia – though why not? Surely, it was not the arrow of ontological universal history that distinguished Venice in 1895. (Which, coincidentally, was the date of the First Sino-Japanese War, and also the beginning of the Japanese expansion that some of the makers/artists convoked by Zoe Butt have addressed in her exhibition.)

Venice was not a neutral location, nor did it exhibit the circumstances and conditions that made it possible. Its intellectual and cultural endeavours were framed by a specific concentration of wealth and distribution of poverty. Europe was booming in 1895 – with resources coming from Asia, Africa, South America and the Caribbean. At Venice, no non-European 'artists' were invited, because beyond Europe, there were no 'artists', just 'makers'. The 'art biennial' was a supreme manifestation of the Western idea of civilisation.[4] But we all know this now. Although, I do think it bears repeated emphasis that when 'art' is limited to the sphere regulated by 'aesthetics' – both concepts being inventions of Western modernity in the eighteenth century – 'art' loses the original meaning of 'skill' that the Latin word *ars* denoted. Consequently, a common human activity is reduced to the provincial meaning of a small sector of the world population. The 'skill to make something' is no longer what the concept of *art* means when it only describes certain types of activity; but more to the point, when it is also used mainly to devaluate and rank the various kinds of activities around the planet.

The call of SB14 to leave the 'echo chamber' is, in my understanding, a call to delink from the traps of *universal* fictions and engage in *pluriversal* world-making. I will elaborate what this entails, but first, let me illustrate it with a simple exercise: What are the words, or the meaning of the words, that in the Arabic language, for instance, would refer to and describe what in the West are named 'art', 'aesthetics' and 'biennial'? To find a one-to-one correspondence is not necessary. To invert the question is prudent: it means to start from Arabic, rather than from any of the six modern Western European languages grounded in Greek and Latin. I did an online search for the meaning of شاعرية (*shaeiria*). I got 135,000,000 links for the singer Shakira. This is what I mean when I talk about being trapped in the echo chamber of Western epistemic concepts, such as 'art' and 'biennial'. When I did the search for فن (fan), I obtained a description of 'fan art'.[5]

Argentine writer Jorge Luis Borges has a memorable short story, 'La Busca de Averroes' or 'Averroes's Search' (1947). In it, Averroes or Ibn Rushd is translating Aristotle's *Poetics* into Arabic. Ibn Rushd has searched all the books he could gather, but hasn't been able to find the way to translate the Greek concept of *tragedy*. Then, he walks to the window and, deep in thought, observes a group of children at play in a garden. Ibn Rushd "sees" them playing, but because the memory of Arabic is not the memory of Greek, he cannot "see" that for Aristotle what the children are doing is *pretending* and pretending is *mimesis*, the foundation of Greek tragedy. Ibn Rushd returns to his desk, and continues his difficult work.

Wided Rihana Khadraoui observes:

> 'Arab art' is a misnomer, as it creates a fabricated homogenous 'Arab culture' that undermines the reality of a diverse region filled with a multitude of unique experiences and ways of seeing the world. It also promotes misleading notions of authenticity. In a globalised world, a dinner of fries, a cheeseburger, and a milk shake is now every bit as 'authentic' as a traditional plate of *kibsa*, even in a city as isolated as Riyadh.[6]

II. Skill to Make: The Work of Makers/Artists

In a series of personal conversations, Skype chats and email exchanges since May 2017, Zoe Butt has explained to me her vision for her segment of SB14, which she summarised as follows:

Journey Beyond the Arrow gives deeper context to the movement of humanity and the tools that have enabled (or hindered) its survival. From spiritual ritual to cultural custom; from technological process to political rule of law; all such practices possess particular tools (object and action), which aid or abet mobility.

> The signs pointing towards the need to shift the geography of sensing, doing and thinking are clear to me here. The above passage takes us out of the 'art' of the echo chamber and into a setting that is larger.

Let us dwell on 'art' for a while. For much of the last two hundred years, the word and concept that were projected unto a global, or universal, sphere were, in fact, regional European ways of conceptualising their own art-making since the eighteenth century. As noted, before the eighteenth century, in Europe, 'art' meant 'skill', the skill to make something. The Greek concept – the term from which 'art' was derived – was *poiesis*, and the maker was a 'poet'. There were no 'artists', as such, in ancient Greece, but there were 'makers' whose 'doing' responded to the expectations and rules of 'poetics'. The legacy of Greek poetics is not in the making of the *artist*, but in the vocabulary that describes and explains what the artist *makes*. Furthermore, the European concept of 'aesthetics' is derived from the Greek *aiesthesis*. Yet whilst *aiesthesis* refers to sense in the Greek context, in Western knowledge, through philosophers such as Kant, aesthetics became the act of sensing and judging the concepts of the beautiful and the sublime.

When I reflect on what Zoe has shared with me about *Journey Beyond the Arrow*, and I search through the profiles of the makers/artists that she has invited, I am left with a deep sensation of a common thread that connects each of them, as well as a sense of the overall or floating framework for the project. What I 'see' may not be what there actually 'is'; but I would like to explain why I see what I see, and in this explanation, reveal my own understanding of the echo chamber, or what I would call, the Colonial Matrix of Power (CMP). Coloniality of power is a decolonial concept. Coloniality and decoloniality exist because of each other; similarly, the unconscious and the psychoanalysis both exist only because of each other: there is no ontological concept of the unconscious without psychoanalysis, and psychoanalysis is predicated on such an ontology.

What I 'see' in the makers/artists convoked in *Journey Beyond the Arrow* is the unavoidable, strong and urgent presence of memories and histories that have coexisted with the intrusion of Westernisation across the planet since 1500. I sense (*aesthesis*) the energy and the dignified anger. I sense the connecting threads, the energies emanating from the power differentials in the borderlands and the borderlines, the differentials that connect and divide; I sense the local histories of North Atlantic colonialisms, their rhetoric of modernity, progress and civilisation; I sense these histories and the rhetoric entangled with local histories, disrupted and derogated, but also entangled with concepts such as 'art', 'aesthetics' and 'biennial'.

If I may, again, bring up a parallel story to elucidate what I am trying to say, this time from Kenyan writer Ngũgĩ wa Thiong'o and his great novel, *The River in Between* (1965). I want to underline a common denominator, even as I would emphasise all the singularities of each maker's/artist's own experience and sense of praxis of living. *The River in Between* tells the story of the interrelated lives of two neighbouring villages: Kameno and Makuyu. In the former, the villagers still strongly believe in traditional practices. In the latter, they have converted to Christianity and embraced the ways of the white settlers. Yet both villages are no longer what they were. Both have been transformed by the intrusion of Western Christianity. If you believe in traditional practices, you sense and know that the villagers of Makuyu have adopted Christian values. But if you are a Makuyu, you cannot ignore either the traditional values of your own community or the traditional values of the villagers across the river. Both dwell in the borderland and the borderline, although differently. Both feel the power differential vis-à-vis the beliefs of the intruding Western Christians.

III. Decolonial Outlets

There are certain statements that anyone can make; however, the density of their meanings is modulated in relation to the teller. Linda T. Smith, a Maori anthropologist, informed her audience at New York University that she learned at school that the Maori had lived on an island, but then when the British arrived, it all changed for the better.[7] The same statement in the mouth of a settler of British descent in New Zealand would have had a different meaning. Decolonial doing and thinking arises when storytellers (thinkers, scholars, artists, activists) appropriate cultural formations (art, disciplines, museums, economies, states) of the invading actors and cultures, and shift them to their own projects of liberation. Steve Biko describes it as the envisioned self: 'We want to attain the envisioned self which is a free self'.[8] What I see in *Journey Beyond the Arrow*, both in Zoe's statement and the artists invited, is a praxis of appropriation and shifting of the meaning of the 'biennial' in the local history of Western tradition: *leaving the echo chamber* in search of envisioned identifications that Western modernity told too many of us that we should despise.[9]

History is neither linear nor circular, but an accumulation of heterogeneous structural entanglements. Is revolution possible, anymore? Today, even revolution is framed by the assumptions and regulations of the nation state, which is utterly corporatist in its outlook: obsessed with accumulation, with a financial and banking system that is predicated on both the belief that only money brings happiness and the willful ignorance that debts are seas of despair. Whether these multiconglomerates are neo-liberal in design or adversely play with the politics of state sovereignty, their structures frame the echo chamber, revealing the borderlines of modernity/coloniality. Consider China's epic 'One Belt, One Road': it is, at once, an initiative and an effort to delink from Western mandates (the IMF, World Bank, US White House), whilst also an attempt to rebuild a national trajectory that was profoundly disturbed by the Opium War of the mid-nineteenth century.

Without the 500 years of Westernisation of the planet, the 'One Belt, One Road' endeavour and its win-win rhetoric may have been unnecessary and, perhaps, unthinkable. China is responding to Western global designs. Hence, it is a state politics of de-Westernisation. Neo-liberal designs have been confronted and are being interrupted by two complementary, although at the same time very distinctive, orientations: one that I would describe as de-Westernisation in international political relations (e.g., China, Russia, Iran), as well as in the general sphere of culture; the other I would describe as decoloniality in all spheres of knowing, sensing and believing.[10] The goals of decoloniality are those of epistemic and aesthetic reconstitution.[11] These imply multiple processes of delinking from both Western epistemology and aesthetics in order to relink with biological cognition and cultural *aesthesis*: biological cognition means that we human beings *know* through the senses of our living organism (*aesthesis*) and translate this knowledge into cultural concepts and theories (aesthetics, epistemology).

Aesthetics has been conceived and formulated in Western philosophy (and not in Rodhesia/Zimbabwe or Bolivia) to highlight the sensation of the beautiful and the sublime, based on Western sensibilities (not based on the sensorium of Southern Africans or South Americans or any other peoples). Western sensibilities are certainly not universal; they are local. Decolonial aesthesis, therefore, expands on the experiences and sensibilities of the non-Western local sensorium (*aesthesis*) entangled with Western philosophical concepts and theories (aesthetics, epistemology) and built on the sensorium of colonial subjects. The entanglement places modern/colonial subjects on the borderlands, whilst imperial/colonial subjects dwell in their territory.[12] Thus, the urgencies of leaving the echo chamber and exiting from the failures of modernisation are multiplying on the planet.

What, then, do 'art', 'biennial' and 'aesthetics' have to do with neo-liberal designs? Surely, they are not independent and untouched by the transformation of the global order under which all of us on the planet live. My own explorations of the splendours of Western aesthetics and artistic cultures went hand in hand with their aberrations: the disavowal of the sensorium that did not correspond with the provincial sensibilities of modern European subjects. The splendours are celebrated in the rhetoric of Western modernity and civilisation. The aberrations materialise in what the rhetoric of Western modernity hides: that aesthetics became the standard to judge and (de)value, on its own terms, the praxis of living and doing of non-Western societies (purported by rulers of Western institutions, such as the conduct of the state, banks, museums and universities). Such aberrations live in the self-conviction of assumption – that what is desired and satisfying to one, is also what will be desired and satisfying to the rest of the people on the planet. That is, in my understanding of what the current echo chamber does to us all. In my vocabulary and conceptual schema, art and aesthetics are fundamental components of the CMP, regulating and managing subjectivities, tastes and sensibilities. The fact that many (including myself) want to delink from the CMP, is the consequence of the repressive dimension of neo-liberal values and beliefs.

What matters now on the planet are the responses to the above in the spheres of art and aesthetics; although not only in art and aesthetics, but also in the entire spheres of sensing, knowing and believing. Which means to focus on power differentials in the modern/colonial entanglement brought about by the processes of Westernisation.[13] I detect two types of response: one I will call cultural de-Westernisation and the other I will call epistemic and aesthetic decolonisation. The first manoeuvre is at the institutional level; the second, at the emerging global political society, of which makers/artists, curators/activists and undisciplined thinkers are a fundamental constitutive dimension.

At the beginning of the essay, I spoke about the call of SB14 to delink from *universal* fictions and engage in *pluriversal* world-making. Let me elaborate on what I mean by the latter term. Elsewhere, I have argued that pluriversality[14] is not a form of cultural relativism, but the entanglement of several cosmologies connected today in a power differential. That power differential is the logic of coloniality covered up by the rhetorical narrative of modernity. Modernity is a fiction that carries in it the seed of the pretense to universality. To think more pluriversally, it is thus necessary to introduce a concept that captures the slash of modernity/coloniality; that is, the '/' of the entanglement and power differential. If a pluriverse is a world not of independent units, as in cultural relativism, but a world entangled through and by the CMP, then it is a way of thinking and understanding that dwells in the entanglement and in the borders. The point is not only to study the borders as such, and not simply to cross the border, but to *dwell* in it, in the territorial epistemology, where you accept a pluriverse as someplace out there that you observe from someplace else outside the pluriverse.

There is precedent in the history of the Sharjah Biennial that elucidates the need and urgency to refashion the dependencies on Western aesthetic, artistic and political imperatives. For instance, the announcements of Yuko Hasegawa, curator of Sharjah Biennial 11, were unmistakable in their response to the historical situation of Sharjah: 'My natural response to its dynamism is to produce a Biennial which asks questions through art, and creates a dialogue that liberates us from Eurocentrism, Globalism, and other relevant isms'.[15]

Seen in parallel (SB14 and SB11), *Leaving the Echo Chamber: Journey Beyond the Arrow* and *Re-Emerging: Towards New Cultural Geographies* are both, in their formulation and acting out, vibrant statements that call for a shift of the geography of sensing, thinking, doing; they are expressions of the desire to delink from the dominant echo chamber/CMP, and to learn/exit from the failures of modernisation, so as to continue the march towards a pluriversal praxis of living beyond the arrow of singular time and the monocultures of the mind.

1 A considerable amount of work has been undertaken on decolonial aesthesis since 2009. Here are some examples and references: Walter Mignolo, 'Aiesthesis decolonial', *Calle 14 revista de investigación en el campo del arte*, vol. 4, no. 4 (2010): 10–25; Aïcha Diallo, 'A conversation with Walter Mignolo: "Decolonial aesthetics/aesthesis has become a connector across the continents"', *C& (Contemporary And)*, 7 August 2014, https://www.contemporaryand.com/magazines/decolonial-aestheticsaesthesis-has-become-a-connector-across-the-continent; Rubén Gaztambide-Fernández, 'Decolonial options and artistic/aestheSic entanglements: An interview with Walter Mignolo', *Decolonization: Indigeneity, Education & Society*, vol. 3, no. 1 (2014): 196–212; Walter Mignolo, 'Re:Emerging, Decentring and Delinking: Shifting the Geographies of Sensing, Believing and Knowing', *Ibraaz*, 8 May 2013, https://www.ibraaz.org/essays/59.

2 Michel-Rolph Trouillot, 'North Atlantic Universals: Analytical Fictions, 1492–1945', *South Atlantic Quarterly*, 101(4) (2002): 839–58.

3 'Sharjah Biennial 14: Leaving the Echo Chamber', press release, Sharjah Art Foundation, accessed 25 January 2019, https://www.e-flux.com/announcements/210307/sharjah-biennial-14leaving-the-echo-chamber.

4 On this topic, see Chris Sharp, 'Are biennials "curatorial mission impossible"? Ahead of the Sharjah Biennial, co-curator Zoe Butt pauses to reflect', *Art/Basel*, accessed 25 January 2019, https://www.artbasel.com/news/zoe-butt-interview-sharjah-biennial-chris-sharp-lulu.

5 See Wided Rihana Khadraoui, 'Arguing Semantics: What Exactly is "Arab Art'?"', accessed 25 January 2019, http://www.mei.edu/content/article/arguing-semantics-what-exactly-arab-art.

6 Ibid.

7 Linda Tuhiwai Smith and Eve Tuck, 'Decolonizing Methodologies', a round table filmed in 2014 at the Graduate Center, CUNY, New York, video, 2:03:50, https://video.search.yahoo.com/search/video;_ylt=A0geK.Fa0UtcGDsAnFNXNyoA;_ylu=X3oDMTE0bWltYTRqBGNvbG8DYmYxBHBvcwMxBHZ0aWQDQjQ4NTNfMQRzZWMDcGl2cw--?p=DECOLONIZING+METHODOLOGY%2C+CUNY&fr2=piv-web&fr=yset_safari_syc_oracle#id=1&vid=af37993e9f95e08dbb62af4e9fc5520c&action=view.

8 Steve Biko, *I write what I like*, 40th anniversary edition (Johannesburg: Pan Macmillan, 2018), 53.

9 Yuko Hasegawa's 2016 exhibition T*he New Sensorium: Exiting from the Failures of Modernization* responds to similar urgencies. See Mylène Ferrand Lointier, 'Yuko Hasegawa: New Sensorium – Exiting from the Failures of Modernization', Seismopolite Journal of Art and Politics (10 August 2016), http://seismopolite.no/yuko-hasegawa-new-sensorium-exiting-from-the-failures-of-modernization. See also Walter Mignolo, 'Re:Emerging, Decentring and Delinking: Shifting the Geographies of Sensing, Believing and Knowing', *Ibraaz*, 8 May 2013, https://www.ibraaz.org/essays/59 .

10 De-Westernisation and decoloniality are neither anti-Western nor anti-colonial. 'Anti' positions are manifestations of 'resistance' to the rules of the game being imposed by imperial forces and local complicities. De-Westernisation and decoloniality are manifestations of *re-existence*: appropriations of the rules of the game to engender and enact what the rules were now made for. De-Westernisation consists of state-led projects. Decoloniality is a project in the hands of the emerging political society (in this case, curator and artists). I see SB14 as both acts of de-Westernisation and decoloniality. I am not saying that *Journey Beyond the Arrow* is decolonial. I am saying that, in my argument, I see it as decolonial.

11 'Aesthetics', since the European Enlightenment, has become part of the philosophical discourse that regulates taste and celebrates the artist-genius. 'Aesthesis' (the manifestation of the sensorium in living organisms) was colonised, as it were. The restitution of aesthesis and the urgency to reduce aesthetics to size (e.g., to decolonise aesthetics) are urgent tasks towards the resurgence of the 'envisioned self'. For the distinction between aestheTics and aestheSis, see the following note.

12 On the biology of cognition, see Humberto Maturana, From Being to Doing: The Origins of the Biology of Cognition, 2nd edition (Heidelberg: Carl Auer International, 2004). On decolonial aesthesis, see Walter Mignolo and Rolando Vazquez, 'Decolonial AestheSis: Colonial Wounds/Decolonial Healings', *Social Text, Periscope* (15 July 2013), https://socialtextjournal.org/periscope_article/decolonial-aesthesis-colonial-woundsdecolonial-healings.

13 Serge Latouche, *L'occidentalisation du monde* (Paris: La Découverte, 1989).

14 See Walter Mignolo, 'On Pluriversality', posted on 20 October 2013, http://waltermignolo.com/on-pluriversality.

15 'Yuko Hasegawa Appointed Curator of Sharjah Biennial 11', e-flux, accessed 30 August 2018, https://www.e-flux.com/announcements/34755/yuko-hasegawa-appointed-curator-of-sharjah-biennial.

J o u r n e y B e y o n d t h
e A r r o w J o u r n e y B e
y o n d t h e A r r o w J o u
r n e y B e y o n d t h e A r
r o w J o u r n e y B e y o n
d t h e A r r o w J o u r n e
y B e y o n d t h e A r r o w
J o u r n e y B e y o n d t h
e A r r o w J o u r n e y B e
y o n d t h e A r r o w J o u
r n e y B e y o n d t h e A r
r o w J o u r n e y B e y o n
d t h e A r r o w J o u r n e
y B e y o n d t h e A r r o w
J o u r n e y B e y o n d t h

e A r r o w J o u r n e y B e

y o n d t h e A r r o w J o u

r n e y B e y o n d t h e A r

r o w J o u r n e y B e y o n

d O n B e c o m i n g A r a b

t h e a n d A r r o w J o u r

n e y B e i n g C r e o l e B

e y o n d t h e A r r o w J o

u r n e y B e y o n d t h e A

r r o w J o u r n e y B e y o

n d t h e A r r o w J o u r n

e y B e y o n d t h e A r r o

w J o u r n e y B e y o n d t

h e A r r o w J o u r n e y B

e y o n d t h e A r r o w J o

Zoe Butt and Lee Weng-Choy interview historian Sumit Mandal about the ideas in *Becoming Arab: Creole Histories and Modern Identity in the Malay World* (Cambridge: Cambridge University Press, 2018), a book that resonates with particular themes of *Journey Beyond the Arrow*.

Zoe Butt (ZB): A common thread throughout the vibrant conversations amongst many of the artworks in *Journey Beyond the Arrow* is the significance of the seas in trans-regionalisms throughout history. What is also strongly evident in the works of many artists is the impact of this body of water on the birthing of creolity and its diaspora as a consequence of not only colonial infrastructure, but also the evolution of local religious beliefs and customs. The Indian Ocean, in particular – or rather, the Indian Ocean Rim – became an important area for me to focus on with this show.

I was interested in bringing you, Sumit, into the publication, because I wanted to discuss the impact of the arrival of Arab peoples in the Malay world, and how the cultures, customs and beliefs of the former have left critical traces in the inherited memories of the latter. In your research, you share your perspective, but also your concerns and cautions, about the application of the term 'Arabisation' to Islamic communities within the Malay world, highlighting the need to have a broader historical view of human flows of differing geographical trajectories and spiritual adherences.

ZB + Lee Weng-Choy (LWC): So, our first cluster of questions concerns the Indian Ocean and the importance of the seas in historic trans-regionalisms. One imagines that you came across some evocative anecdotes about the Indian Ocean in the course of your research – could you share one with us? In the book, you talk about how the Arab communities and economies in the Malay world shifted from being maritime to being land-based. What were some of the significant consequences of that shift? Also, you mostly discuss migration from the Arabian peninsula to the Malay world. What about movements in the opposite direction – from East to West?

Sumit Mandal (SM): Standing on the shoreline of Batavia in the eighteenth century, a Hadrami man flung sacks of money into the sea. People gathered around him, flabbergasted at the sight. They asked him what he was doing and he replied that he was dispatching money to his mother in the Hadramaut. Batavia was the Dutch colonial name of Jakarta, the capital of Indonesia today, and the Hadramaut is a valley in Yemen. The Hadrami man was no ordinary individual but someone revered by the community of Muslims around him for the qualities of sainthood that he possessed. Sayyid Husein Alaydrus, like many others from the Hadramaut, had travelled across the Indian Ocean to the Malay world, the archipelago that spreads out from the southernmost point of the Asian continent and today falls mostly within the sovereign boundaries of three nation-states: Indonesia, Malaysia and the Philippines. Plying their knowledge of commercial affairs, diplomacy, languages and Islam, Hadramis became integral to the coastal polities of the oceanic expanse. Sayyid Husein came to be regarded as a saint, not only because of his extraordinary piety, but also for defending his community in the face of oppressive actions taken by the Dutch rulers of Batavia. He drew the awe and respect of the Dutch over time by performing a number of miraculous acts. The governor rewarded Sayyid Husein with a sum of money when the latter correctly predicted the former's rise to his position when he was but a child. It was this money that Sayyid Husein promptly dispatched to his mother by sea. This is the story told of the man whose gravesite is still a site of commemoration of his piety and miraculous acts today. In the story, the mother receives the sacks of money safely on the very same day.

My book begins with an account of the above individual to bring to mind the trans-regional Islamic space that was constituted across the Indian Ocean from the sixteenth century onwards. Countless geographical landmarks, institutions, legal frameworks, commercial arrangements and faith practices were shared across the vast oceanic expanse and were familiar to seagoing travellers of the time. Gravesite shrines were but one example of such recognisable elements in the social landscape. The saints buried at these sites were, in every likelihood, adherents of Sufism – the mystical tradition in Islam – who are said to have played a large role in the conversion to Islam of people in the Malay world. Like Sayyid Husein, saints are remembered in places that dot the Indian Ocean Rim, not only for their piety and miraculous acts, but also for their interventions in the lives of local communities. Besides coming to the defense of these communities, the saints introduced new skills, crops and technologies. One Sufi is said to have introduced coffee beans from India to Aceh, and another taught people of the same region in North Sumatra to cast cannons. Stories of such extraordinary individuals as these are commemorated by oral and written hagiographies – and in growing online versions – recounted in conjunction with their gravesites. The latter serve as inscriptions on the landscape of their exceptional lives and the miracles they performed.

The story of Sayyid Husein does not end with the dispatch of funds by sea, but also relates his time in Gujarat before coming to Batavia. Upon arriving in Surat, the western Indian region's well-known cosmopolitan coastal city, he found a people suffering from severe drought and cholera. Their troubles were over once they collectively agreed to convert to Islam, and the well and pond that were built following Sayyid Husein's instructions began to fill with the heavy rainfall that followed. Gujarat was thereby turned from a parched area to a fertile land. By recalling his time in Gujarat, the stories told in Jakarta today reiterate trans-regional histories. That past was a time when the sea was not only the means by which commercial and cultural exchange had expanded in scope across the world, but it also infused the imagination of people far and wide as a space of connectivity.

Rulers of the Malay world who rose in power and wealth as the Islamic space of commercial and cultural exchange was developing across the Indian Ocean recognised the significance of the sea in the world. This recognition is nicely captured in a letter written by the Sultan of Malacca to the King of Ryukyu, south of Japan, in the fifteenth century: 'We have learned that to master the blue oceans people must engage in commerce. All the lands within the seas are united in one body. Life has never been so affluent in preceding generations as it is today'.[1]

The Malaccan Empire, whose eponymous capital lay at the crossroads of trade between the Indian Ocean and the South China Sea, was newly emerging and recently integrated into maritime trade on a global scale. The idea of connectivity is not purely instrumental in this instance, but, as the quote suggests, a profoundly encompassing and mobile vision. The sea appears to be at the centre of this vision as it is through the sea that the lands come together.

But the story of Sayyid Husein marks the beginning of the decline of the sea as a space of connectivity, and the rise of land-centred concentrations of power and wealth with which my book is concerned. In *Becoming Arab*, I explore, in depth, the creation of the colonial state and the instruments of immobility it produced, namely, categorisation and control on the basis of race. Migrants from the Hadramaut formed creole communities in the Malay world that were intimately tied to the sea. The sea was the medium that magically transported sacks of money across the Indian Ocean. The sea was also the means by which creole Hadramis traded throughout the archipelago, immersed in and extending the reach of Malay, itself a creole language, and contributing to its rise as the lingua franca of the region. The land-based categories of the colonial state constrained mobility with lasting consequences. Racialised identities became part of the social landscape of the region and were eventually adopted by anti-colonial nationalists in the twentieth century. The independent states of Indonesia, Malaysia and Singapore reinforced the borders between their respective nations and ethnic categories.

Recounting the maritime past is an act of acknowledgement of the trans-regional connections through the sea. But it is more than that. This act opens up the possibility of seeing the constitution of contemporary nation-states as intimately tied to the inflow of people and cultural influences across borders, sometimes from places a great distance away. As it turns out, the traces of creole Hadrami histories of the maritime past persist in the fluid interactions and intermixing that continues in Indonesia, Malaysia and Singapore. The end of the Cold War and the fall, in 1990, of the Marxist regime that ruled the Hadramaut meant that families of creole Hadramis could, and have, embarked on 'journeys of return' to the other homeland, whose language and people were barely familiar to them. They travelled by aeroplanes rather than ships, but two-way connections have been established that have returned to both societies what are potentially more expansive and inclusive notions of self and belonging. That we may belong to many places and have more than one homeland is an idea that might have begun to germinate for the many peoples of the Malay world.

ZB + LWC: In the book, you discuss the intersections of creolity, diaspora and modernity; for example, the role of print in the construction of cultural identities. The book offers lessons about creolity for the present day – at least that's one way of putting it into conversation with the contemporary art world. The point is not to mythologise a precolonial ideal, but to listen to what history can teach us about writing alternatives to the current hegemonies of racialised nationalisms. First of all, is creolity predicated on diaspora? And how did histories of creolity, movement and exchange sit with histories of policing purity in the Arab Malay world? How does an understanding of these histories help to contextualise present-day expressions of Islam that are deemed isolationist and extremist, such as in Afghanistan, for instance?

SM: Creole societies offer narratives of multifarious rather than linear histories. They carry within them experiences grounded in more than one cultural geography. The biographies and stories that constitute them offer material evidence of complex pathways and cultural outcomes across the world, and defy the neatly ordered narratives of racialised nationalisms. The grounded and multifarious stories of creoles cannot get fully assimilated into racial categories. The latter are an abstraction that is sustained through the deployment of political instruments and the ongoing mobilisation of ideas and people.

My own research has drawn on the experience of Hadrami interaction with the Malay world and the creole histories produced to offer a more expansive and multifarious vocabulary of belonging than the prevailing ethno-national terms. Creole societies are only one pathway to understanding what a human history of interaction is. I see *Becoming Arab* thus sitting alongside not just other works uncovering creole histories and the diasporas from which they arise, but other books that explore the human condition as an intersection and outcome of multiple genealogies.

ZB + LWC: You make the point that colonial maps were necessary fictions. Our final question concerns the epistemological and the historiographical. Your work was based on interrogating existing sources – revisiting and revising colonial histories. Back then, scholar bureaucrats and business merchants determined, to a large degree, the production of knowledge. Don't they still, in some ways? How can we move past this kind of instrumentalisation of knowledge? Professional historians don't usually speculate on what could have been. Though that's precisely what some artists do, often as a way of reimagining not so much the past, but the future. We'd like to end by asking you to reflect personally on the state of the academic enterprise of history.

SM: My argument is that colonial rule produced consequential, but not totalizing, racial categorisations. The production of racial subjects was a project that was not only constrained by political and pragmatic considerations, but negotiated and resisted by Hadramis themselves. Although the range of roles in society played by Hadramis became narrower over the course of racialization, their versatility was not entirely eliminated. The instrumentalisation of knowledge cannot be viewed in terms of the changes proposed, but how ideas come to be implemented; it has to be historicised.

The instrumentalisation of knowledge has parallels in present times, most certainly in relation to Arabs and Islam. Bodies of scholarship have emerged in conjunction with the securitisation of states following the aeroplane attacks on the United States in September 2001. The 'War on Terror' policy of the United States encouraged and provided the impetus for funding for research on terrorism that came to be focused on Arabs and Islam.

Drawing from established traditions of independent inquiry in a variety of disciplines, scholars have produced work that stands in sharp contrast to the frequently uncritical and ahistorical instances of 'terrorism studies'. *Becoming Arab* ends by highlighting a concern about the use of the term 'Arabisation' to describe the growth of politically radical and socially conservative forms of Islam in Indonesia and Malaysia. This term does little to render the nuanced and complex interactions of Arabs with the Malay world over the course of centuries. By attributing the growth of radicalisation and conservatism to 'Arabs', the term also dangerously ethnicises ideologically driven changes that could have travelled through a number of networks of people and organisations, including amongst them people of different ethnic backgrounds. The proponents of radical and conservative thinking are frequently responding to political acts, such as what they perceive as aggression against Muslims by the United States and other powers across the world.

Historians reimagine the past in ways that allow us to be able to see a range of possibilities for the present and the future. By envisioning the trans-regional, we are opening up the scales of our understanding of belonging to a variety of different historical imaginaries: the Malay world, Bay of Bengal, Indian Ocean and so forth. This permits us to see the connections between what we were once taught to regard as separate and distinct regions such as the 'Middle East', 'South Asia' and 'Southeast Asia'. The connections, in turn, open up potentially exciting channels for imagining human mobility as well as commercial and cultural exchange. The attention to time and space – contextualisation – remains very important, because it offers the necessary fine-grained texture to the imaginative leaps of scale that are now possible. When Arabisation is bandied about, for instance, it renders a complex and nuanced trans-regional space into an ahistorical abstraction. The trans-regional scale becomes a liberating and creative space in the study of humanity when it is grounded in history.

1 Craig Lockard, *Societies, Networks, and Transitions: A Global History, Volume I: To 1500* (Boston: Houghton Mifflin Company, 2008), 380.

J o u r n e y B e y o n d t h
e A r r o w J o u r n e y B e
y o n d t h e A r r o w J o u
r n e y B e y o n d t h e A r
r o w J o u r n e y B e y o n
d t h e A r r o w J o u r n e
y B e y o n d t h e A r r o w
J o u r n e y B e y o n d t h
e A r r o w J o u r n e y B e
y o n d t h e A r r o w J o u
r n e y B e y o n d t h e A r
r o w J o u r n e y B e y o n
d t h e A r r o w J o u r n e
y B e y o n d t h e A r r o w
J o u r n e y B e y o n d t h

e A r r o w J o u r n e y B e

y o n d t h e A r r o w J o u

r n e y B e y o n d t h e A r

r o w I S e e M y s e l f J o

u r n e y B e y o n d t h e A

r r o w J o u r n e y B e y o

n d t h e A r r o w J o u r n

e y G e o g r a p h y B e y o

n d t h e o f L i g h t s A r

r o w J o u r n e y B e y o n

d t h e A r r o w J o u r n e

y B e y o n d t h e A r r o w

J o u r n e y B e y o n d t h

e A r r o w J o u r n e y B e

y o n d t h e A r r o w J o u

I see myself

I see myself
And the apprehensive people
Amidst what appears to be the crossroads
of a labyrinth
We step forwards hesitantly
And anguish over other times
Haunted by prosperity
We stray into a deep hole
Snared by the history they, themselves,
unearthed
No one truly meant to dig
So that we might excavate their corpses
Even though no one reads the future
It is there in proximity
Like the reflection off a piece of glass
The shattered and fragmented whole
If there is some imagination left
Even without a discernable future
The lucid present emanates from our
eyes

I see myself
And those mired by cynicism and
disorder
An epidemic of doubt
Thought on the verge of collapse
Like a defiant horse from a fairy tale
Galloping through a sacred forest
A wooded canopy of fury in the shrieking
wind
A whistling reverberation throughout the
mountain pass
Some of us enter the trees to find
ourselves
But find neither we nor others
Some are transfixed by the luminous blur

of the city
Only to discover
Alienation inside the crowd
Of people with shattered hearts

I see myself
And the possession of the headless crowd
Shouldering the unbearable density of
doubt and interrogation
Comprised of sides and criticism
Mere expression, impression,
confinement
Within the fetters of fear, obscurity
An exquisite field of black envelops us
More terrifying than its guiding light
With a headless projection
The parade advances as thought retreats
In the same direction
To become an ordinary story
Who will dare to wander astray
Only to appear the abject delinquent
Cast out in bitterness for all eternity?

I see myself
And those who lack a spine of one's own
The ones who pack an idea and build a
boat around it
To float across the sea of eternity
With no spine
It's tiring to persevere in dignity
When every position is exhausted
What is the point of a victory without a
position
When the spirit is stained?
Lofty ideals tarnished by lowly tactics

I see myself
And those who cling to their clan

Ethnicity and established borders
Are projecting walls across the horizon
A religious vision fenced in barbed wire
In the foreground, a mirror
I try to forget it all
The entirety of my education
All of the words of Ustaz Ustazah
Liberated into the blackness of the mind
So I ask myself ؟ كامو سياف
เจ้าคือใคร คุณคือใคร เธอคือใคร
Who are you? Who art thou? من أنت؟
Everything still makes sense
But you may not like the point
All of the answers remain
But you may not welcome the response

I see myself
Like a blank page inserted into a book
I desire, I want it filled with confessions
Sentences, lyrical oratory, symbolism and
various analogies
But perhaps it's best to leave it blank
I see myself
And I see all of you watching me write this
But looking into your own words would
suit you better

Zakariya Amataya

Translated from Thai by Noah Viernes

Geography of Lights

In the eye's retina
An inverted global image
Like a surreal poem
We look at the inverted world obliviously
Do we see the world through our eyes
Or through the refractions of light?
The duration of imaginary travel
Ever swifter than the truth
Sometimes more real
Until it becomes delusional
Haunted in myth
Swayed towards that which does not exist
Bringing us to the castle in the sky
The majestic kingdom
Is intoxicated, decadent, delirious
Towards prosperity
The imaginary world we create
Is safer than the one that exists
We dig, we dig, we dig into ourselves
To become bunkers
Wherever refuge might be had
Tranquility beyond disorder
Equal to our own bunkers

The geography of light
Is difficult to discover and possess
Many travellers and seekers
Try to engage the vast world
But no one can turn back to seize the light
The aesthetics of illumination
Might be discovered in darkness
Surrounding each one of us
Or inside of our own confusion
No matter how gloomy
No matter the proximity to the truth
There is the relationship between light
and colour
When light changes, colour changes
Truth changes
Beauty changes
When the sun sets
Everything breaks apart into blackness
Leaving only the bare truth
The desolate solitude
Precarious emotions
Born of silence from within
God hath bestowed darkness unto us
That He might also grant us vision

Zakariya Amataya

Translated from Thai by Noah Viernes

J o u r n e y B e y o n d t h
e A r r o w J o u r n e y B e
y o n d t h e A r r o w J o u
r n e y B e y o n d t h e A r
r o w J o u r n e y B e y o n
d t h e A r r o w J o u r n e
y B e y o n d t h e A r r o w
J o u r n e y B e y o n d t h
e A r r o w J o u r n e y B e
y o n d t h e A r r o w J o u
r n e y B e y o n d t h e A r
r o w J o u r n e y B e y o n
d t h e A r r o w J o u r n e
y B e y o n d t h e A r r o w
J o u r n e y B e y o n d t h

The foragers are the provocateurs who reveal trajectories of human movement, illustrating human trails of bounty whose histories have failed to enter the macro imagination of our globalising echo chamber. These foragers of transversals narrate sociopolitical comparisons behind their culture's human action and ritual, refreshing/redrawing a line connecting cause to effect.

The foragers are the provocateurs who reveal trajectories of human movement, illustrating human trails of bounty whose histories have failed to enter the macro imagination of our globalising echo chamber. These foragers of transversals narrate sociopolitical comparisons behind their culture's human action and ritual, refreshing/redrawing a line connecting cause to effect.

e A r r o w T h e J o u r n e
y B e y o n d F o r a g e r s
t h e A r r o w J o u r n e y
B e y o n d t h e A r r o w J
o u r n e y B e y o n d t h e
A r r o w J o u r n e y B e y
o n d t h e A r r o w J o u r
n e y B e y o n d t h e A r r
o w J o u r n e y B e y o n d
t h e A r r o w J o u r n e y
B e y o n d t h e A r r o w J
o u r n e y B e y o n d t h e
A r r o w J o u r n e y B e y
o n d t h e A r r o w J o u r
n e y B e y o n d t h e A r r

Tuấn Andrew Nguyễn

The Specter of Ancestors Becoming, 2019

French colonial subjects – *tirailleurs Sénégalais* and *tirailleurs Indochinois* – defended France in world wars far from home, until the mid-twentieth century. When the Vietnamese rose up against French colonial rule, French colonial forces from West Africa were shipped to help quell the uprising. There are stories of *tirailleurs Sénégalais* defecting from their positions on the battlefield to join the Vietnamese revolutionary soldiers. These stories of 'solidarity' exist as hearsay, as unrecorded and invalid myths.

Throughout the war and after the defeat of the French at Dien Bien Phu in 1954 – the moment philosopher Frantz Fanon declared to be the beginning of the end of the French Empire – hundreds of Vietnamese women and their children migrated to Senegal with their Senegalese husbands, colonial soldiers of the French Army who had been stationed in Indochina. Many other soldiers left their wives and took only their children. Still others took children not their own, some of whom were *metis* and others who were completely Vietnamese – the latter, raised as Senegalese, often without knowledge of their origins.

Within this largely unwritten history, personal stories and incomplete secrets come to undermine the monolithic quality of established historical narratives. In *The Specter of Ancestors Becoming*, the Senegalese-Vietnamese community reveals the resonating effects of colonialism, migration, memory and identity through the bridges and gaps formed from generation to generation.

Initially drawn to the possibilities of solidarity amidst colonial conditions – and upon hearing the particular stories of Merry Bey Diouf, Anne Marie Niane and Macodou Ndiaye – I soon came to realise that the non-existence of such camaraderie arose from an indoctrinated 'colonial mentality'. Here, prejudice based on colour, class and faith continues to complicate the power play between native, colonial subjects and their offspring. I worked with these Vietnamese-Senegalese descendants to write fictional scenes based on their desire to activate the past and to relook at the relationships that have defined their lives today. *The Specter of Ancestors Becoming* thus imagines, and reimagines, the birthing of this *other metis* community, offering space in which to destabilise colonial understandings of race, identity, nationalism and the culture of recorded history.

Tuấn Andrew Nguyễn

In the 'Specter of Ancestors Becoming', three Vietnamese-Senegalese individuals share their own imagined conversations between/with their parents or grandparents. These carfully nuanced tales reveal their complex desire to forget and to remember, as they remain deeply aware of how each of their ancestral journeys and cultural roots set them forever (metaphysically) apart. In this four-channel installation, the voices of these descendents are given double power play – as narrator and actor – begging acknowledgement of the voices (of relation and its experience) that embody intangible, oral, and imagined historical conscience. Such forms should be considered primary evidence that can challenge the dominant hegemonic understandings of decolonising societies.

In the 'Specter of Ancestors Becoming,' three Vietnamese-Senegalese individuals share their own imagined conversations between/with their parents or grandparents. These carefully nuanced tales reveal their complex desire to forget and to remember, as they remain deeply aware of how each of their ancestral journeys and cultural roots set them forever (metaphysically) apart. In this four-channel installation, the voices of these descendants are given double power play – as narrator and actor – begging acknowledgement of the voices (of relation and its experience) that embody intangible, oral, and imagined historical conscience. Such forms should be considered primary evidence that can challenge the dominant hegemonic understandings of decolonising societies.

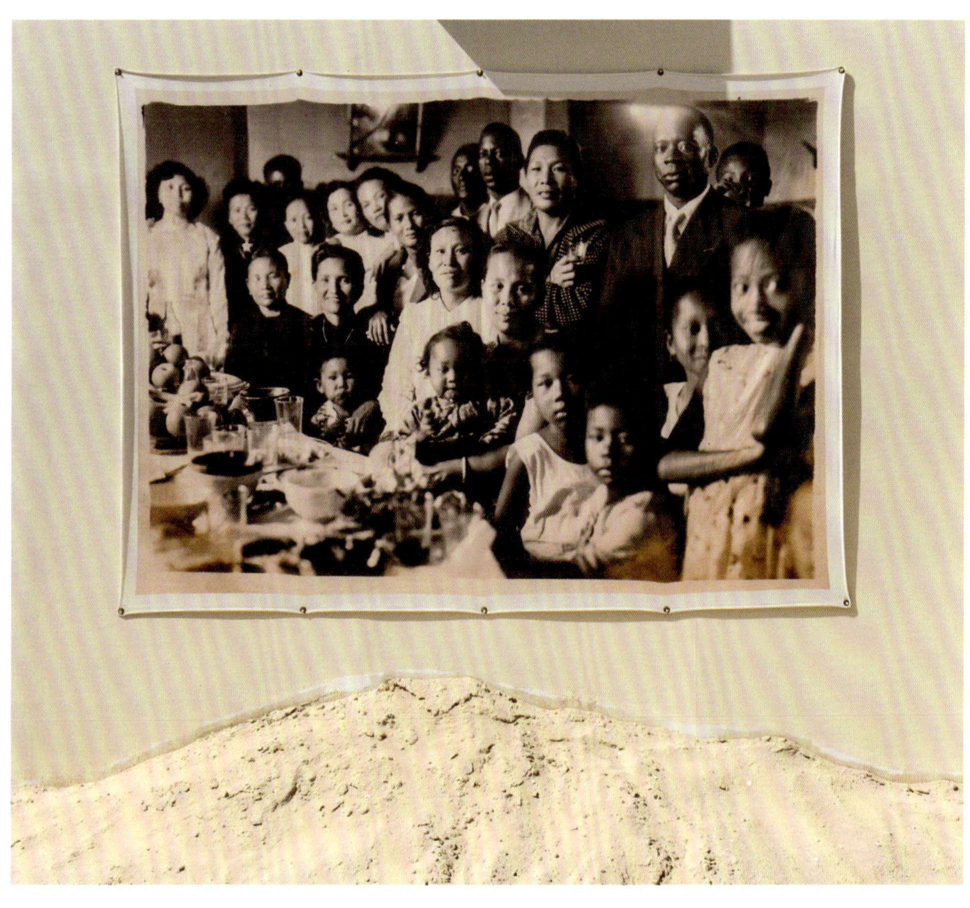

The Specter of Ancestors Becoming
2019
4-channel video installation: colour, 7.1 surround sound; inkjet on canvas, oil on canvas, graphite on paper, C-prints, sand
28 minutes; dimensions variable
Commissioned by Sharjah Art Foundation
Produced by Sharjah Art Foundation with additional production support from the San Francisco Museum of Modern Art
Courtesy of the artist and James Cohan, New York

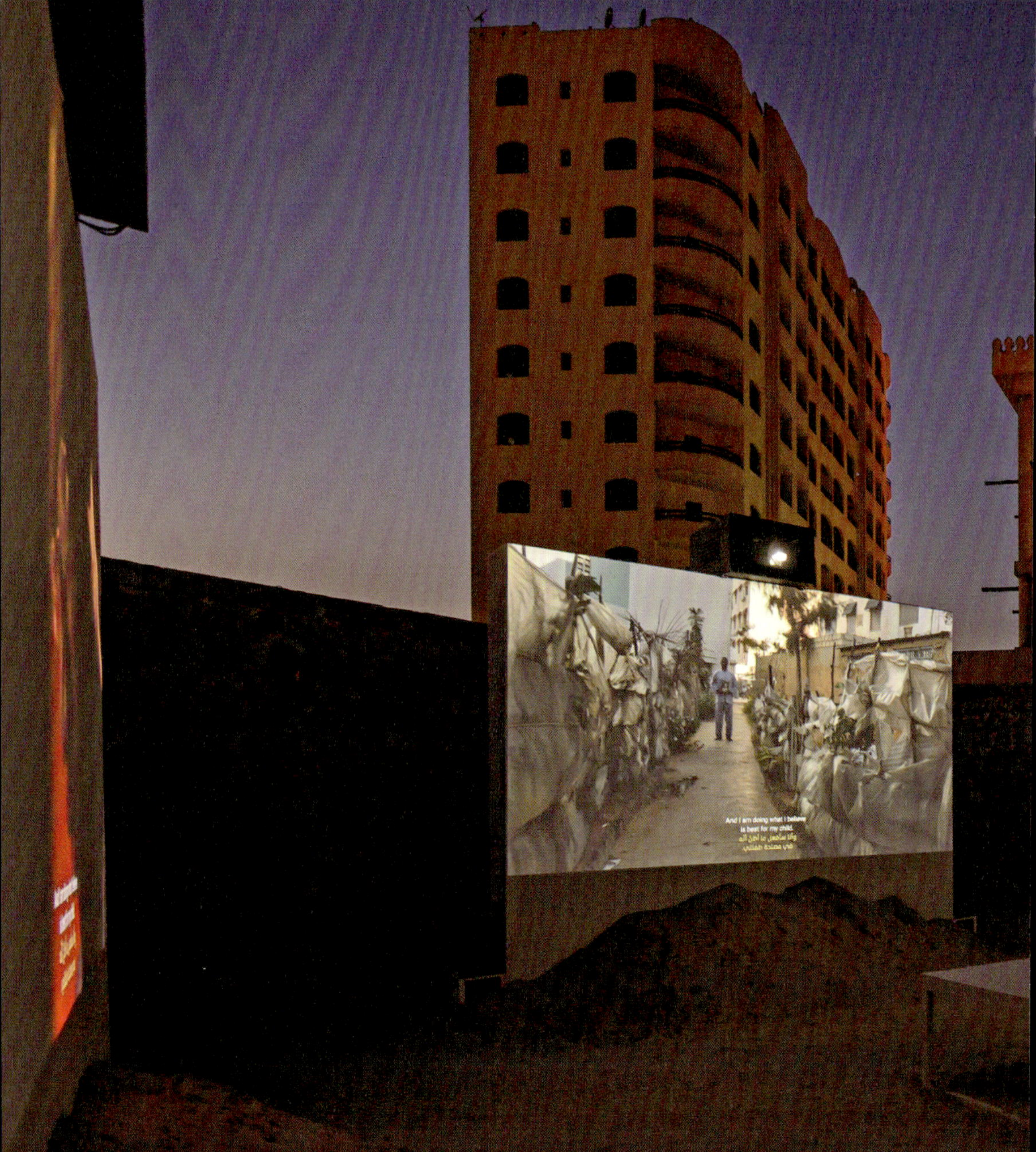
And I am doing what I believe
is best for my child.

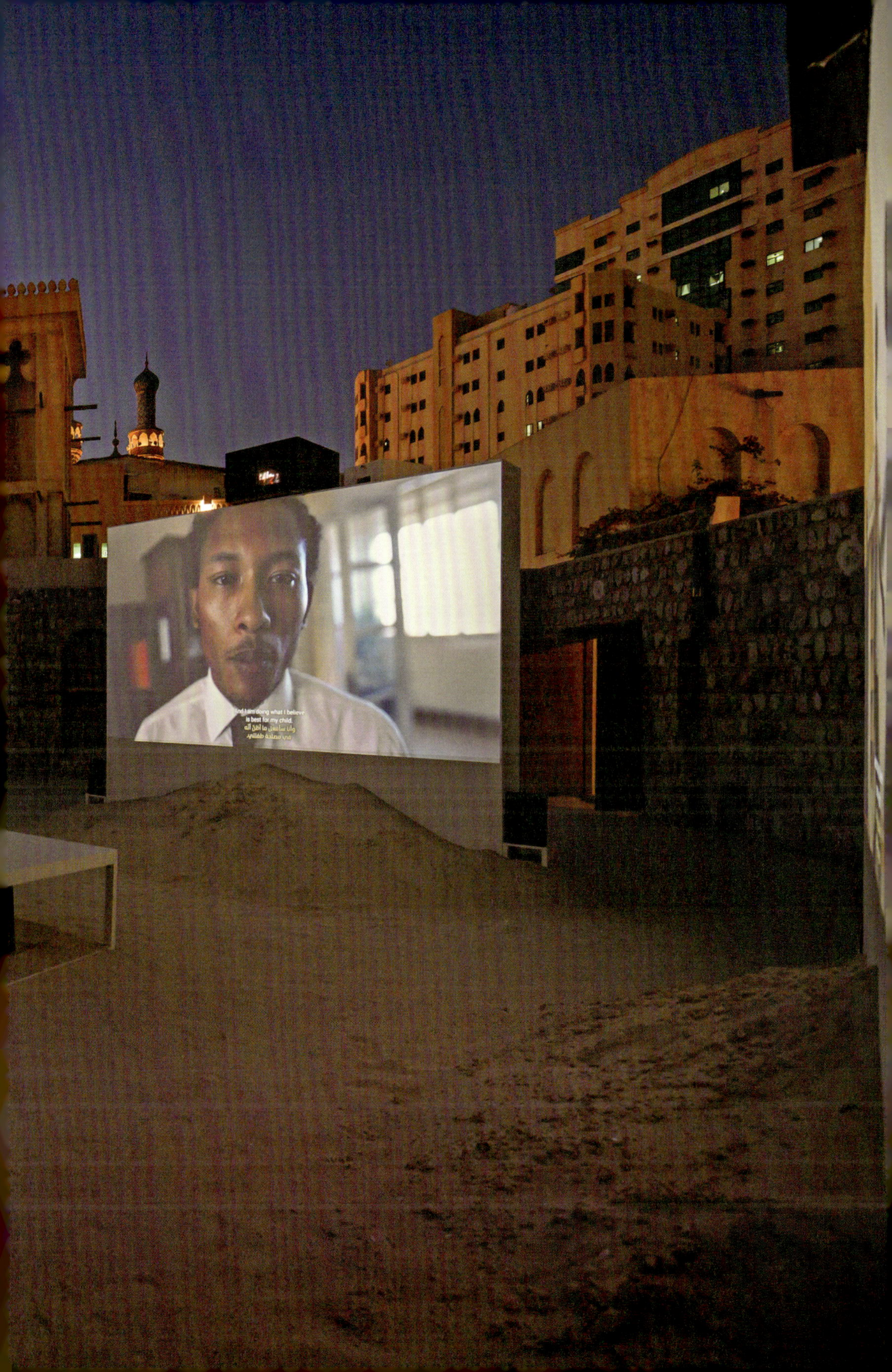
nd I am doing what I believe
is best for my child.

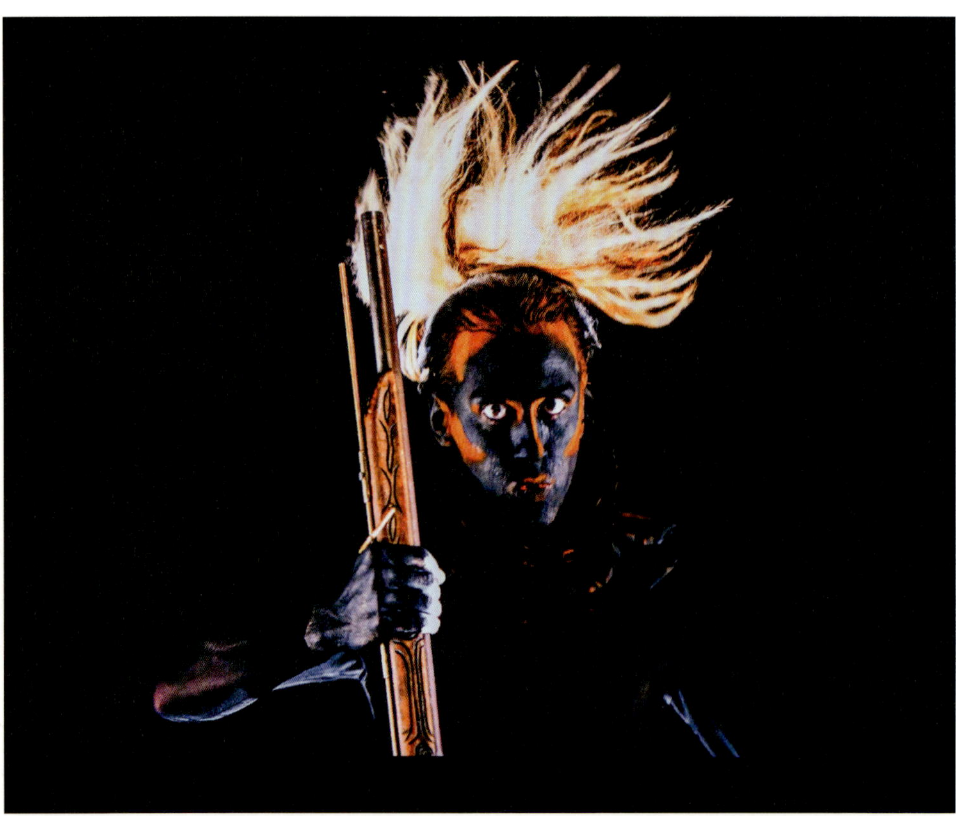

Nomads of the Sea
2019
4-channel 3D UHD video: multi-channel audio, steel, lighting installation with sculptural components
19 minutes; dimensions variable
Co-commissioned by Sharjah Art Foundation and Creative New Zealand, Nga Aho Whakaari, Te Taura Whiri Maori Language Commission and Jan Warburton Charitable Trust.
Co-produced by Artprojects and Reihanamations Ltd
Courtesy of the artist and Artprojects, Aotearoa/New Zealand

ARTPROJECTS

In 'Nomads of the Sea', the traditional role of women in Aotearoa (New Zealand) – as matriarchs, owners of property and spiritual custodians – is contested with the arrival of a favoured escaped convict and the material wealth of the colonising 'junks of England. Lisa provides insight into the valuing of the musket as synonymous with the female body, revealing the social tensions between cultural leadership, spiritual custom and egotistical desire in the face of foreign political challenge. This 3-D immersive installation is narrated via 'Storyteller', a mythical figure who guides viewers through a voyage of recall of the past via oral, performed and written histories.

In 'Nomads of the Sea', the traditional role of women in Aotearoa (New Zealand) – as matriarchs, owners of property and spiritual custodians – is contested with the arrival of a favoured escaped convict and the material wealth of the colonising 'Dukes of England'. Lisa provides insight into the valuing of the musket as synonymous with the female body, revealing the social tensions between cultural leadership, spiritual custom and egotistical desire in the face of foreign political challenge. This 3-D immersive installation is narrated via 'Storyteller', a mythical figure who guides viewers through a voyage of recall of the past via oral, performed and written histories.

Lisa Reihana

Nomads of the Sea, 2019

Nomads of the Sea weaves historical fact with fiction, connecting the tale of a Pakeha (Western/English) female mutineer, Charlotte Badger, with Puhi, a proud woman of Ngāpuhi descent. Charlotte lives under the protection of the Maori chief, Huri Waka; however, she is caught between Huri Waka and Puhi, who is jealous of her rising status. Why would a Maori chief welcome a fugitive, the first European woman, into his tribal homeland? Charlotte is a survivor and Puhi is ambitious, but they must both prove their value in the early days of colonisation, when intermarriage, trade and the procurement of muskets were seen as essential to the survival of Maori society. Between insults and blows, the story of these two women is revealed – it is an unborn child that is traded, as payment, for ultimate survival.

As I'm of mixed race, the circumstances of the very first child of both Maori and British descent appeals to me. This story slips between a masculine and a feminine voice, as experiences from 1800s New Zealand are narrated. As a musket is raised, we learn about Pakeha Maori – Europeans who were adopted and co-opted by Maori to increase prowess, gain strategic ability and, ultimately, counteract the spread of Western dominance and power. *He wai ngunguru,* the centrepiece of this installation, explores the cultural circumstances surrounding women during the early nineteenth century, contrasting European law with Maori culture and morality.

Lisa Reihana

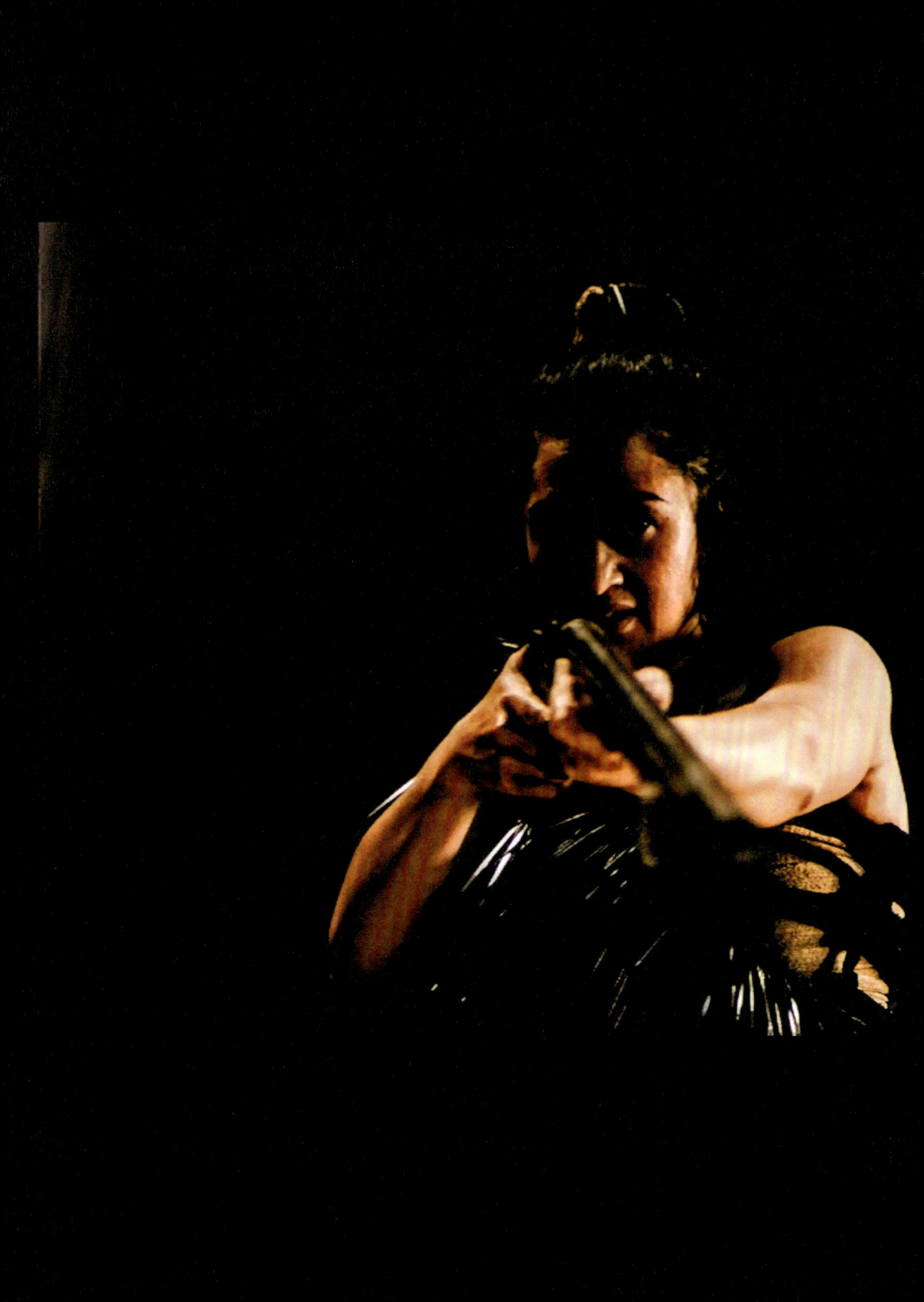

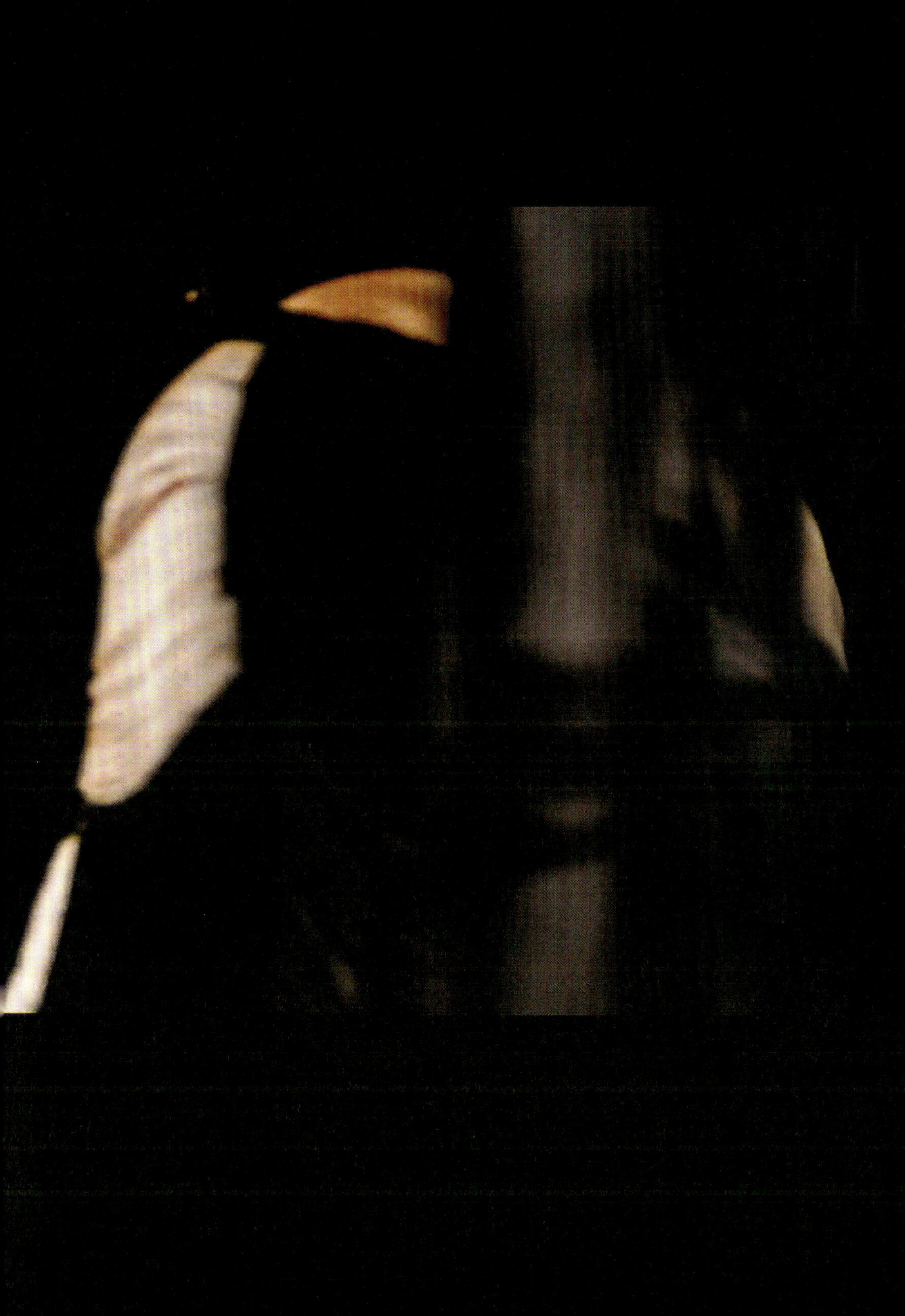

Meiro Koizumi

The Angels of Testimony, 2019

How do we inherit guilt? If I were to experience the killing of another human, I would be traumatised for the rest of my life. I would suffer from feelings of shame; my trauma would recur with flashbacks that I would be unable to control.

Guilt is based on a private mechanism of psychology, in which one understands they have done something wrong. However, collective emotions, such as the 'war guilt of a nation', are not based on such mechanisms. It is always someone else who committed the dirty crime. Your hands are clean whilst you are still entitled to feel the shame. So, there is a gap between the emotions you are supposed to have and your private, psychological reality. This is where ritual kicks in – ritual as a transformative method that is used to change one's identity from outside and also from within. For example, through a funeral, I officially become a dead person; the ritual is an obligatory(?) process that my loved ones enact, so as to let me go.

The Angels of Testimony attempts to make visceral this gap, between experiential and obligatory emotions, by inviting eleven Japanese youth to consciously create a collective way to inherit the guilt of a World War II soldier who has agonisingly held inside the war crimes he committed in China during the Second Sino-Japanese War (1937–45). The work is an attempt to engrave a sense of guilt onto our cultural DNA through a newly created ritual. But is such a devised act a kind of brainwashing?

In much of my work, I create public performances with ordinary citizens, in a way 'testing' their awareness of conditioned and innate behaviours. As a result, I have realised that Japanese people are particularly ready to adapt to any kind of formalistic ritual. We are accustomed to doing this in school and at home. Since we were children, our bodies have become ritualistic vessels, in a prescribed sense.

Meiro Koizumi

Meiro's artistic practice often touches on the malleable fragility of the human mental world. Most recently, he has undertaken an exploration of the effects of modern technological warfare (particularly in contexts such as Iraq and Japan), making visible the impact of merciless mechanical violence upon the human body and how the latter remembers and internalises trauma. The artist's fascination with this theme was initiated by his experience of growing up in a country that has often silenced its own role in historical atrocities. In 1937, the Empire of Japan brutally captured Shanghai and Nanjing as part of an imperialist agenda to secure access to raw reserves, food and labour. This invasion was the beginning of a ruthless campaign, which by 1940 also included the occupation of many parts of South East Asia. The violence of Japanese militarism during World War II is still a sensitive issue today, and is rarely discussed publicly in Japan.

A disturbing silence is similarly found throughout South East Asia, whose people have arguably also refrained from analysing the full impact of the Japanese occupation — anecdotes of which can be found in the works of Phan Thao Nguyen (pg.190) and Antariksa (pg.208)

Meiro's artistic practice often touches on the malleable fragility of the human mental world. Most recently, he has undertaken an exploration of the effects of modern technological warfare (particularly in contexts such as Iraq and Japan), making visible the impact of merciless mechanical violence upon the human body and how the latter remembers and internalises trauma. The artist's fascination with this theme was initiated by his experience of growing up in a country that has often silenced its own role in historical atrocities. In 1937, the Empire of Japan brutally captured Shanghai and Nanjing as part of an imperialist agenda to secure access to raw reserves, food and labour. This invasion was the beginning of a ruthless campaign, which by 1940 also included the occupation of many parts of South East Asia. The violence of Japanese militarism during World War II is still a sensitive issue today, and is rarely discussed publicly in Japan.

A disturbing silence is similarly found throughout South East Asia, whose people have arguably also refrained from analysing the full impact of the Japanese occupation — anecdotes of which can be found in the works of Phan Thao Nguyen (pg 190) and Arahmaiani (pg 208)

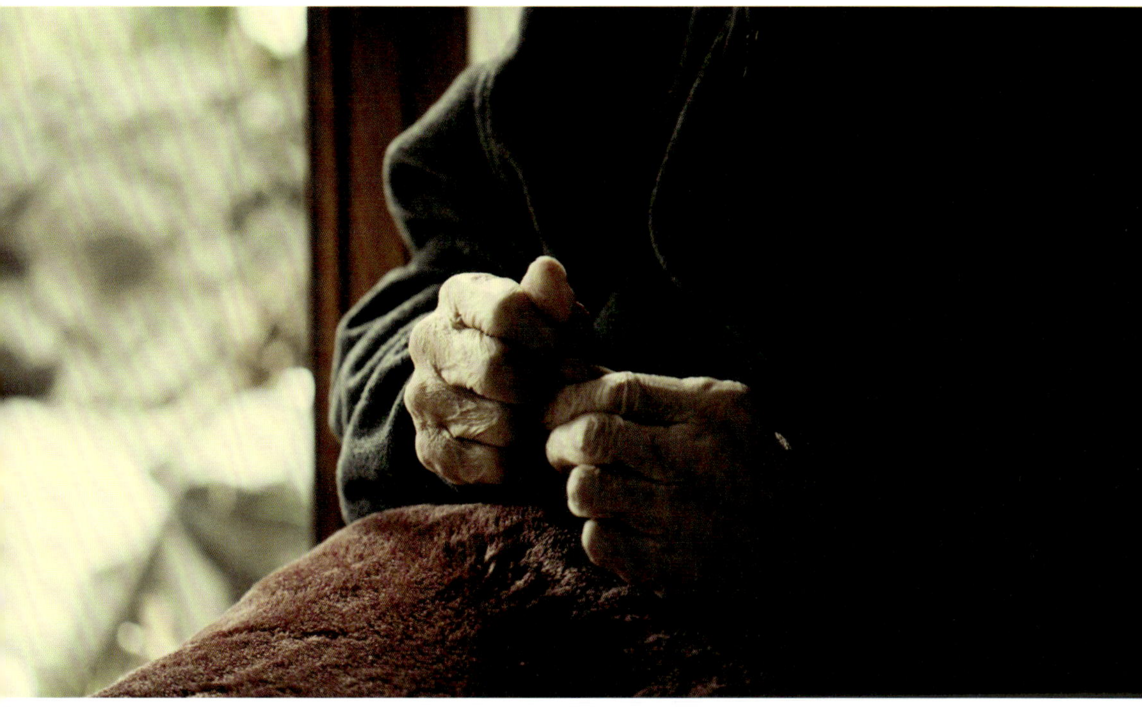

The Angels of Testimony
2019
3-channel video installation: colour, sound; archival materials
47 minutes; dimensions variable
Commissioned by Sharjah Art Foundation
Courtesy of the artist, Annet Gelink Gallery, Amsterdam and MUJIN-TO Production, Tokyo

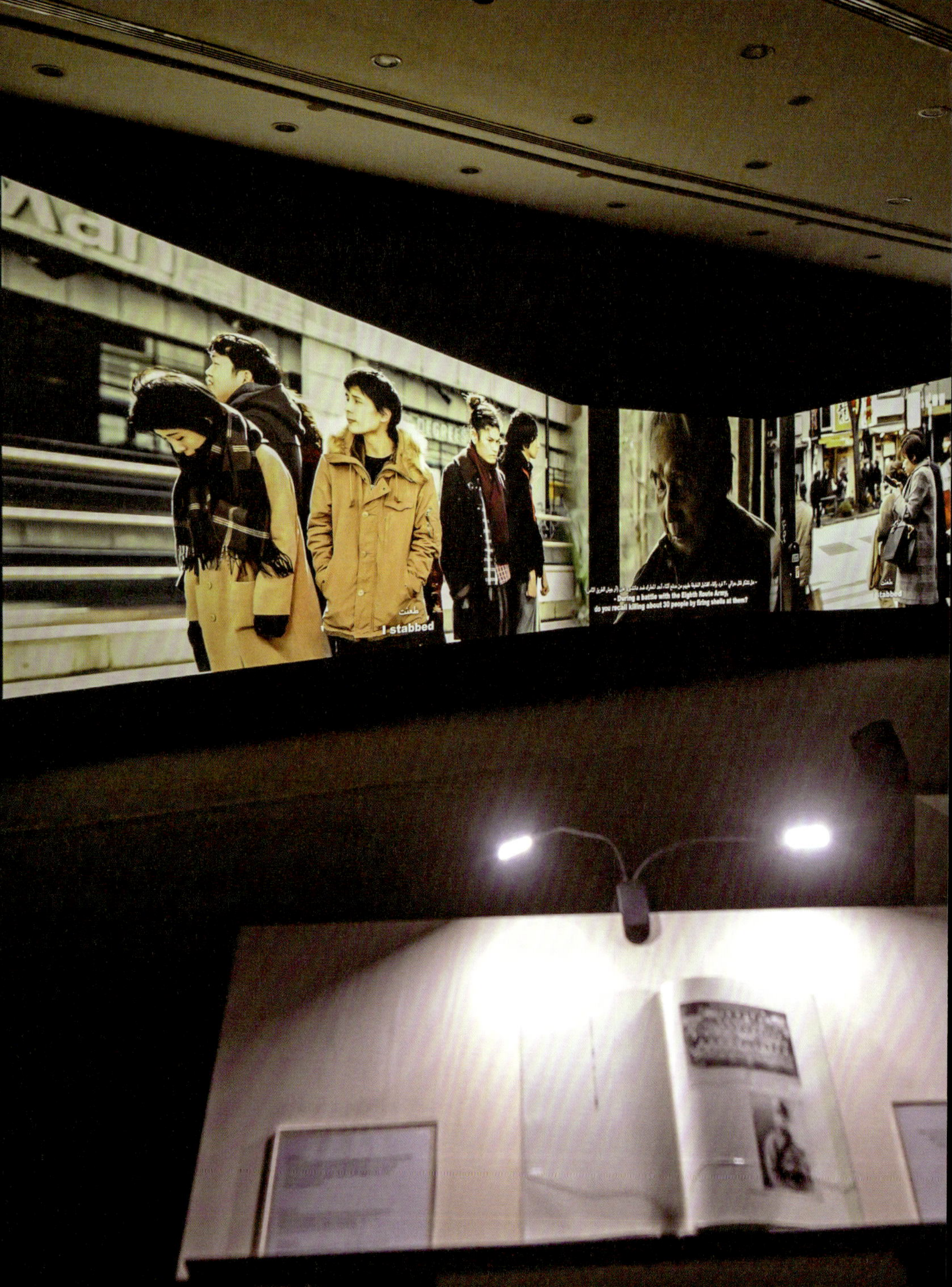
طعنت
I stabbed
- During a battle with the Eighth Route Army,
do you recall killing about 30 people by firing shells at them?

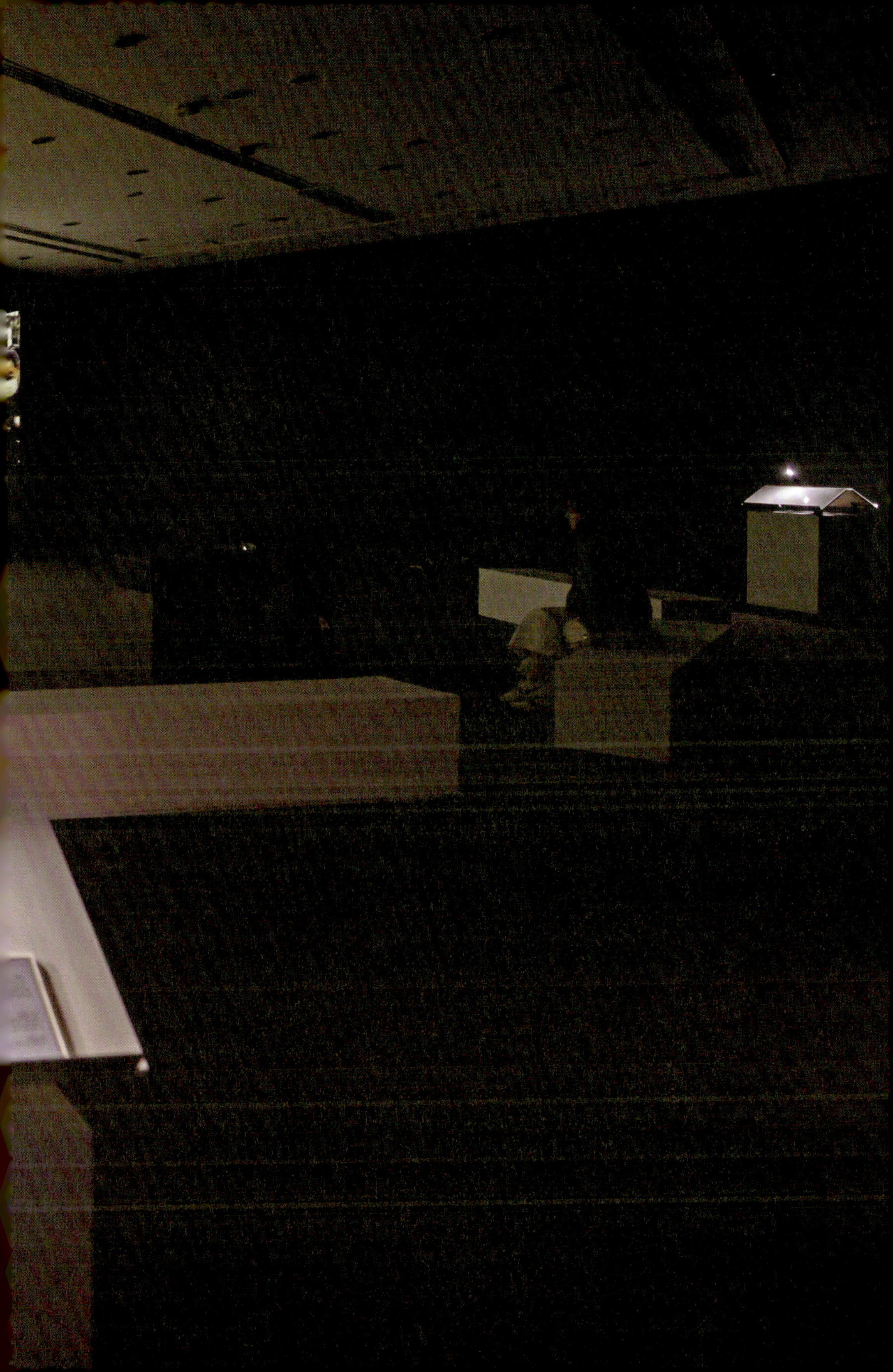

Qiu Zhijie

We live among quotidian systems of concepts, expressions, visual customs as well as habits of thought; we are always in the midst of their latent or apparent effects. The domination over human beings of this sort of habituation is sometimes very apparent. People within these systems may speak as if they are having an outer-body experience. Other times people haven't the faintest idea that they are being controlled by the power of these systems ... Habituation, custom, and belief encourage people to not think, so that they mistakenly deem these cultural instantiations inevitable instead of man-made.

Everyday life becomes a trap — becoming habituated to things and forgetting that truth can be different ... To break out of the trap, you must first become aware of these limitations ... you must carefully observe with a self-critical eye and never doubt your suspicions. This process of self-critical observation has become a trendy practice known as 'cultural studies'. Hence art that labors to break out of the trap has no choice but to treat cultural studies as its starting point.

We are in an era of fundamental division; our cultural values are fragmented. Our individual honor is divided from social obligation. Our labor is divided from creation. Our art is divided from life. Our radicalism is divided from compromise. Our cities are divided from the countryside. The self is divided from the other. These various predicaments are the symptoms of a grave spiritual illness. It is the peculiar psychosis of our times. We should first become conscious of and acknowledge the symptoms of our own schizophrenia and then begin to change this form of psychosis. Those who do not seek connections will not be connected. Those who do not seek unity will have no unity.

Proposing a new way is based then on the critique of habit. It is a disruption of everyday life and of all power, authority and order that purports to be unquestionably extant ... We must launch training into how to err: relating at random, opening up genealogies, zen, post-perception, etc.

Total art is a tool for assisting the evolution of human beings and the world.

Qiu Zhijie

Qiu Zhijie is a polymath whose insatiable desire to explore the presumed limits of possibility continues to shape his life's practice. The ~~above~~ text is an excerpt from the artist's thesis on 'Total Art' (2012), a concept that has self-cultivated his social role as artist and teacher. For Qiu, art and thus life, must be full of the labor of imagination, and thus an engagement with the everyday presumed and hidden. For SB14, Qiu thinks through, and thwarts, the boundaries of cartography, not only the psychogeographies of the Discipline itself, its mapping of conquest, study and control, but also its casting of a history of exchange and relation between China and the Arab world. These inked studies reveal alternate windows of learning, human action and its production, in all its interconnected and interdependent manifestations.

Qiu Zhijie is a polymath whose insatiable desire to explore the presumed limits of possibility continues to shape his life's practice. The ~~above~~ text is an excerpt from the artist's thesis on 'Total Art' (2012), a concept that has self-cultivated his social role as artist and teacher. For Qiu, art and thus life, must be full of the labor of imagination, and thus an engagement with the everyday presumed and hidden. For SB14, Qiu thinks through, and thwarts, the boundaries of cartography, not only the psychogeographies of the Discipline itself, its mapping of conquest, study and control, but also its casting of a history of exchange and relation between China and the Arab world. These linked studies reveal alternate windows of learning, human action and its production, in all its interconnected and interdependent manifestations.

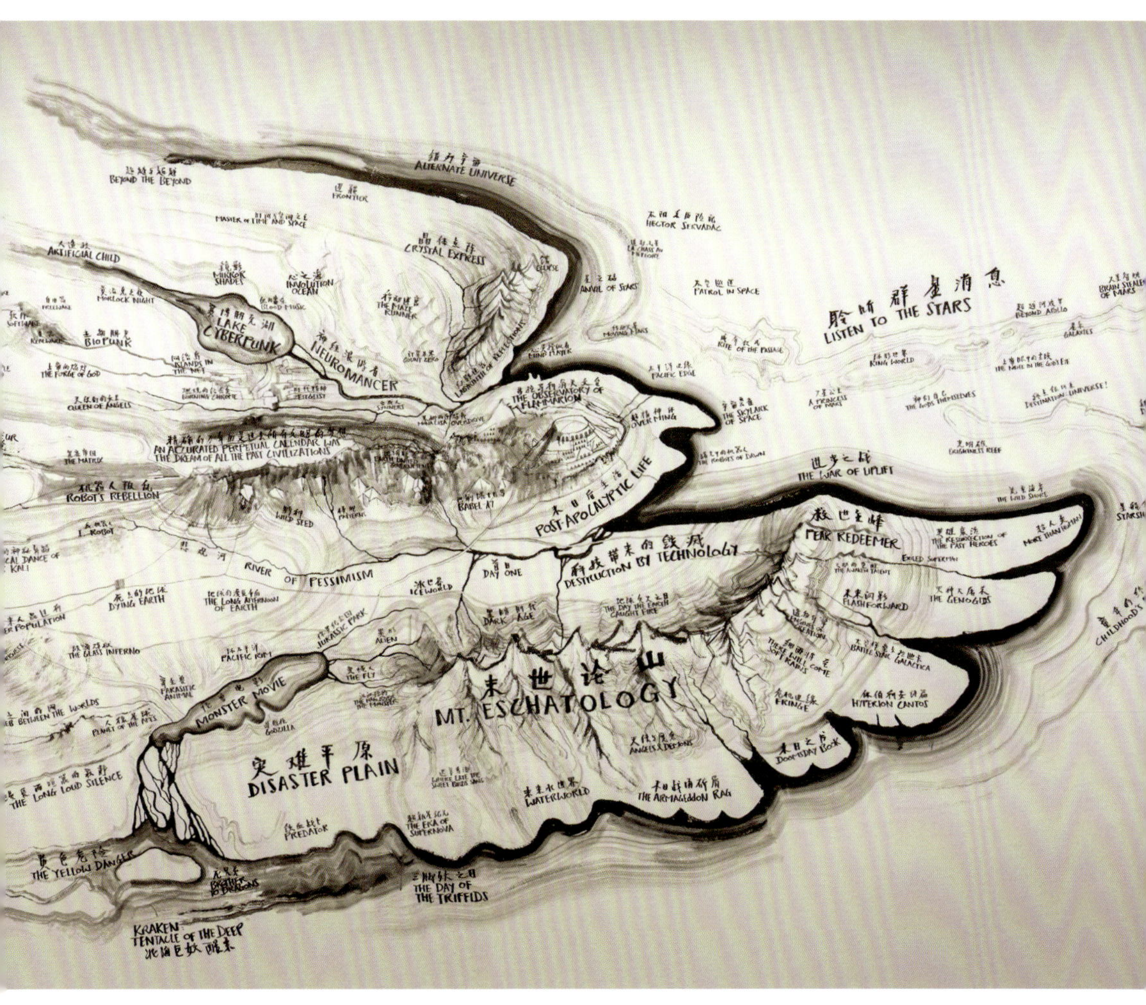

Various works
2015–2019
35 colour-print scrolls
Dimensions variable
Partially commissioned by Sharjah Art Foundation.
Courtesy of the artist

Page 110:
Map of Religion - Some People Always Tend to Believe
2015
Ink on paper
300 x 126 cm

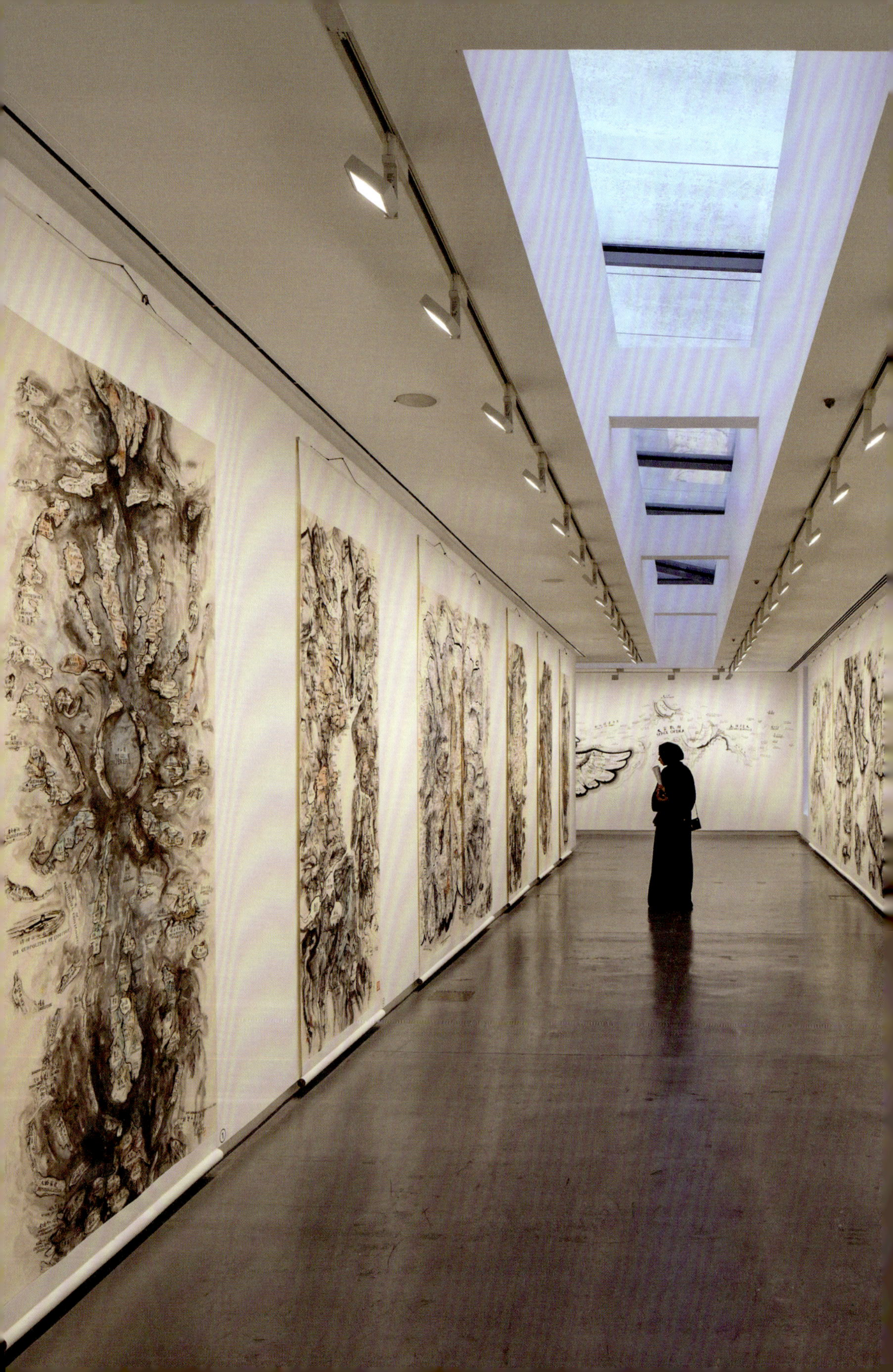

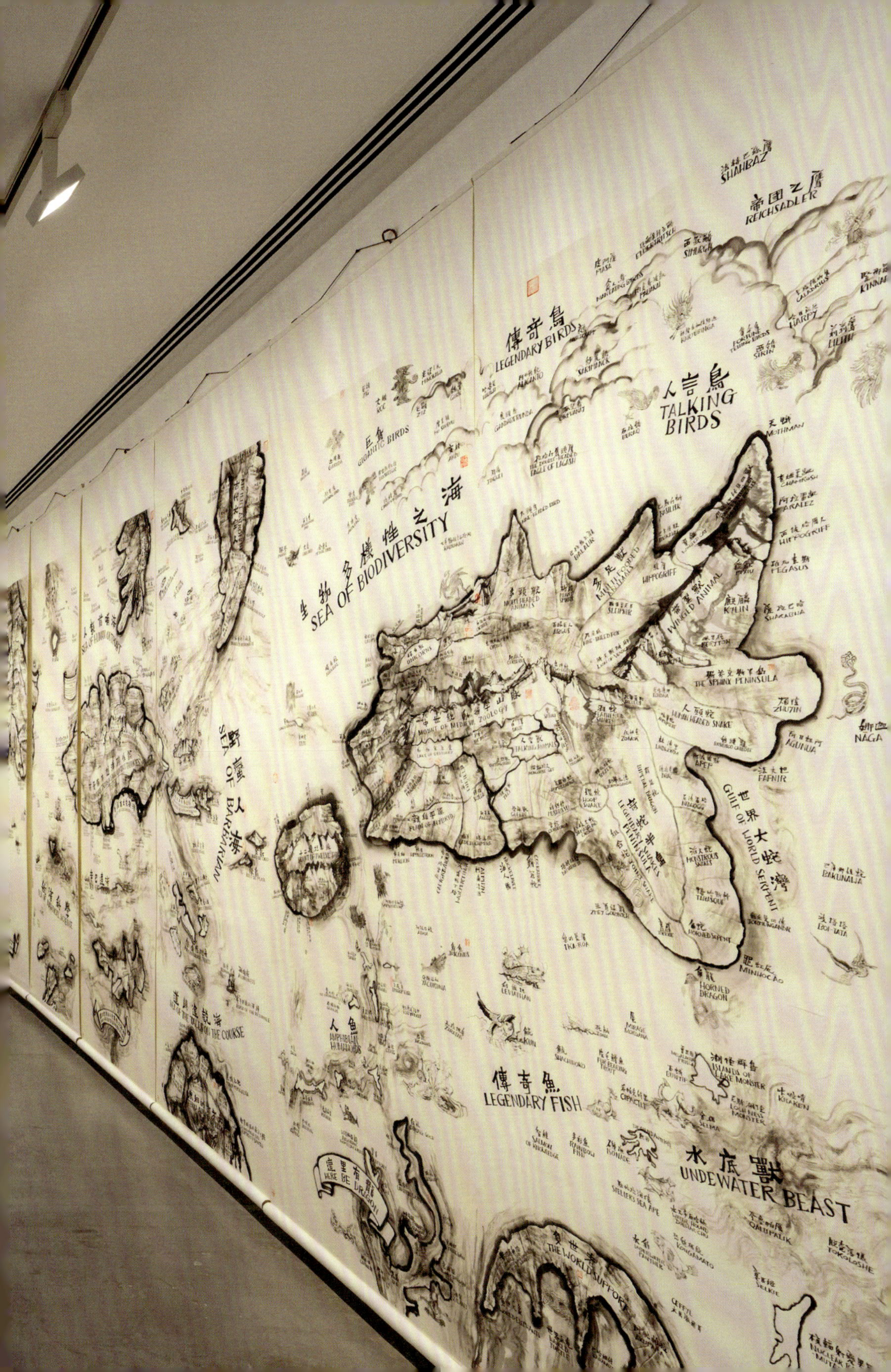

SHAHBAZ
帝国之鹰
REICHSADLER
傳奇鳥
LEGENDARY BIRDS
人言鳥
TALKING BIRDS
巨鳥
GIGANTIC BIRDS
HARPY
MOTHMAN
HIPPOGRIFF
PEGASUS
KILIN
生物多樣性之海
SEA OF BIODIVERSITY
WINGED ANIMAL
THE SPHINX PENINSULA
NAGA
FAFNIR
世界大蛇灣
GULF OF WORLD SERPENT
HORNED SERPENT
HORNED DRAGON
野蠻人海
SEA OF BARBARIAN
人魚
傳奇魚
LEGENDARY FISH
KRAKEN
水底獸
UNDEWATER BEAST
HERE BE DRAGON

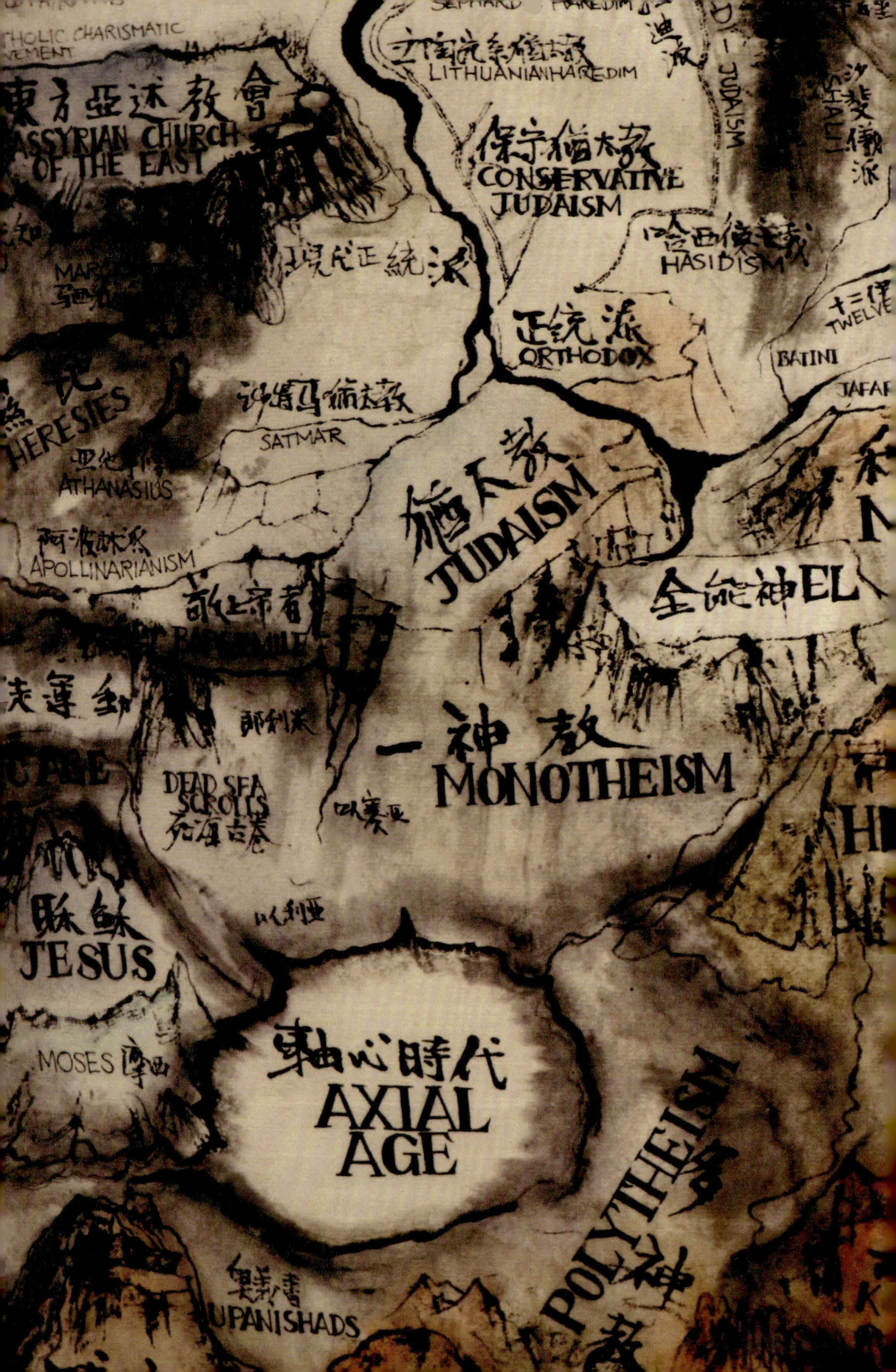

東方亞述教會
ASSYRIAN CHURCH OF THE EAST
LITHUANIAN HAREDIM
CONSERVATIVE JUDAISM
HASIDISM
正統派
ORTHODOX
TWELVE
BATINI
HERESIES
SATMAR
猶太教
JUDAISM
ATHANASIUS
APOLLINARIANISM
全能神 EL
一神教
MONOTHEISM
DEAD SEA SCROLLS
JESUS
MOSES 摩西
軸心時代
AXIAL AGE
POLYTHEISM
UPANISHADS

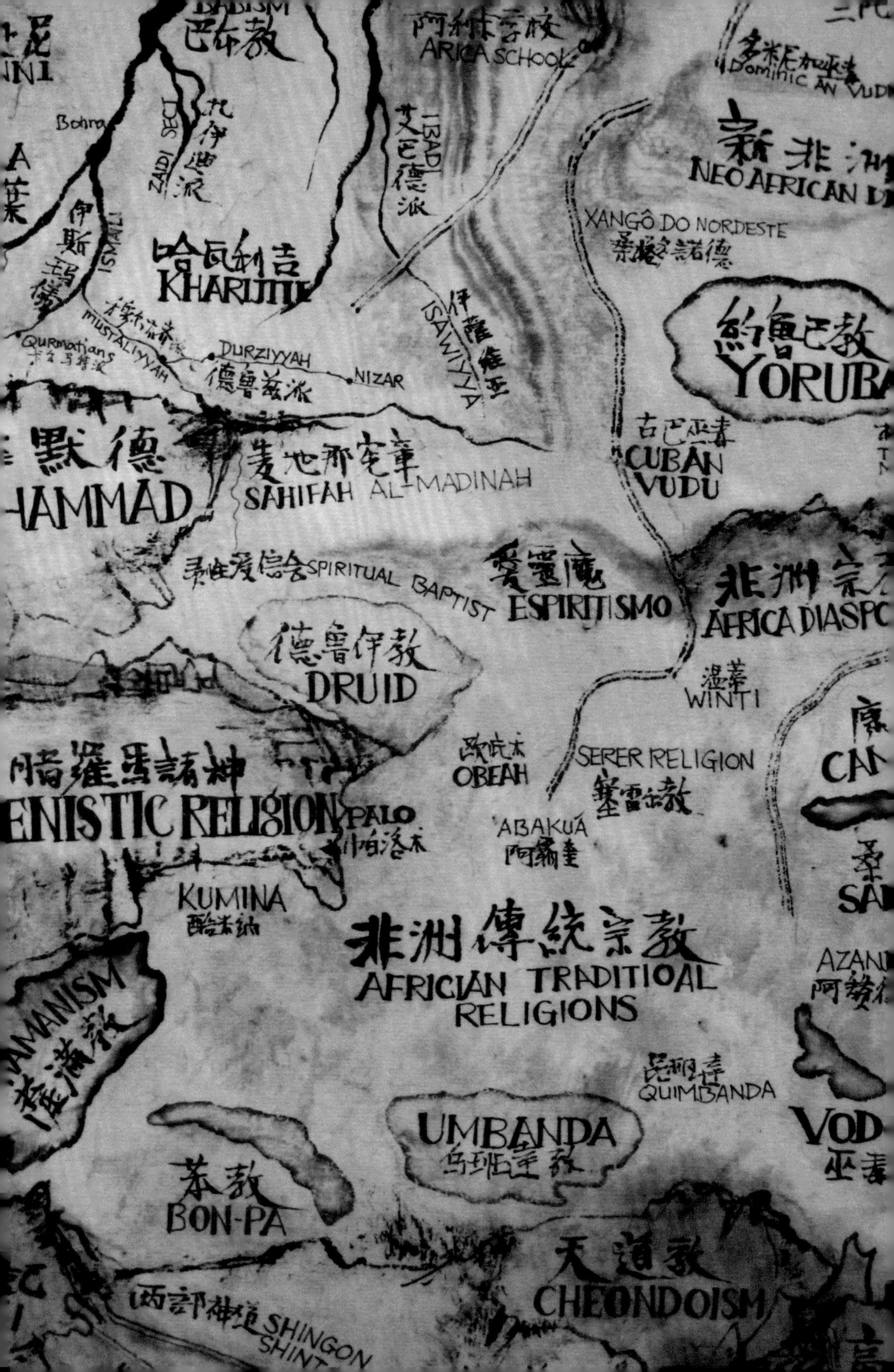

BABISM
巴布教

阿利卡学校
ARICA SCHOOL

多米尼加巫毒
DOMINIC AN VUDU

Bohra

ZADI SECT

ISMAILI

伊斯玛仪

IBADI
艾巴德派

新非洲
NEO AFRICAN

XANGÔ DO NORDESTE

哈瓦利吉
KHARIJITE

ISAWIYYA
伊薩維亞

MUSTALIYYAH

Qurmatians

DURZIYYAH
德魯兹派

NIZAR

約魯巴教
YORUBA

古巴巫毒
CUBAN
VUDU

默德
HAMMAD

麦地那宪章
SAHIFAH AL-MADINAH

SPIRITUAL BAPTIST

愛靈魔
ESPIRITISMO

非洲宗
AFRICA DIASPO

德魯伊教
DRUID

WINTI

OBEAH

SERER RELIGION

ENISTIC RELIGION

PALO
帕洛木

ABAKUÁ
阿爾奎

KUMINA

非洲傳統宗教
AFRICIAN TRADITIOAL
RELIGIONS

AZAN

AMANISM
薩滿教

QUIMBANDA

UMBANDA

VOD
巫毒

苯教
BON-PA

天道教
CHEONDOISM

西部神道 SHINGON
SHINT

Jompet Kuswidananto

Keroncong Concordia, 2019

In 1879, a group of wealthy Dutch East Indies colonial elites founded a social club in Bandung, Indonesia. Named 'Sociëteit Concordia', the club contributed to the popularity of *keroncong* music, a style initially developed by Indo-Europeans and rooted in the Portuguese *fado* (initially played in Indonesia by seventeenth-century slaves). *Keroncong* was considered lower-class music during much of the Dutch era, but after decades of musical development and social change, the Dutch came to consider it as one of their most valuable cultural contributions.

Permission to enter particular areas of Sociëteit Concordia was restricted according to race and class, thus dividing Dutch, Indo-Dutch, Indo-African, Chinese descendants, native Indonesians and other mixed-blood communities. (Ironically, it is to these discriminated-against people that *keroncong* owes its legacy.) In many ways, this privileged and prejudiced society enacted and harboured the beginnings of the racial violence that would consume Indonesia in years to come.

In 1945, Indonesia proclaimed its independence, but the bloody conflict between Indonesian nationalists and the Dutch Empire was just beginning. The conflict was often framed in terms of Tanah Air ('land and water'), a deeper Malay concept of 'hometown' and a reference to the mixed-blood community that included the Indo-African Royal Netherlands East Indies Army (KNIL) soldiers, who were eventually forced to flee the archipelago.

As a glass bird crashes to the ground – its colonial dreams in shattered luxury - personal stories of this *Keroncong Concordia* community who desire a decolonised Indonesia are sung, offering different perspectives, from Indo-African KNIL soldiers to National Army veterans. *Keroncong Concordia* projects a dystopic glance at colonial greed and the desire for social control, thinly veiled by the sounds of folk tunes, whose residual histories carry little-known counter-memories.

Jompet Kuswidananto

Keroncong Concordia
2019
Sculptural video installation: 3-channel video: colour, sound; glass, metal, light, carpets
15 minutes 33 seconds; dimensions variable
Commissioned by Sharjah Art Foundation
Courtesy of the artist

Page 114–117:
Photo: readsreads.info

In 2015, I visited Elmina Fort, off the coast of Accra, Ghana, where I found myself in a state of violent helplessness, incredulous over the conditions, in this Dutch-created hell, where thousands were 'processed' as slaves to cross the Atlantic. In Elmina, I also visited the Java Museum, with its batiks and wayang puppetry, and mildewing photographs of a Ghanaian prince and his Indonesian wives. There, the Belanda Hitam, or Black Dutchmen, are given memorial, the story of their trade as 'trophies' to the Dutch East Indies recorded in this little-known house on a hill. 'Keroncong Concordia', while anchored metaphorically in Bandung (a club whose building hosted the Bandung Conference in 1955), is also an artistic gesture that speaks to a broader community, whose experience of assimiliation as '<u>inter-colonial subjects</u>' deserves further visibility and consideration.

For a glance at another 'inter-colonial' community (between Vietnam and Senegal), see the work of Tuan Andrew Nguyen on pg. 94

In 2015, I visited Elmina Fort, off the coast of Accra, Ghana, where I found myself in a state of violent helplessness, incredulous over the conditions, in this Dutch-created hell, where thousands were 'processed' as slaves to cross the Atlantic. In Elmina, I also visited the Java Museum, with its batiks and wayang puppetry, and mildewing photographs of a Ghanaian prince and his Indonesian wives. There, the Belanda Hitam, or Black Dutchmen, are given memorial, the story of their trade as 'trophies' to the Dutch East Indies recorded in this little-known house on a hill. 'Keroncong Concordia', while anchored metaphorically in Bandung (a club whose building hosted the Bandung Conference in 1955), is also an artistic gesture that speaks to a broader community, whose experience of assimilation as '<u>inter-colonial subjects</u>' deserves further visibility and consideration.

For a glance at another 'inter-colonial' community (between Vietnam and Senegal), see the work of Tuan Andrew Nguyen on pg. 94

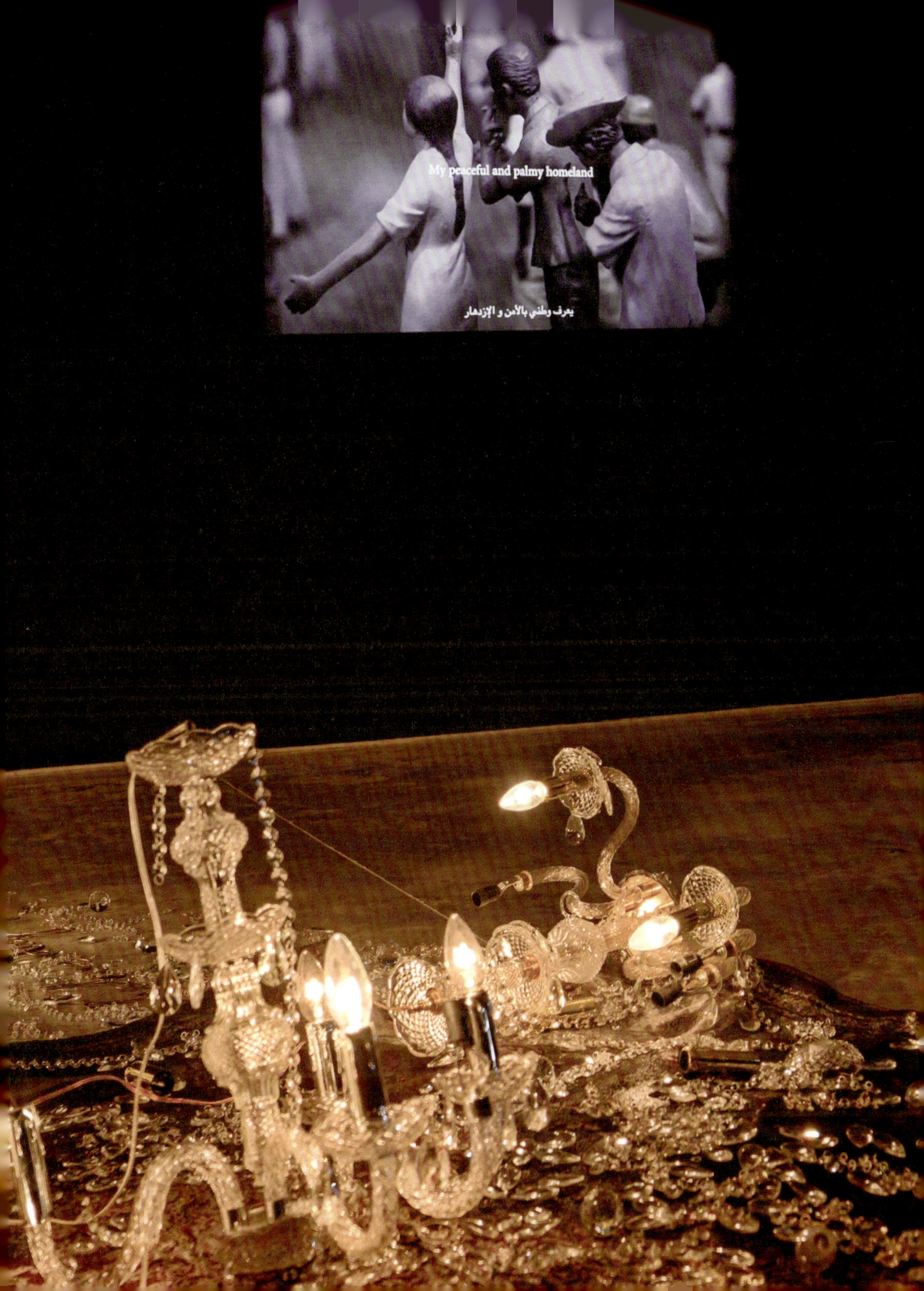

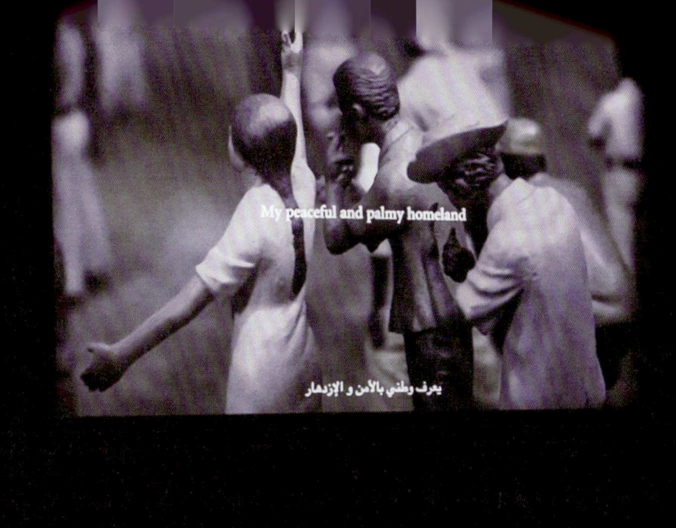
My peaceful and palmy homeland
يعرف وطني بالامن و الإزدهار

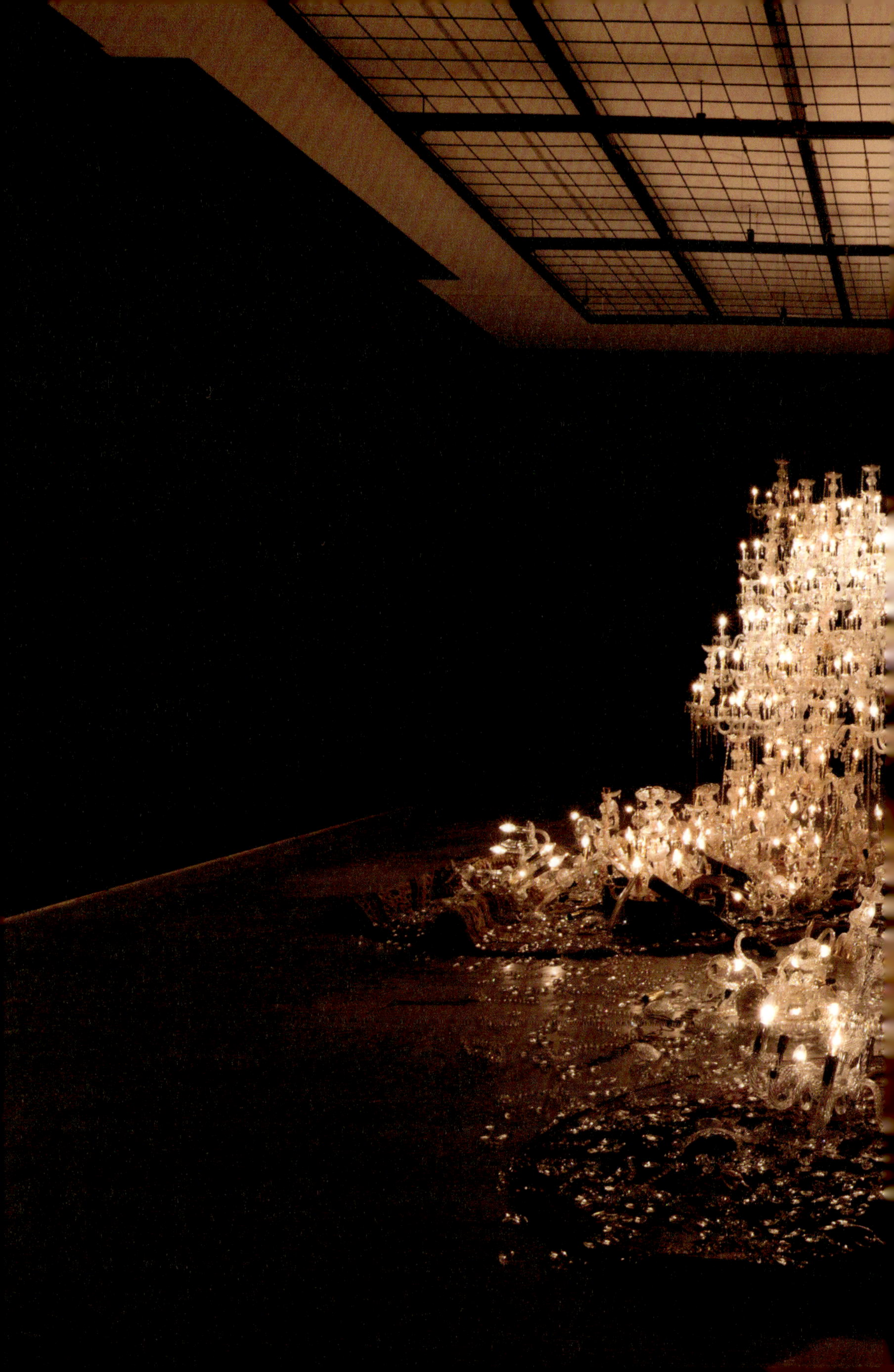

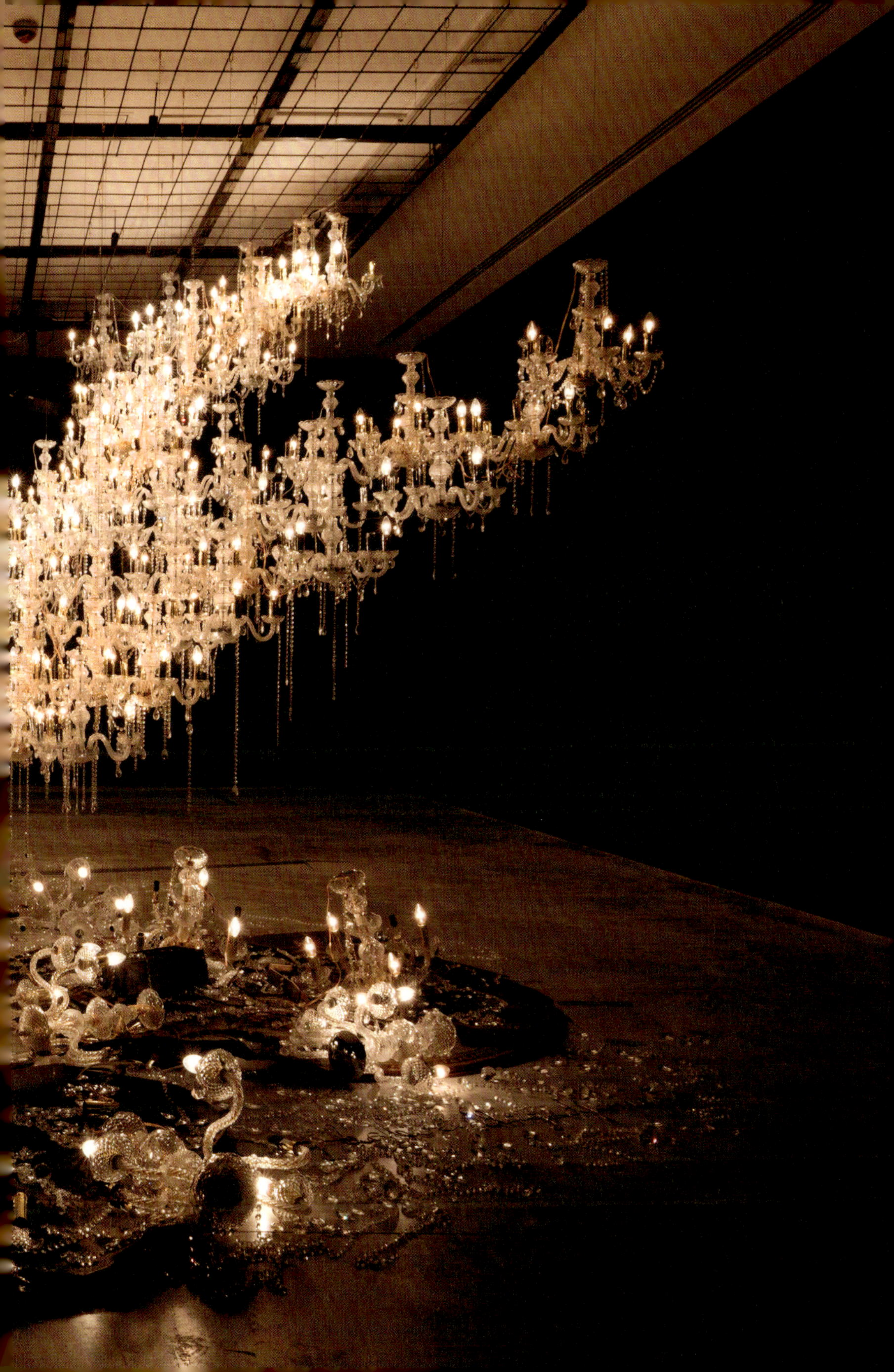

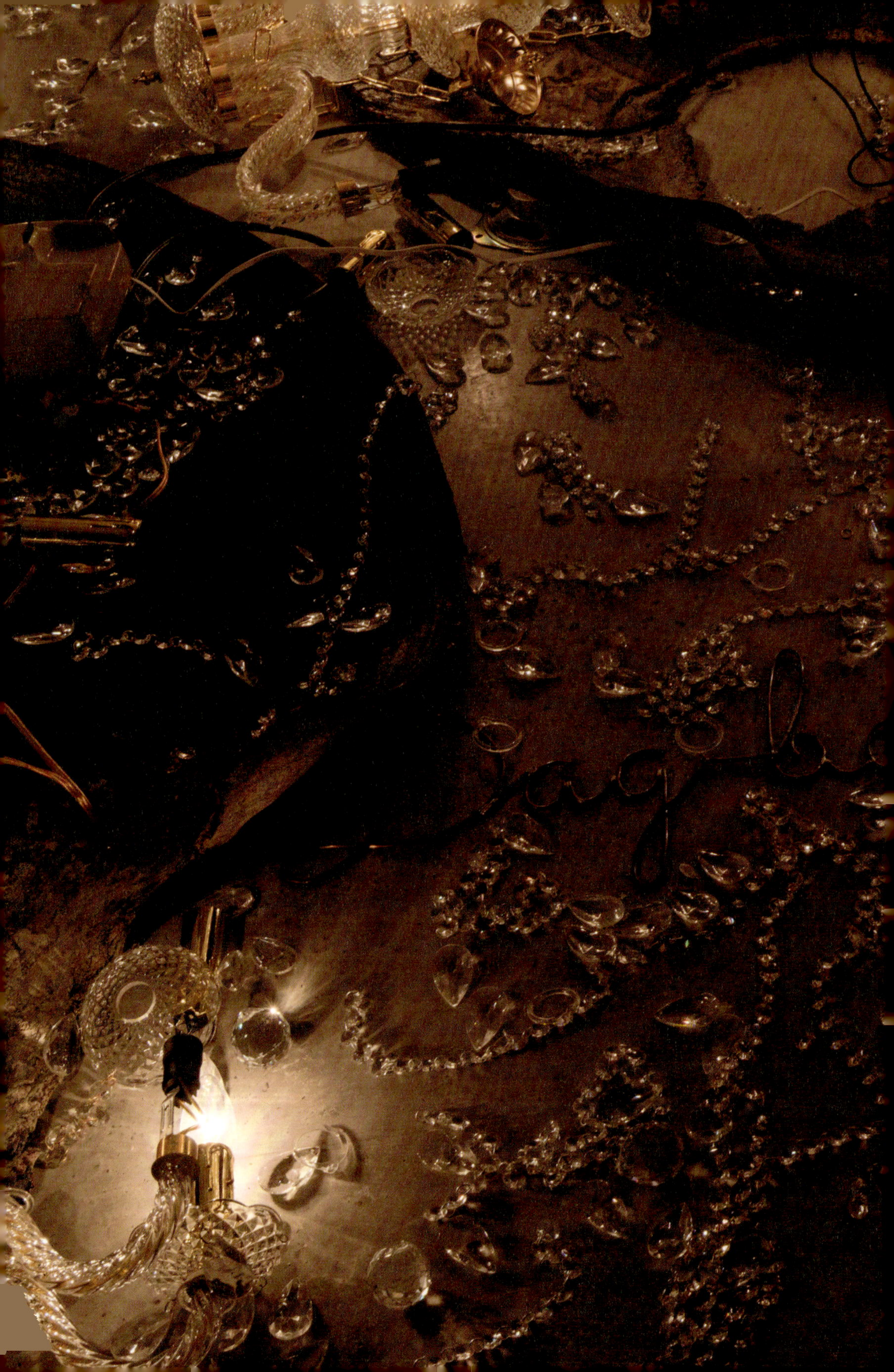

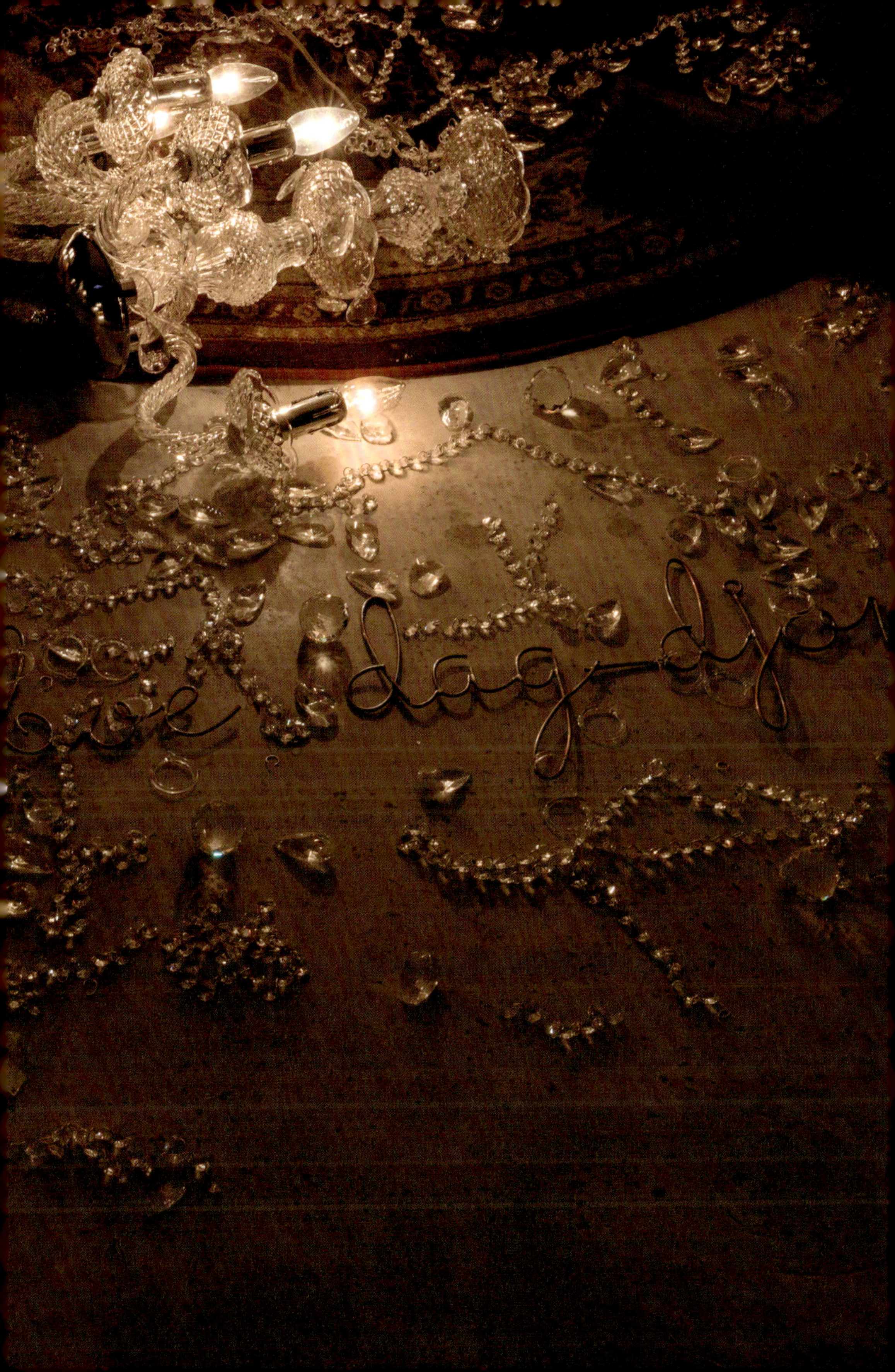

Ho Tzu Nyen

R for Resonance (The Critical Dictionary of Southeast Asia, Vol. 9), 2019

R for Resonance (The Critical Dictionary of Southeast Asia, Vol. 9) is a story about South East Asia, a geopolitical concept that connects societies and individuals – though here it is mapped as an interconnected sequence of symbols, landscapes, music and rituals that recalls human fallibility in its search for sacred and mythological worlds. One powerful symbol here is the gong, a tool of political power, whose presence and practice reflect a geography of ghosts and a history of violence, whilst charting kingship, empires and the cosmos.

Here, in this world of Resonance, I dream not only in bronze, but also in the fluid, the viscous, the molten, the moment when the bronze possesses the possibility of metamorphosis, before it is forged into shape. Entering this virtual world, the gong – whose potential influence is represented by certain objects or concepts that recall specific dictionary terms – operates as a portal to human memory, each pulse a doorway into a human landscape of resource, innovation and intrigue. To resonate, rather than to reason, is to be connected across space by circular rings of vibrations, rather than to be tied by lines of reason. It is not so much what you hear, but how you hear, like how the vibrations of a gong turn your entire body into a single, vibrating ear.

The first use of the term 'Southeast Asia', in a fully modern sense, can be traced to the book *Progress and Welfare in Southeast Asia* (1941) by the British-born colonial public servant and writer, John Sydenham Furnivall. During the Second World War, South East Asia was, for the first time in its history, virtually occupied by a single rule, that of the Japanese. Consequently, in 1944, Lord Louis Mountbatten and his allied South East Asia Command produced the first map of the region, visualised as a geographic reality.

The Critical Dictionary of Southeast Asia begins with a question: What is South East Asia? It was, after all, a 'region' that had never been unified by language, religion or political structures. The *Dictionary* consists of twenty-six entries, one for each letter of the alphabet, each of which is an idea, a motif or a biography that allows us to reframe and reimagine this region that is not 'one'.

Ho Tzu Nyen

In approximately 500 BCE, the rise of the Iron Age gave birth to technology that saw a consolidation of power in a select social elite across the communities now known as South East Asia. Subsequent kingdoms – think Funan, Champa, Angkor – produced various gong designs, whose differentiating sounds rang with known (sacred and, thus influential) significance.

Tzu Nyen's 'Critical Dictionary of South East Asia' gives wonder to a deeper trajectory of human society and the interconnected material spaces its members inhabit. The work thus reminds us of the impact of systemic and colonial mechanisations of power on this part of the world; here, they largely foreclose the innovative synergy and respect between and across South East Asia's vastly differing communities.

In approximately 500 BCE, the rise of the Iron Age gave birth to technology that saw a consolidation of power in a select social elite across the communities now known as South East Asia. Subsequent kingdoms – think Funan, Champa, Angkor – produced various gong designs, whose differentiating sounds rang with known (sacred and, thus influential) significance.

Tzu Nyen's 'Critical Dictionary of South East Asia' gives wonder to a deeper trajectory of human society and the interconnected material spaces its members inhabit. The work thus reminds us of the impact of systemic and colonial mechanisations of power on this part of the world; here, they largely foreclose the innovative synergy and respect between and across South East Asia's vastly differing communities.

R for Resonance
The Critical Dictionary of Southeast Asia Vol. 9

+++

A for Alliteration
A for Altitude
A for Anarchism
A for Archipelagoes
A for Attitude

+++

B for Bamboo
B for Bronze

+++

C for Casting
C for Circle of Kings
C for Civilization
C for Cognatic Kinship
C for Conquest
C for Contagion
C for Copper
C for Corruption
C for Cosmology

+++

D for Decay
D for Decenter
D for Disaggregate
D for Disperse
D for Dissimulate

+++

E for Eradicate
E for Erasure
E for Evanescent
E for Evasion

+++

F for Fiction
F for Flee
F for Forest
F for Friction
F for Friend
F for Frontier

+++

G for Geobody
G for Geography
G for Ghosts
G for Ghostwriter
G for Gong
G for Goong

+++

H for History
H for Hydraulics
H for Hydrography
H for Hydrology
H for Humidity

+++

I for Identity
I for Imitation
I for Inscription
I for Irresolution
I for Irrigation

+++

J for Jellyfish
J for Jellyfish tribes

+++

K for Kingship
K for Kinship

+++

L for Labour
L for Lai Teck
L for Language
L for Layering
L for Legibility
L for Localization

+++

M for Mandala
M for Manpower
M for Map
M for Mobility

+++

N for Names
N for Narcosis
N for Narration
N for Nation

+++

O for Ocean
O for Onomatopoeia
O for Opium
O for Oral
O for Origin
O for Osmosis

+++

P for Padi
P for Parastic
P for Peasant
P for Planting
P for Periphery
P for Politics
P for Puppet

+++

Q for Quaking
Q for Queen
Q for Question
Q for Quotation

+++

R for Region
R for Reason
R for Resonance
R for Ritual
R for Rain

+++

S for Sea
S for Slave
S for Soul
S for Soul-stuff
S for State
S for Stratification

+++

T for Theater
T for Theater-state

+++

U for Unheard

+++

V for Vampire
V for Voice

+++

W for War
W for Weretiger

+++

X for Xenocracy
X for Xenodochial
X for Xenagogue
X for Xenophilia
X for Xenophobia
X for Xenomania
X for Xenogamy

+++

Y for Yearning
Y for Yielding
Y for Yes

+++

Z for Zombie
Z for Zomia
Z for Zones of refuge
Z for Zoomorphic
Z for Zoophilia

R for Resonance
2019
From 'Critical Dictionary of South East Asia', 2012–ongoing
Installation with VR 360-degree video, ambisonic sound through headphones, single-channel HD video projection, 5-channel sound
Dimensions variable
Commissioned by Sharjah Art Foundation
Courtesy of the artist and Edouard Malingue Gallery, Hong Kong

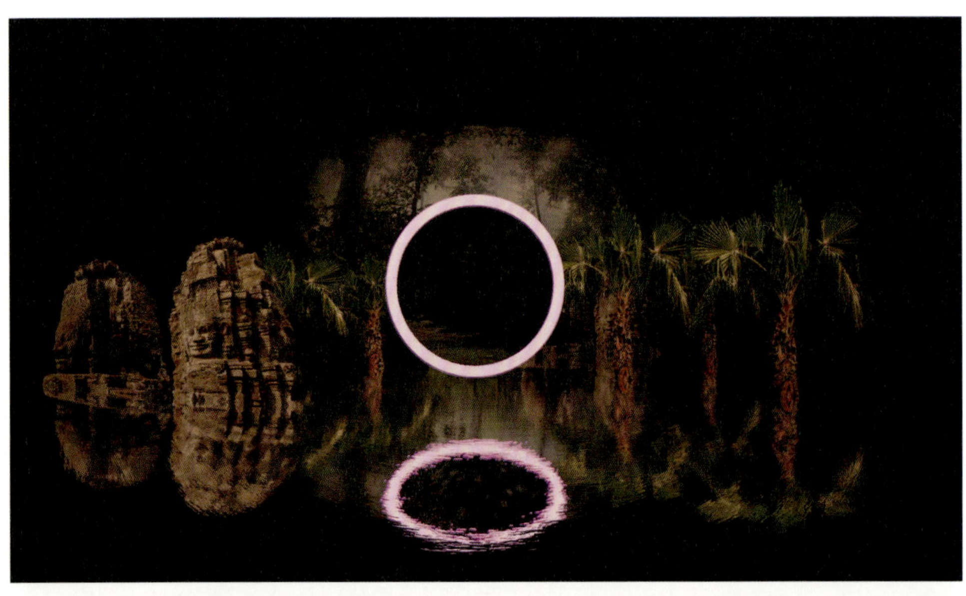

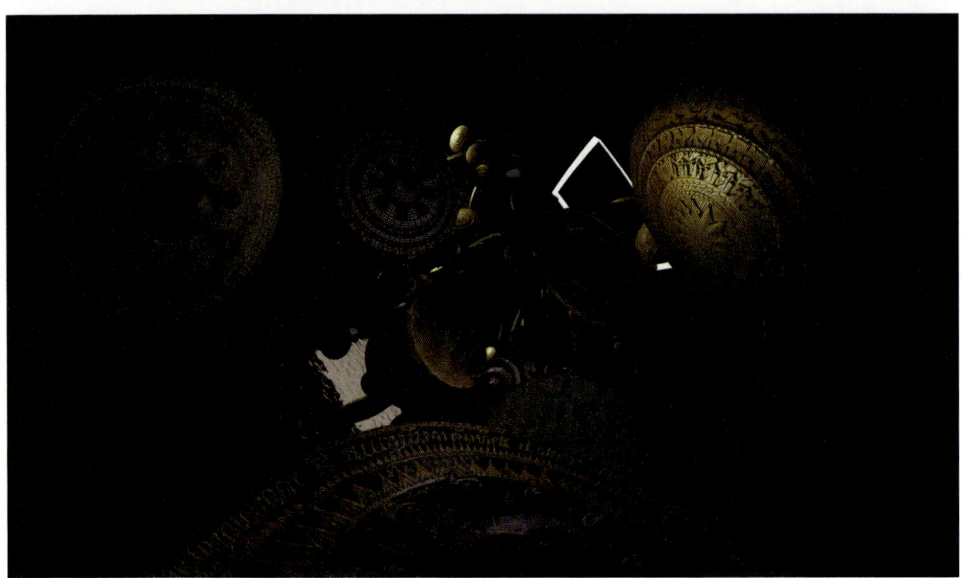

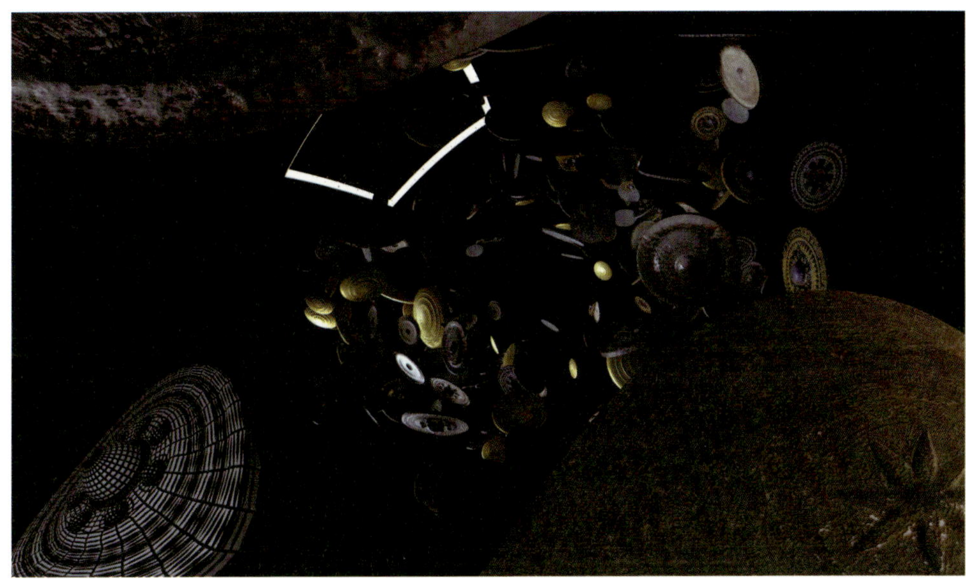

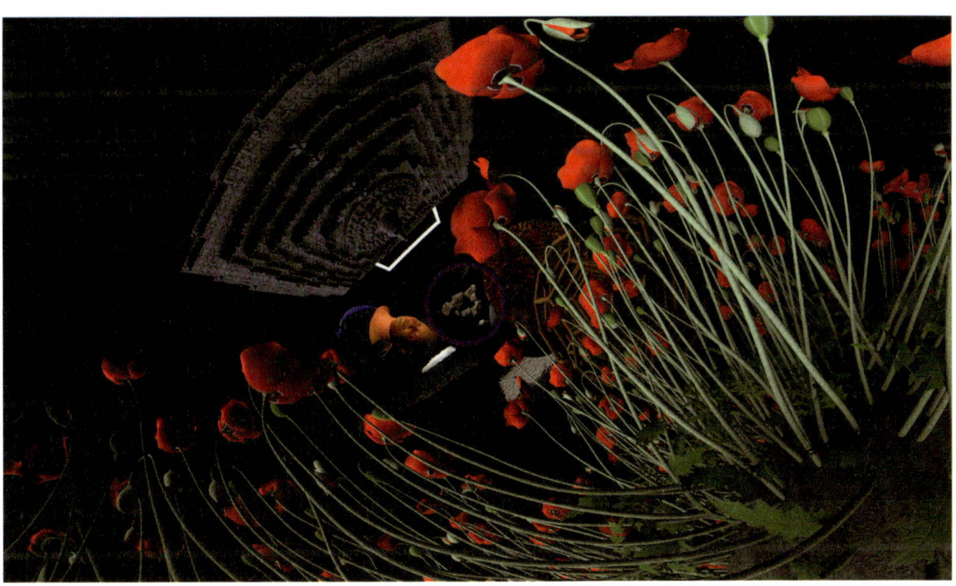

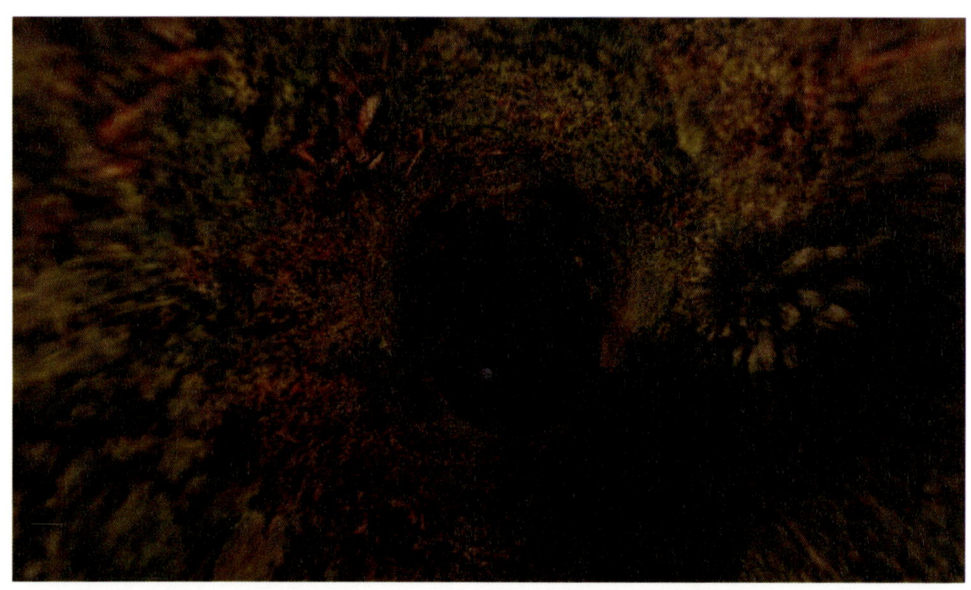

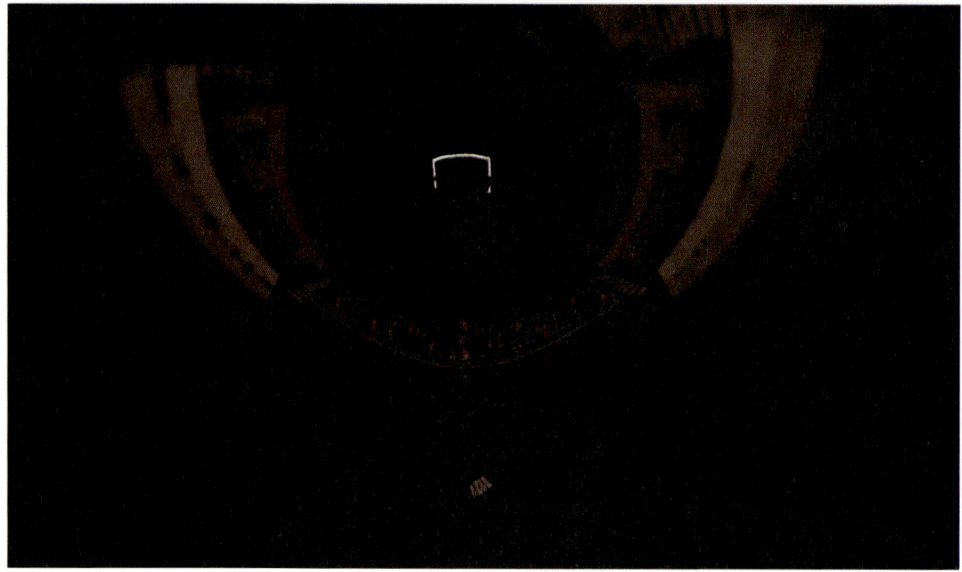

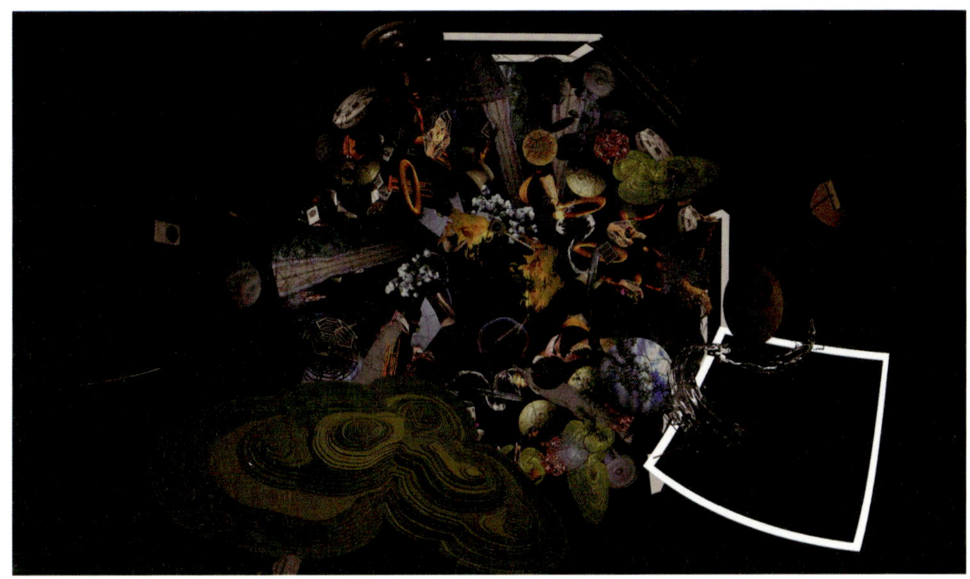

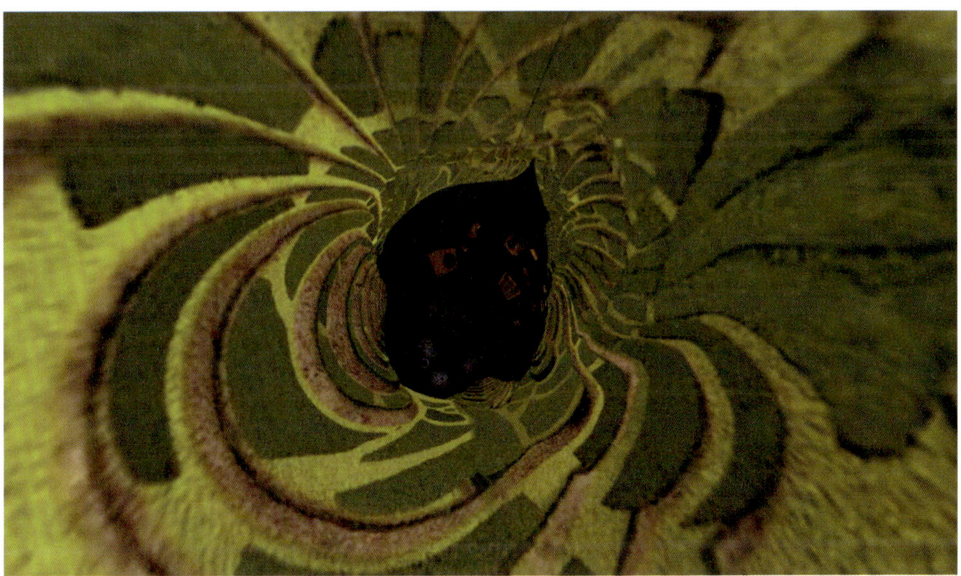

Adriana Bustos

Vision Machine, 2019

Vision Machine is an installation made up of multiple devices (drawings, watercolours, heliographs and paintings), whose function is 'to make one see'. The objective of this machine is to provide the broadest possible vision of particular social issues, by juxtaposing images (sometimes hidden) that present a knowledge of its historical roots. This 'machine' provides an opportunity for me to multiply panoramas of reference that synchronise my past and present projects, which in some way all revolve around concepts of colonialism, racism and patriarchy.

Here, you will find references to the superimposition of old colonial trade routes and current drug-trafficking rings in Latin America; also present is the globe's thirst to consume, with particular intensity, the jungles of Bolivia where human and natural resources were colonially exploited across Latin America. The imposition of a white, European, patriarchal, scientific model of discovery in Latin America – and how this 'gaze' contrasts with local cosmologies prior to colonialism – is detailed in the work. This issue dovetails with the linear depiction, since the fifteenth century, of the slave trade in the Americas, as an enduring calamity that gave foundation to today's planetary capitalism and the biologisation of inequality.

I believe that art produces singular forms of knowledge. Therefore, the type of research that involves the revision of history in non-linear terms and its articulation with the present comprises the substrate of my work. Strategies of anthropology, history, science, popular culture, fiction, biographical writings, and academic and intuitive knowledge are laid as fragmentary and linear; objective and subjective; in juxtaposition, and often in montage. My multiple devices, which at times also include film and sculpture, are the tools that I use to speak about political and social issues, predominantly beginning within the context of Latin America.

Adriana Bustos

Various works
2019
Watercolour on paper, photograph and graphite on paper, graphite, acrylic, silver leaf on canvas,
Dimensions variable
Courtesy of the artist

Page 126–127:
Photo: readsreads.info

In the adjacent room to the main gallery, are two 'celestial' maps. One refers to History as it is writen, its drawings detailed in red, recalling the blood and violence of the history of patriarchy. The other map recovers the feminine participation in that History, its drawings detailed in black graphite. A standing red glass sits in the middle of the room – if you see through this glass towards each work, history is no longer History: as the red lines of patriarchy disappear, only the graphite remains.

In the adjacent room to the main gallery, are two 'celestial' maps. One refers to History as it is written; its drawings detailed in red, recalling the blood and violence of the history of patriarchy. The other map recovers the feminine participation in that History; its drawings detailed in black graphite. A standing red glass sits in the middle of the room – if you see through this glass towards each work, history is no longer History: as the red lines of patriarchy disappear, only the graphite remains.

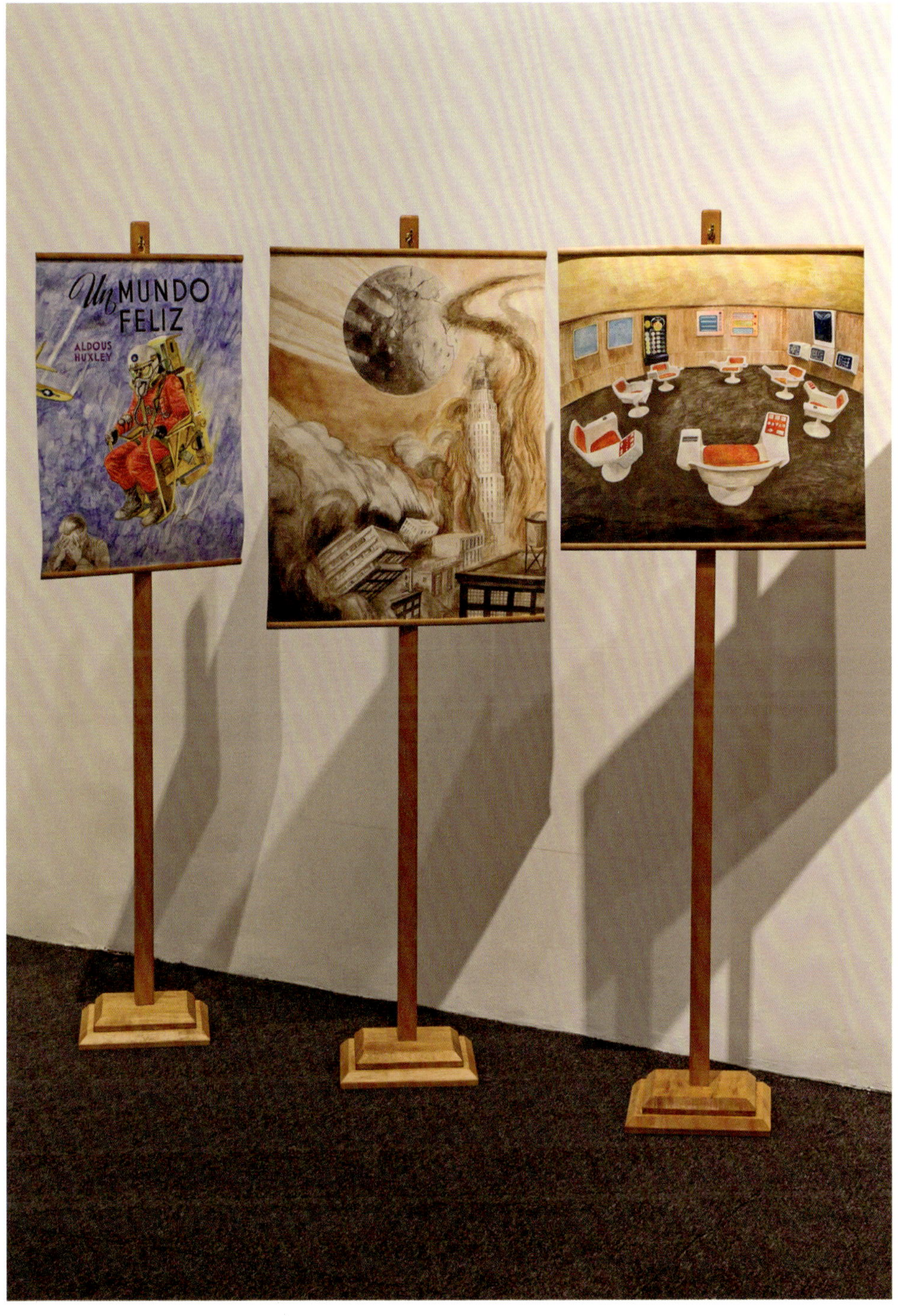
Un MUNDO FELIZ
ALDOUS HUXLEY

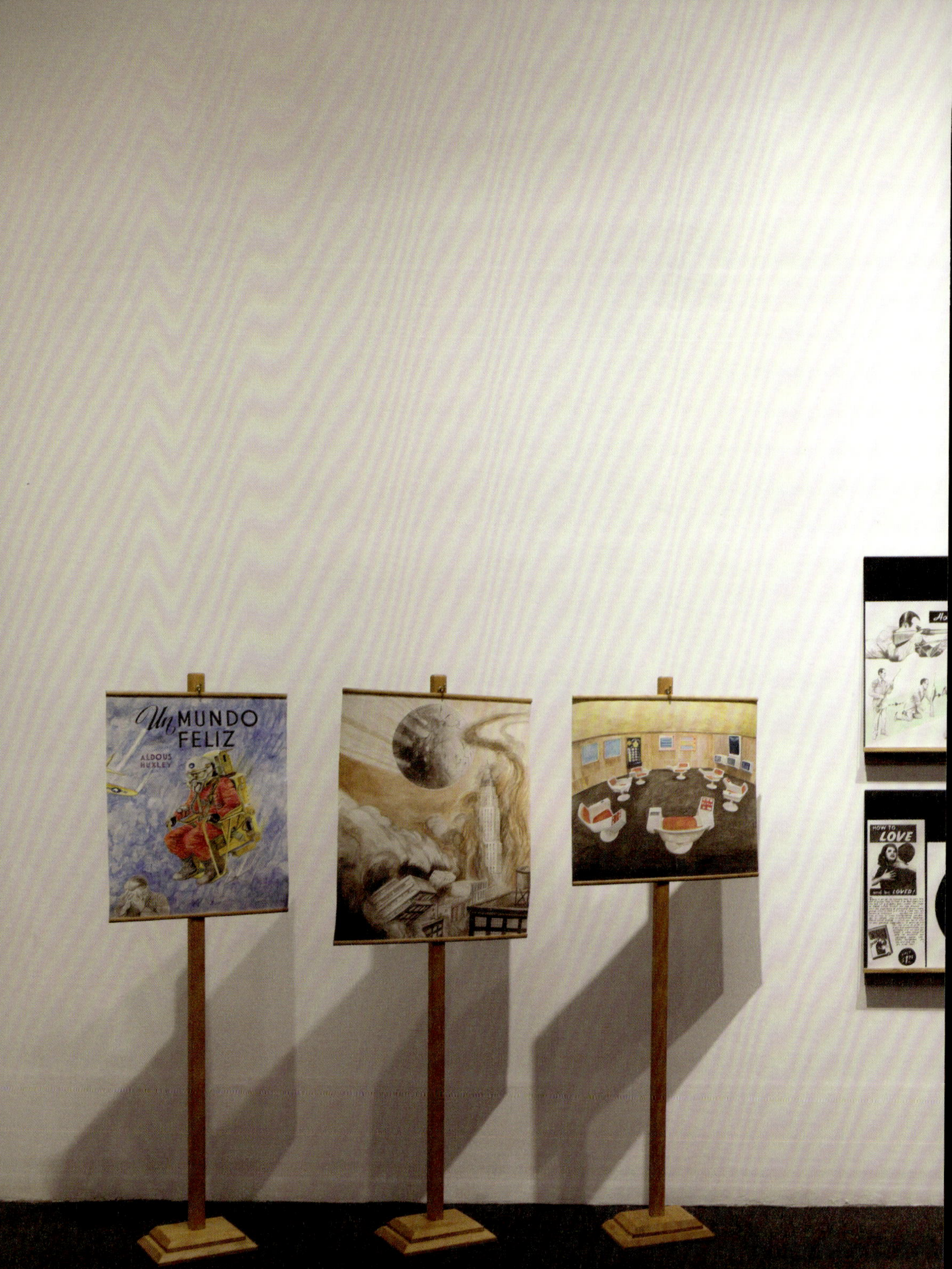
Un MUNDO FELIZ
ALDOUS HUXLEY
HOW TO
LOVE

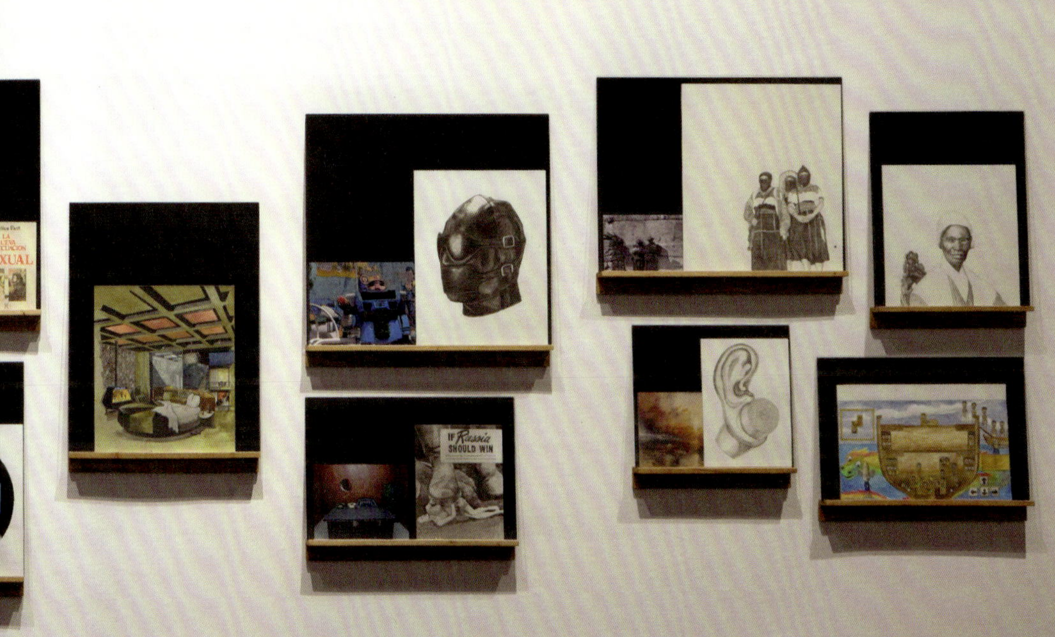
IF Russia
SHOULD WIN

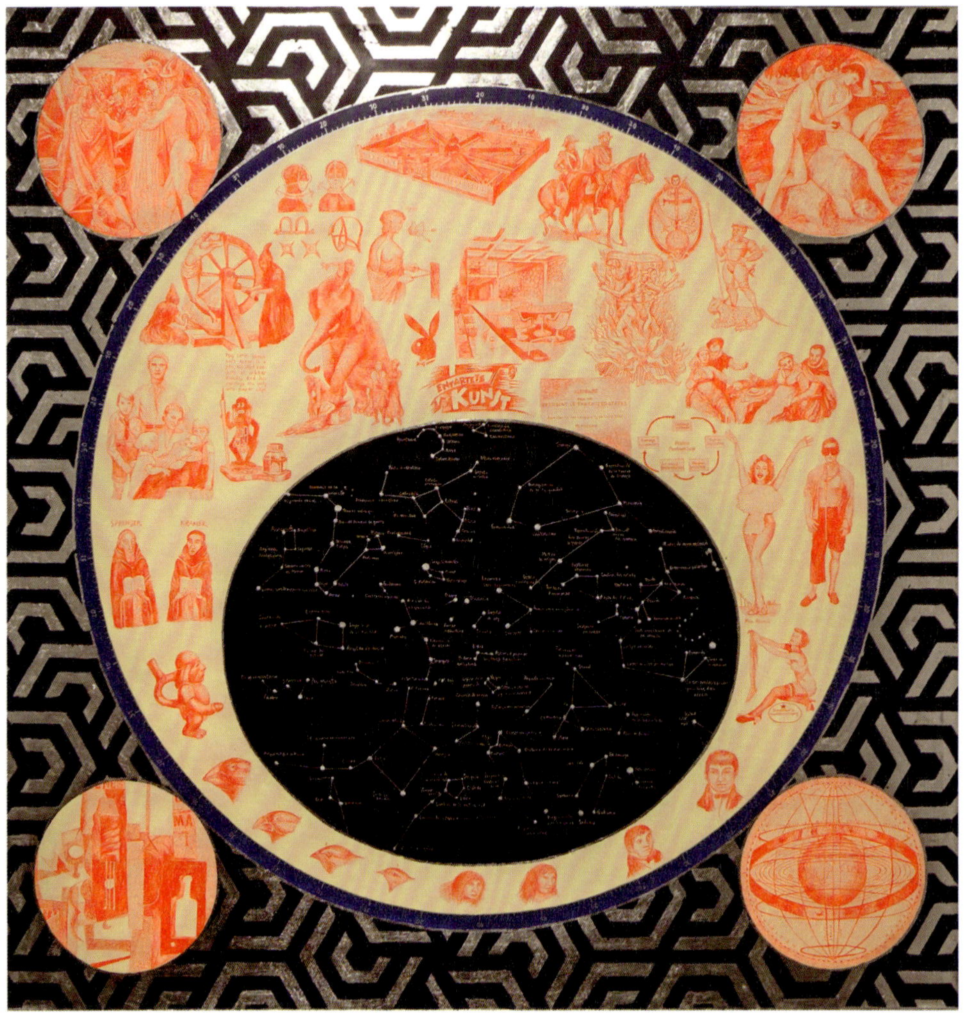
ENTARTETE
KUNST
SPRENGER
KRAMER

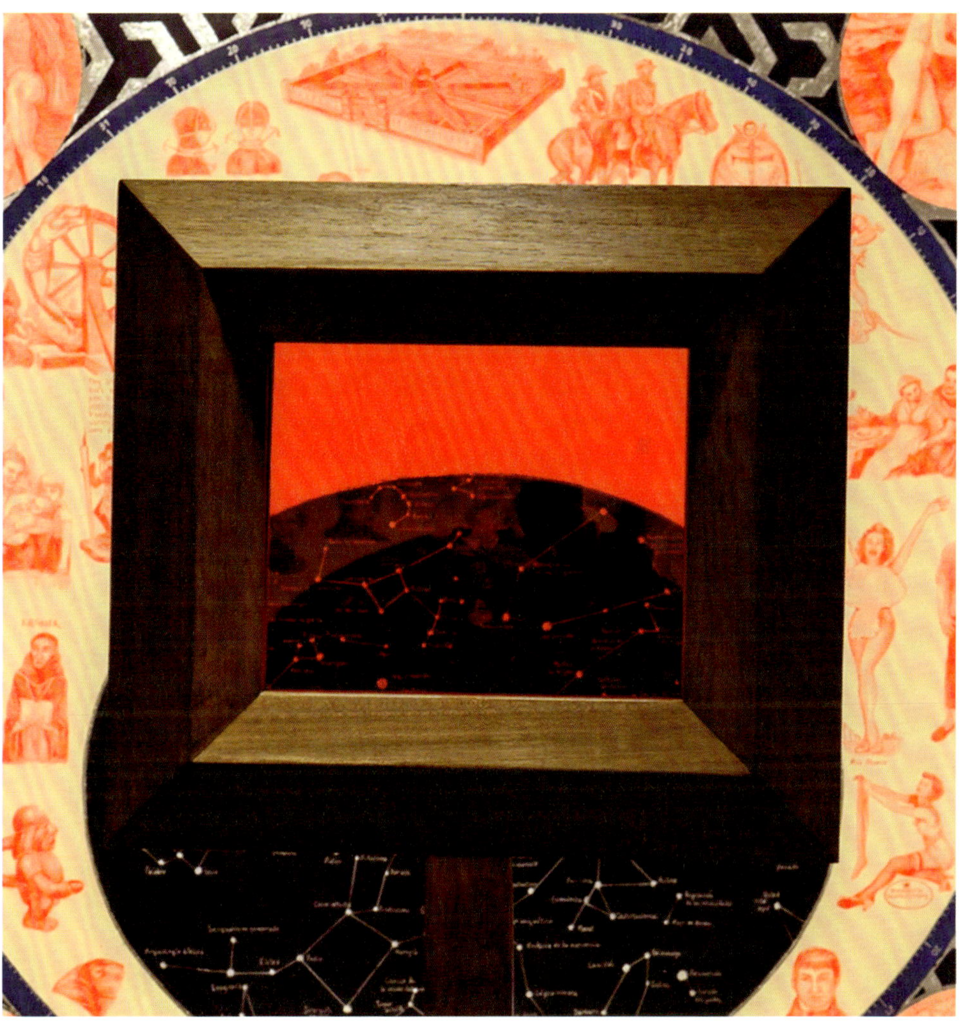

Official Territory 2018
2019
From 'Vision Machine'
Acrylic, graphite, silver leaf on canvas
180 x 180 cm
Courtesy of the artist and Nora Fisch Contemporary Art, Buenos Aires

Khadim Ali

Flowers of Evil, 2019

Symbols, characters and generational sayings have been defined and redefined in various periods. For example, the stories of the *Shahnameh*, written in the court of Mahmud Ghaznavi (971–1030) and used as a motivational text for the sultan's warriors, were deeply rooted in the collective experiences of the region. In the twentieth century, historical stories alongside religious tales were used to legitimise violence. For example, the Taliban refer to themselves as 'Rustam of Islam'; Rustam was a popular hero from the *Shahnameh* who ruthlessly eliminated the enemies of the king.

The experience, effects and imagery of war always make their way into the minds of the people. In the tapestries and handicrafts of Afghanistan, produced during the entanglements with the Soviet Union as well as the aftermath of 9/11, pictures of tanks, airplanes, grenades and guns can be found. Many tapestries were woven by displaced children, who lived in Afghan refugee camps along the Pakistan border. These children were socially, politically and psychologically uninformed; yet without training, they possessed adept weaving skills, and were not bound by traditional methods and designs of the craft.

During the Soviet invasion of Afghanistan in 1979, international aid agencies opened schools for these displaced children. The content of their textbooks, created by Western aid agencies, consisted of information such as: 'I for infidel, J for Jihad and K for Kalashnikov'. These schools dictated that political violence and unpunished killings were revolutionary acts. Weapons of war became symbols of fashion and beauty; firing weapons became commonplace during the celebration of births, weddings and festivals; and the possession of firearms came to contribute to one's social status and its affiliated political alliances. Consequently, these children would eventually join the mujahedeen to fight the Soviet Union, and are now warlords holding governmental positions.

Page 132:
In collaboration with
Bamyan Art Space
Standing Flames
2019
From 'Flowers of Evil'
Acrylic, industrial paints, Dutch metal gold leaf on MDF
1785 x 539 cm
Commissioned by Sharjah Art Foundation
Courtesy of the artist

From the employment of flags as questionably 'national' in aid assistance, to the monumentalization of the bomb; from the large-scale mural emblems of Rustam, to the painterly collage of military tools; from the sound of repetitive propaganda songs, to the archival documents that visualize recurring political histories – Khadim's ambitious body of work in 'Flowers of Evil' gives pause to the exploitation of faith and charity as political agents of social influence. Is such normalisation of violence supported by or challenged in its aestheticisation as Art? The artist believes that it is his fundamental duty to critically examine the relationship between past and present, to remember the intention behind image-making and to remind us about the transference of history and the fickle power of its interpretation.

From the employment of flags as questionably 'national' in aid assistance, to the monumentalization of the bomb; from the large-scale mural emblems of Rustam, to the painterly collage of military tools; from the sound of repetitive propaganda songs, to the archival documents that visualize recurring political histories – Khadim's ambitious body of work in 'Flowers of Evil' gives pause to the exploitation of faith and charity as political aspects of social influence. Is such normalisation of violence supported by or challenged in its aestheticisation as Art? The artist believes that it is his fundamental duty to critically examine the relationship between past and present, to remember the intention behind image-making and to remind us about the transference of history and the fickle power of its interpretation.

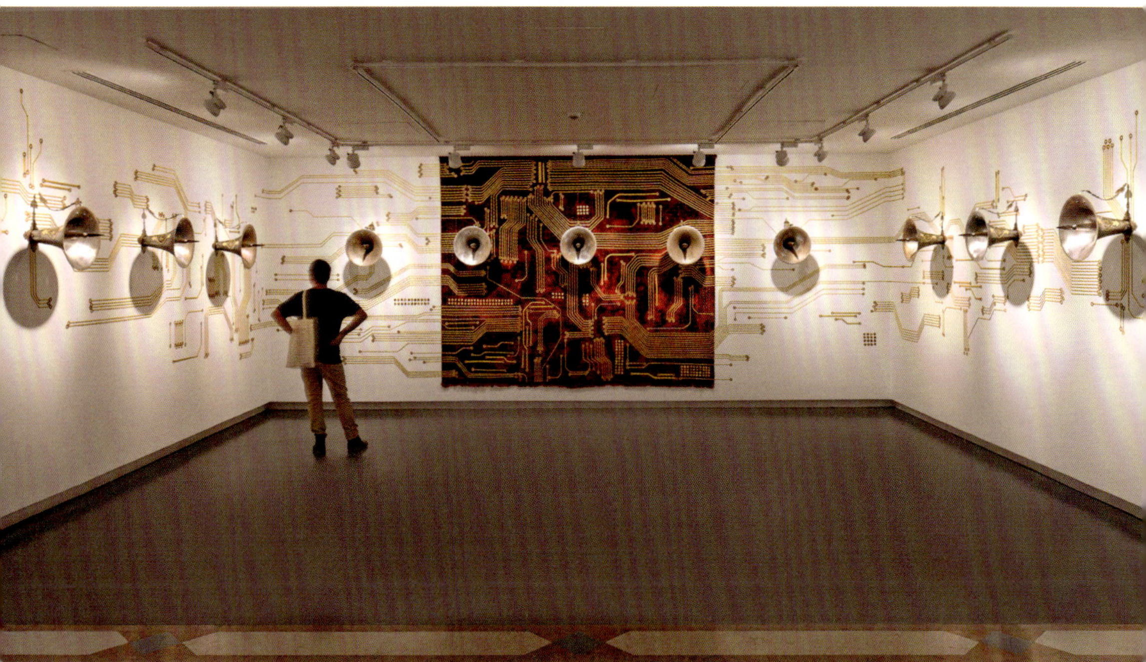

Flowers of Evil recalls the work of French poet Charles Baudelaire (1821–1867), in that it complicates the estrangement of modern life amidst the endangering of traditional and religious law, as well as the plight of the everyday person. Baudelaire, unlike other philosophers, considered death decadent and erotic, potentially glorious and cheerful. Within the Islamic world today, for someone to wear a bomb around their waist and blow himself up amongst people, death does not have just a moral meaning. Such dramatic murder intimidates via its aesthetic impact, and is brutally effective in the way it instills fear.

Khadim Ali

In collaboration with
Sher Ali
Urbicide
2019
From 'Flowers of Evil'
11-channel sound: steel, metal, gold leaf; nylon thread on machine woven rug
Dimensions variable
Commissioned by Sharjah Art Foundation
Courtesy of the artist

This work was co-facilitated by the Bamyan Cultural Centre (of which Khadim Ali is a founding member), and reflects the ingenuity of craftsmanship from Isfahan, Bamiyan, Kabul and Yogyakarta. The artist wishes to thank Ali Baba Aurang, Atika Hussain, Aziz Hazara, Golsom Haidary, Mohammad Hadi Rahnaward, Razia Haidary, Sher Ali Hussainy, Art Merdeka Yogyakarta, Jafarian Crafts Isfahan, Milani Gallery Brisbane and A3 Art Agency Berlin.

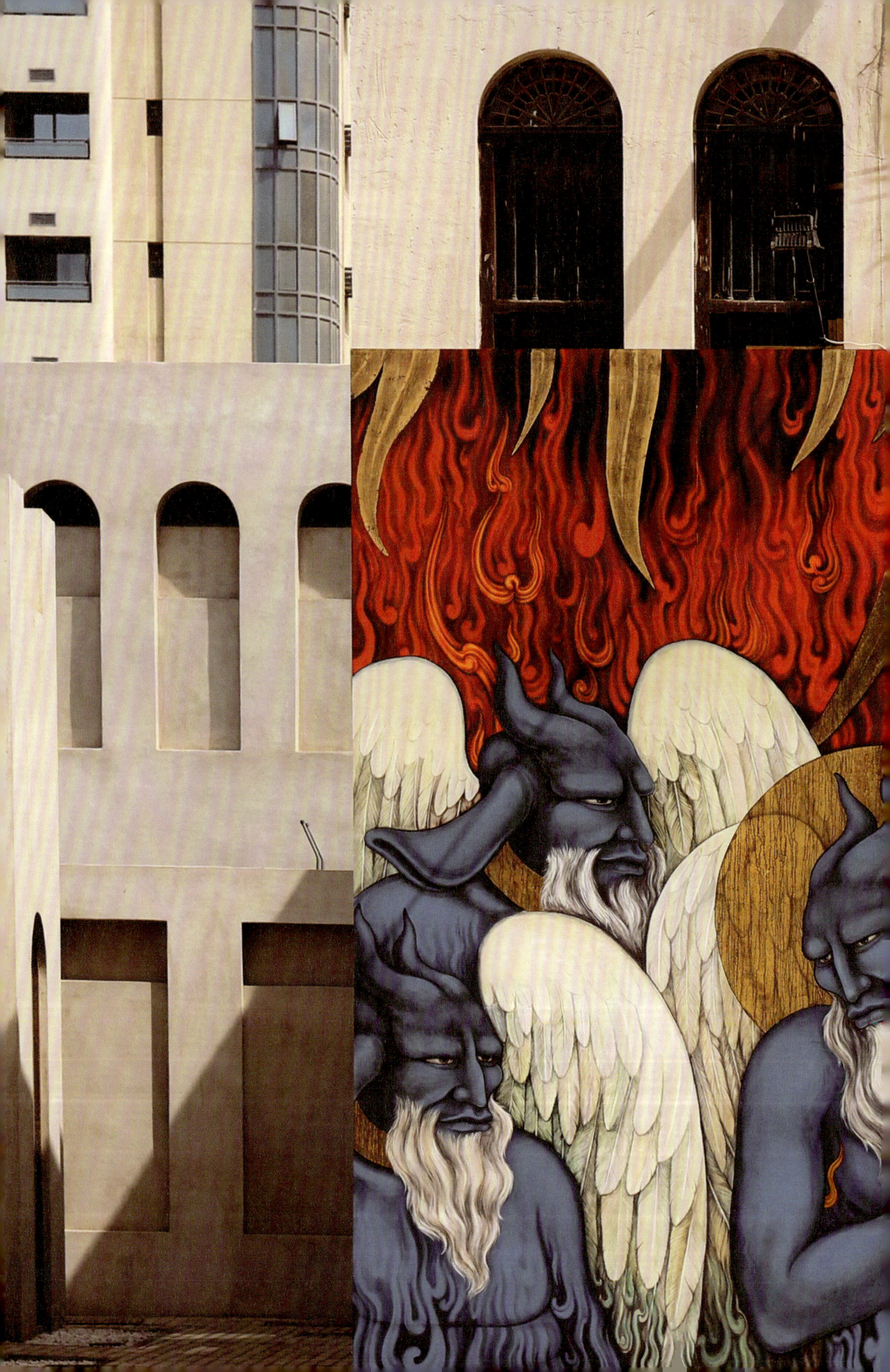

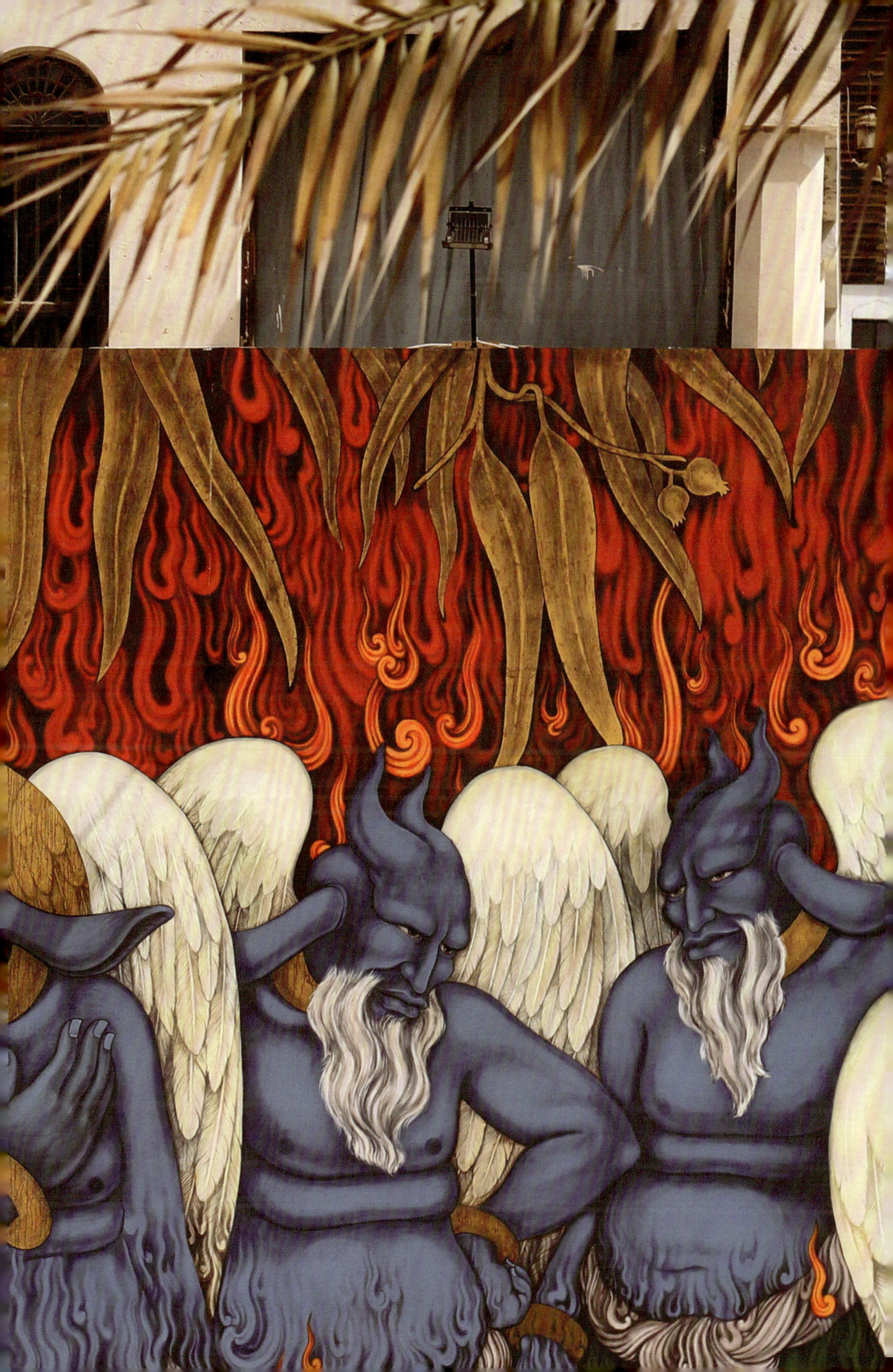

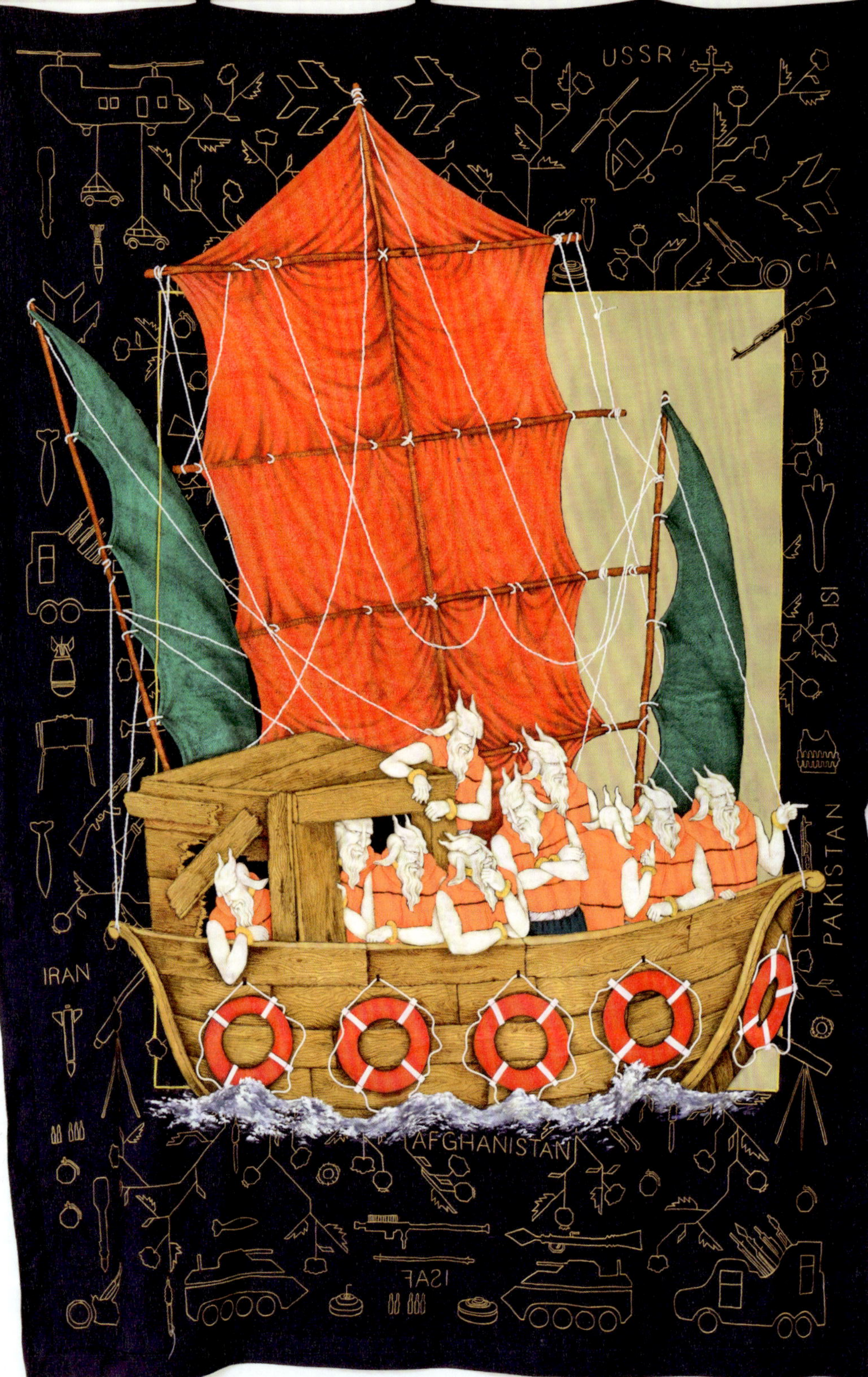
USSR
CIA
ISI
PAKISTAN
IRAN
AFGHANISTAN
ISAF

Untitled 18
2019
From 'Flowers of Evil'
Hand and machine
embroidery stitched on
fabric and dye
220 x 153 cm
Commissioned by Sharjah
Art Foundation
Courtesy of the artist

Urbicide

Within me, there is a dystopia,
A destroyed Kabul
A Baghdad with mad caliphs,
A wounded Aleppo,
A Tehran with many prisons
An Islamabad overflowing with terror schools,
A Bamiyan without Buddhas
The corpses on the road of Damascus
And the Mediterranean with thousands of refugees.

When I was born, I rejected by father,
Who blamed me a demon child,
Abandoned me on the top of Alborz Mountain,
When back to Kabul,
They taught me how to throw stone at the windows,
At birds, cats, flaneur and strangers.
At the eyes of the beautiful Rudabah, who was watching me
with love from behind the windows.
To become an expert and learn the latest techniques of
killing cities,
They send me to religious schools,
In my school book T was terror,
B bomb and bullet,
K Kalashnikov and killing of the city,
G Gun and Genocide,
R rocket
M Mohammad, Mujahedeen, mother bomb, Missile and massacre,
I learned Alphabet, with the taste of paradise angels' breast,
who was flying in the sky of our muddy schools.
I read a holy book, with Taste of Thousands of imaginary
naked women,
I swam across the rivers of wine and milk, smoked hash with
God and Prophets,
It was possible to have all these blessings if I could destroy
cities, and kill humanity in my mind and to remove love from
my heart,
Genocide was not enough, my duty was to kill the built
environment,

I destroyed Kabul and Bamiyan many times in my imagination,
almost in every line of the Quran.

I grew up,
Bullets and rockets took the place of stones,
I shot all the bullets to the Almond eyes of Rudabah.
And no longer any eyes watched me from behind the windows,
Now Kabul is a ghost
Speaks with the language of the dead
smoke and fire,
حي على الفلاح!
Again, the Suicide attack happened in the city,
One of my classmates is going to paradise, to sleep with the
promised virgin angels,
And scatters his bones flying in the air,
We float in the hunted valley of blood and bodies,
Verses of darkness, migration, and massacre
Everywhere is dark,
Houses have no Windows,
People have no eyes,
The blind man runs the city, the citizen, and whatever it is.

Kabul is a Rudabah that Prophets and Imams go to Paradise
from the ladder of her hair,
the Afghan honor, covered her beauty under mud, dust and Burqa,
Islam stoned her
Colonialism plundered her,
Afghan communist parties invested her through their personal
bank accounts,
Mujahideen shot their faith with Kalashnikov on her eyes,
Intellectuals vomited god on her lips,
Taliban beheaded her on the way,
And the liberals burned her in public.

Kabul is the city of madmen
The city there one-eyed is Amir al-Mu'minin and the eyes of eyes,
Development is a manual bomb,
Justice is a project,
Human rights an industry,
Fraud is the meaning of Democracy,

And the demons are poets and painters they trying to take away
the built and stones from the eyes Rudabah,
Everything follows and the destruction rules,
Even poetry, prose and painting.
Every poem is a ruin,
Every prose is capturing the corpses,
A captive demon who writes not to be killed,
And every painting is a wounded eye,
A house without any windows,
An intangible prophet who hide bodies with light and colours.
A Tahamina's dream who was killed by his father at the
young age
Don't tell anything,
Don't show or express anything,

Kabul is Aleppo
Damascus
Baghdad
A city which is the battlefield of the holy cows
The bloody fingers of the painter cannot make it colorful,
cannot hide the ruins,
It is not possible to go up with a ladder of any poem and colors
from the empty curves of Bamiyan Buddhas,
Only Kalashnikov rods can sing the urbicide age with children's
blood on the wall of Palmyra.

Within me, there is a destroyed city,
In which the windows of its houses are stoning at least five
times every day.
And I do not write a poem,
Not sing a song,
Not draw a dream,
From Kabul to Damascus, I put the dead bodies beside each other,
Words are nothing against stone and guns,
Painting cannot wash the bloody earth
It takes a long time for the earth to give birth
to Bamiyan mountains.
And the Middle East is too wounded
That give birth to the Palmyra once more.

If I sometimes draw.
If I sometimes wash red-colored pepper in klärälven,
It's because I committed to diversity, the earth as it was without any political borders.
If I sometimes play with words,
It's because I have nostalgia of the future,
Nostalgia of being demon child,
Nostalgia of Gulbigum, Tabassom, Leyla, Amina and Saheb-dad.
The nostalgia of reading the diary of the beautiful Rudabah, who was watching me
From the windows and how stupidly I threw stones at her almond eyes.

Asad Buddha and Khadim Ali

J o u r n e y B e y o n d t h

e A r r o w J o u r n e y B e

y o n d t h e A r r o w J o u

r n e y B e y o n d t h e A r

r o w J o u r n e y B e y o n

d t h e A r r o w J o u r n e

y B e y o n d t h e A r r o w

J o u r n e y B e y o n d t h

e A r r o w J o u r n e y B e

y o n d t h e A r r o w J o u

r n e y B e y o n d t h e A r

r o w J o u r n e y B e y o n

d t h e A r r o w J o u r n e

y B e y o n d t h e A r r o w

J o u r n e y B e y o n d t h

History refers to events as signposts of time, the interpretation of these signposts often the determining factor in delineating between the victim and the conqueror, between the provocateur and the duped, between the traitorous and the loyal. Here, artists offer a different highway, a pause in the road of 'History', sharing a set of poetic reflections on this 'road' that can reveal contradictions in humanity's presumption of telling and reading Time.

History refers to events as signposts of time, the interpretation of these signposts often the determining factor in delineating between the victim and the conqueror, between the provocateur and the duped, between the traitorous and the loyal. Here, artists offer a different highway, a pause in the road of 'History', sharing a set of poetic reflections on this 'road' that can reveal contradictions in humanity's presumption of telling and reading Time.

e A r r o w T h e J o u r n e

y B e y o n d t h e P o s t s

A r r o w J o u r n e y B e y

o n d t h e A r r o w J o u r

n e y B e y o n d t h e A r r

o w J o u r n e y B e y o n d

t h e A r r o w J o u r e y B

e y o n d t h e A r r o w J o

u r n e y B e y o n d t h e A

r r o w J o u r n e y B e y o

n d t h e A r r o w J o u r n

e y B e y o n d t h e A r r o

w J o u r n e y B e y o n d t

h e A r r o w J o u r n e y B

e y o n d t h e A r r o w J o

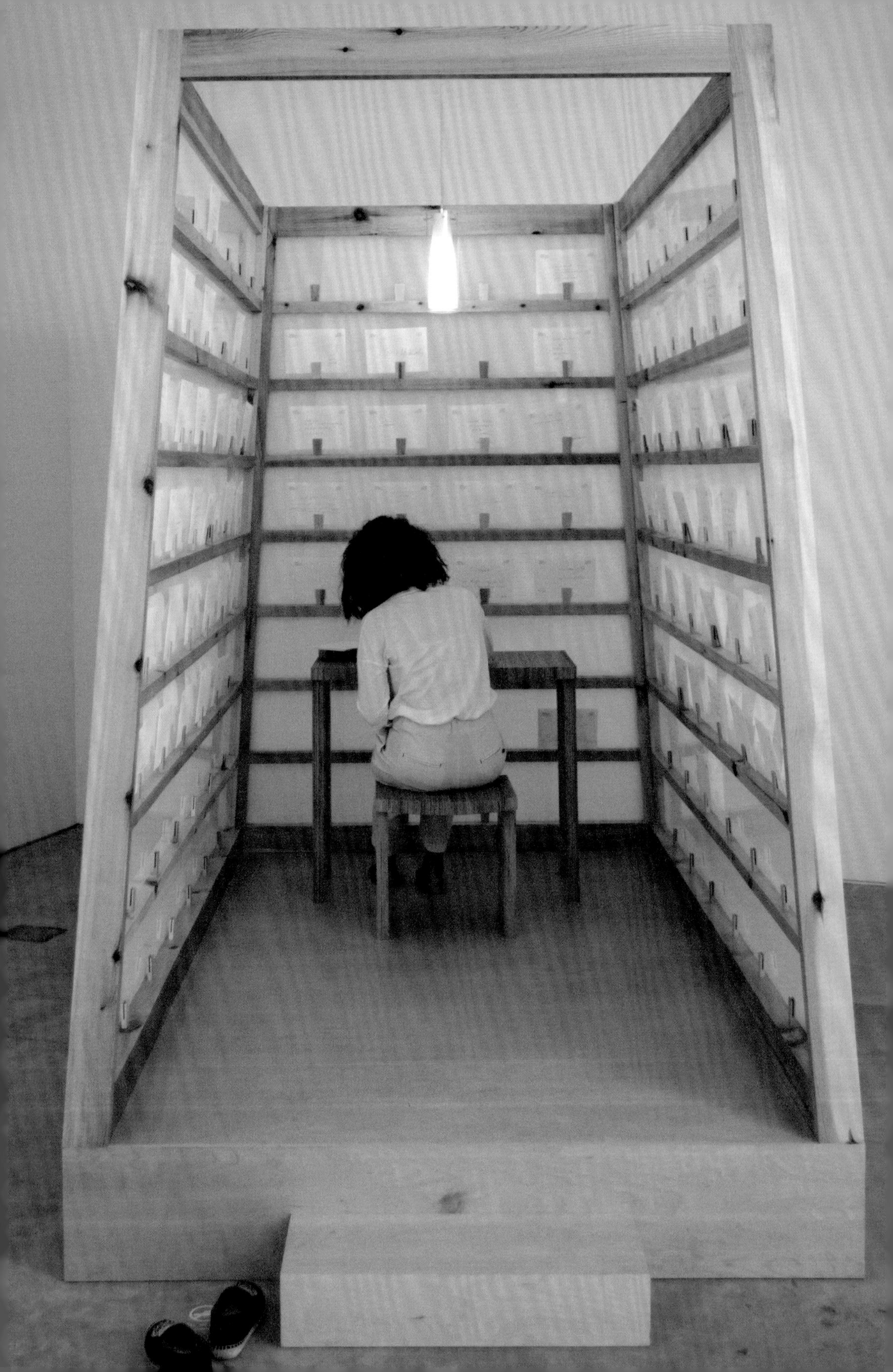

This is the first time that 'The Letter Writing Project' is taking place in the Middle East and in the region's multifarious languages, which include Arabic, Urdu, Hindi, Tagalog, Malayalam and so many more, building on previous versions in Australia, Germany, Korea, Indonesia, Japan, New Zealand, Taiwan, the United Kingdom and the United States. As a participatory artwork in the language of the audience's choosing, it begs the engagement of the viewer in order to be effectual as it continues to travel across the world, possessing its own journey of human catharsis – a critical process of ongoing reflection that has criss-crossed the globe

This is the first time that 'The Letter Writing Project' is taking place in the Middle East and in the region's multifarious languages, which include Arabic, Urdu, Hindi, Tagalog, Malayalam and so many more, building on previous versions in Australia, Germany, Korea, Indonesia, Japan, New Zealand, Taiwan, the United Kingdom and the United States. As a participatory artwork in the language of the audience's choosing, it begs the engagement of the viewer in order to be effectuated as it continues to travel across the world, possessing its own journey of human catharsis – a critical process of ongoing reflection that has criss-crossed the globe

Lee Mingwei

The Letter Writing Project, 1998–ongoing

When my maternal grandmother passed away, I still had many things to say to her, but it was too late. For the next year and a half, I wrote many letters to her, as if she were still alive, in order to share my thoughts and feelings with her.

For *The Letter Writing Project*, I invite visitors to write the letters they had always meant to, but never made the time for. Each of three writing booths, constructed of wood and translucent glass, contains a desk and writing materials. Visitors can enter any of these booths and write a letter to a deceased or otherwise absent loved one, offering previously unexpressed gratitude or forgiveness, or even an apology. They can then seal and address their letters (for posting by the host museum), or leave them unsealed in one of the slots on the wall of the booth, where subsequent visitors can read them. Many later visitors come to realise, through reading the letters of others, that they, too, carry unexpressed emotions, which they would feel relieved to write down and, perhaps, share. In this way, a chain of feeling is created, reminding visitors of the larger world of emotions in which we all participate. In the end, it is the spirit of the writer that is comforted, whether or not the intended recipient (or others) ever even reads the letter.

Lee Mingwei

The Letter Writing Project
1998/2019
Mixed media interactive installation, 3 wooden booths, writing paper, envelopes
290 x 170 x 231 cm each
Produced by Sharjah Art Foundation
Courtesy of the artist

Page 144–145:
Photo: readsreads.info

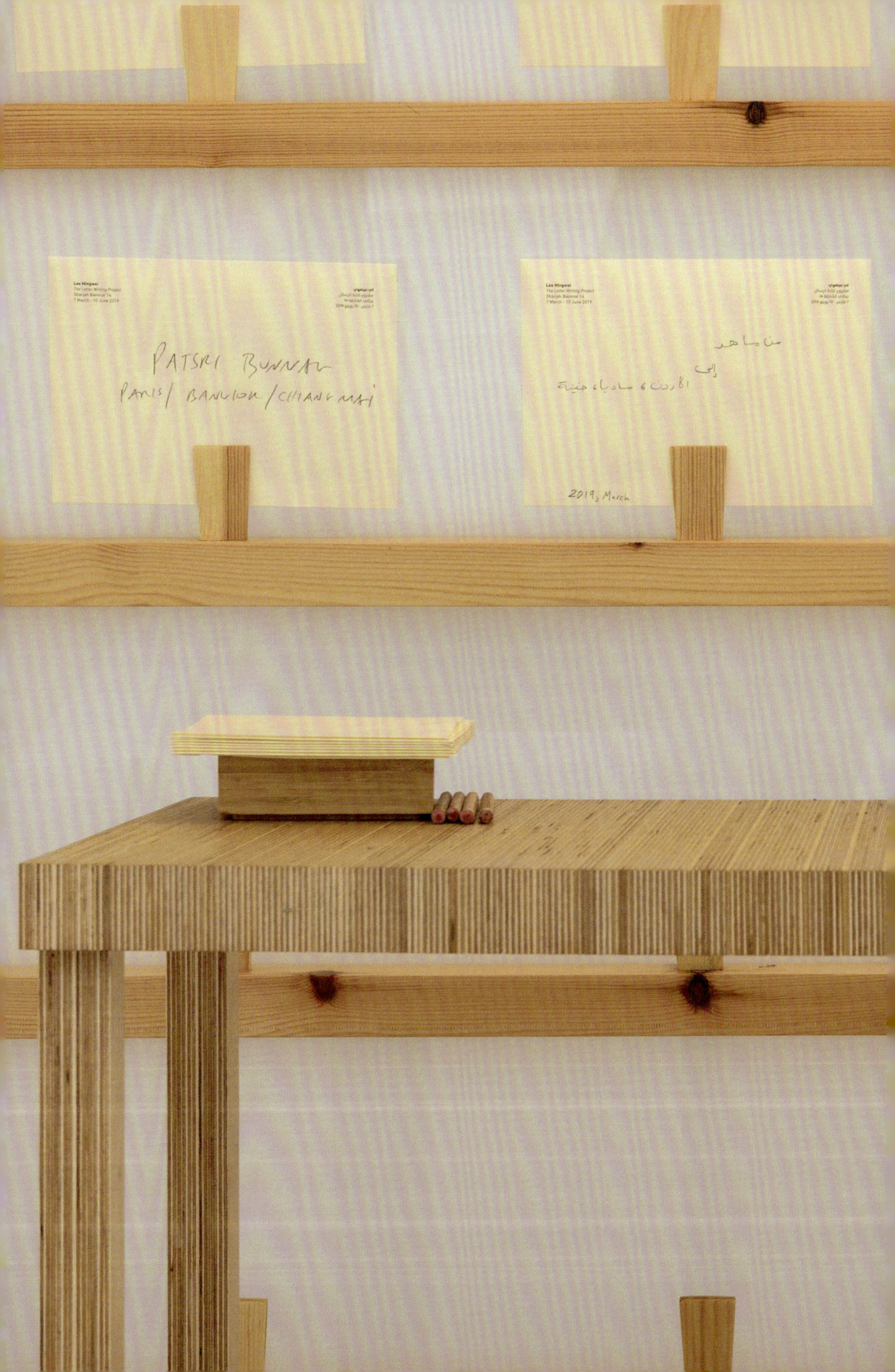
Lee Mingwei
The Letter Writing Project
Sharjah Biennial 14
7 March – 10 June 2019
PATSRI BUNNAG
PARIS/ BANGKOK/CHIANG MAI
Lee Mingwei
The Letter Writing Project
Sharjah Biennial 14
7 March – 10 June 2019
من ماهر
إلى
2019, March

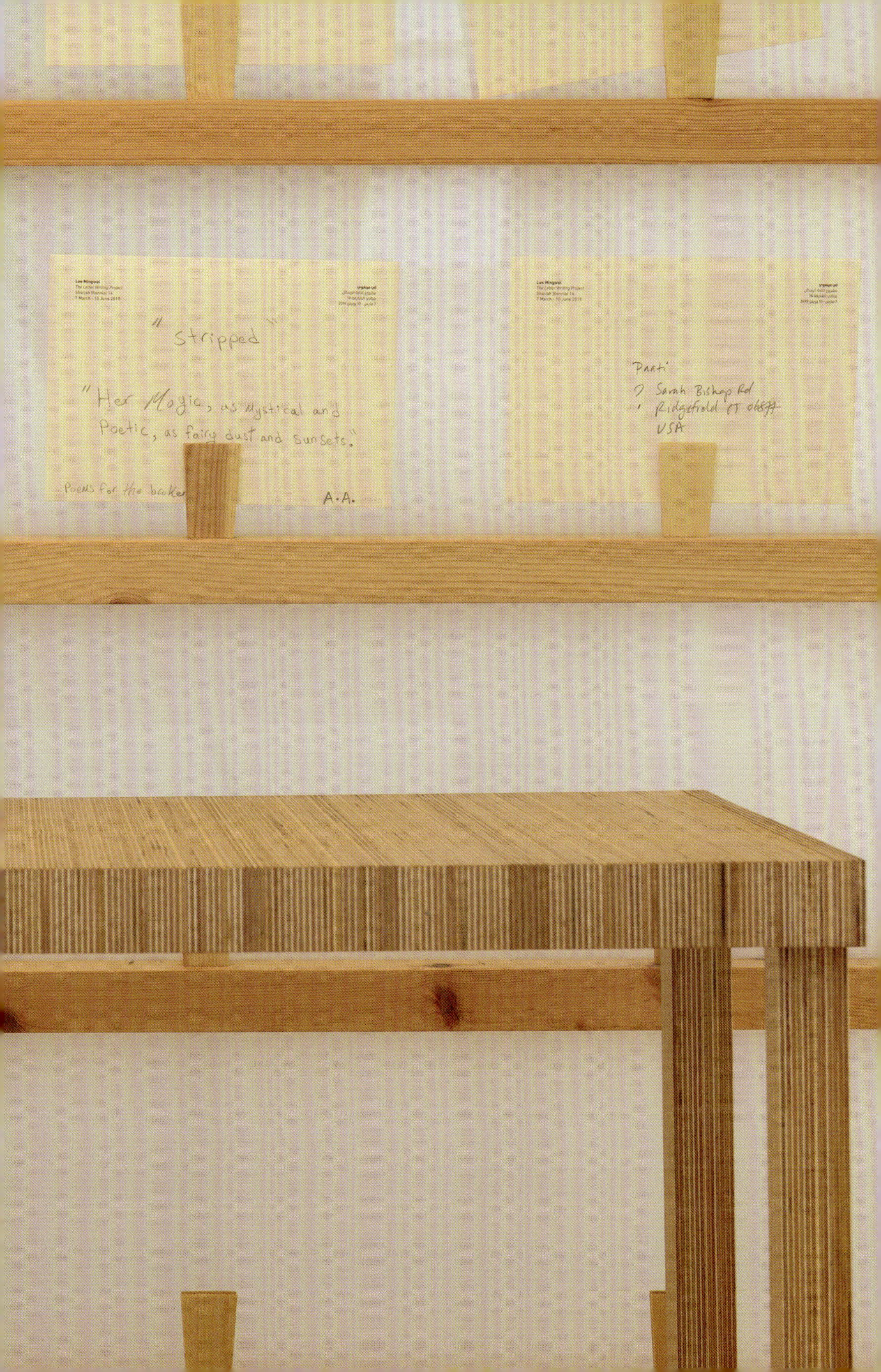
Lee Mingwei
The Letter Writing Project
Sharjah Biennial 14
7 March – 10 June 2019
"Stripped"
"Her Magic, as Mystical and
Poetic, as fairy dust and sunsets."
Poems for the broken
A.A.
Paati
Sarah Bishop Rd
USA

Kidlat Tahimik

Ang Ma-bagyong Sabungan ng 2 Bathala ng Hangin, A Stormy Clash between Two Goddesses of the Winds (WW III – the Protracted Kultur War), 2019

Framing the Legend

Surfing on a coastal wave, the Ifugao legend *Inhabian* weaves a G-string on her back-strap loom. The gods decide to test her with wind-tunnel gusts. She survives – thanks to the back-strap, which serves as a seatbelt. Impressed, the gods anoint her *Ifugao Goddess of the Winds*, and tribal folk invoke her for protection from typhoons.

Enter the invading tsunami: *Marilyn M* with her iconic windblown pose, our *Hollywood Goddess of the Winds*. She leans against the howling winds from the lips of *Inhabian* to stand her ground, lest the weaver's gales launch her into lunar orbit.

This is no windsurfing *kampf*. Yet it is the fight of the *quincentenary*, since Magellan colonised the Philippines in 1521. Yes, in 1898, Filipino revolutionaries threw out the Cross-bearing colonial masters. Then in 1992, we kicked out the squatting American B-52 air bases. However, fighting the enemy nesting in our gut culture (slay the fast-food Father) and detoxing our brains of blazing-gun heroes may be the most elusive victory we have yet to achieve.

Inhabian and *Marilyn M* face off in World War III – a protracted *kultur* clash. No A-bombs. No ICBMs. Just the sound and fury of *Inhabian's* focused winds – '*Whewww!!*' – to stave off penetrant images of the Dream Factory. 'Stay away! We've overdosed with HollyWood *(HW)* Superheroes!' More ferociously, she bellows, '*Whewwww!!!* Be gone! Let our homegrown heroes and heroines regreen our own voices!'

Ang Ma-bagyong Sabungan ng 2 Bathala ng Hangin, A Stormy Clash Between 2 Goddesses of the Winds (WW III – the Protracted Kultur *War)*
2019
Wooden carved icons, ritual objects, interwoven C-print photographs, projected images, audio, mosaic, rattan-basket figurines, back-strap bamboo loom, wrought-iron launch-pads, fibreglass, root sculptures, rotten fishing boats, sawdust, bamboo fences and runo-reed fauna
Dimensions variable
Commissioned by Sharjah Art Foundation
Courtesy of the artist

Kidlat's life's work strongly influenced my conceptualisation of 'Journey Beyond the Arrow'. <u>Not only are his film sets and props compelling artworks and installations in their own right</u>, but his ethos towards the spirit of improvisational skill and his inherent ability to cope with constant change, what he calls 'Bathala Na' ('leave the final outcome to the Cosmos'), is an inspiration to all twenty-first-century cultural workers, especially given the technological arrogance of the era. Our denial of the interdependent diversity of human production and habitat – its 'kapwa' orientation ('myself is in the other') – has been reflected in our histories of countless acts of repression, pain and violence.

The wooden carved objects in Kidlat's daily life are found in his home and the community arts centres he has founded in Baguio – firstly the Victor Oteyza Community Art Space and secondly, the Ili Likha Artist Village

Kidlat is popularly pigeon-holed as a Third Cinema practitioner, as someone who started his journey as an economist in the West, who went on to 'discover' celluloid reels and their ability to tell stories that do not need a singular time or end. His essayist oeuvre is articulated not only in his films and art as genre, but as a philosophical mode in his critical yet deeply respectful relationships with the Cordilleran indigenous community of the Phillippines: as father, husband, friend and mentor.

The wooden carved objects in Kidlat's daily life are found in his home and the community arts centres he has founded in Baguio – firstly the Victor Oteyza Community Art Space and secondly, the Ili Likha Artist Village

Kidlat's life's work strongly influenced my conceptualisation of 'Journey Beyond the Arrow'. Not only are his film sets and props compelling artworks and installations in their own right, but his ethos towards the spirit of improvisational skill and his inherent ability to cope with constant change, what he calls 'Bathala Na' ('leave the final outcome to the Cosmos'), is an inspiration to all twenty-first-century cultural workers, especially given the technological arrogance of the era. Our denial of the interdependent diversity of human production and habitat – its 'kapwa' orientation ('my self is in the other') – has been reflected in our histories of countless acts of repression, pain and violence.

Kidlat is popularly pigeon-holed as a Third Cinema practitioner, as someone who started his journey as an economist in the West, who went on to 'discover' celluloid reels and their ability to tell stories that do not need a singular time or end. His essayist oeuvre is articulated not only in his films and art as a genre, but as a philosophical mode in his critical yet deeply respectful relationships with the Cordilleran indigenous community of the Philippines: as father, husband, friend and mentor.

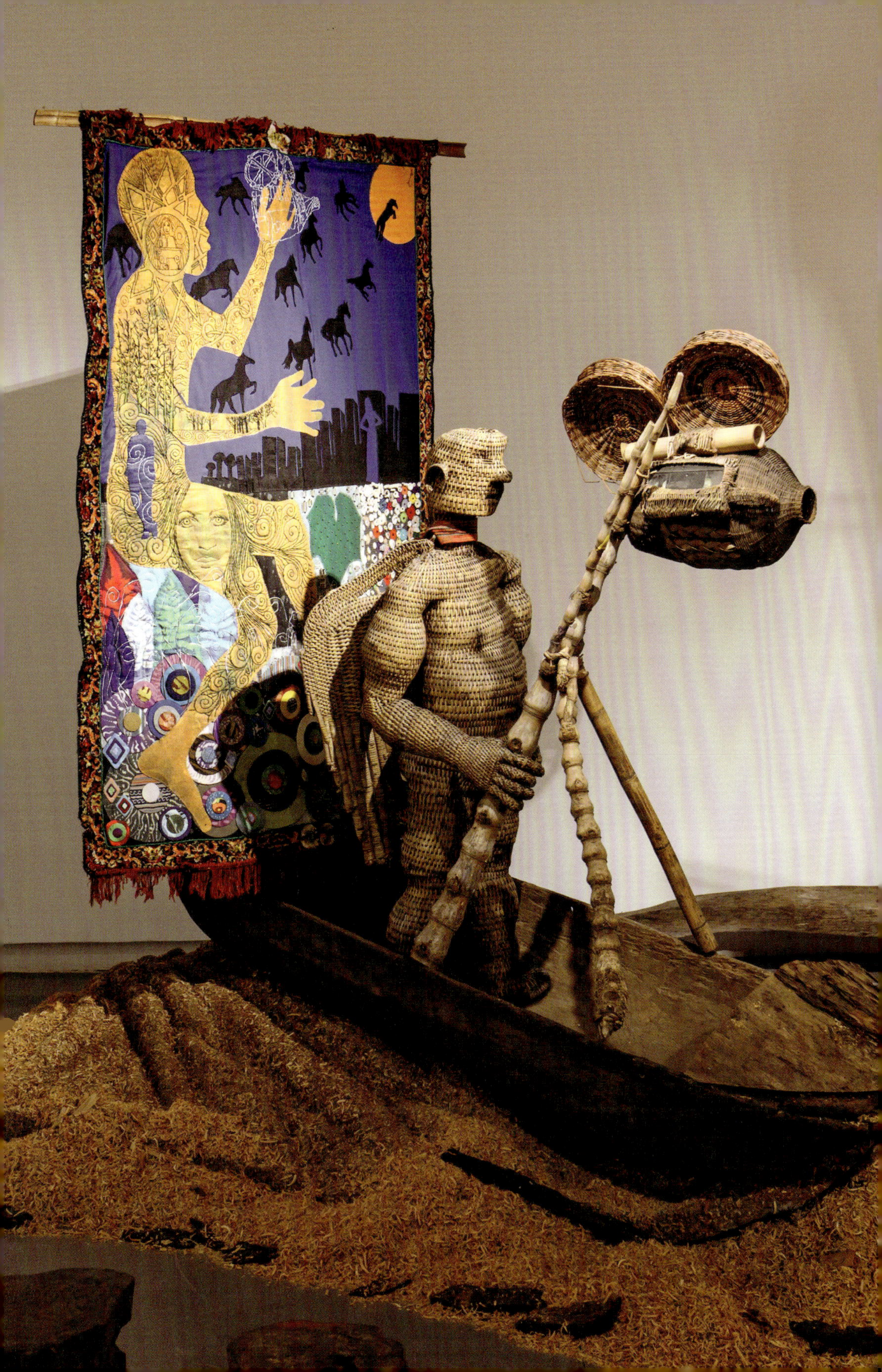

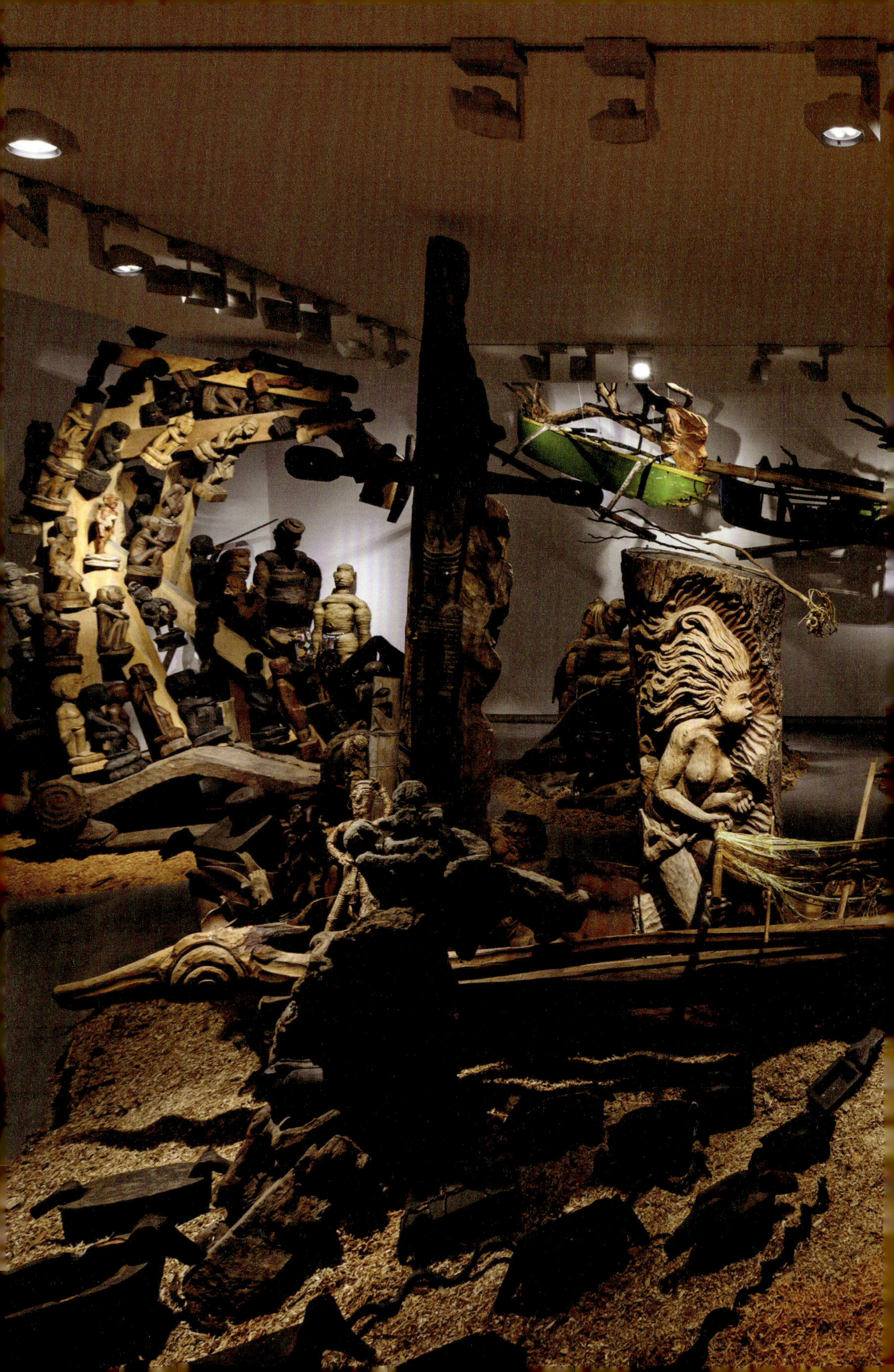

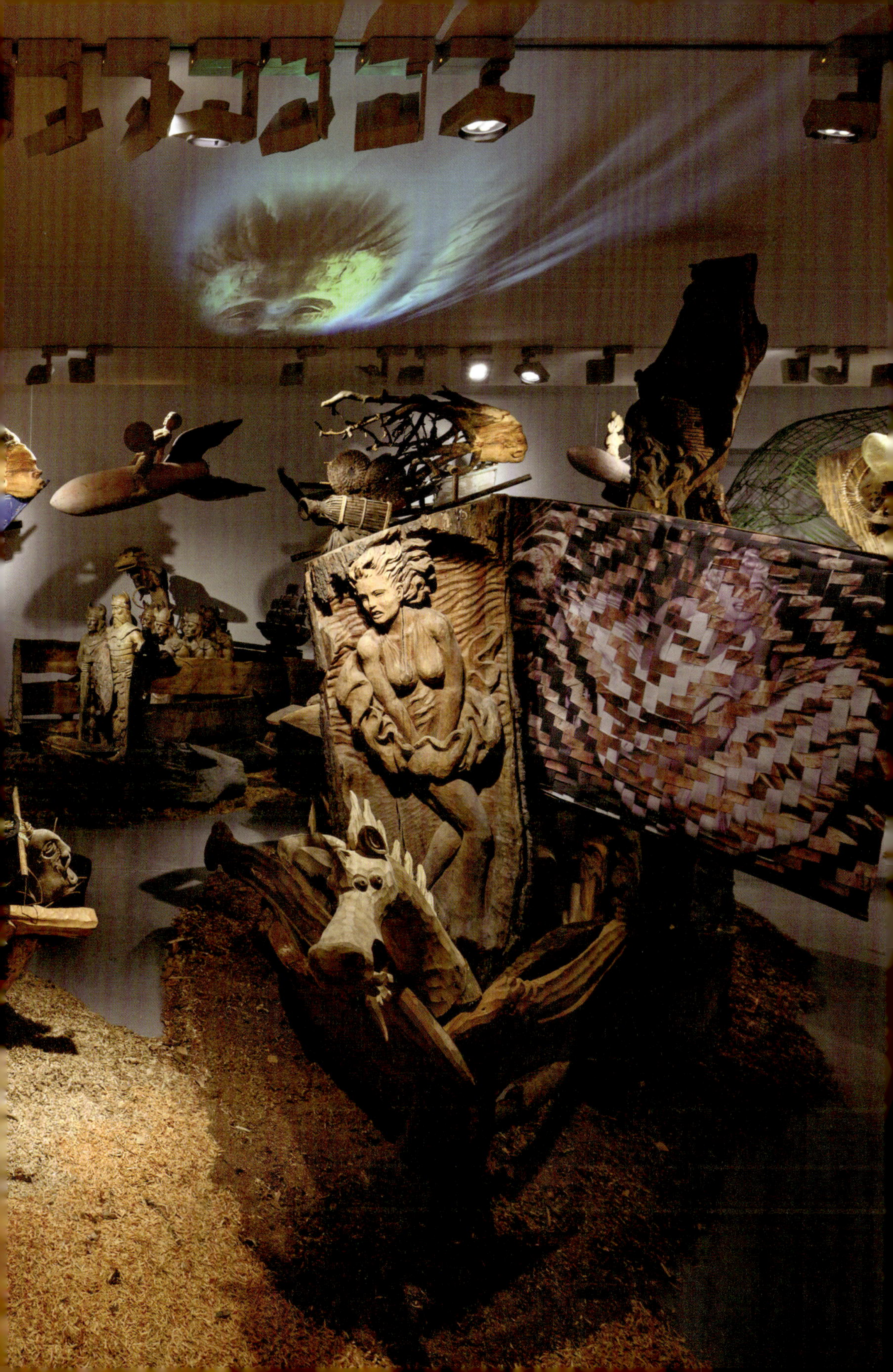

Framing the Auteur

Kidlat's boyhood visuals were fed by the *Big-HW blockbusters*, the spiciest celluloid dishes cooked by HollyWood chefs. As their menus *blocked/busted* the minds of young Filipinos, producers were siphoning off film profits to America (starving out the local storyteller cineastes). Long before Kidlat was alphabetised, his homeland's values were molded by *American Idol* flicks (and yes, of the H. Weinstein kind).

Kidlat was born/bred in Baguio, America's colonial hill station, the bastion of 'West-meets-East' culture. After sleeping for one-third of a century in a 'cocoon of American dreams', the artist's butterfly spirit bolted from its *colonial echo chamber* – in search of its indigenous voice. Uncaged in 1977 from his MBA diploma, the freed *kultur* warrior managed to *stray on track*. By pioneering Filipino indie cinema (outside the *HW* echo chamber), Kidlat worked out his colonial contradictions.

Four decades later, a detour: 'I refuse to be boxed-in as a *filmmaker*. This *WW III* work is my coming-out party'.

This sculptural installation explores issues (and objects) prominent in his films: the *local* story, the indigenous and the personal – why are they sacrificed to *HW*'s no-brainer formulas? Western values are fed to us on a daily dose of Trojan images: junk-food bytes in our age of visual fast food, or cancerous diets for creators and consumers of art?

We see *Inhabian* blow away the boatload of Marilyn's Trojan cargo (film projector, jeep, jukebox, Gutenberg Bible) in order to protect the ancient wisdom of her island people. In the skies above, her Divine-Wind allies (a.k.a. Kami-Kazi) engage invading superhero missiles in 'dog fights'. The Bamboo Kamera shoots a *counter-narrative*. This is the indie's tool that challenges the echo chamber of colonial historians – those chauvinist casting directors who continue *caste-ing* the slave/master hierarchies. Pray tell: Who, then, are the *cocooned slaves*? And who are the *spiritually* free?

Kidlat Tahimik, a.k.a. Eric O. de Guia (colonial name...)

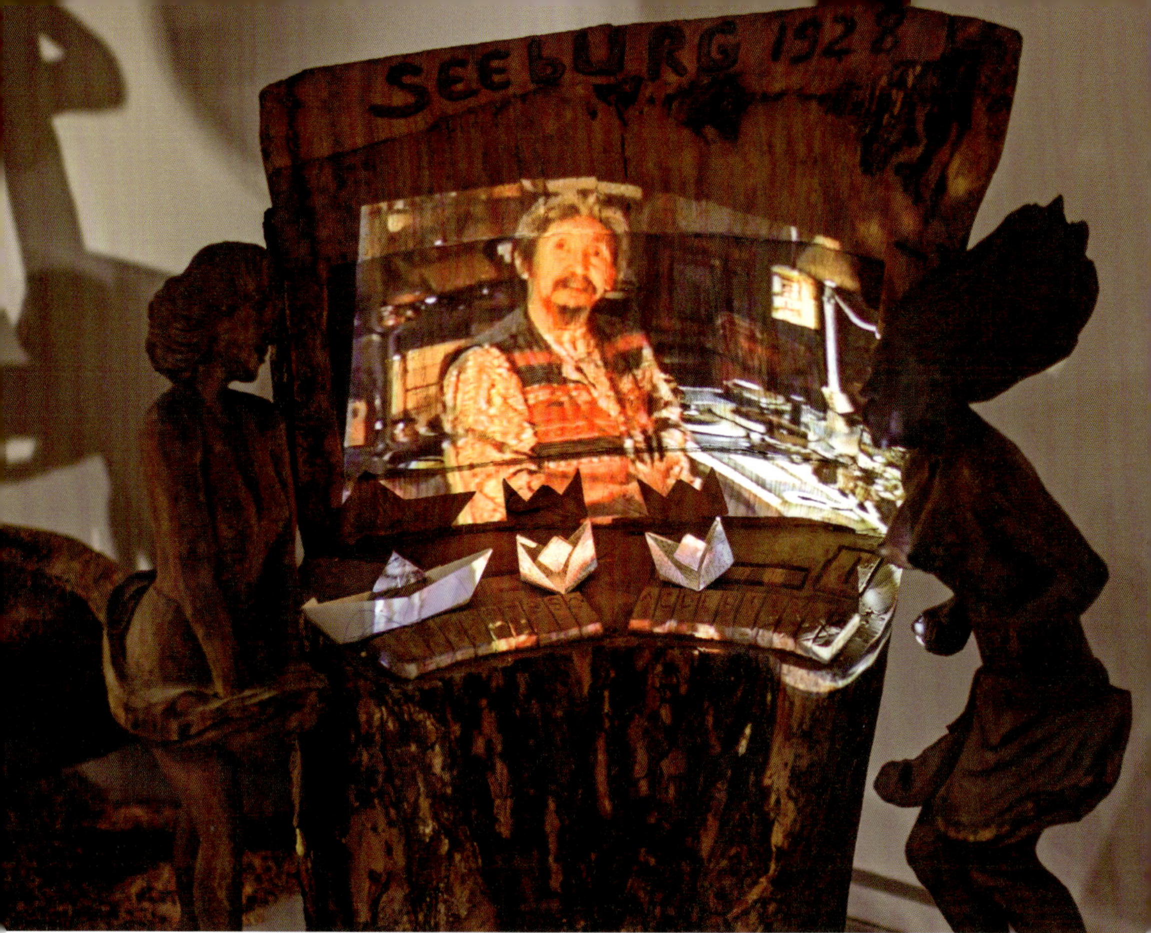

Framing the Cosmic Collaborators
(acknowledgements...muchas gracias!)

Ifugao Wood-Art Storytellers:
Goddess *meister*-carvers: Chris Matiwon and Jason Taguyongon
Ancient ritual-object carvers: [unknown, but revered]
Basket Tribe blind sculptor: Rogelio Ginanoy
Bontoc rattan weaver: Jason Domling
Sea monster coconut mosaic-er: Jun Ritumalta

Homage to the Creativity of His Artist KKKK Family:
Interwoven-photograph sails: Kidlat de Guia
Flying boats and missiles: Kawayan de Guia
Mosaic sea monsters and missile launchpad: Kabunyan de Guia
Kapwa seafarers storyteller: Katrin de Guia

Ancient Wind Goddess Casting Director:
Ritualist/narrator of *Inhabian's* legend: Lopes Nauyac

Nalini Malani

All We Imagine as Light, 2017

All We Imagine as Light is an eleven-panel reverse painting that captures the pain of parting, as well as the deep human conditions of affinity and affection that bind people together. Created as a response to today's ruptured, riven geography and traumatic imaginary, the work is part of an eponymous series that refers to the Kashmiri poet Agha Shahid Ali (1949–2001). In his poems, which combine his Hindu, Muslim and Western heritage, everyday feelings about death and memory are put into words with profound effect. My painting is based on a longing for, and belonging to, those from whom one cannot bear to be apart. As with my two other multi-panel paintings, *Splitting the Other* (2007) and *Twice Upon a Time* (2014), the narrative in this work is built through a number of figures who connect to each other in an undefined space, floating as if in a dream-state galaxy. Unlike the written standard of left to right, top to bottom, or right to left, this narrative can unfold from any starting point. Off-centre in *All We Imagine as Light*, three children bend over a sphere, which appears as a hole in the earth, showing them the damaged landscape of Kashmir. They are surrounded by an endless series of colour graphs, as if humankind were reducible to appealing statistics. Below them, the cryptic lines of Ali read: 'I am everything you lost. My memory keeps getting in the way of your history'.

Nalini Malani

Divisions between people, throughout history, have caused (and continue to cause) great, painful unrest. Kashmir, historically part of the Mughal and Durrani (Afghan) empires, became territory contested by India, Pakistan and China, following the collapse of British-occupied India in 1947. The region remains in limbo – a land for countless individuals seeking differing sovereignty – and is considered one of the most militarised regions of the world. In 'All We Imagine as Light', Nalini alludes to the building blocks of humanity (human touch & heart, memorialisation of courage) that persist amongst destructive pathologies of violence (soldiers, death and weapons). Of ultimate lamentation is the dilemma of measuring equals across ideological and political divides, poetically quoted as, 'You needed me. You needed to perfect me'.

Divisions between people, throughout history, have caused (and continue to cause) great, painful unrest. Kashmir, historically part of the Mughal and Durrani (Afghan) empires, became territory contested by India, Pakistan and China, following the collapse of British-occupied India in 1947. The region remains in limbo – a land for countless individuals seeking differing sovereignty – and is considered one of the most militarised regions of the world. In 'All We Imagine as Light', Nahiri alludes to the building blocks of humanity (human touch, heart, memorialisation of courage) that persist amongst destructive pathologies of violence (soldiers, death and weapons). Of ultimate lamentation is the dilemma of measuring equals across ideological and political divides, poetically quoted as, 'You needed me. You needed to protect me'.

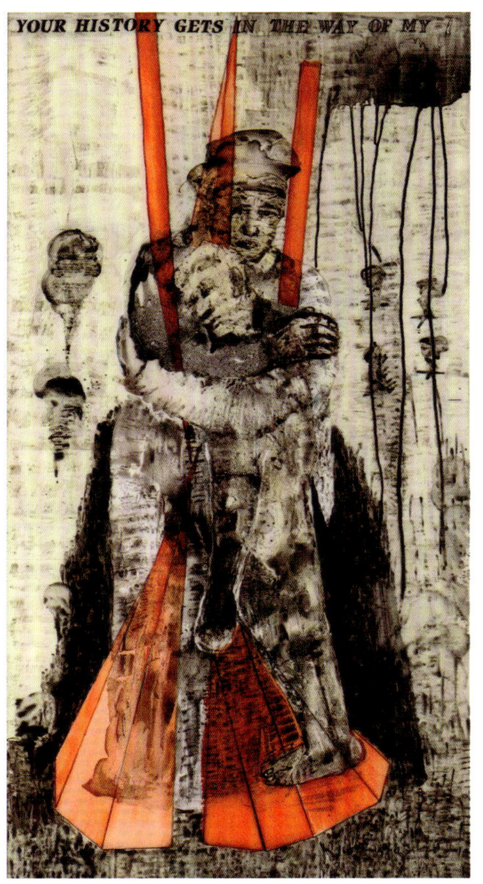

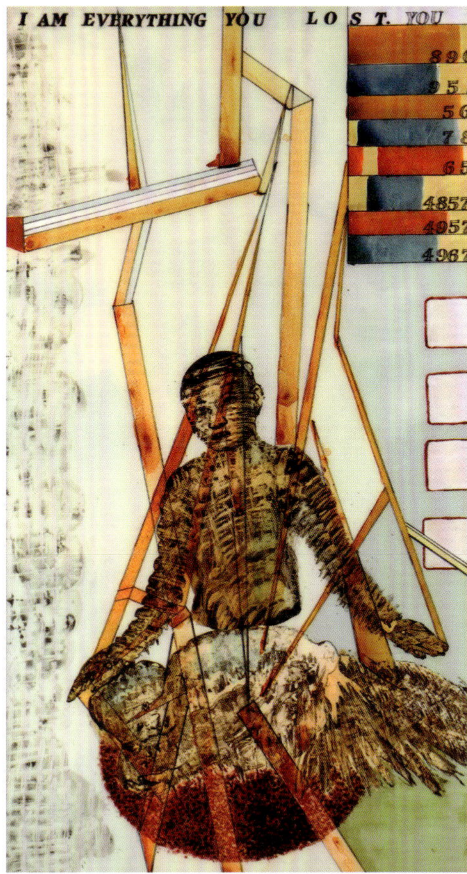

All We Imagine as Light
2017
11-panel reverse paintings
on acrylic
187 x 106 cm each
Burger Collection,
Hong Kong
Courtesy of the artist and
Burger Collection,
Hong Kong

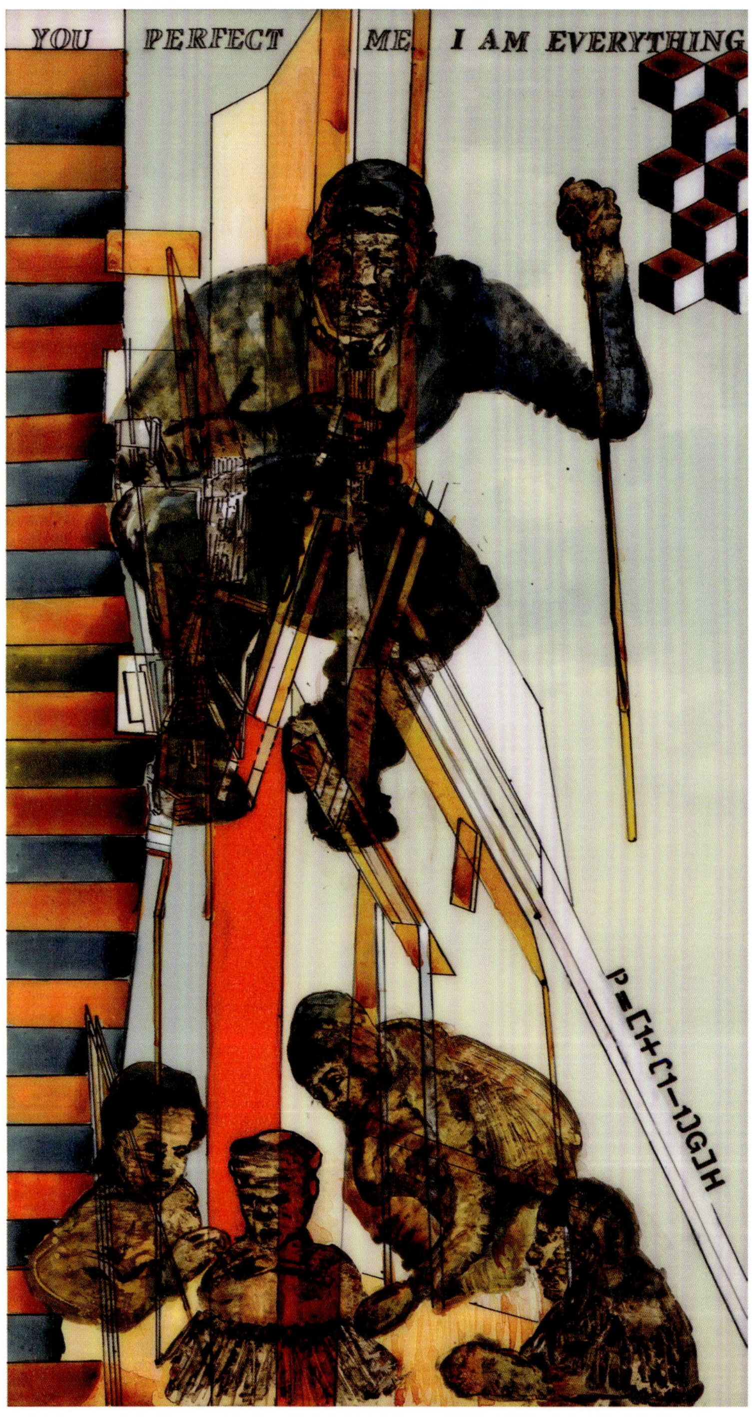
YOU
PERFECT
ME
I AM EVERYTHING
P=[1+[1-1]G]H

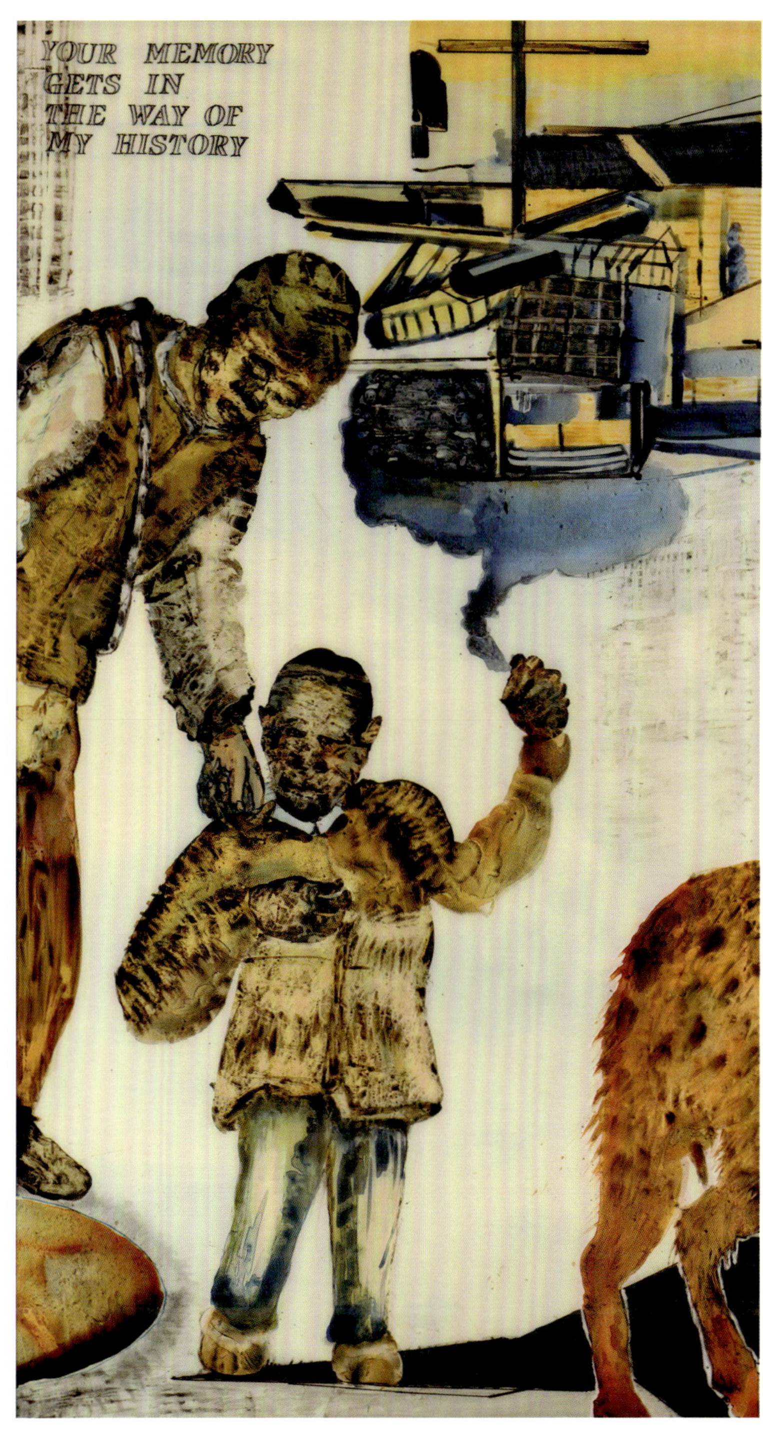
YOUR MEMORY
GETS IN
THE WAY OF
MY HISTORY

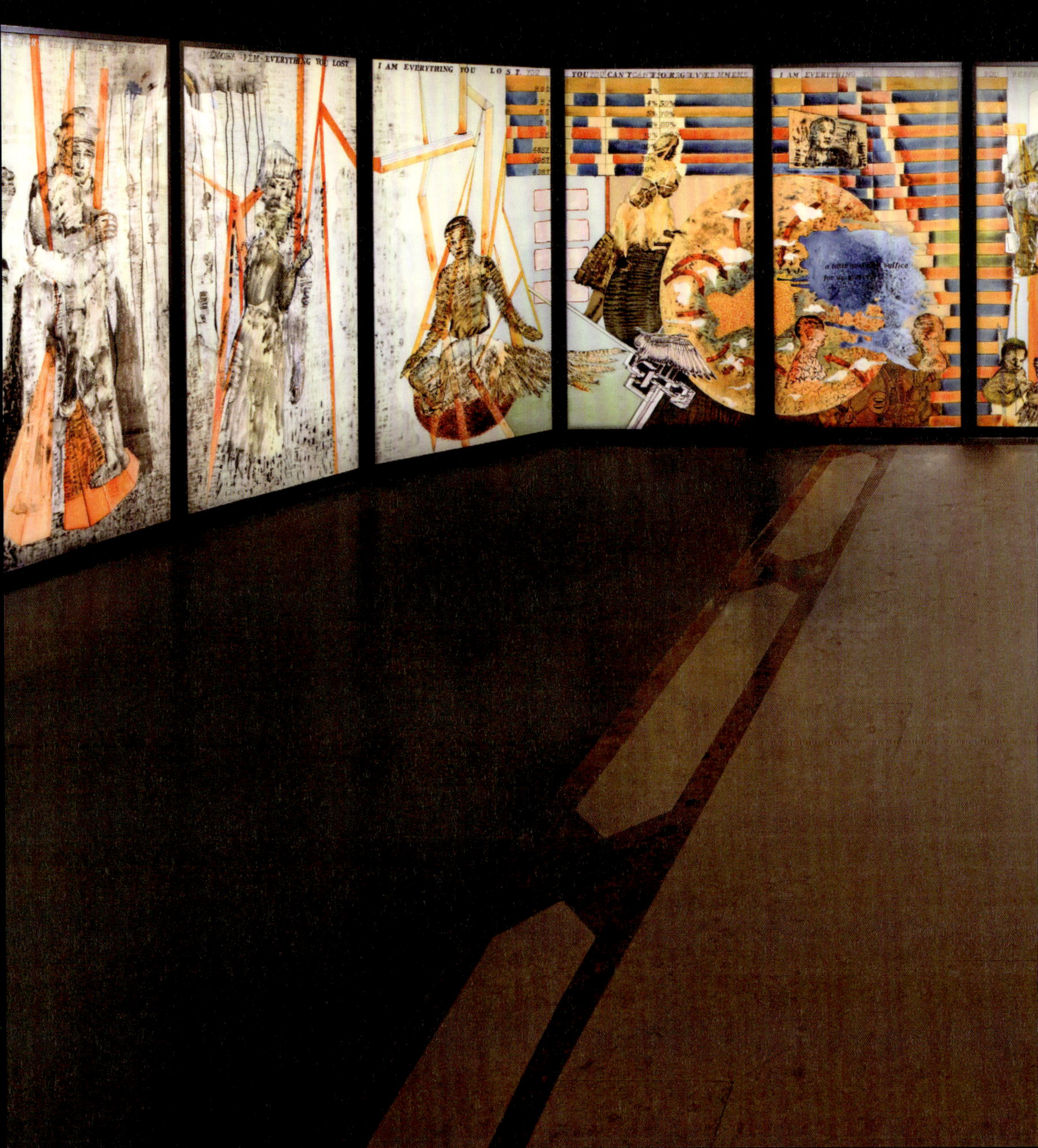
EVERYTHING YOU LOST
I AM EVERYTHING YOU LOST
I AM EVERYTHING

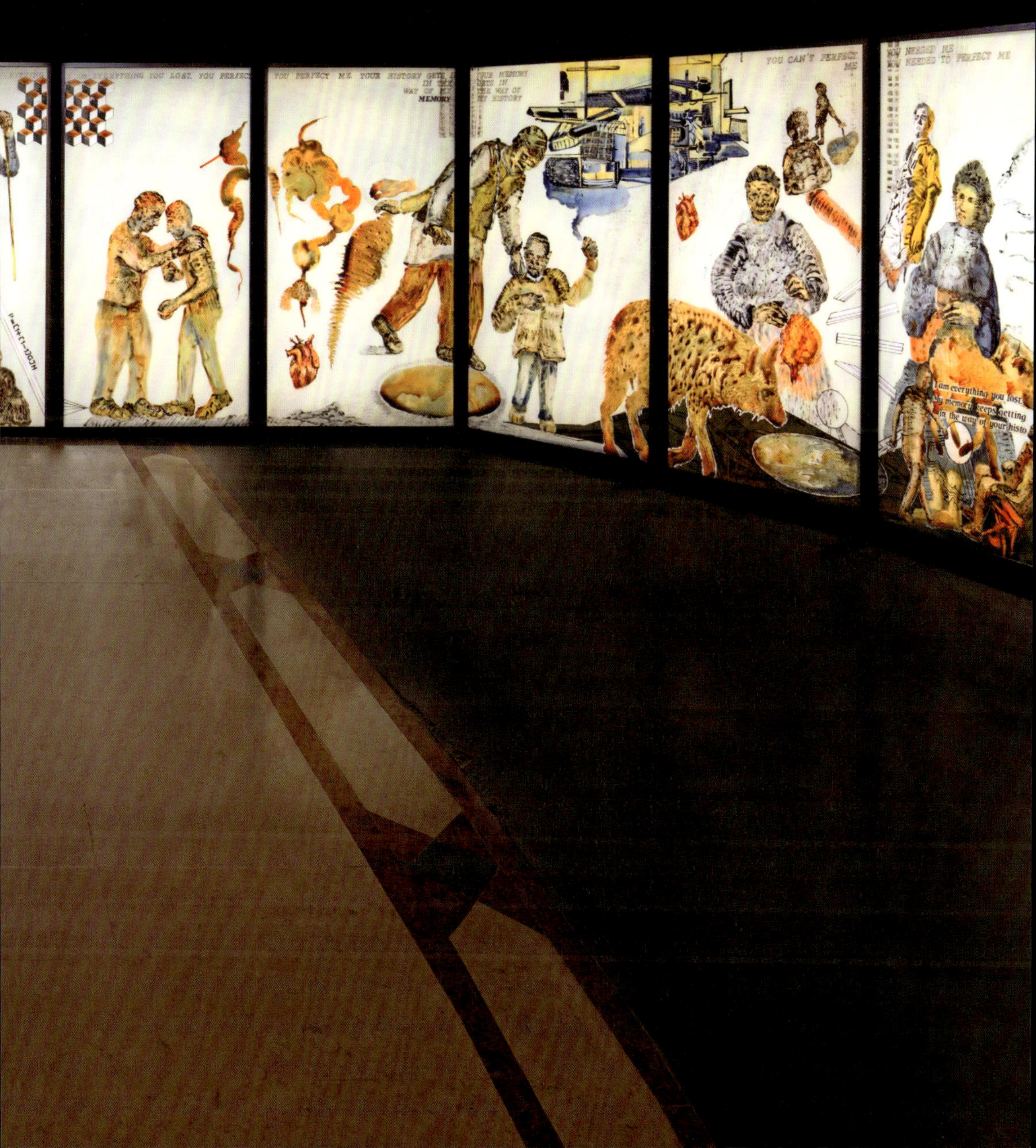
YOU LOST. YOU
YOU PERFECT ME. YOUR HISTORY
MEMORY
YOUR MEMORY
GETS IN
THE WAY OF
MY HISTORY
YOU CAN'T PERFECT
ME
NEEDED ME
NEEDED TO PERFECT ME
I am everything you lost.
in the way of your

Carlos Garaicoa

Yo nunca he sido surrealista hasta el día de hoy (III) / I've Never Been a Surrealist until Today (III), (unrealized)

The language of architecture has allowed me to develop methodologies that attempt to connect the rationality of geometry with the creation of fictitious worlds. In such a universe, the image of a certain reality is completed with the interplay of the impossible, and the calling into question of that particular reality is compounded by the introduction of a history based on subjectivity. This use of subjectivity was already masterfully put into practice by historical Surrealism. In that case, and my own, we do not try to expose what we see, but what we feel and what we think we should say. Although my work is not affiliated with the precepts of Surrealism, its strategies can be useful in putting observed reality into crisis. In a situation of an excess of objectivity (the circulation of capital, for example), I have been interested in applying an excess of possible subjectivity, an idea that already existed in surrealist games such as *Cadavre Exquis* (Exquisite Corpse).

For SB14, I continue my interest in public space – a preoccupation I've had since the beginning of my career – and the interaction of citizens in the public realm who are not conscious that they are entering an artistic space. In *I've Never Been a Surrealist until Today (III)*, the route of the pedestrian in Sharjah is revealed, giving wonder to the immersion of a street underpass as an oasis of vegetation: this quiet and fertile space thus becoming a visual, and perhaps rational, contradiction to the noisy, crowded and hot desert city.

Elements and materials exclusive to the world of architects, urbanists and gardeners (those beings of reality) are arranged here in such a way that they manage to make a claim on a more dreamlike world. The placement of these materials proposes a reordering of this world, denying the logic of our Western culture. Art functions here as a way to create new meanings and change the perception of walking through the city as part of daily life. This site-specific installation comments on the historical reality of art, appropriating a certain avant-garde spirit in its questioning of the logic of observation; it attempts to reveal, like a mirror, the limitations of our interactions and analyses of the environment.

Carlos Garaicoa

It is with great disappointment that this project could not be realized for SB14 (largely due to financial limitations), however it remains a critical and integral conceptual node of my mapping 'Journey Beyond the Arrow', and thus you find it visualized here in this book. The everyday person who would have utilized this immersive artistic environment would largely not be accustomed with the world of 'Art', nor likely knowing why such a field of human production could be inclusive of their presence. It is Garaicoa's reference to the 'surreal' that I understand as the anomaly of Capital. For me, artists are crucial provocateurs of assumed privilege, often playfully disturbing the presumed means and methods of engaging imagination and innovation, across class, social prejudice and political dogma.

It is with great disappointment that this project could not be realized for SB14 (largely due to financial limitations), however it remains a critical and integral conceptual node of my mapping 'Journey Beyond the Arrow', and thus you find it visualized here in this book. The everyday person who would have utilized this immersive artistic environment would largely not be accustomed with the world of 'Art', nor likely knowing why such a field of human production could be inclusive of their presence. It is Lovaccoin's reference to the 'surreal' that I understand as the anomaly of Capital. For me, artists are crucial provocateurs of assumed privilege, often playfully disturbing the presumed means and methods of engaging imagination and innovation, across class, social prejudice and political dogma.

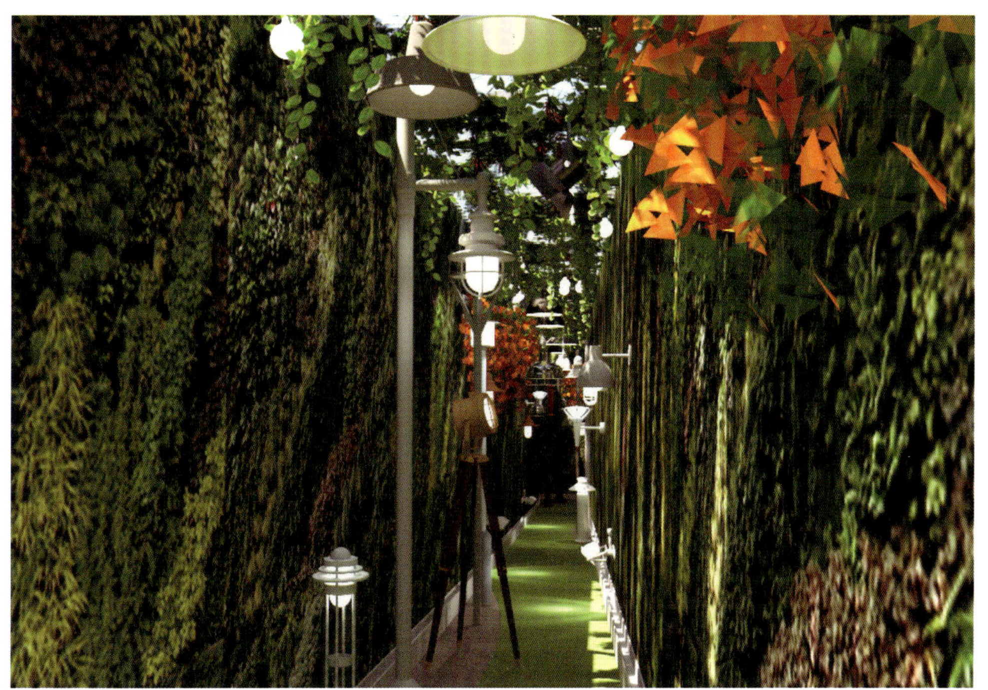

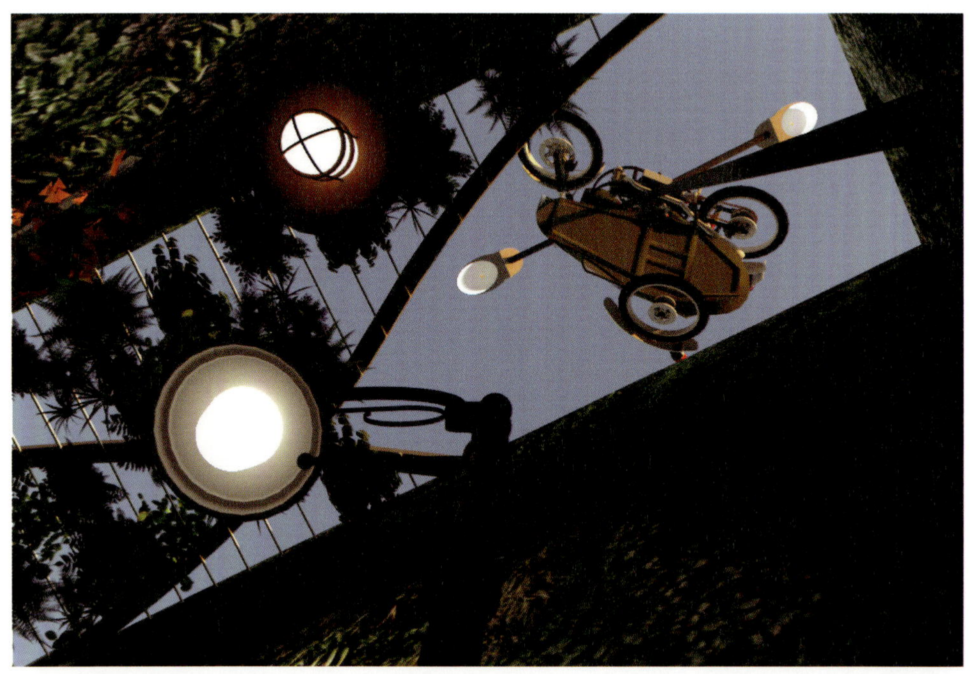

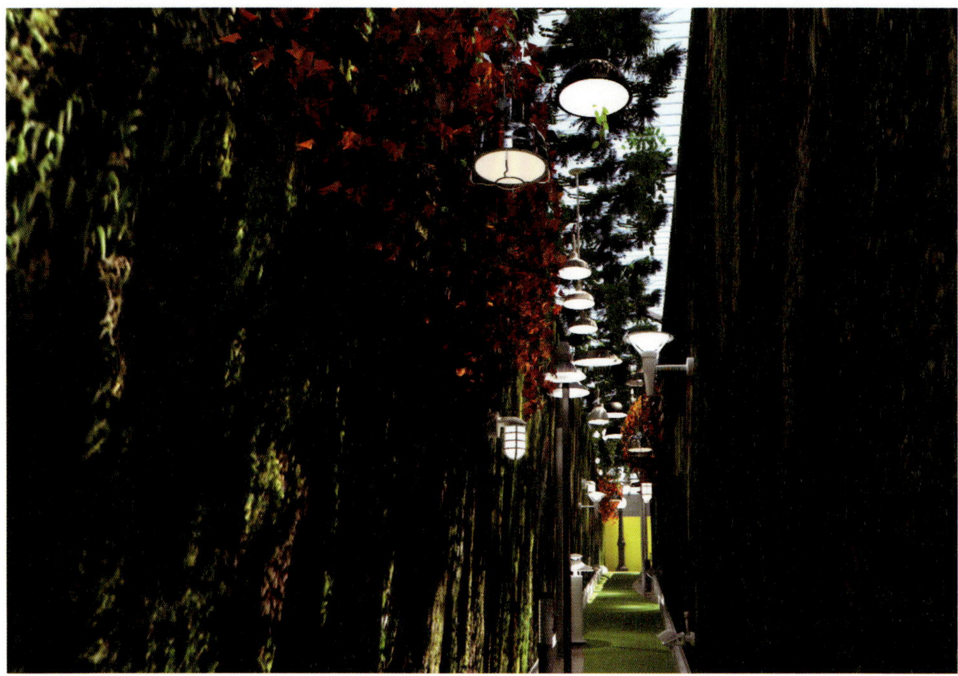

Xu Zhen

The Starving of Sudan, 2008

When 'The Starving of Sudan' was first staged in Beijing at Long March Space in 2008, it was met by a most vocal public reaction. This performance installation takes as its subject and visual frame the 1994 Pulitzer Prize – winning photograph by South African photographer Kevin Carter (1960 – 1994). Shot in famine-stricken Sudan, Carter's image shows a vulture lurking in the rear, its eyes fixed on a young Sudanese baby, waiting for it to die. Xu Zhen recreates this scene in 'The Starving of Sudan.'

Walking into the brightly lit Chinese gallery space, one was immediately confronted by the heat and smell of organic matter, as it must have been like in that horrific moment. It was quite apparent that this piece hit an intrinsic human nerve: hearing the sudden, rapid intake of breath or seeing the hands that fluttered to the mouths of those who stumbled into the space, providing testament to a kind of universal understanding of human value. Still, there were those who gleefully took snapshots of the performance, excitedly loading their images to social media, their comments at times insensitive, and dangerously close to racist, in their assessment of the scene. Many in the local art community, women in particular, were angered by the employment of this Chinese migrant child – too young to understand what she was being asked to do – in the artist's piece.

After receiving the Pulitzer, Carter rose to the top of journalism fame overnight, only to be found two months later, dead in Johannesburg, from self-inflicted carbon monoxide poisoning. It is said that he was a highly competitive man who craved professional recognition. His death was mired in guilt,

When 'The Starving of Sudan' was first staged in Beijing at Long March Space in 2008, it was met by a most vocal public reaction. This performance installation takes as its subject and visual frame from the 1994 Pulitzer Prize-winning photograph by South African photographer Kevin Carter (1960-1994). Shot in famine-stricken Sudan, Carter's image shows a vulture lurking in the rear, its eyes fixed on a young Sudanese baby, waiting for it to die. Xu Zhen recreates this scene in 'The Starving of Sudan'.

Walking into the brightly lit Chinese gallery space, one was immediately confronted by the heat and smell of organic matter, as it must have been like in that horrific moment. It was quite apparent that this piece hit an intrinsic human nerve: hearing the sudden, rapid intake of breath or seeing the hands that fluttered to the mouths of those who stumbled into the space, providing testament to a kind of universal understanding of human value. Still, there were those who gleefully took snapshots of the performance, excitedly loading their images to social media, their comments at times insensitive, and dangerously close to racist, in their assessment of the scene. Many in the local art community, women in particular, were angered by the employment of this Guinean migrant child – too young to understand what she was being asked to do – in the artist's piece.

After receiving the Pulitzer, Carter rose to the top of journalism fame overnight, only to be found two months later, dead in Johannesburg, from self-inflicted carbon monoxide poisoning. It is said that he was a highly competitive man who craved professional recognition. His death was mired in guilt, his conscience heavily exacerbated by the press, which soon came to question the ethical difference between voyeurism and journalism: How could he leave the scene without knowing the fate of the child? It is this dark side of 'truth' and 'conscience' that Xu prods, confronts and, wilfully, perhaps sadistically, inserts into his own artistic practice.

Xu's art has always tested our ethical assumptions and notions of human limits; however, with this particular work, he controversially challenges and implicates his own artistic profession as possible farce. What, quite ironically, saves it from pure spectacle are the subjects he forces his viewers and, indeed, himself to confront. By manipulating the platform of art at his disposal, perhaps seeking some kind of reconciliation with his own involvement in a visual system of knowledge (and, thus, with its own rubric of power in its representation), he surreptitiously plants a question in everyone's mind about the meaning of contemporary art and its ability to provoke our own understanding of passive participation in the world's chronic tragedies.

The 'Starving of Sudan' has remained with me ever since 2008. I was particularly confounded by the conditions of the general Chinese audience and its lack of comparative international query. Xu's work makes me deeply aware of how the online bubble of information in China today remains one of the most controlled in the world, its citizens increasingly monitored for signs of any outspoken, independent thinking.

his conscience heavily exacerbated by the press, which soon came to question the ethical difference between voyeurism and journalism: How could he leave the scene without knowing the fate of the child? It is this dark side of 'truth' and 'conscience' that Xu prods, confronts and, wilfully, perhaps sadistically, inserts into his own artistic practice.

Xu's art has always tested our ethical assumptions and notions of human limits; however, with this particular work, he controversially challenges and implicates his own artistic profession as possible force. What, quite ironically, saves it from pure spectacle are the subjects he forces his viewers and, indeed, himself to confront. By manipulating the platform of art at his disposal, perhaps seeking some kind of reconciliation with his own involvement in a visual system of knowledge (and, thus, with its own rubric of power in its representation), he surreptitiously plants a question in everyone's mind about the meaning of contemporary art and its ability to provoke our own understanding of passive participation in the world's chronic tragedies.

The 'Starving of Sudan' has remained with me ever since 2008. I was particularly confounded by the conditions of the general Chinese audience and its lack of comparative international query. Xu's work makes me deeply aware of how the online bubble of information in China today remains one of the most controlled in the world, its citizens increasingly monitored for signs of any outspoken, independent thinking.

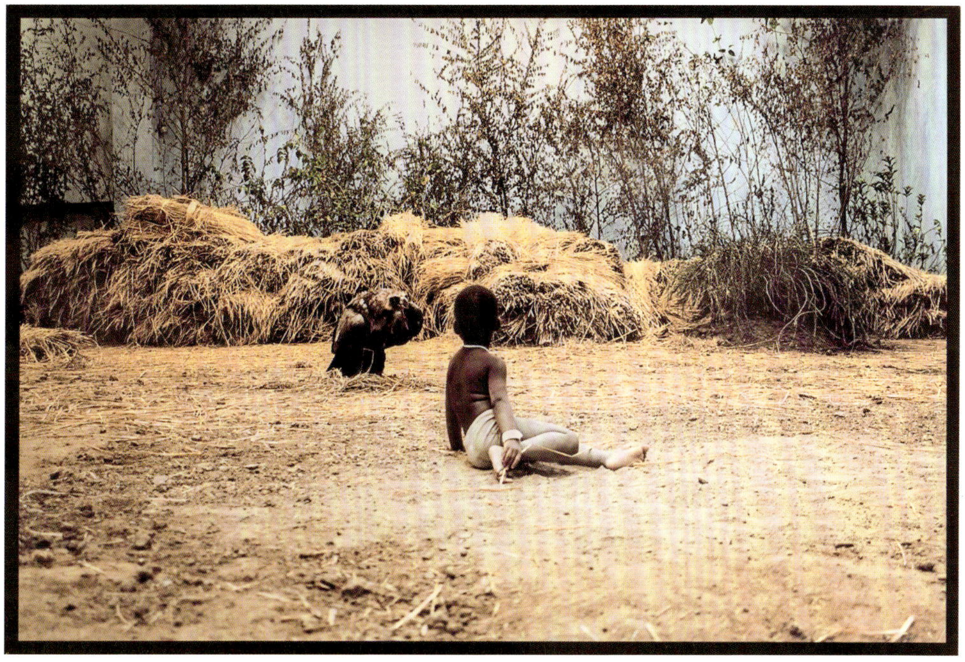

The Starving of Sudan
2008
21 C-print on Dibond
120 x 80 cm each
Courtesy of the artist and
Long March Space, Beijing

Page 164–165:
The Starving of Sudan
2008
Single-channel video:
colour, sound
12 minutes 11 seconds
Courtesy of the artist and
Long March Space, Beijing

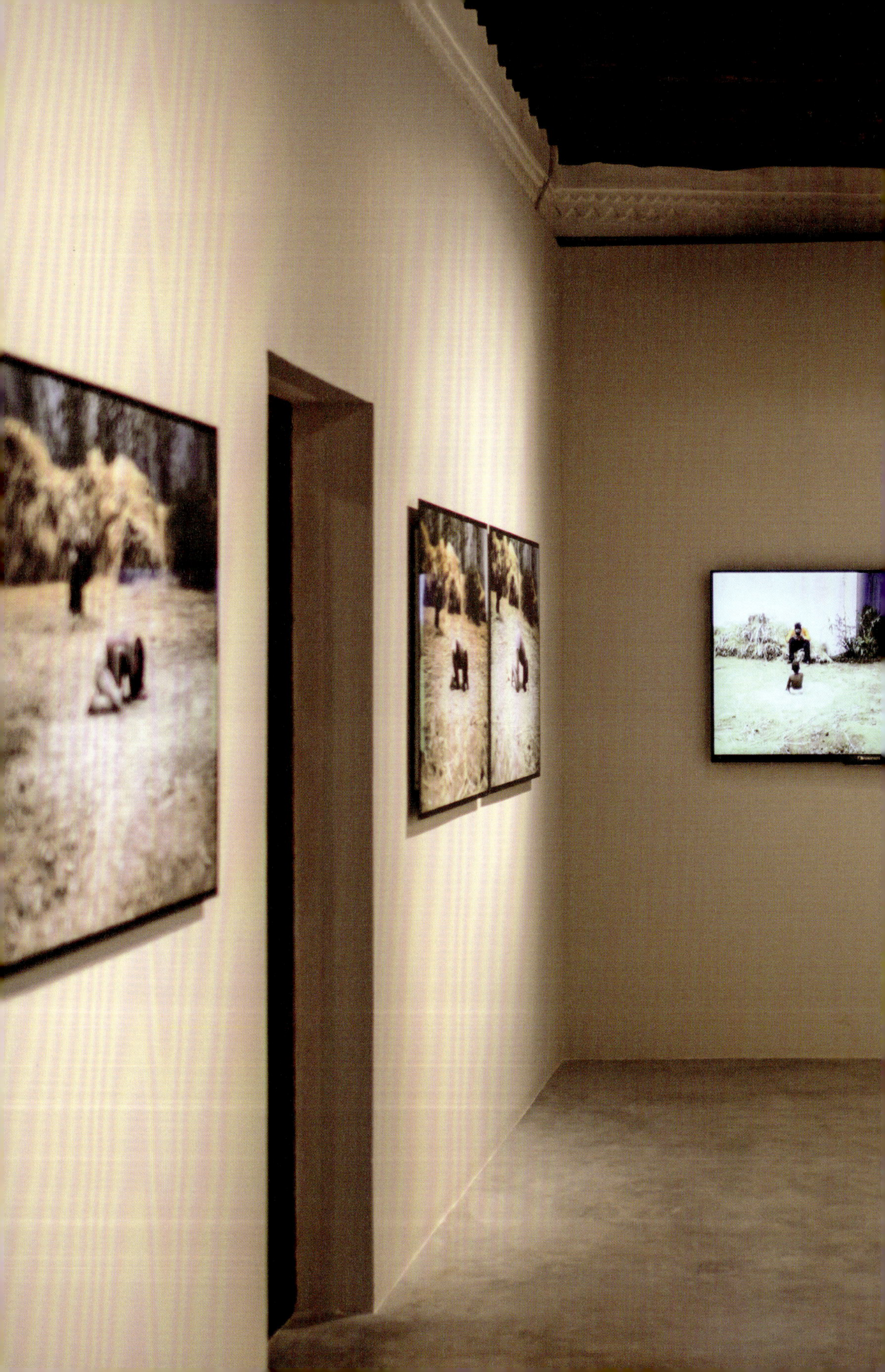

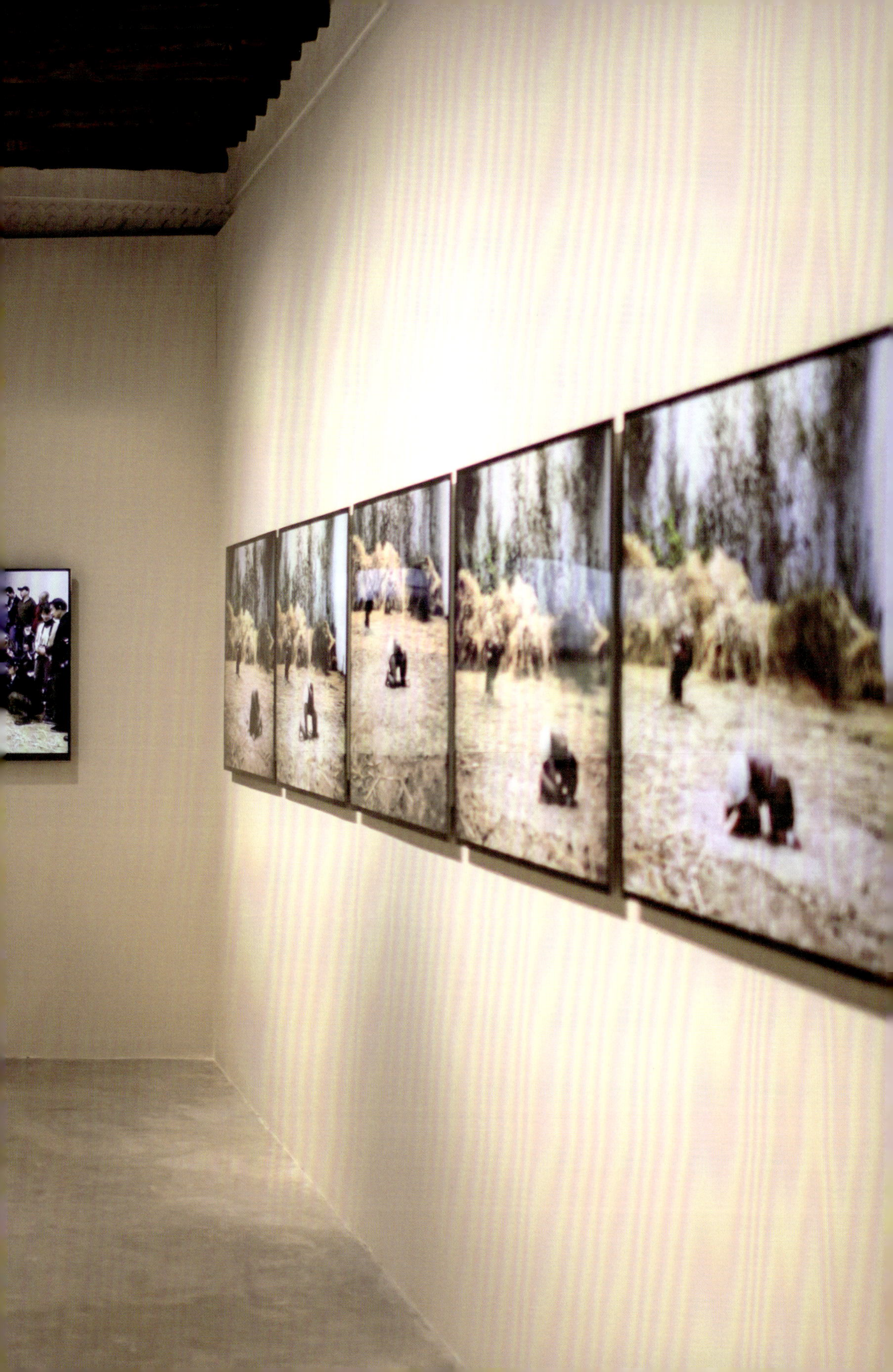

Rohini Devasher

Spheres, 2017

Spheres explores ideas of interiority, inversion and the construction of a 'climate' that evokes a strangeness, not of haunting, but of wonder. Studies on creative problem-solving show that finding new perspectives can be achieved by juxtaposing one problem with something completely unrelated, thereby making the familiar, strange. 'Strange-ing' thus becomes a strategy for encountering, observing and, finally, recording both environment and experience, whilst walking a fine line between wonder and the uncanny. The result is somewhat unclassifiable, a category unto itself.

A work in four parts, *Spheres* seeks this unclassifiable space. We first see a crater, standing as monument to past upheaval, with mist, cloud and fog; with a distant horizon, an atmosphere. Then a cylindrical sea, rising overhead as artificial suns simulate daylight, by turns illuminating and obscuring the landscape. Finally, geographic metaphors of 'the valley' and the 'cloud-maker' imply the unobservable (i.e., in comparison with what can be observed). These conjured images are a species of 'chimera'. They stand in for something else, pushing the limits of the known and the imagined. The landscape, because of its projected scale, provides an almost mythic realisation of oneself within this environment.

This work takes inspiration from Jules Verne's series of novels titled *Voyages Extraordinaires* (1863–1905). The French writer's meticulous attention to detail and scientific trivia particularly influenced my drawing, which forms the screen for this video that brings together moments of our planet as a sphere or a whole. For instance, *Spheres* refers to the Hollow Earth theory that asserts another Earth exists at the centre of our planet, in a place accessible via one-way volcanic shafts. It also considers the Homeric view of the Earth as a flat, circular disc of land surrounded by a continuous ocean-stream.

With *Spheres,* I am interested in juxtaposing these ideas of the Earth with those of author Arthur C. Clarke, specifically in his *Rendezvous with Rama* (1973), in which an unidentified object enters our solar system. What follows (in his story and mine) is a world turned outside-in, with a cylindrical sea that arches above the explorers, possibly cities lit by three linear suns.

Rohini Devasher

The video of this site-specific installation was shot on Mount Aso, Japan's largest and most active volcano, at the lip of its caldera (the hollow crater formation that resulted from a volcanic eruption between 30,000 and 90,000 years ago). For Rohini, humanity has spent much of its resources creating tools to study outer space from Earth; but here, in 'Spheres', she inverts that gaze, reminding us to journey inwards, to reassess the cycles and structures of the very world we physically inhabit.

The video of this site-specific installation was shot on Mount Aso, Japan's largest and most active volcano, at the lip of its caldera (the hollow crater formation that resulted from a volcanic eruption between 30,000 and 90,000 years ago). For Rohini, humanity has spent much of its resources creating tools to study outer space from Earth; but here, in 'Spheres', she inverts that gaze, reminding us to journey inwards, to reassess the cycles and structures of the very world we physically inhabit.

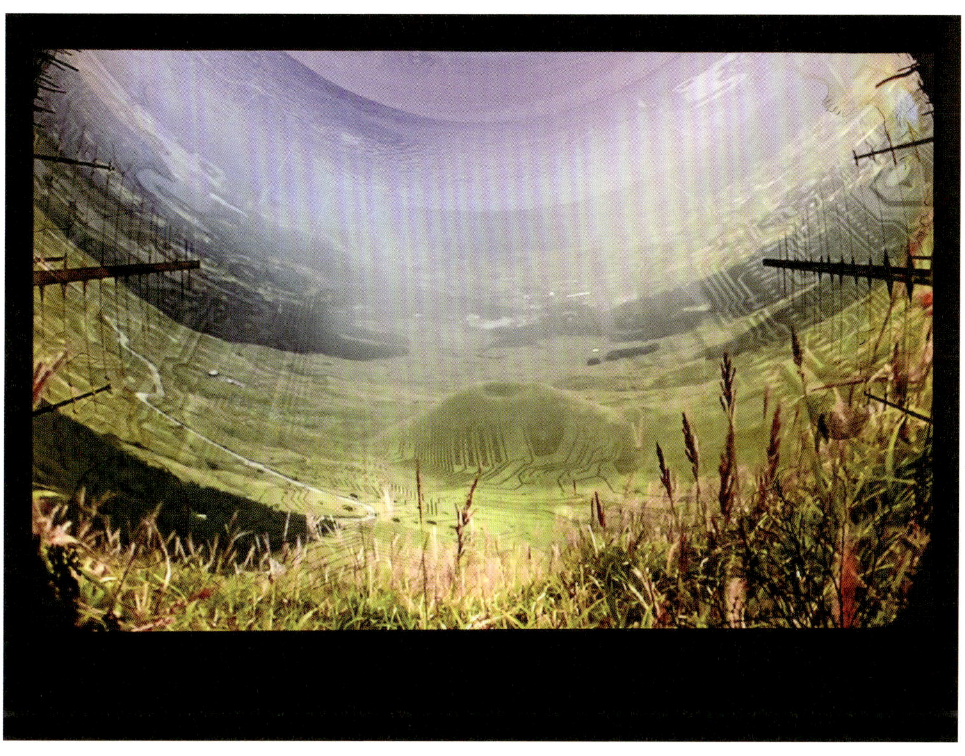

Spheres
2017
Single-channel video projection: colour, sound; metallic paint, pan pastel, dry pastel, acrylic, charcoal, pencil, colour pencil on wall
22 minutes; dimensions variable
Courtesy of the artist and Project 88, Mumbai

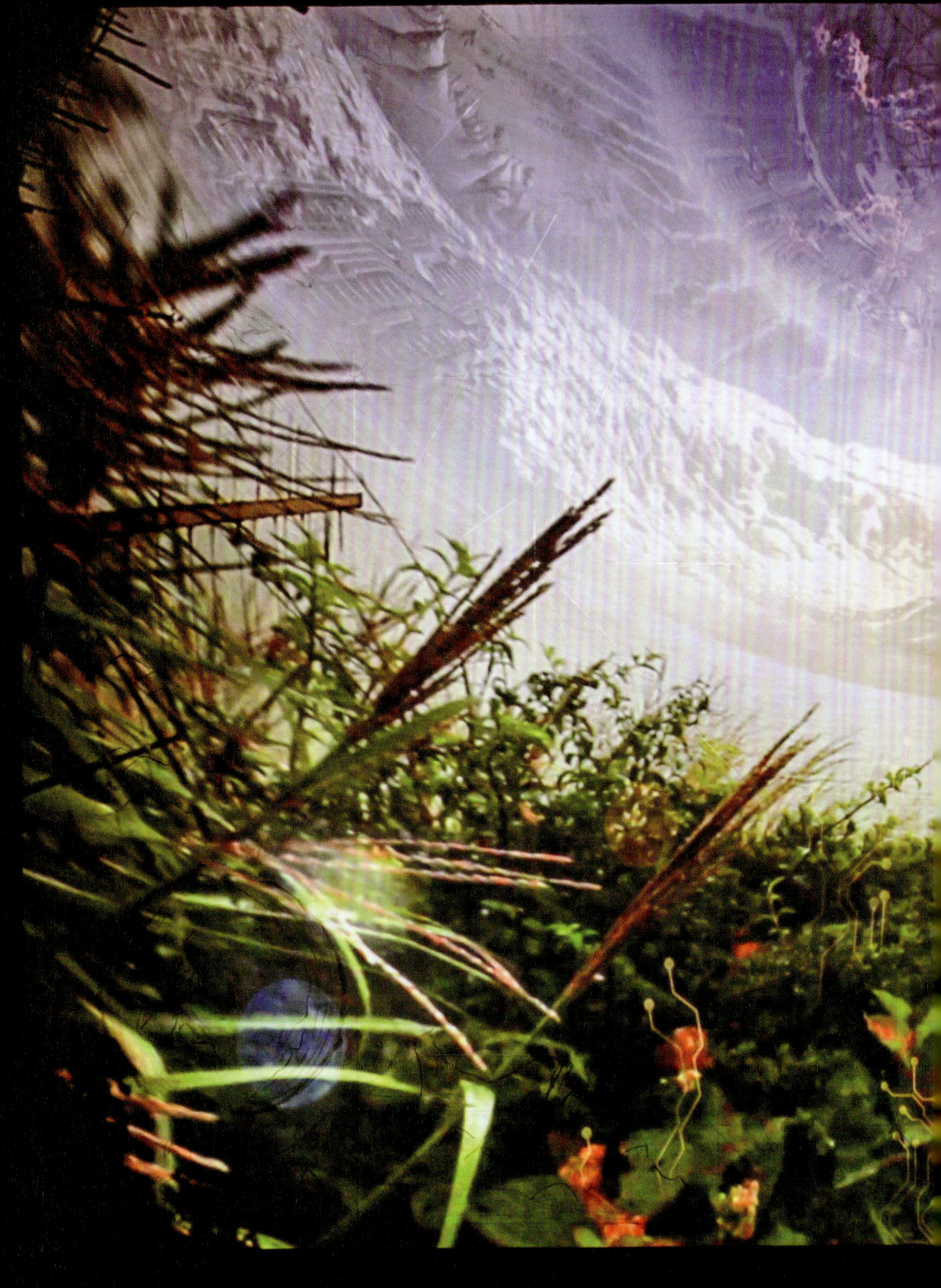

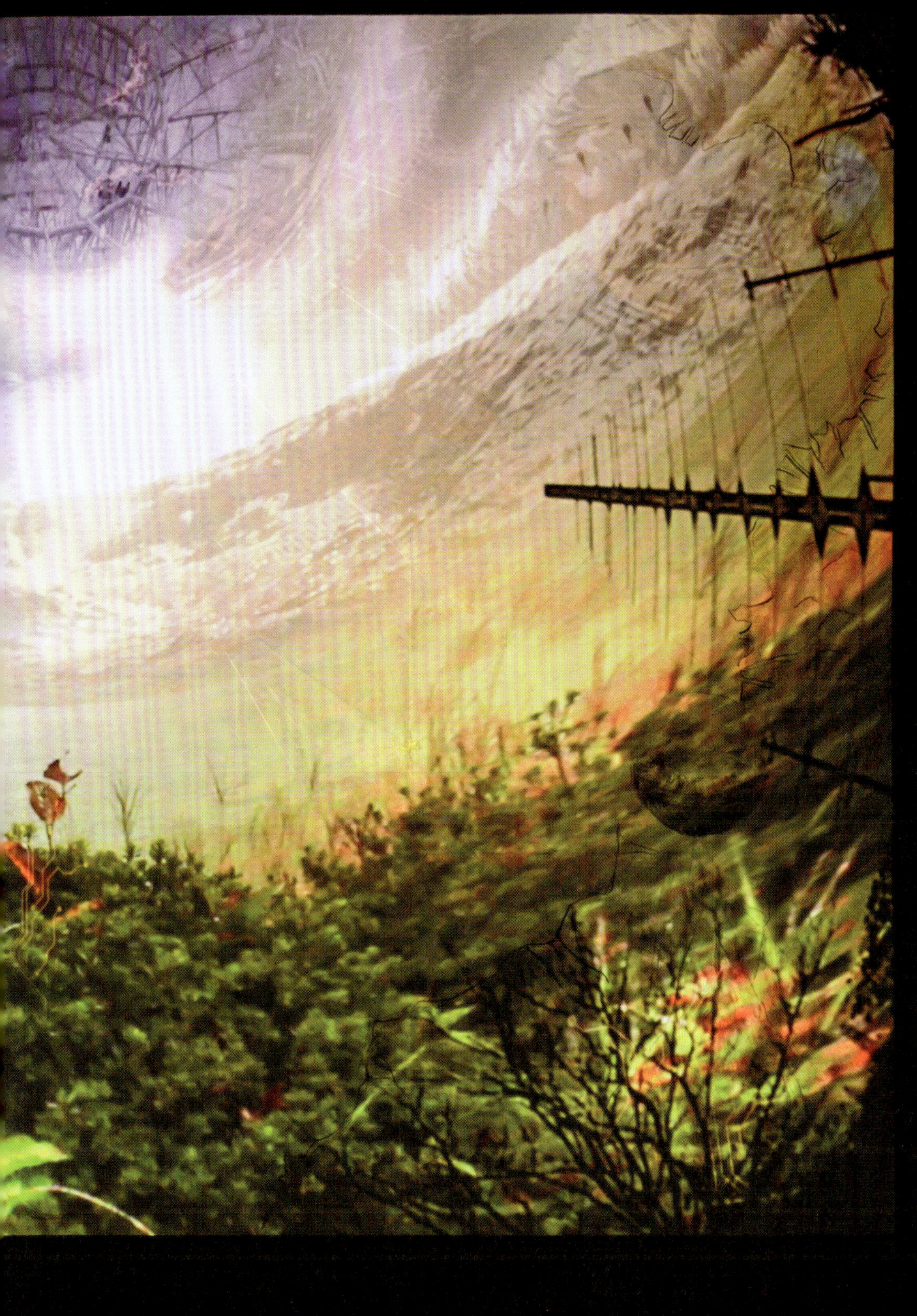

Kawayan de Guia

Popular Extinctions, 2019

In the Philippines, around every New Year, we see trumpets made from film in the streets. My curiosity was drawn to these instruments, wanting to know what was in this film. As I investigated, I soon found myself in Tondo, one of the most densely populated suburbs of Manila. This is the location of the infamous 'Smokey Mountain', a toxic landfill where many have died at the whim of flammable fumes that can cause rotting waste to ignite.

It turns out that these film negatives, often dumped in Tondo, are from old Filipino movies. If we look at film as the great recorder of time and history, it means that we have been burning our history for the past fifty or so years. No wonder we Filipinos are in a state of cultural amnesia, where history tends to repeat itself! Yet it also shows how the Filipino people are able to turn nothing into something.

These sculptures share my fascination with celluloid, a craft in which my father (Kidlat Tahimik) has made many innovations. Although here, I am a film-maker working not on a film that will be projected, but one that is tangible. Reminiscent of an oil spill, these loitering, slick-black structures are composed of reels and reels of negatives – 35mm Filipino B-grade movies shot in the 1980s and '90s (found footage, predestined to recycle the sounds of a New Year).

The accompanying video shares a fragmentary glimpse of what lies within this glorified waste.

Kawayan de Guia

In 'Popular Extinctions', the wealth of dreams in film is aestheticised as a liquid economy, seemingly with power over its own visibility and circulation. Just as oil fuels the (privileged) connectivity of the planet, so does it conquer our equanimity, as our dreams are given image, and thus pregudiced, circulated and boot-legged. Our dreams are therefore commodified and, ultimately, end as the potentially flammable waste that Kawayan redeems as a repository of popular memory — an ironic memorial to the power of the moving image that here melts beyond representation.

See the work of Lantian Xie and Mark Salvatus, who both also refer to the circulation and repercussion of the boot-leg, but this time as a curious extrapolation of (national) identity.

In 'Popular Extinctions', the wealth of dreams in film is aestheticised as a liquid economy, seemingly with power over its own visibility and circulation. Just as oil fuels the (privileged) connectivity of the planet, so does it conquer our equanimity, as our dreams are given image, and thus prejudiced, circulated and boot-legged. Our dreams are therefore commodified and, ultimately, and as the potentially flammable waste that Kawayan redeems as a repository of popular memory — an ironic memorial to the power of the moving image that here melts beyond representation.

See the work of Lantian Xie and Mark Salvatus, who both also refer to the circulation and reproduction of the boot-leg, but this time as a cursory extrapolation of (national) identity.

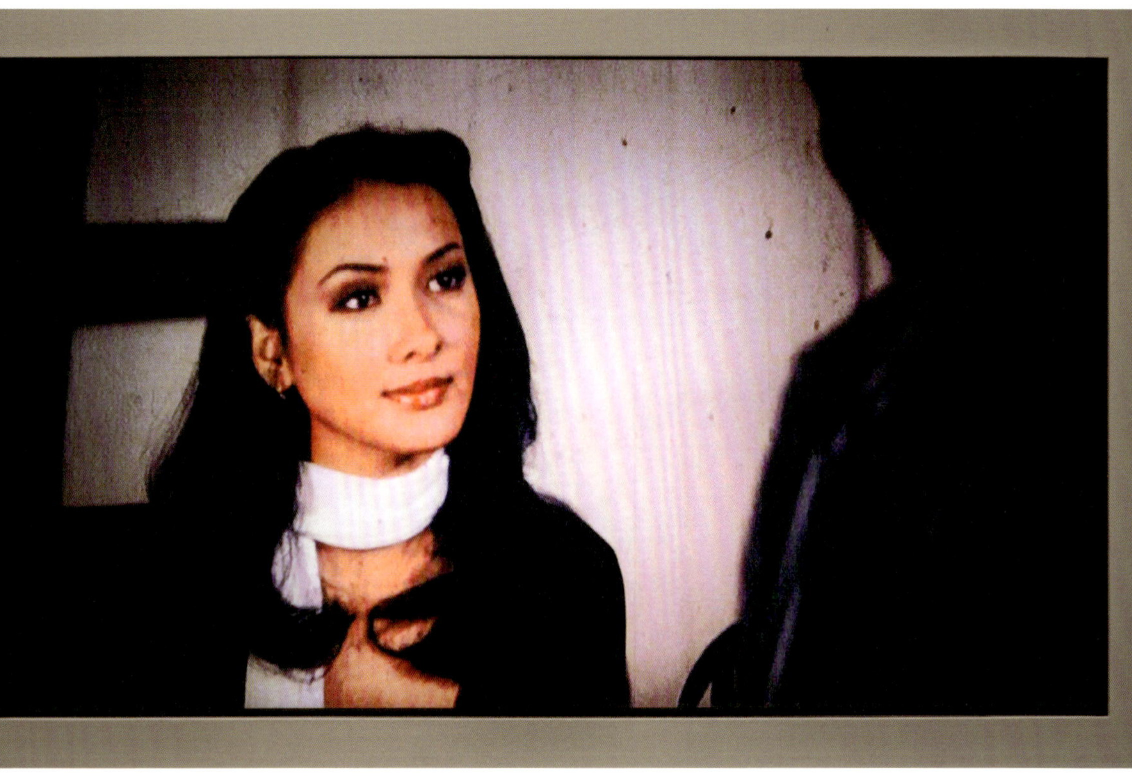

Popular Extinctions
2019
35 mm celluloid film, metal, wood; single-channel video: colour
11 minutes; Dimensions variable
Commissioned by Sharjah Art Foundation
Courtesy of the artist

Pg. 172-173:
Popular Extinctions
2019
35 mm celluloid film, metal, wood; single-channel video: colour
11 minutes; Dimensions variable
Commissioned by Sharjah Art Foundation
Courtesy of the artist

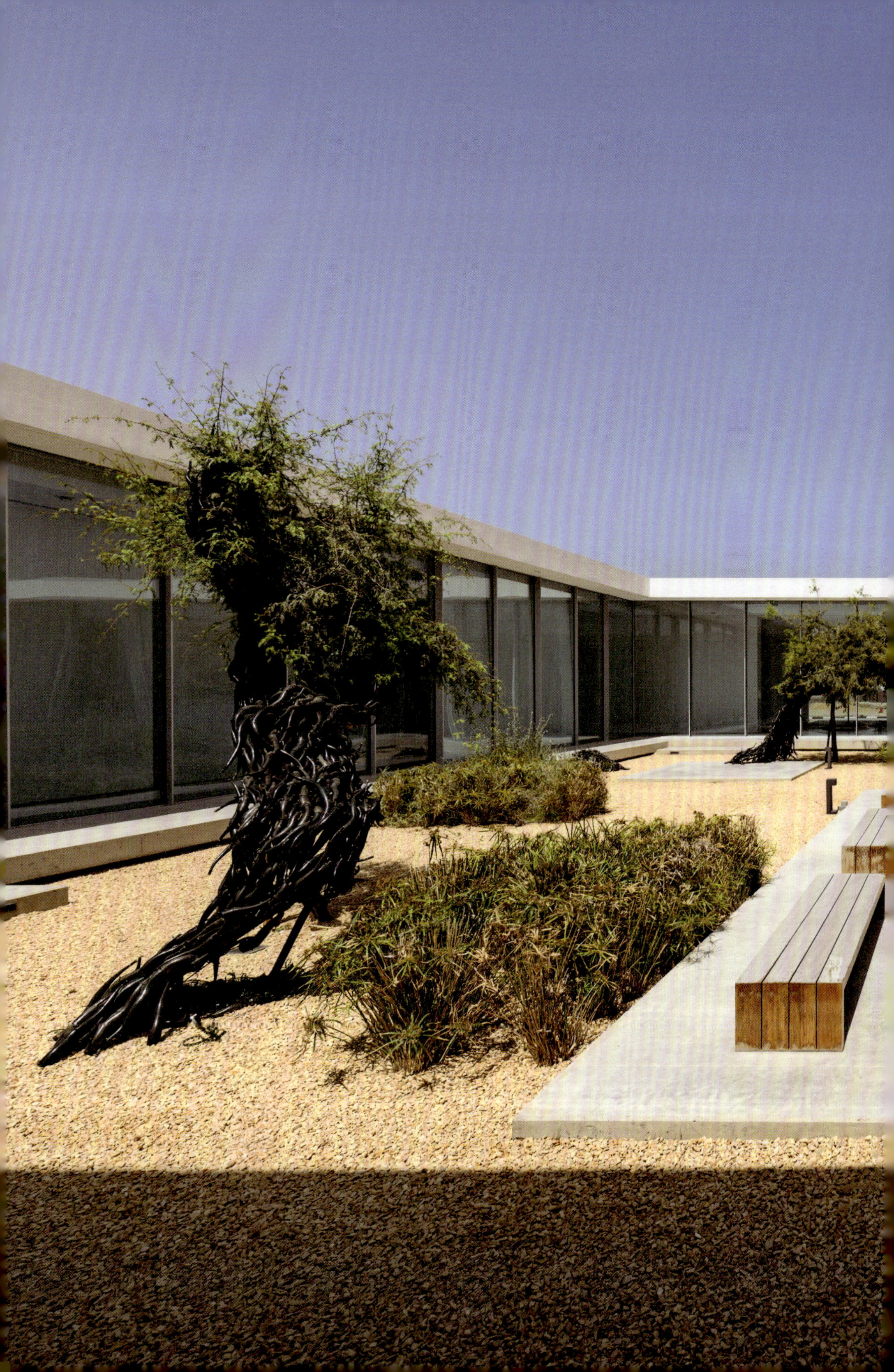

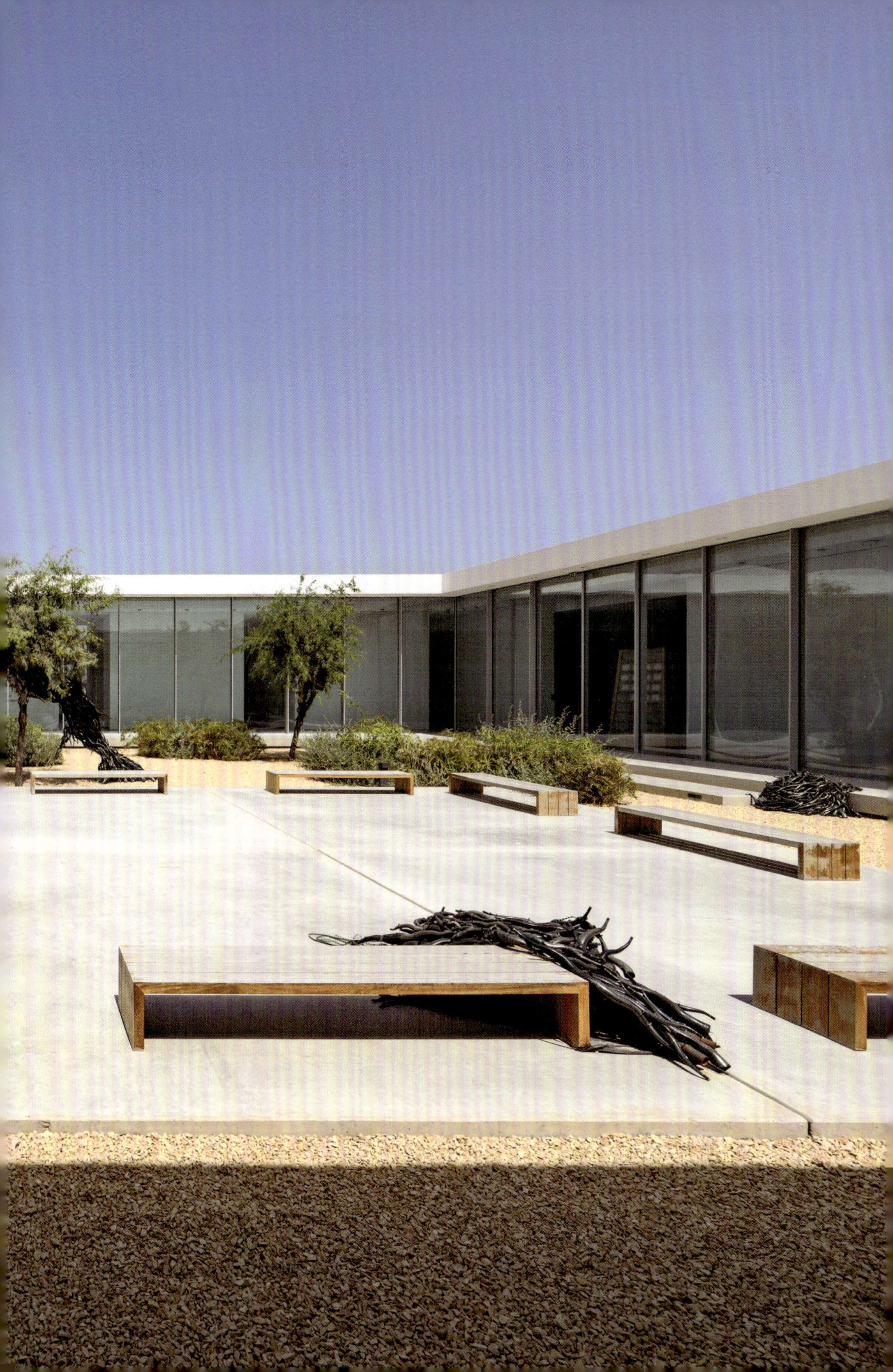

Neo Muyanga

House of MAKEdbA, 2019

Miriam Makeba 'happened' to Euro-America at a time when the world woke up to an Africa emerging from centuries of colonial paternalism. In her own biography, Makeba writes:

> Three hundred years have passed, but the weight of oppression is still on our backs. It has not grown lighter. The taste of dirt, flavoured with our tears and our blood, is still bitter.

Using her inimitable voice and style, Makeba performed the role of translator, not only of the South African struggle against apartheid, but also of the intricate contingencies of what it meant to be a postcolonial pan-African, for overseas governments, the diplomatic corps of the United Nations and her global fans. Much has been written and said of Makeba since her worldwide debut as a jazz singer inside that hub of intellectual exploits. Sadly, however, her role as one of the primary translators of what it meant to be an African in a world where empire was in the process of crumbling has been reduced to a footnote of modern history, and as such, has been largely obfuscated and 'domesticated'.

Unable to return home due to her outspoken views on apartheid, Makeba lived for a time in 'Muslim Africa', performing, for example, at the All-Africa Games in Algiers in 1978. Such appearances elevated the minority view of Guinea (her then host country), which insisted on the inclusion of countries of the Maghreb, such as Morocco, Egypt, and Libya, as well as Algeria itself, under the banner of pan-African solidarity.

The value of a Miriam Makeba to us all today, I would argue, is that she points us to a global future of contingency, of exile-for-all. She disabuses us of the fallacious assumption of a home that is static, homogenous and hermetically secured.

Neo Muyanga

Miriam Makeba (1932-2008) was a South African singer, songwriter, actress and civil rights activist. Her music – crossing Afropop, jazz and world music – won awards alongside fellow superstars such as Harry Belafonte. She faced hostility for her personal connections with the Black Panther Party, but was also showcased at several independence celebrations across Africa, marking her as 'tour de force', a politically conscionable, singular individual in acknowledgement of all souls displaced, oppressed or in exile.

In 'House of MAKEdbA', Neo performs in memory of Makeba (this installation was first activated by a performance during SB14's opening week). Weaving her voice between his own compositions, the artist imagines this work as the space of a healer, a shrine to Makeba's cultural legacy – her words and music in catharsis with the diaspora of humanity; beyond ideas of nation, race and faith, towards our vital need for inclusivity, equality and humility.

Miriam Makeba (1932-2008) was a South African singer, songwriter, actress and civil rights activist. Her music – crossing Afropop, jazz and world music – won awards alongside fellow superstars such as Harry Belafonte. She faced hostility for her personal connections with the Black Panther Party, but was also showcased at several independence celebrations across Africa, marking her as 'tour de force', a politically conscionable, singular individual in acknowledgement of all souls displaced, oppressed or in exile.

In 'Home of MAKEBA', Neo performs in memory of Makeba (this installation was first activated by a performance during SB14's opening week). Weaving her voice between his own compositions, the artist imagines this work as the space of a healer, a shrine to Makeba's cultural legacy – her words and music in catharsis with the diaspora of humanity; beyond ideas of nation, race and faith, towards our vital need for inclusivity, equality and humility.

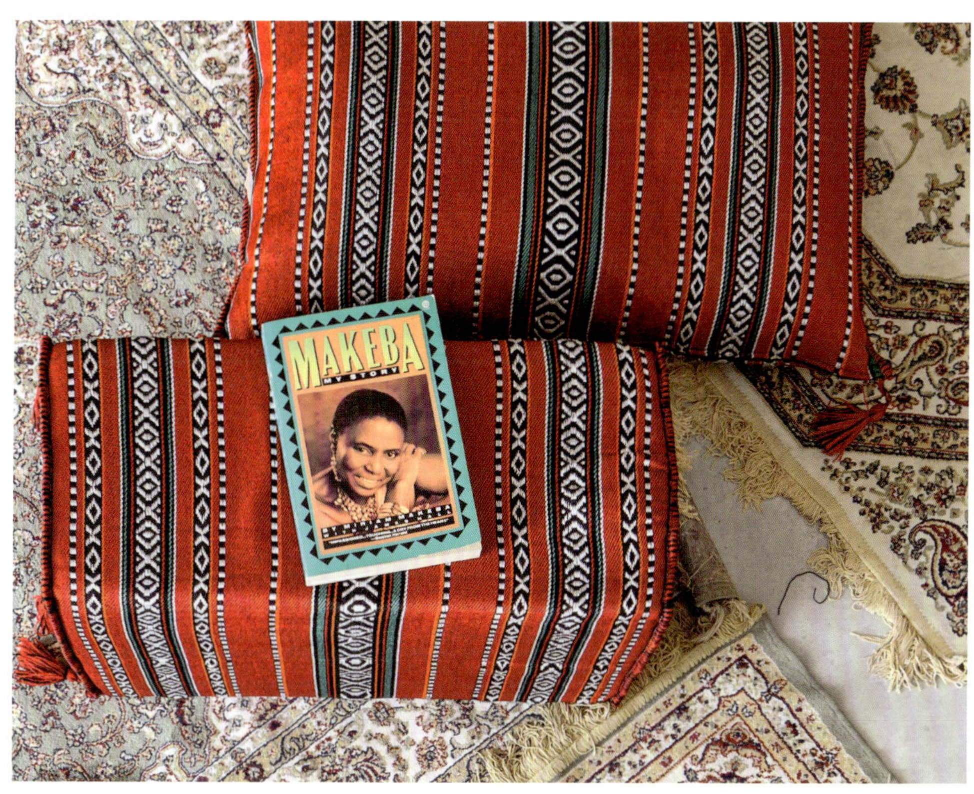

house of MAKEdbA
2019
Interactive installation:
2 record players, sound,
animated photograph,
objects, furniture, lamps
Dimensions variable; 15
minutes loop
Commissioned by Sharjah
Art Foundation
Courtesy of the artist

Page 176–177:
Neo Muyanga performing
on the opening day of
Sharjah Biennial 14

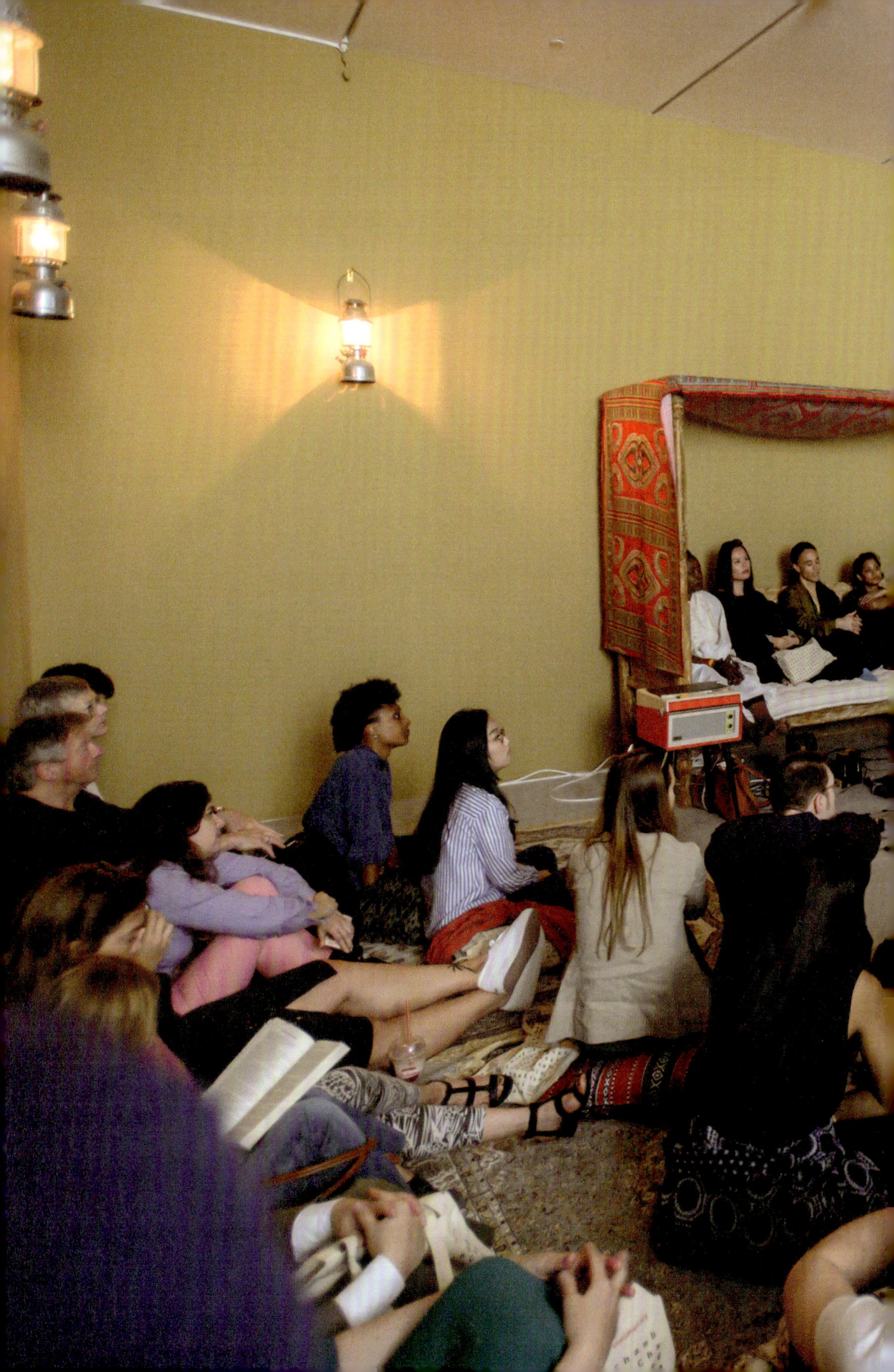

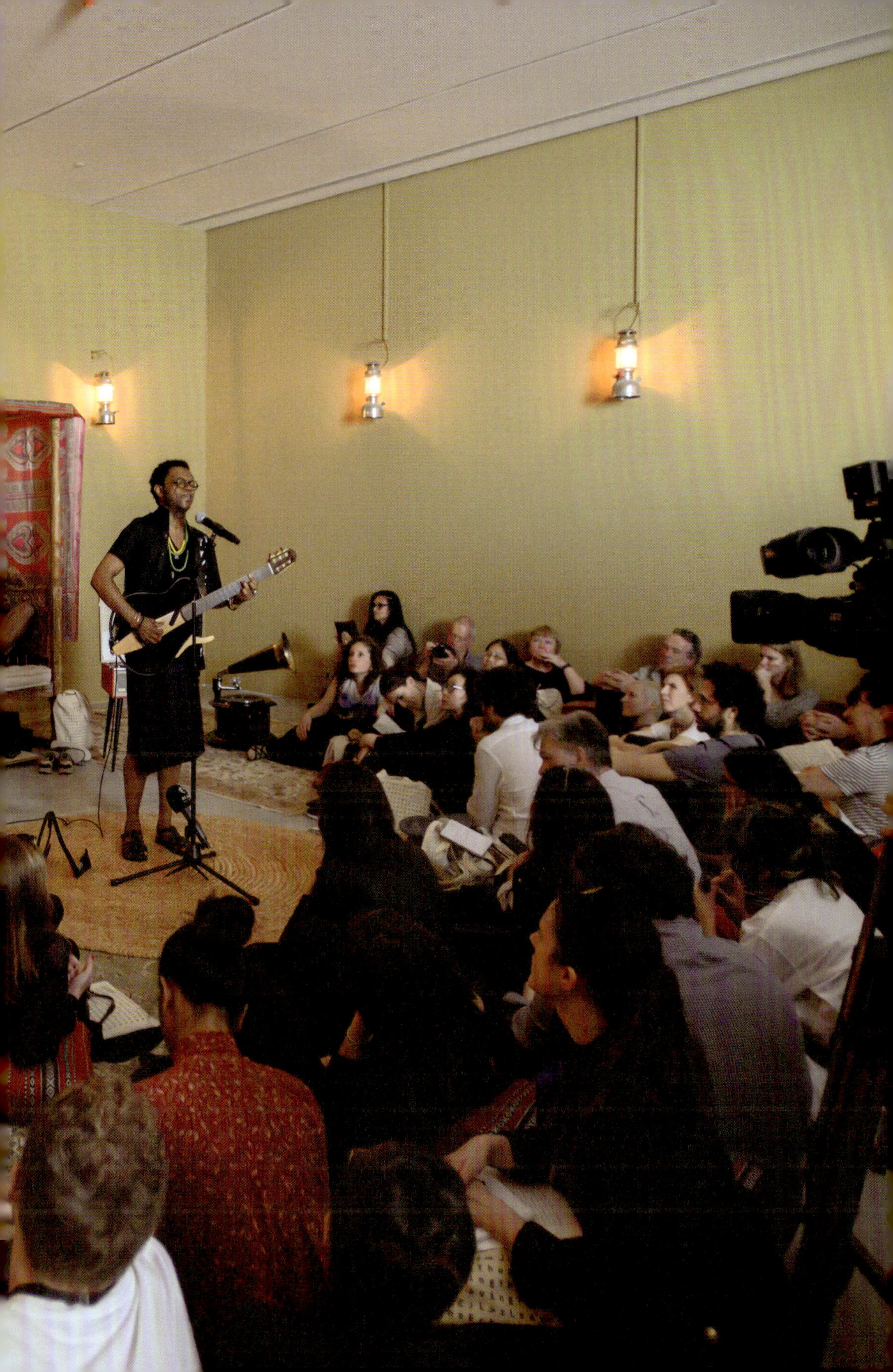

Speech of A Simple Citizen

I am just a citizen
Just a simple citizen
All I want is
To cut that ribbon
Not on the opening
Of my new factory
For in the factory I am
Driven in chains
And in the street
Driven in chains
Within myself
Driven in chains
So am I so are all my relatives
All my friends
Ever since we were born
All our families and us
All our people and us
Except for the flunkies
And the tyrants...
To them belong the nation and the
population
History and glorification
While in lamentation
We cringe in the graves
To them belong the palaces
I do not want palaces
I do not want that history to pass
I'm just a simple citizen

All I want is
To cut that ribbon
All I want is
My right to dream
That I live in my country
Without fear and injustice
That you don't confiscate my thoughts
That you don't blockade my narrative
That you let people's awareness be free
That if one says no
You don't lug him to the lockup like a log
That my crime would not consist
Of thinking too much
That my calamity would not consist
Of being conscientious
In our countries, ideas are destroyed
And subjugated are the ones who revolt
Dreamers are turned into apostates
And oppositionists into villains
I'm just a simple citizen
And all I want is a life
Not in worship of rulers in my country
But in worship of the Divine
What makes you kings
And makes us rats
We all come from Adam
We all are human

Anis Chouchene

Translated from Arabic by Jacques Aswad

J o u r n e y B e y o n d t h
e A r r o w J o u r n e y B e
y o n d t h e A r r o w J o u
r n e y B e y o n d t h e A r
r o w J o u r n e y B e y o n
d t h e A r r o w J o u r n e
y B e y o n d t h e A r r o w
J o u r n e y B e y o n d t h
e A r r o w J o u r n e y B e
y o n d t h e A r r o w J o u
r n e y B e y o n d t h e A r
r o w J o u r n e y B e y o n
d t h e A r r o w J o u r n e
y B e y o n d t h e A r r o w
J o u r n e y B e y o n d t h

The cataloguers are the recorders of time, gathering and documenting the artefacts that determine and challenge reason and categorisation, troubling the shaping of human exigency and often revealing resilience and thus wonder in the capacity of the human spirit to adapt and persevere.

The cataloguers are the recorders of time, gathering and documenting the artefacts that determine and challenge reason and categorisation, troubling the shaping of human exigency and often revealing resilience and thus wonder in the capacity of the human spirit to adapt and persevere.

e A r r o w T h e J o u r n e
y B e y o n d t h e A r r o w
J o u r n e y B e y o n d t h
e A r r o w J o u r n e y B e
y o n d C a t a l o g u e r s
t h e A r r o w J o u r n e y
B e y o n d t h e A r r o w J
o u r n e y B e y o n d t h e
A r r o w J o u r n e y B e y
o n d t h e A r r o w J o u r
n e y B e y o n d t h e A r r
o w J o u r n e y B e y o n d
t h e A r r o w J o u r n e y
B e y o n d t h e A r r o w J
o u r n e y B e y o n d t h e

Anawana Haloba

Reconstructing Histories: China in Africa, Myths and Facts (A Dragon King in Sleepy Pride Rock), 2019

Reconstructing Histories: China in Africa, Myths and Facts (A Dragon King in Sleepy Pride Rock) explores China's presence in Africa – in Zambia, in particular – taking into consideration historical and present-day myths and facts. My interest in researching this theme is partly inspired by all the media buzz touting China's 'new inroads' into the developing world.

I should clarify that this project does not aim to engage China's presence in Africa from the Tang dynasty (618–907) through to the last imperial dynasty of the Qing (1644–1912). Rather, here, I am interested in exploring China's modern relations with Africa commencing in the 1950s, during the Cold War era, and throughout the '60s and '70s, and examining their social and political implications. What did this solidarity, or 'friendship of economics' – whose core agenda was to eradicate colonialism and forge a common front to safeguard sovereignty of emerging nations against Cold War politics – *mean* to a newly independent Africa?

It was in this modern mindset that the TAZARA Railway was realised; built between 1968 and 1975, it was China's first (and biggest) aid project on the African continent. This railway was a critical link to the sea, one that landlocked Zambia desperately needed in order to break free from its dependency on Ian Smith's Rhodesia and apartheid-era South Africa's rails and ports. TAZARA thus became a strong anti-apartheid statement, a symbol of freedom (*Uhuru*, in Swahili), as well as a revolutionary gesture of solidarity with resistance to the forces of imperialism, colonialism and neocolonialism.

Since 2016, I have journeyed numerous times along the poorly maintained TAZARA Railway, its trains rusting and in dangerously deteriorating states. I have spent time at various stations, recording stories from railway passengers, deeply intrigued by their perceptions of China and views of its role in their country. Reconjuring postcards and maps of the train's route from Livingstone to Dar es Salaam, I also revisited the revolutionary liberation period of the '60s and '70s using song, thus drawing metaphorical connections to the African Spring movement. I was curious to see if any relationship could be found between the political implications of China's presence in Africa today and its socio-economic impact on the lives of the African people.

Anawana Haloba

Today, China's One Belt, One Road initiative is arguably the successor to the TAZARA Railway – a remarkable indication of how a former socialist motivation has since become capitalised and imperialistic. This network of land and sea corridors has been popularised as the 'twenty-first century Silk Road,' linking South East Asia to Eastern Europe and Africa, affecting seventy-one countries in total. This gargantuan blueprint for trade gives startling political and, surely, military leverage to China, whose control of foreign debt today has sparked global concern. This suggests an image of 'Tianxia' (a Chinese term meaning 'all under heaven') as the realm of the historical Chinese Middle Kingdom, with the administration of its people – of their access to differing realities, of their impact on other parts of the world – being of utmost importance, a control that must be concealed.

In the adjacent gallery the work of Xu Zhen reflects on these problems from within China.

Today, China's One Belt, One Road initiative is arguably the successor to the TAZARA Railway – a remarkable indication of how a former socialist motivation has since become capitalised and imperialistic. This network of land and sea corridors has been popularised as the 'twenty-first century Silk Road', linking South East Asia to Eastern Europe and Africa, affecting seventy-one countries in total. This gargantuan blueprint for trade gives startling political and, surely, military leverage to China, whose control of foreign debt today has sparked global concern. This suggests an image of 'Tianxia' (a Chinese term meaning 'all under heaven') as the realm of the historical Chinese Middle Kingdom, with the administration of its people – of their access to differing realities, of their impact on other parts of the world – being of utmost importance, a control that must be concealed.

In the adjacent gallery the work of Xu Zhen reflects on these problems from within China.

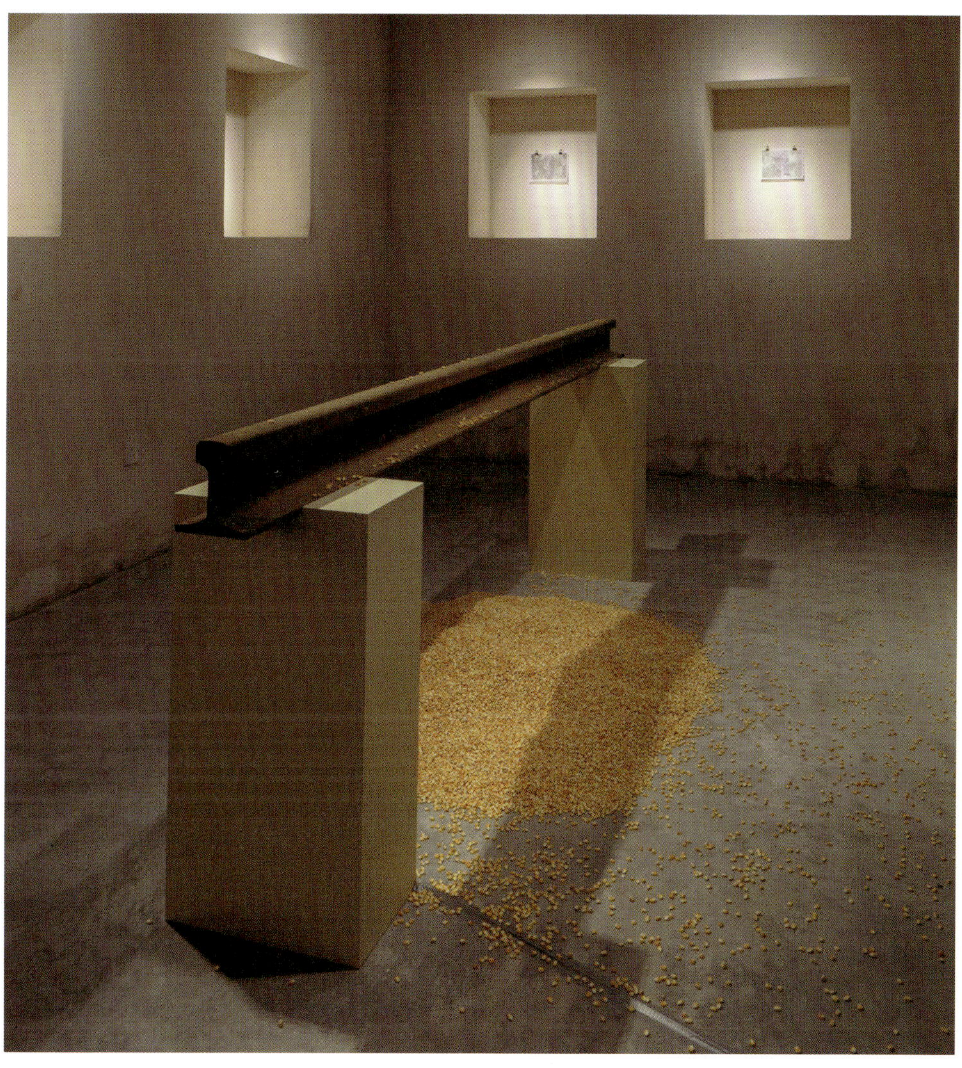

A Dragon King in Sleepy Pride Rock
2019
Installation: synchronised animations with sound, postcards, prints, old televisions, train rail, dried maize cobs
Dimensions variable
Commissioned by Sharjah Art Foundation
Courtesy of the artist and Norsk Kulturråd, Oslo
Photo: readsreads.info

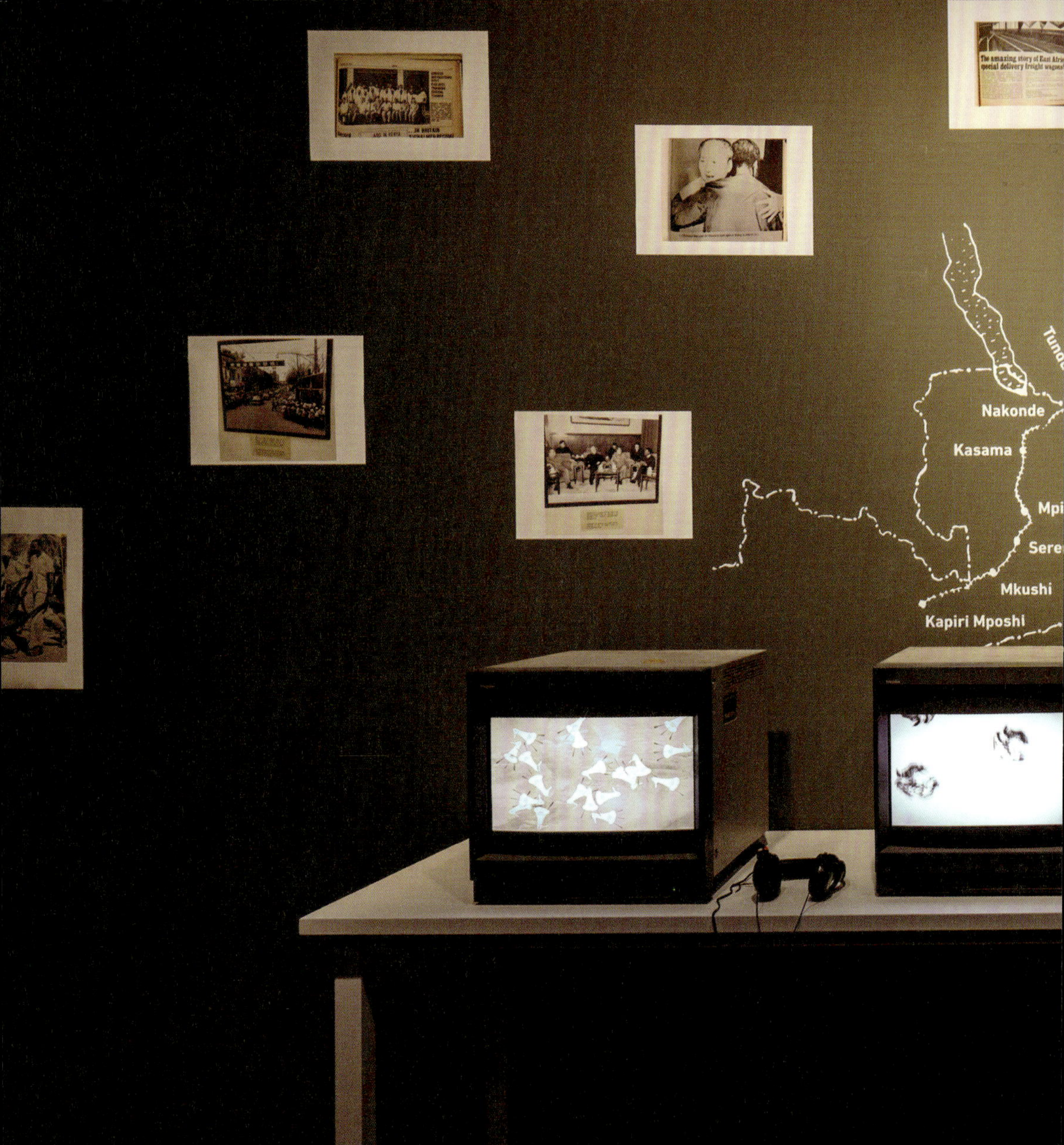
Nakonde
Kasama
Mkushi
Kapiri Mposhi

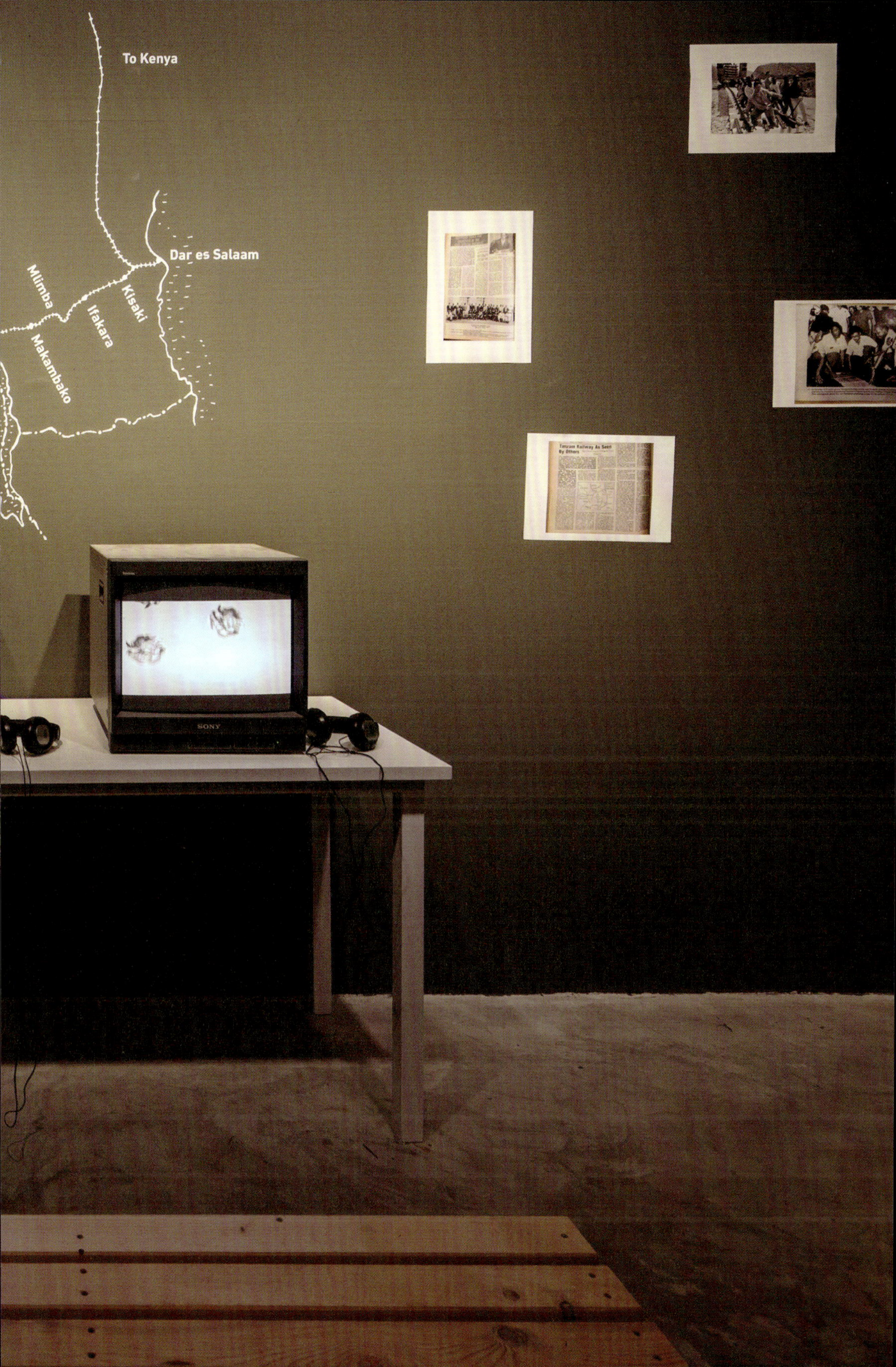
To Kenya
Dar es Salaam
Mlimba
Ifakara
Kisaki
Makambako
Tanzam Railway As Seen By Others
SONY

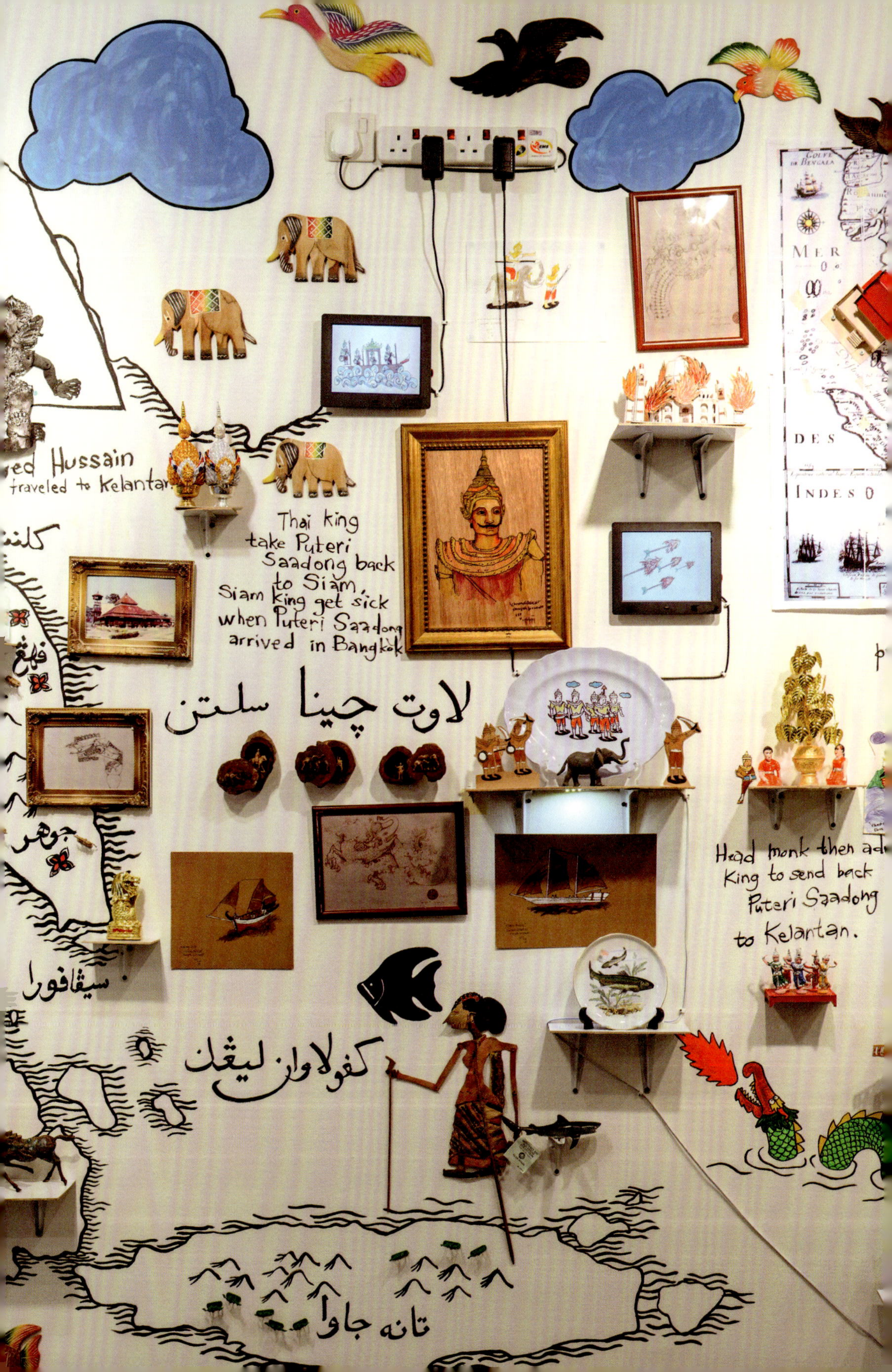

GOLFE DE BENGALA
MER
DES
INDES O
ed Hussain
traveled to Kelantan
Thai King take Puteri Saadong back to Siam, Siam king get sick when Puteri Saadong arrived in Bangkok
لاوت چينا سلتن
فهڠ
جوهر
سيڠافورا
كفولاوان ليڠڬ
تانه جاوا
Head monk then ad
King to send back Puteri Saadong to Kelantan.

Around the ninth century, merchants from the Arab World began arriving in the Malay Archipelago – what is today Malaysia, The Philippines and Indonesia – having crossed the Indian Ocean from Hadhramaut in Yemen. This seafaring, largely nomadic community also anchored itself in East Africa and the Indian subcontinent, from Morocco to Mauritania, and even in Europe and China. Engaging in commerce, scholarship and diplomacy and, eventually, entering local politics, these communities gained particular local influence through marriage, often using genealogical claims to wield influence over the local nobility.

Mapping this cultural ancestry, ISE's 'chronoLOGICal' offers a personal history of the kingdom of Kelantan (descendants of this Yemeni migration) in the north-eastern peninsula of Malaysia. Working with oral histories recorded within his local community – by friends and family, rural teachers and village elders, as well as local imams and historians – the artist created this hand-drawn map, replete with miniature souvenirs, animations of historical accounts and textual drama. These artistic elements both illustrate and narrate the various conflicts and claims of this largely Islamic territory, between ancient kingdoms such as Siam (present-day Thailand) and the Sultanate of Malacca (present-day Malaysia).

As the storms brewed and the floods ensued, as the ships arrived carrying intrigue and political distress, ISE seeks to remind us that a mapping of time can never be logical, linear and certain. Rather, such an endeavour gives credibility to the lore of old, mythical legends and childhood tales – their histories determined by the voices that echo beyond the centralised tomes of doctrine and academia.

Around the ninth century, merchants from the Arab World began arriving in the Malay Archipelago – what is today Malaysia, The Philippines and Indonesia – having crossed the Indian Ocean from Hadhramaut in Yemen. This seafaring, largely nomadic community also anchored itself in East Africa and the Indian subcontinent, from Morocco to Mauritania, and even in Europe and China. Engaging in commerce, scholarship and diplomacy and, eventually, entering local politics, these communities gained particular local influence through marriage, often using genealogical claims to wield influence over the local nobility.

Mapping this cultural ancestry, ISE's 'chronological' offers a personal history of the kingdom of Kelantan (descendants of this Yemeni migration) in the north-eastern peninsula of Malaysia. Working with oral histories recorded within his local community – by friends and family, rural teachers and village elders, as well as local imams and historians – the artist created this hand-drawn map, replete with miniature souvenirs, animations of historical accounts and textual drama. These artistic elements both illustrate and narrate the various conflicts and claims of this largely Islamic territory, between ancient kingdoms such as Siam (present-day Thailand) and the Sultanate of Malacca (present-day Malaysia).

As the storms brewed and the floods ensued, as the ships arrived carrying intrigue and political distress, ISE seeks to remind us that a mapping of time can never be logical, linear and certain. Rather, such an endeavour gives credibility to the lore of old, mythical legends and childhood tales – their histories determined by the voices that echo beyond the centralised forms of doctrine and academia.

Roslisham (ISE) Ismail

chronoLOGICal, 2015

ChronoLOGICal
2015
Mixed media
Dimensions variable
Courtesy of the artist

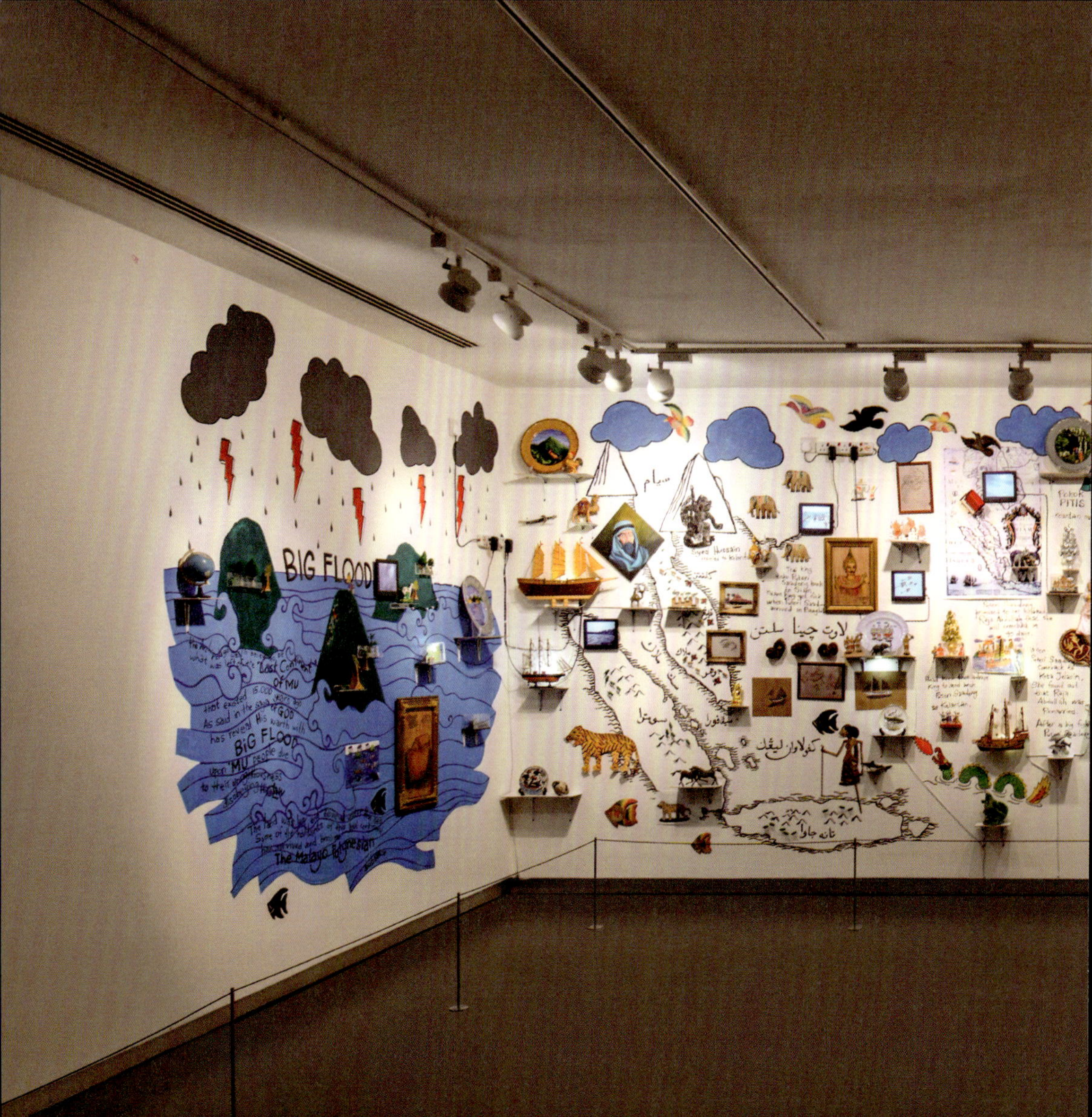
BIG FLOOD
Lost Continent
OF MU
BiG FLOOD
The Malayo Polynesian
لاوت چينا سلتن
PITIS

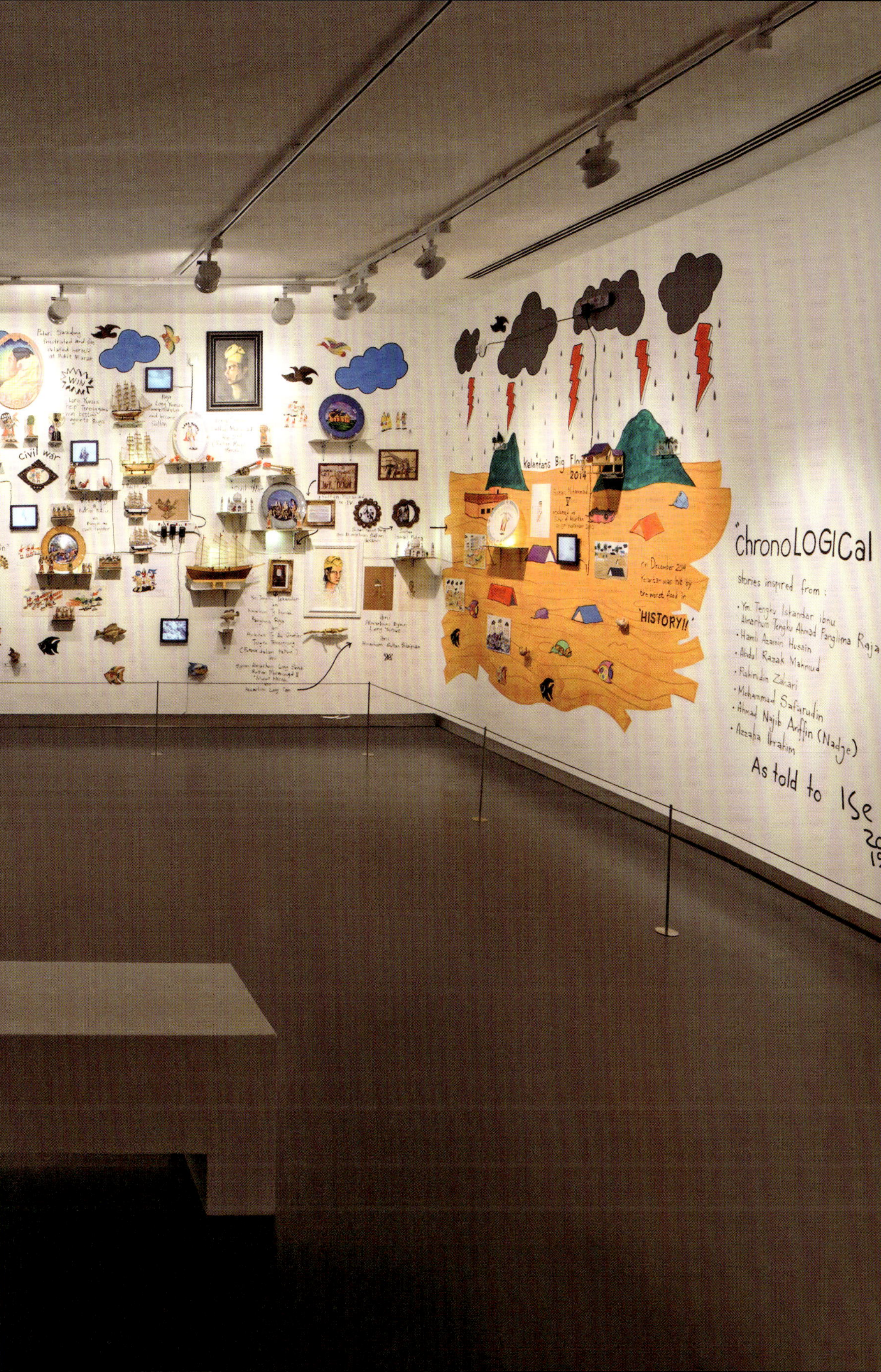
"chronoLOGICal
stories inspired from :
• Ym. Tengku Iskandar ibnu Almarhum Tengku Ahmad Panglima Raja
• Hamli Azamin Husain
• Abdul Razak Mahmud
• Fakhrudin Zakari
• Mohammad Safarudin
• Ahmad Najib Ariffin (Nadje)
• Azzaha Ibrahim
As told to ISe
Kelantan's Big Flood 2014
"HISTORY!!"
Civil war

Phan Thảo Nguyên

Mute Grain, 2019

Mute Grain is a personal interpretation of the little-discussed 1945 famine in Vietnam, which took place during the Japanese occupation of French Indochina (1940–45). This famine is believed to have caused the death of more than two million people in the Red River Delta of North Vietnam.

Years ago, I read a short prose piece titled *Starved* (2003) by To Hoai. I was an adolescent, and the agony of this famine, compressed in a few printed pages, left a lasting impression on me. My curiosity about how historical events are treated – how one event can be glorified when another is forgotten – has since developed into a constant question for me.

Mute Grain weaves oral histories (research undertaken by historian Van Tao, who donated his oral recordings to the Vietnam Museum of Revolution in Hanoi) with magical elements borrowed from Vietnamese folk tales and chronicles. Told from the perspective of two adolescents, the work is expressed in a lyrical language inspired by Japanese post-war writer Yasunari Kawabata's *Palm-of-the-Hand Stories* (first published in Japanese in the 1920s).

The narrative of *Mute Grain* relays the story of the unjustified death of a young woman named Tám, who is unable to move on to the next life, and thus becomes a hungry ghost. She keeps her human form, appearing between layers of time and space, across silk screens and cinematic frames, together with her brother, Ba, who floats anxiously, searching for her. This story of March (Ba) and August (Tám) reflects the poorest months of the lunar calendar, a fragile time when farmers once had to borrow money and find side jobs to sustain themselves. Intertwined between these fictional imaginations are the stories of those who endured these grueling times, serving as unreconciled witnesses not only to famine, but to the ensuing communist violence of the land reform/subsidy era (1954–75), when Vietnam was politically divided in two.

In studying this Japanese-occupied era, it became clear to me that food security is (and always has been), a never-ending episodic tragicomedy, the final act that robs humanity and corrodes both culture and nature. In today's global political situation, with famine still raging in different parts of the world, the story of *Mute Grain* remains of great exigency.

Phan Thảo Nguyên

The catastrophic famine of 1945 is still hardly discussed in Vietnam today – it's not prohibited or taboo, just rarely mentioned throughout <u>official history</u> – and thus, young generations are ill informed about the impact of a number of major issues: the crop failures during the period of French economic and agricultural reform; the Japanese demands on local farmers to replace rice with jute to support their war effort; and the calamitous typhoons and ensuing floods that left millions destitute during that time.

This tension, between official and unofficial histories, continues in the projects of Antariksa and Ahmad Fuad Osman in the neighboring galleries

The Vietnamese countryside often figures in the art of Nguyen, becoming a dreamlike landscape where cultural and political histories are replayed through the eyes of traumatised youth. In her work, we learn of the past through historical fiction, a mode that questions our reliance on material archives, in which cultural memory instead searches for a means to include the experiences of those who are often overlooked.

The catastrophic famine of 1945 is still hardly discussed in Vietnam today – it's not prohibited or taboo; just rarely mentioned throughout official history – and thus, young generations are ill informed about the impact of a number of major issues: the crop failures during the period of French economic and agricultural reform; the Japanese demands on local farmers to replace rice with jute to support their war effort; and the calamitous typhoons and ensuing floods that left millions destitute during that time.

The Vietnamese countryside often figures in the art of Nguyen, becoming a dreamlike landscape where cultural and political histories are replayed through the eyes of traumatised youth. In her work, we learn of the past through historical fiction, a mode that questions our reliance on material archives, in which cultural memory instead searches for a means to include the experiences of those who are often overlooked.

This tension, between official and unofficial histories, continues in the projects of Antariksa and Ahmad Fuad Osman in the neighbouring galleries

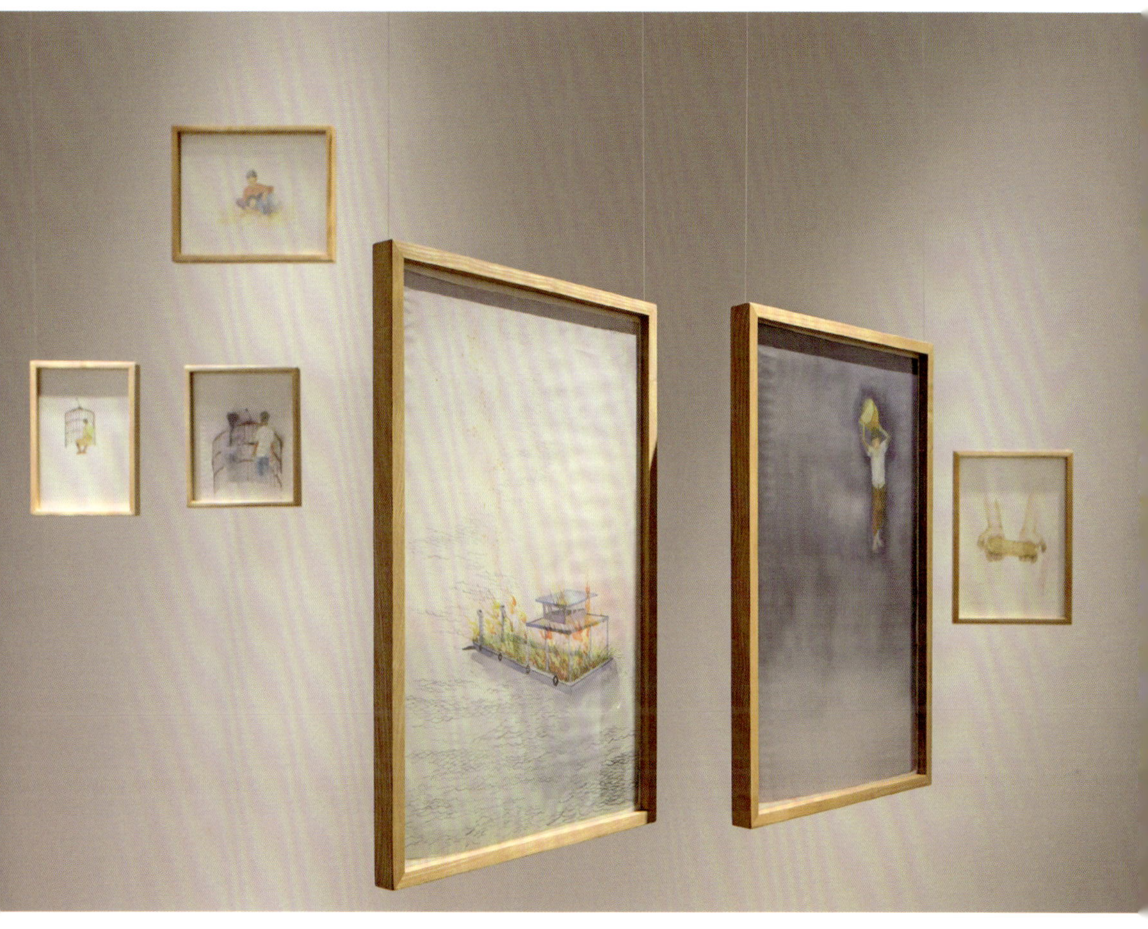

Dream of March and August
2019
From 'Mute Grain'
Watercolour on silk
14 diptychs, 1 triptych;
dimensions variable
Commissioned by Sharjah
Art Foundation
Courtesy of the artist
Photo: readsreads.info

Page 194–195:
Mute Grain
2019
From 'Mute Grain'
Three-channel video
installation: colour, sound
15 minutes 45 seconds
Commissioned by Sharjah
Art Foundation
Courtesy of the artist

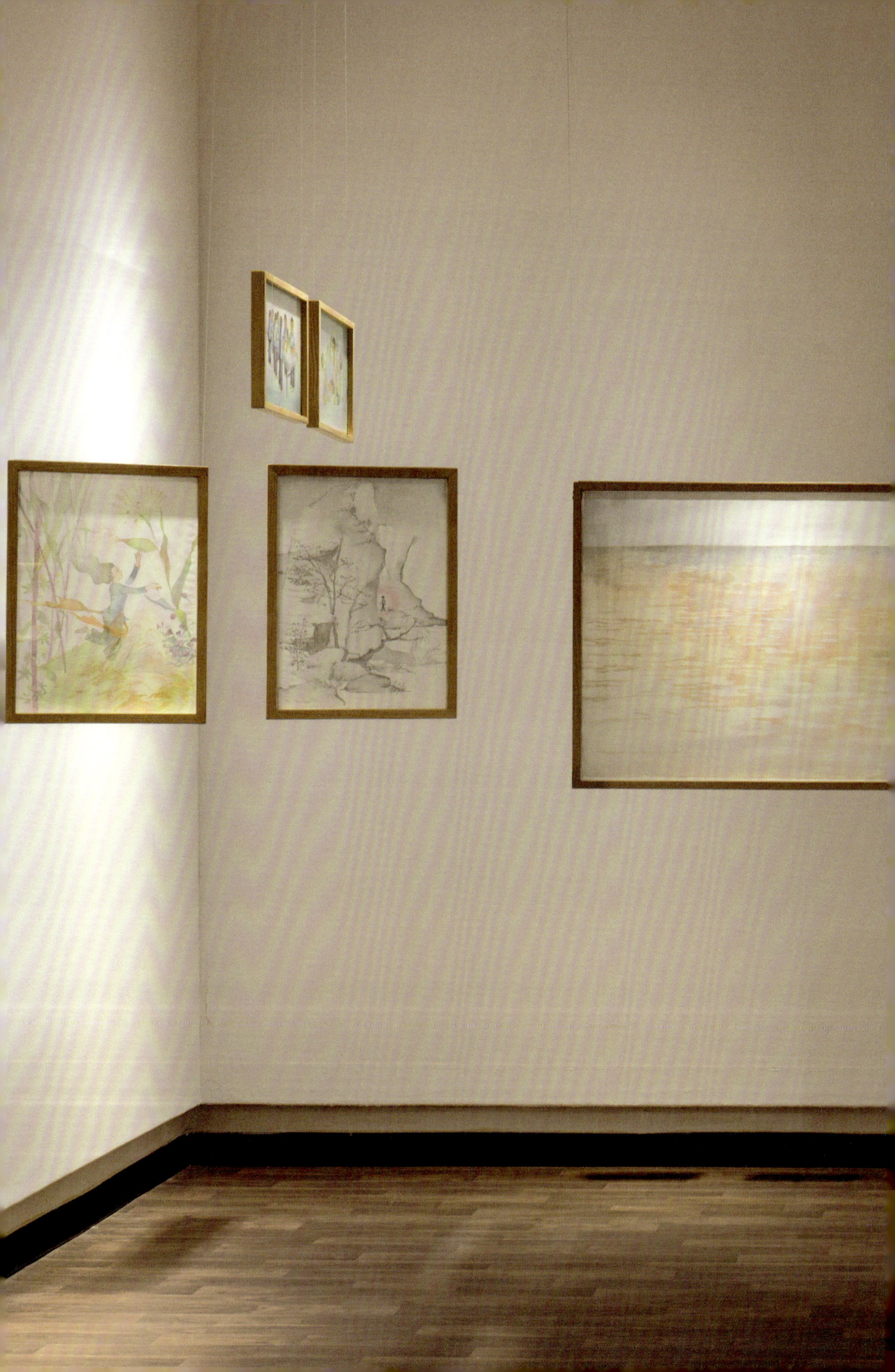

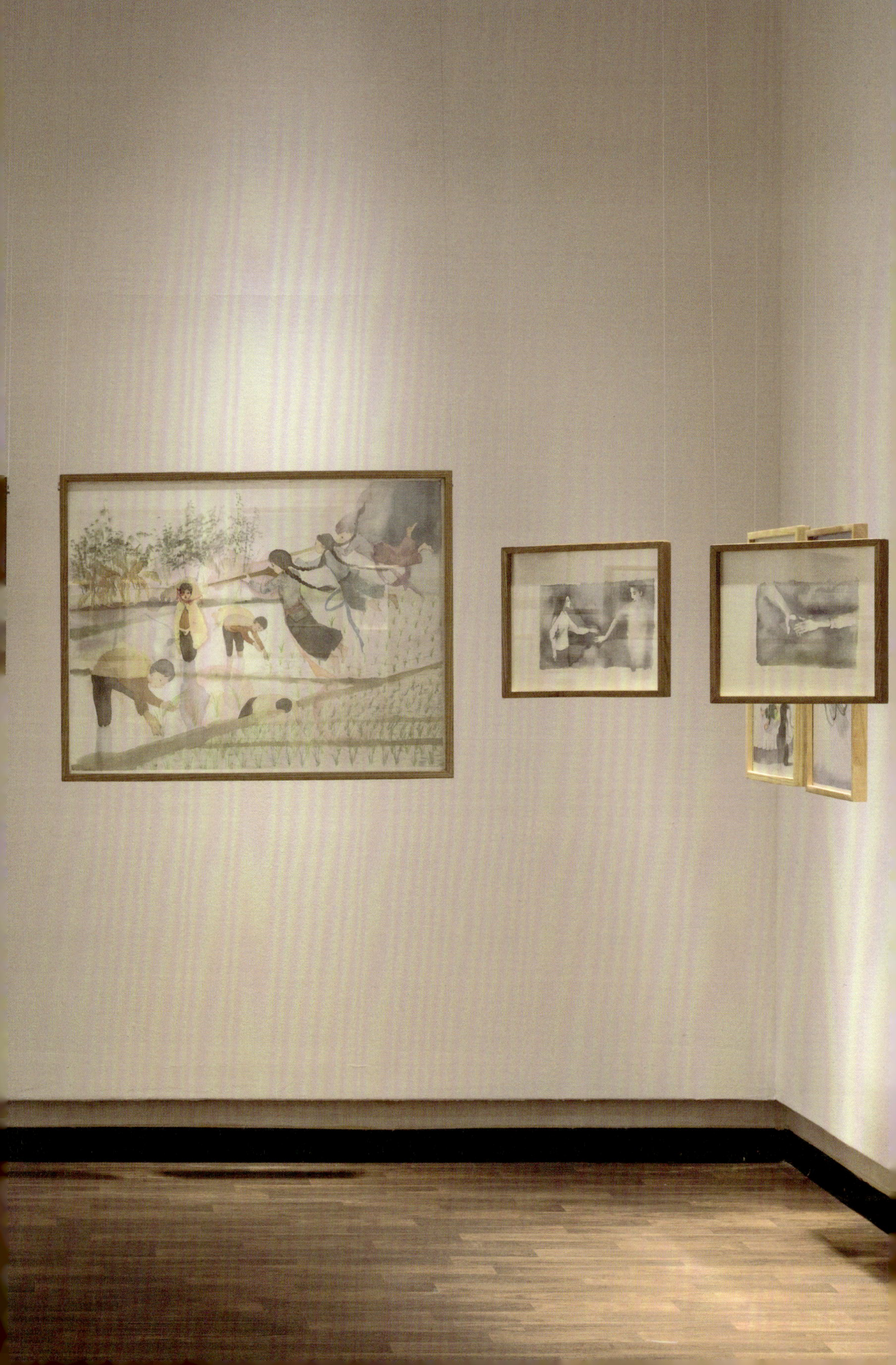

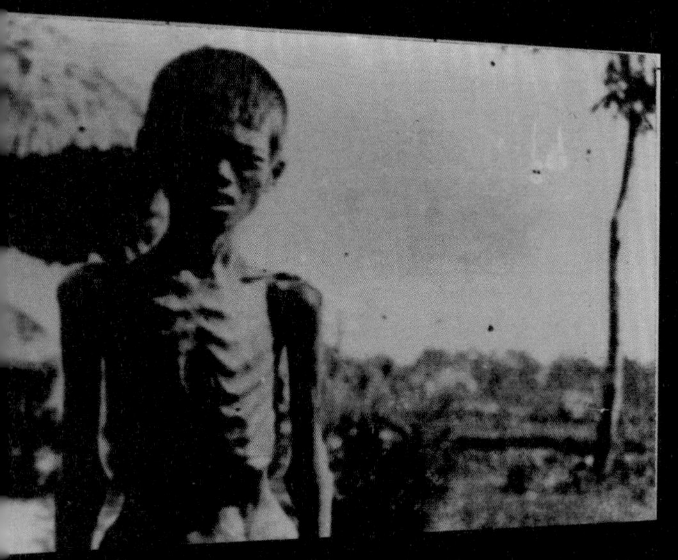

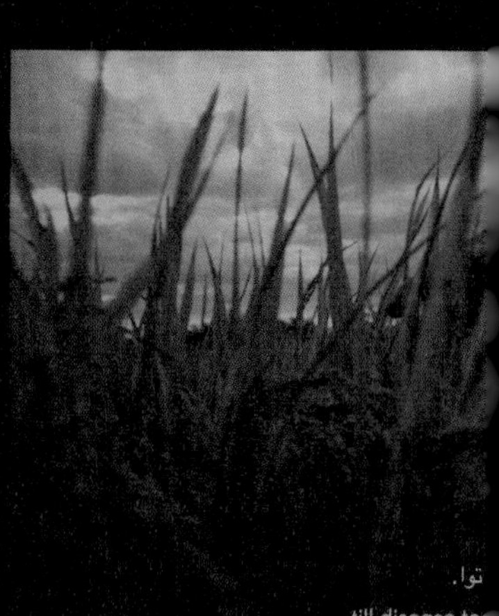
توا.
till disease

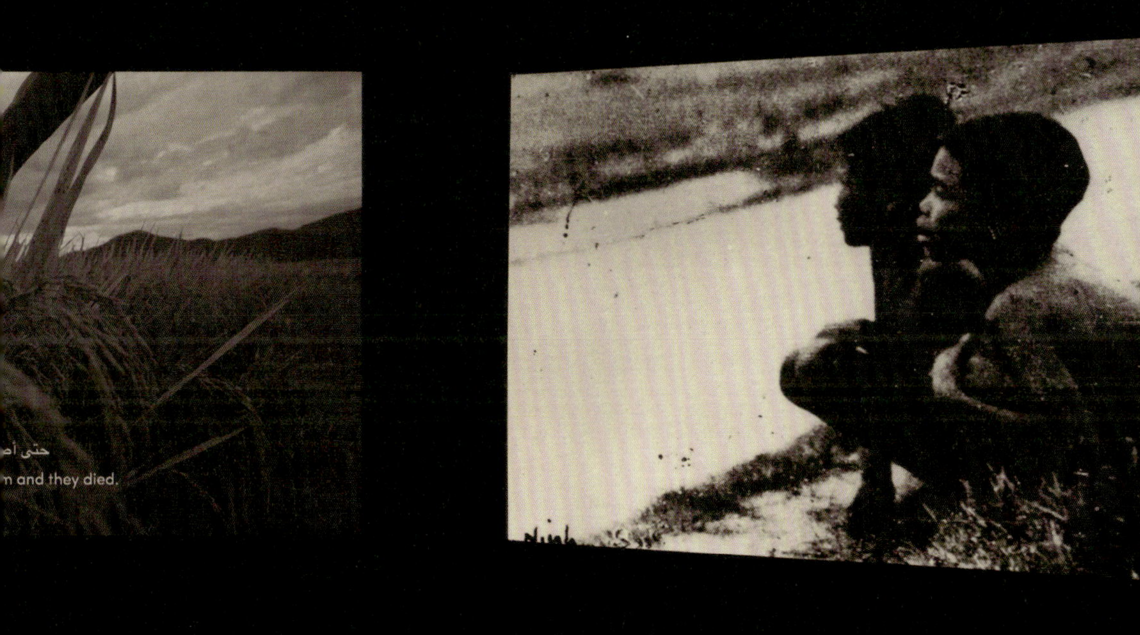
and they died.

Mark Salvatus

Notes from the New World, 2015-2019

The Philippine Constabulary Band was formed in 1901, three years after Spain sold the Philippines to the United States under the Treaty of Paris, an agreement in 1898 that involved Spain relinquishing nearly all of its empire, also ceding Puerto Rico and Guam to the US. Formed in Manila, the band's first members were recruited from community ensembles in Luzon that previously included musicians from Spanish Army bands.

Wanting to show its might as a nation, the US had a huge presence in the 1904 St. Louis World's Fair, showcasing a 'human zoo' of indigenous people from their newly acquired territories. More than 1,000 Filipinos were forced onto boats, from Luzon, Visayas and Mindanao, and instructed to dance, sing and perform rituals daily. Not many know that the Philippine Constabulary Band was part of this live exhibit. It was the group's performance of Gioachino Rossini's 1829 'William Tell Overture' that got the attention of John Philip Sousa (the American composer and conductor also known as the King of Marches). The band subsequently went on to perform at illustrious political events, including the 1939 Golden Gate International Exposition, the inauguration of US President William Howard Taft, as well as for Emperor Meiji of Japan and Queen Liliuokalani of Hawaii.

In 2015, I discovered the Philippine Constabulary Band's vinyl record in my father's collection – 111 years after the group's performance in St. Louis. I then asked the band (previously the Philippine Constabulary Band, now under the Philippine Army) to play 'Rossini's Overture'; this performance is observed here as *Notes from the New World*, projected alongside vinyl records and archival material that I inherited from my father's collection. While the Philippine Army Band is imprinted with a particular colonial past, my father's vinyl collection is equally interwoven, reflecting the rise of America, beginning with the Marcos era and its love of Hollywood and American icons, and then on to the dispersal of my country's labour via the Overseas Filipino Workers and their resulting eclectic music tastes, which have made their way back home (here, alluding particularly to vinyl records with Middle Eastern influence, or from the Middle East, which I intersperse with drawings based on performances I attended by Filipino bands in Dubai).

Mark Salvatus

Interested in the migration of labour through music and its tenuous ties to the politics of entertainment, Mark spent time for SB14 with Overseas Filipino Workers (OFW) who, as musicians in Dubai's hotels and bars, croon with a repertoire of American covers. The Phillipine Constabulary Band may have basked in the glow of their US masters, but the artist asks, has anything really changed? Are these OFW workers similarly bound (or blind) to their contribution to what has become a nationalised system of labour for the Philippines?

Interested in the migration of labour through music and its tenuous ties to the politics of entertainment, Mark spent time for SB14 with Overseas Filipino Workers (OFW) who, as musicians in Dubai's hotels and bars, croon with a repertoire of American covers. The Philippine Constabulary Band may have basked in the glow of their US masters, but the artist asks, has anything really changed? Are these OFW workers similarly bound (or blind) to their contribution to what has become a nationalised system of labour for the Philippines?

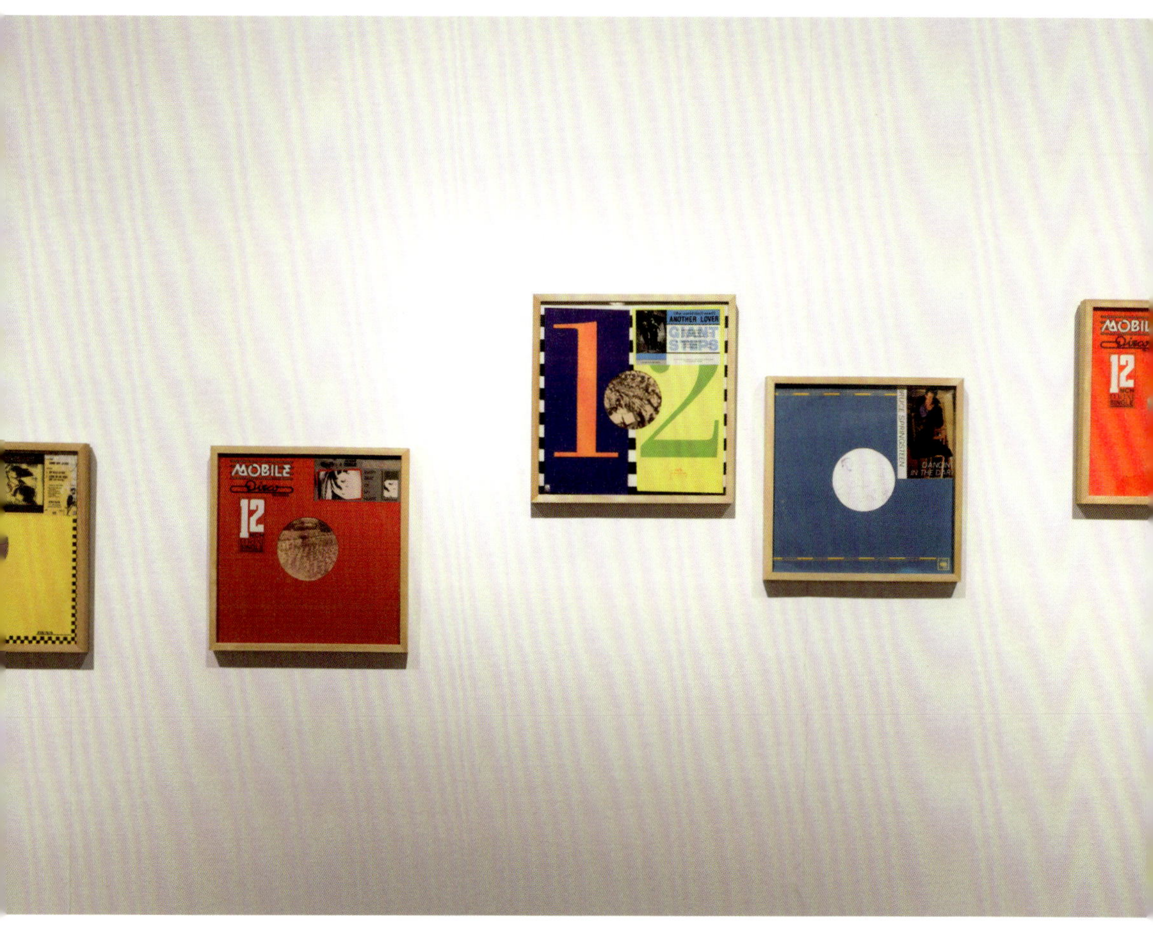

Notes from the New World
2015–2019
Multimedia installation with 2-channel video; assemblage and collage of magazine clippings; books; archival photographs from Lopez Museum & Library in Manila; drawings; found vinyl records; vinyl covers, vinyl players
12 minutes 24 seconds; dimensions variable
Partially commissioned by Sharjah Art Foundation
Courtesy of the artist and Salvage Projects
Photo: readsreads.info

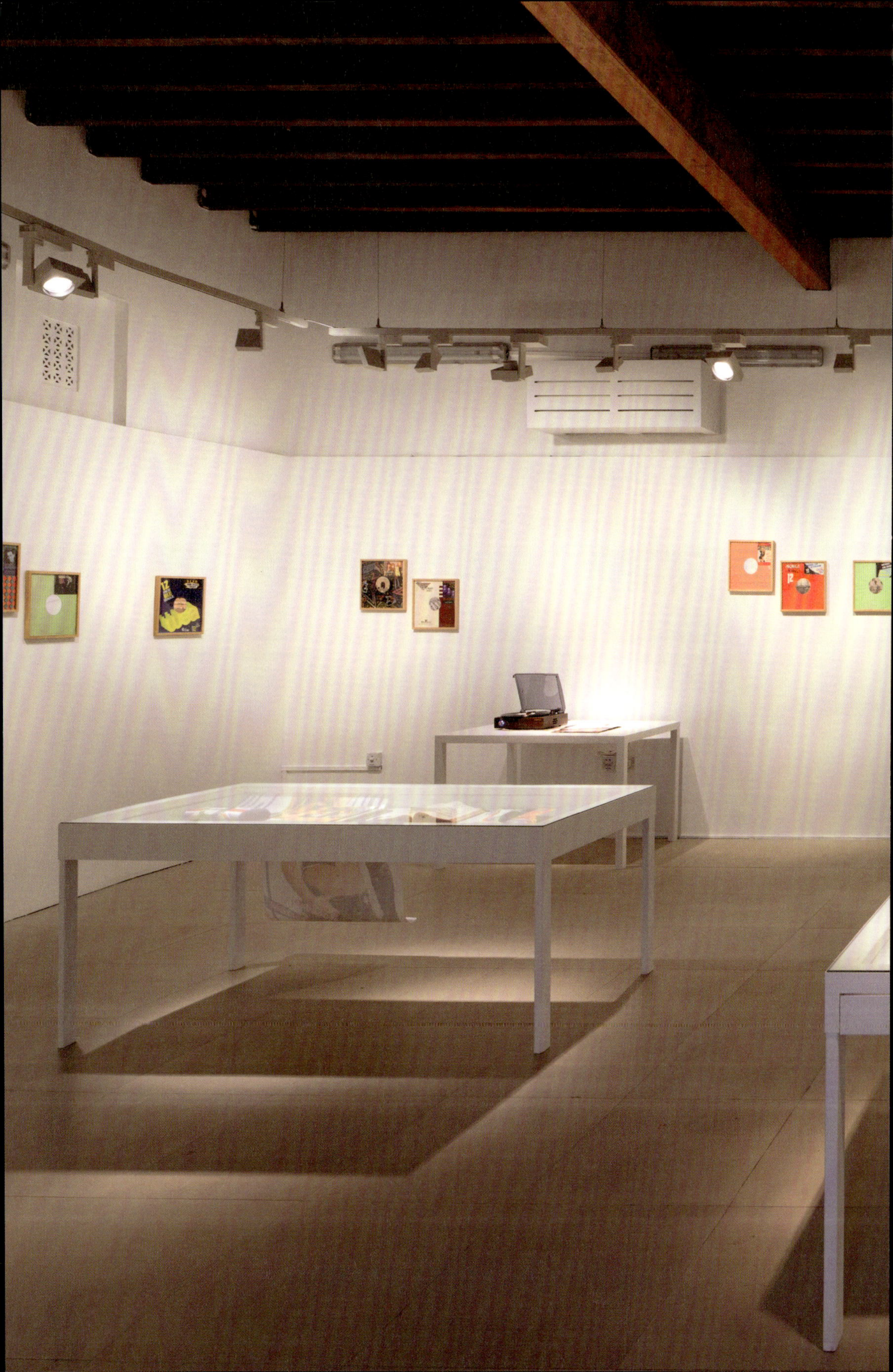

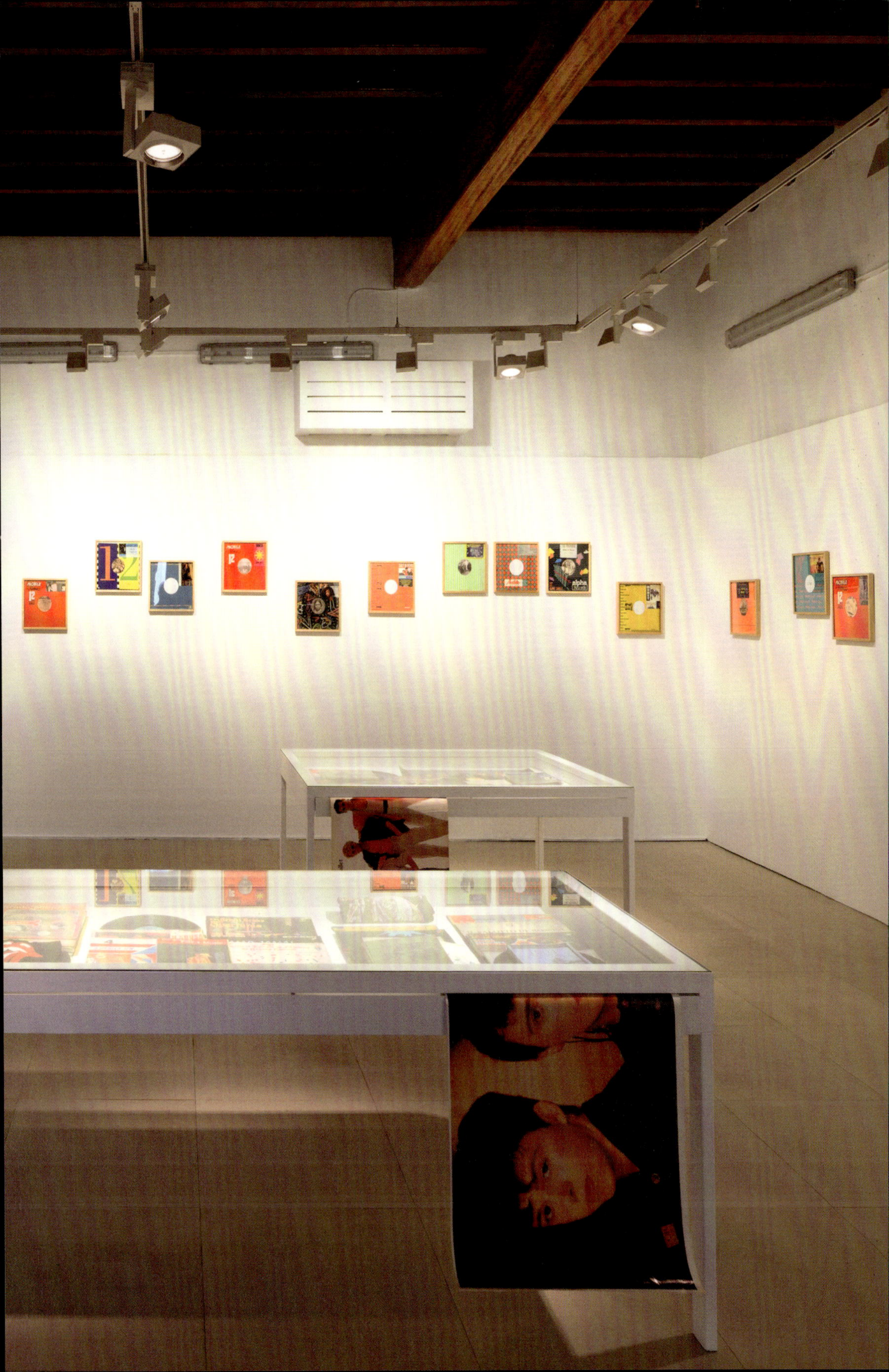

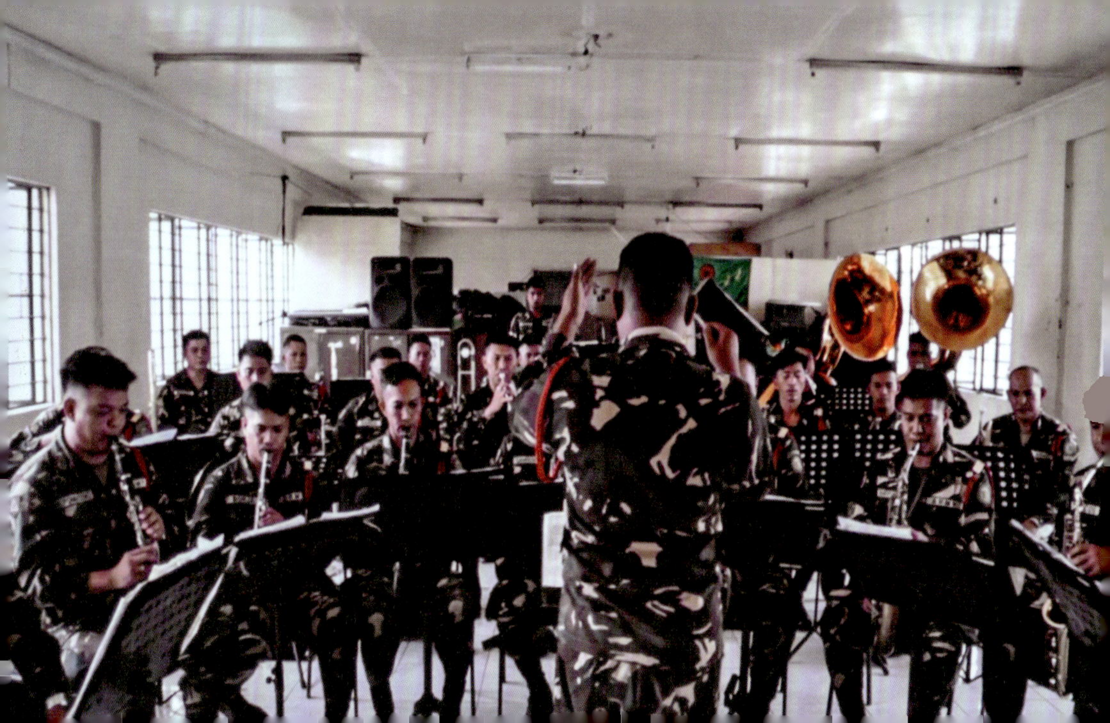

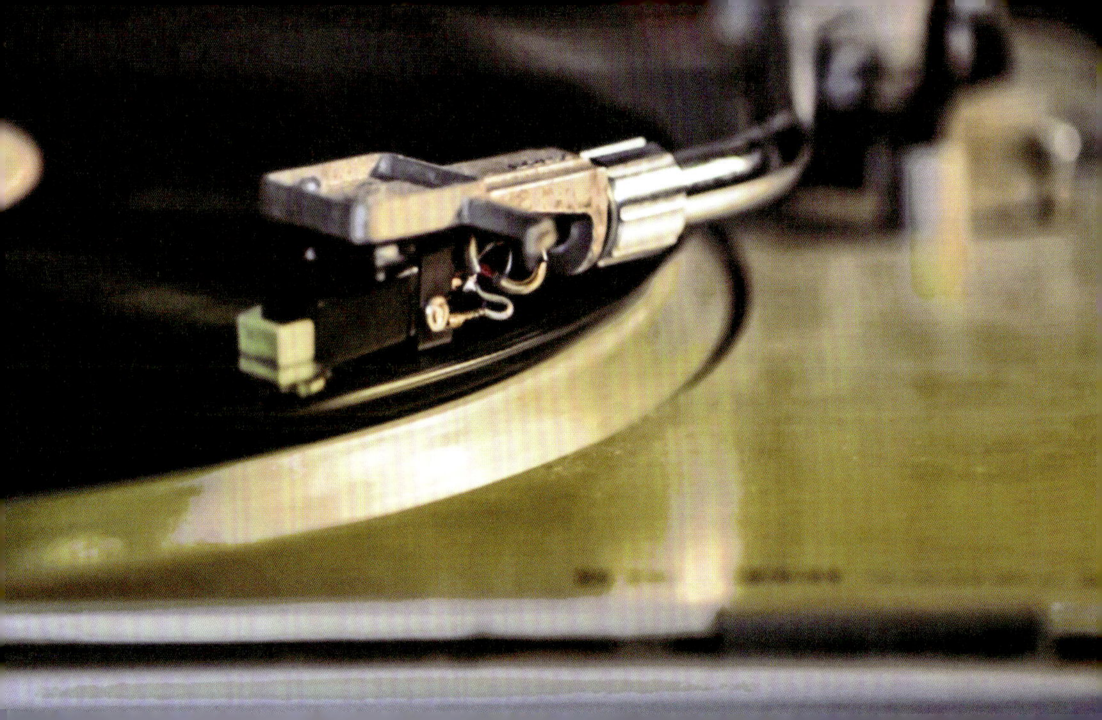

Ahmad Fuad Osman

Enrique de Malacca Memorial Project, 2016–ongoing

At times, history functions like a mirror; while we depend on it to show us to ourselves, its reflective surfaces are not always reliable – they echo, skew, magnify and invert. If history is really written by the victors/winners, then how truthful can it be?

I discovered Enrique de Malacca in 1985 through a novel amongst my mother's small collection of old books, *Panglima Awang* (1958) by Harun Aminurrashid. The tale it recounts, summarised below, was my first introduction to an alternate history, which spurred the eventual creation of this ongoing memorial project.

Ferdinand Magellan is commonly acknowledged as the first to circumnavigate the world. However, few realise that the explorer was killed in a bloody armed conflict on the island of Mactan on 27 April 1521 – and never completed the voyage around the world. (Only two of his ships, travelling on without him, eventually reached their destination, the Moluccas.) Antonio Pigafetta, a Venetian scholar and explorer who accompanied Magellan throughout this journey, recorded Magellan's demise in his journal.

Magellan's last will and testament mentions that a man named Enrique – a slave who Magellan had captured in Malacca in 1511 and sailed with throughout the three-year journey – was to be made a 'free man' upon his death. Could it therefore be that Enrique, who possibly outlived his master, is the one who actually deserves to be credited as the first to circle the globe? After Mactan, Enrique's whereabouts remain unknown, a factual void that has shaped a near-mythical historical legacy surrounding his identity, allegiance and reputation. Who was this man before he was baptized as 'Enrique'? Was he a Muslim, or perceived as heathen? Where did he come from? Why did Magellan decide to take him back to Portugal, Azemmour (Morocco) and Spain, and then return with him to the Malay Archipelago ten years later? What made him so special to Magellan? Where did he go after the massacre at Mactan?

The *Enrique de Malacca Memorial Project* is a fictional memorial, built from fragments of historical evidence, scholarly interviews and oral religious histories. It is an attempt to reconstruct a lost character, a vanished archive; an undertaking to negotiate the identity of a man celebrated today in Malaysia, Indonesia and the Philippines.

Ahmad Fuad Osman

This vast collection of tools and observations that Fuad has assembled may be fictional and speculative, but its accrual of narrative – supported by multiple sources, across geographies that are historically and culturally intertwined – significantly questions how History, with a capital 'H', determines value (in terms of History, as always written, and thus controlled, by the conquerors).

Ahmad Fuad Osman's focus on Enrique de Malacca resonates with the work of Kidlat Tahimik (see pg. 146) this vast collection of tools and observations that Fuad has assembled may be fictional and speculative, but its accrual of narrative – supported by multiple sources, across geographies that are historically and culturally intertwined – significantly questions how History, with a capital 'H', determines value (in terms of History, as always written, and thus controlled, by the conquerors).

Ahmad Fuad Osman's focus on Enrique de Malacca resonates with the work of Kidlat Tahimik (see pg. 146)

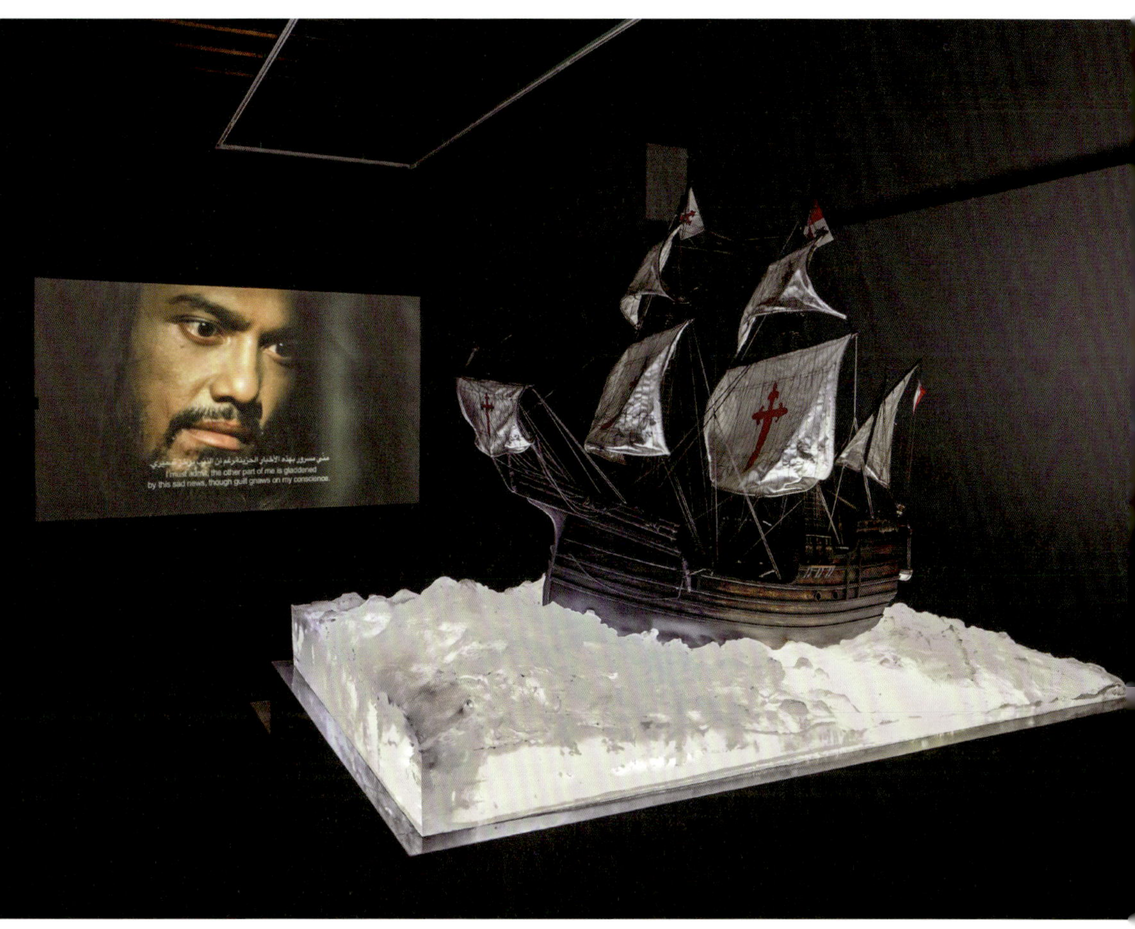

Enrique de Malacca Memorial Project
2016–ongoing
Mixed media installation: 73 objects; two single-channel videos: colour, sound; 33 interactive video interviews, archival materials
Dimensions variable
Partially commissioned by Sharjah Art Foundation
Courtesy of the artist

Page 205–207:
Photo: readsreads.info

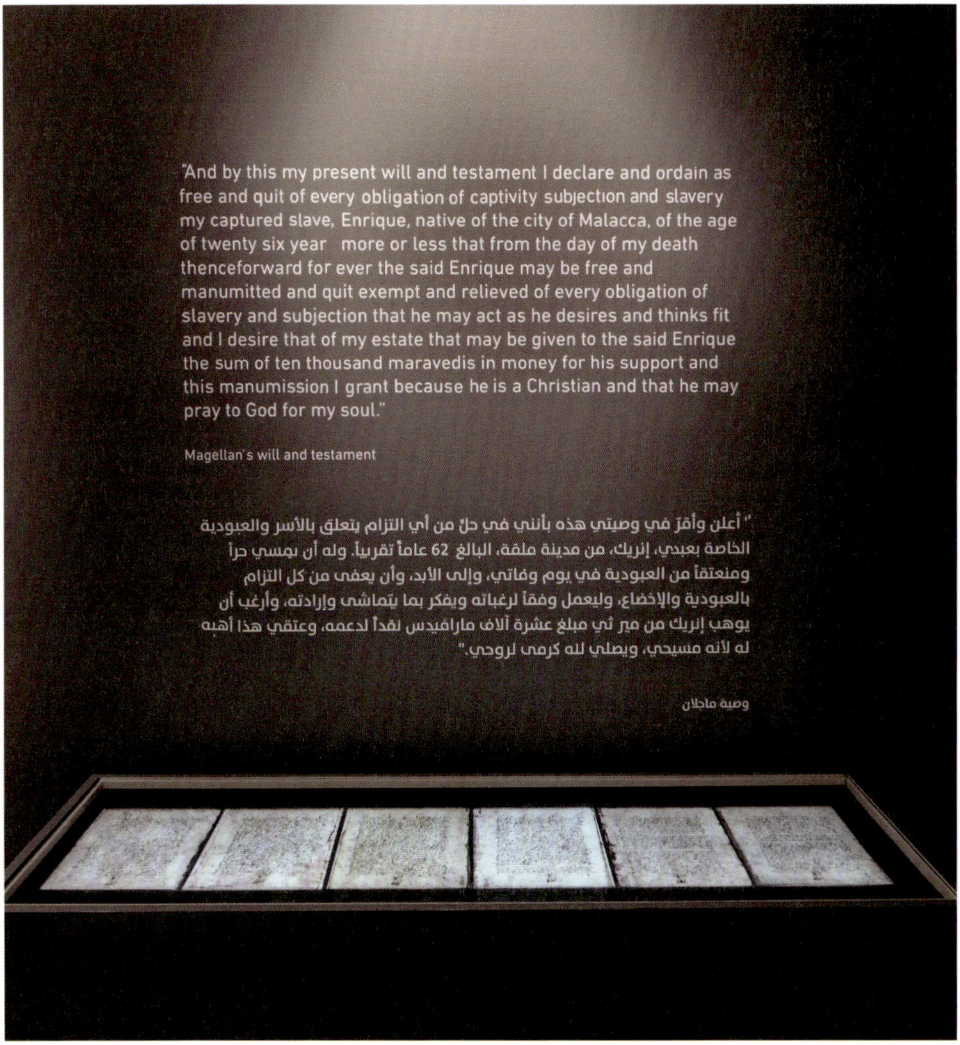

"And by this my present will and testament I declare and ordain as free and quit of every obligation of captivity subjection and slavery my captured slave, Enrique, native of the city of Malacca, of the age of twenty six year more or less that from the day of my death thenceforward for ever the said Enrique may be free and manumitted and quit exempt and relieved of every obligation of slavery and subjection that he may act as he desires and thinks fit and I desire that of my estate that may be given to the said Enrique the sum of ten thousand maravedis in money for his support and this manumission I grant because he is a Christian and that he may pray to God for my soul."

Magellan's will and testament

" أعلن وأقرّ في وصيتي هذه بأنني في حلٍّ من أي التزام يتعلق بالأسر والعبودية الخاصة بعبدي، إنريك، من مدينة ملقة، البالغ 62 عاماً تقريباً. وله أن يمسي حراً ومنعتقاً من العبودية في يوم وفاتي، وإلى الأبد، وأن يعفى من كل التزام بالعبودية والإخضاع، وليعمل وفقاً لرغباته ويفكر بما يتماشى وإرادته، وأرغب أن يوهب إنريك من مير ثي مبلغ عشرة آلاف مارافيدس نقداً لدعمه، وعتقي هذا أهبه له لأنه مسيحي، ويصلي لله كرمى لروحي."

وصية ماجلان

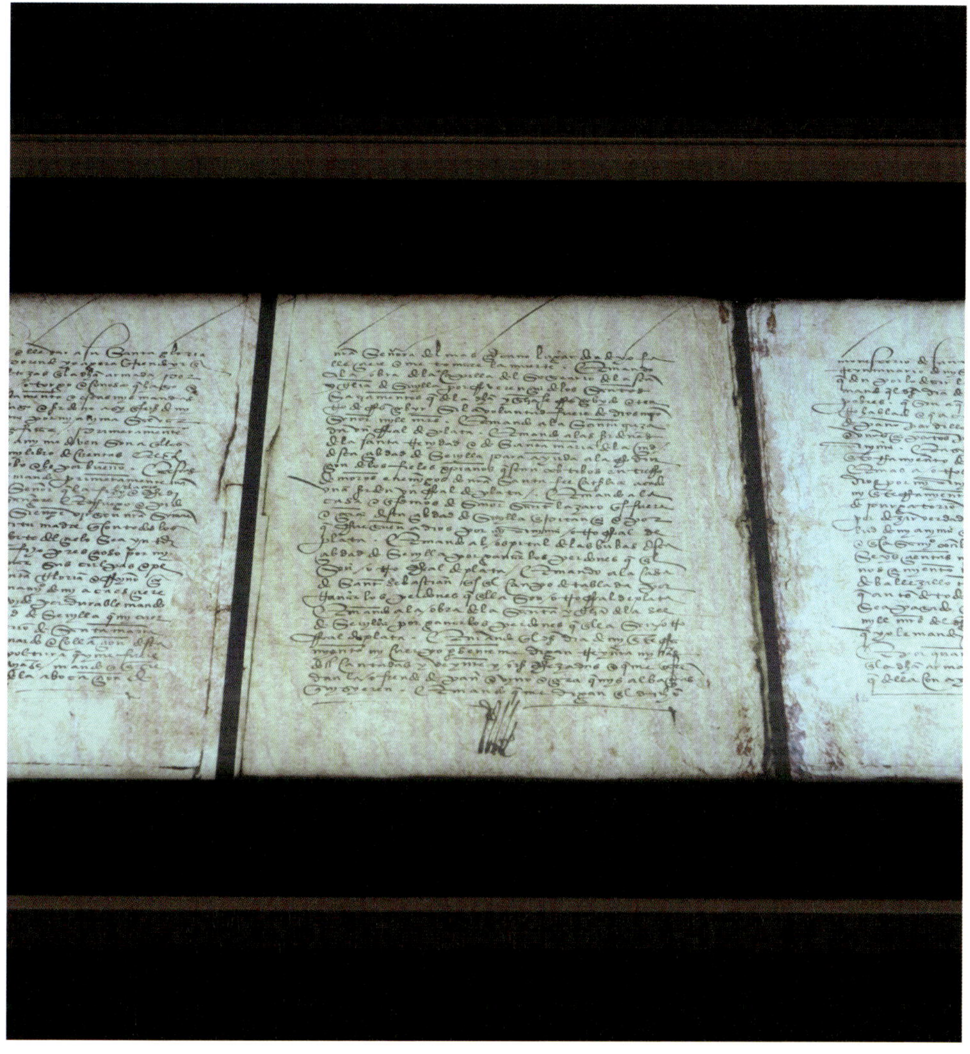

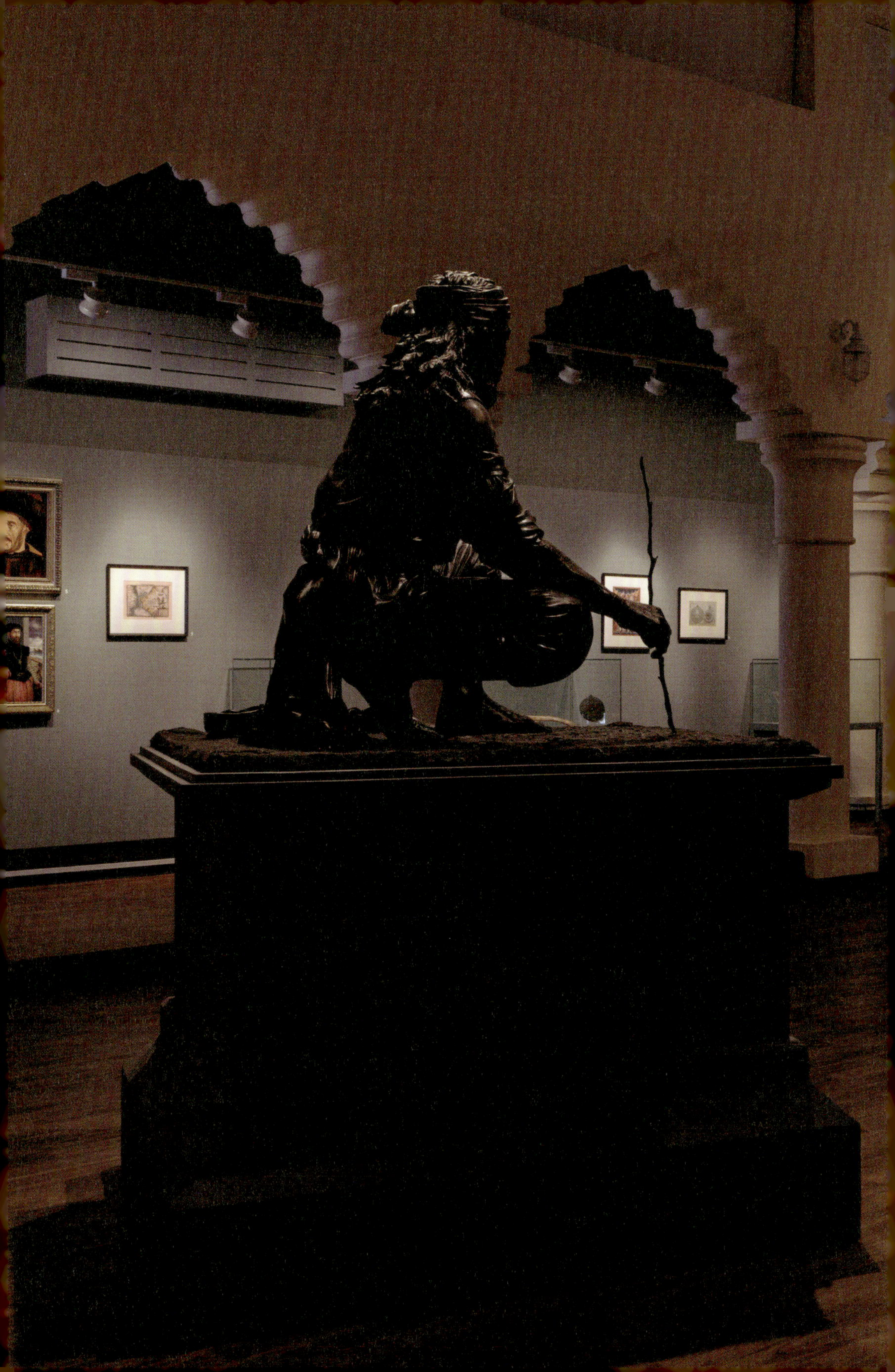

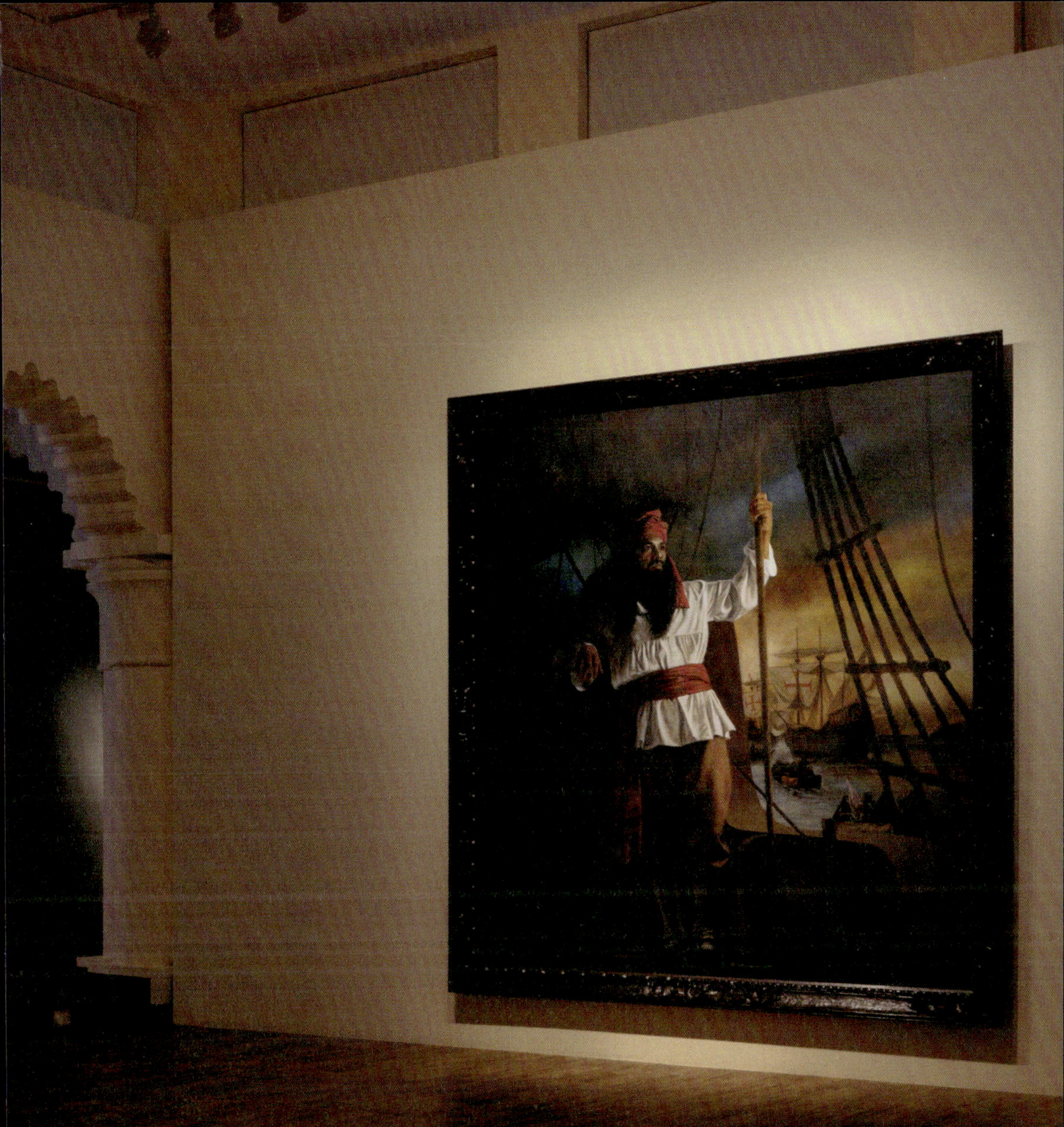

Antariksa

Co-Prosperity #3

Japanese artists had already been sent to the battlefields to create images in the first Sino-Japanese War (1894-1895) and the Ruso-Japanese War, ten years later. But the practice was expanded on an unprecedented scale in the late 1930s and early 1940s, when hundreds of Japanese artists served in the military. About a third of that figure were sent to work with the *Sendenbu* (propaganda department) in Japanese-occupied Indonesia from 1942 to 1945. The *Sendenbu* recruited hundreds of Indonesian artists and intellectuals for propaganda activities in Indonesia. Their works were exhibited in large war-art exhibitions in Japan, which were attended by the Japanese emperor himself, and attracted the general public in record numbers. Their propaganda value was further amplified through the dissemination of printed reproductions in the mass media.

I have created an installation around these artists' biographies, their works and their documentation—both the biography of *jūgun gaka* (official war painters) and unofficial artists in war-time Japan and Japanese-occupied Indonesia. A biography, especially a military one, may be read or experienced as hard historical evidence. However, I seek to challenge the conventions by which historians narrate the past by using *only* hard historical evidence—to challenge the equation of such 'hard evidence' with objectivity, and 'objectivity' as being without feeling. This notion of 'objectivity' is not without bias; perhaps it is this objective language that fools us. If we take this language away, what would we find?

My tools are our senses; my approach to interrogate (and sometimes speculate) using "soft evidence" as a counter to the language of hard historical evidence as we know it. Through this process, I seek to continue my experiments in developing audiences' sensory experiences toward the subjects presented in my installation, and to continue rethinking the ways in which the public can participate with and intervene into history, interpreting the past based on their own new present, their perceptions and sensory experiences. In a similar way, I have included works by Japanese friends and colleagues, artists Makoto Murata and Tsuyoshi Ozawa; they too have intervened to subvert the 'hard' narratives of war. Murata-san eases these narratives from the controlled spaces of censorship, stigma and shame, through questioning the authorship of histories and playing with scale to induce intimacy and feeling; while Ozawa-san speculates on the biography and post-war experience of a famous Japanese war painter, via his own contemporary adventure.

Antariksa

In the first room of Antariksa's installation, our senses are challenged; we enter a space bathed in UV light, as we find stacks of paper piled on a low-level shelf. On these pages, written in ink only visible in UV light, are the biographies of artists from Japanese-occupied Indonesia. As an archival display, Antariksa questions the privilege of sight in according factual evidence. This provocation, juxtaposed with the work of other contemporary artists who also 'play' with history and its fictions, is exemplary of how artists have re-conjured historical narratives that can challenge the official stories.

In the first room of Antariksa's installation, our senses are challenged; we enter a space bathed in UV light, as we find stacks of paper piled on a low-level shelf. On these pages, written in ink only visible in UV light, are the biographies of artists from Japanese-occupied Indonesia. As an archival display, Antariksa questions the privilege of sight in according factual evidence. This provocation, juxtaposed with the work of other contemporary artists who also 'play' with history and its fictions, is exemplary of how artists have re-conjured historical narratives that can challenge the official stories.

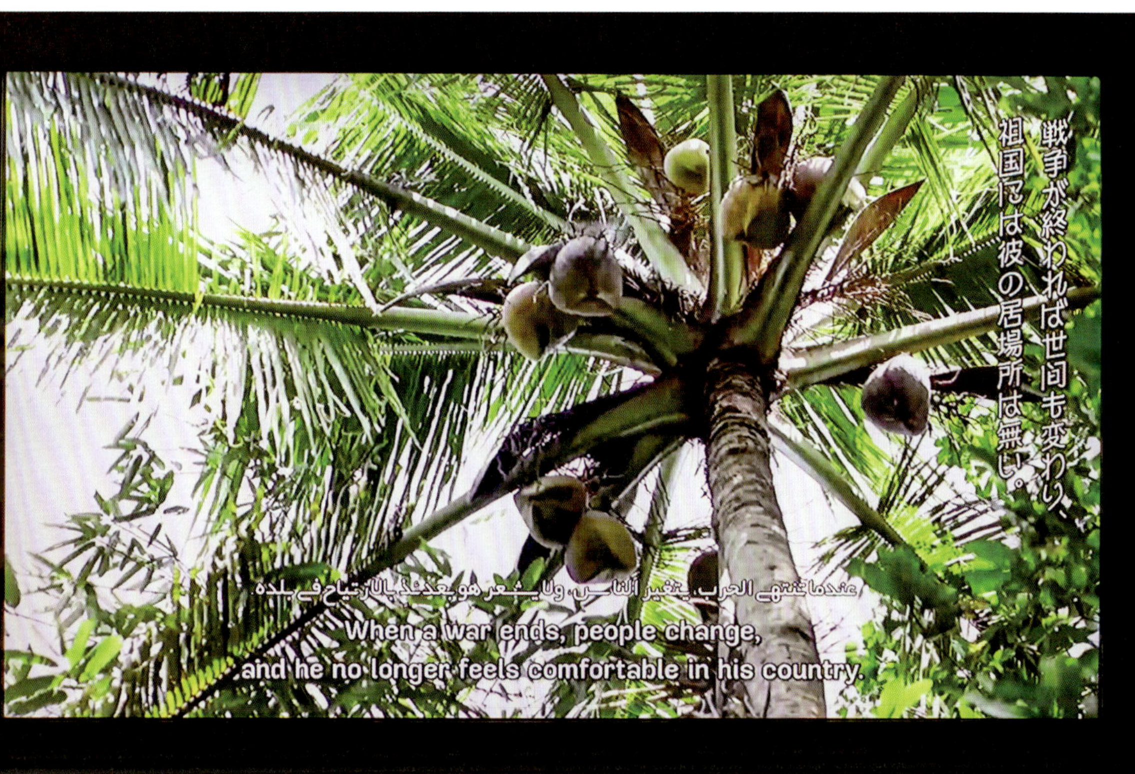

Tsuyoshi Ozawa
'Painter F Song' from 'The Return of Painter F'
2015
Single channel video: colour, sound
12 minutes 13 seconds
Courtesy of Tsuyoshi Ozawa

Page 210–211:
Co-Prosperity #3
2019
Curated display of artwork and archival material
Commissioned by Sharjah Art Foundation

Page 212–213:
Makoto Murata
Petit Senso-ga
2016
153 miniature paintings: oil on board
Dimensions variable
Courtesy of Makoto Murata and SNOW Contemporary, Tokyo

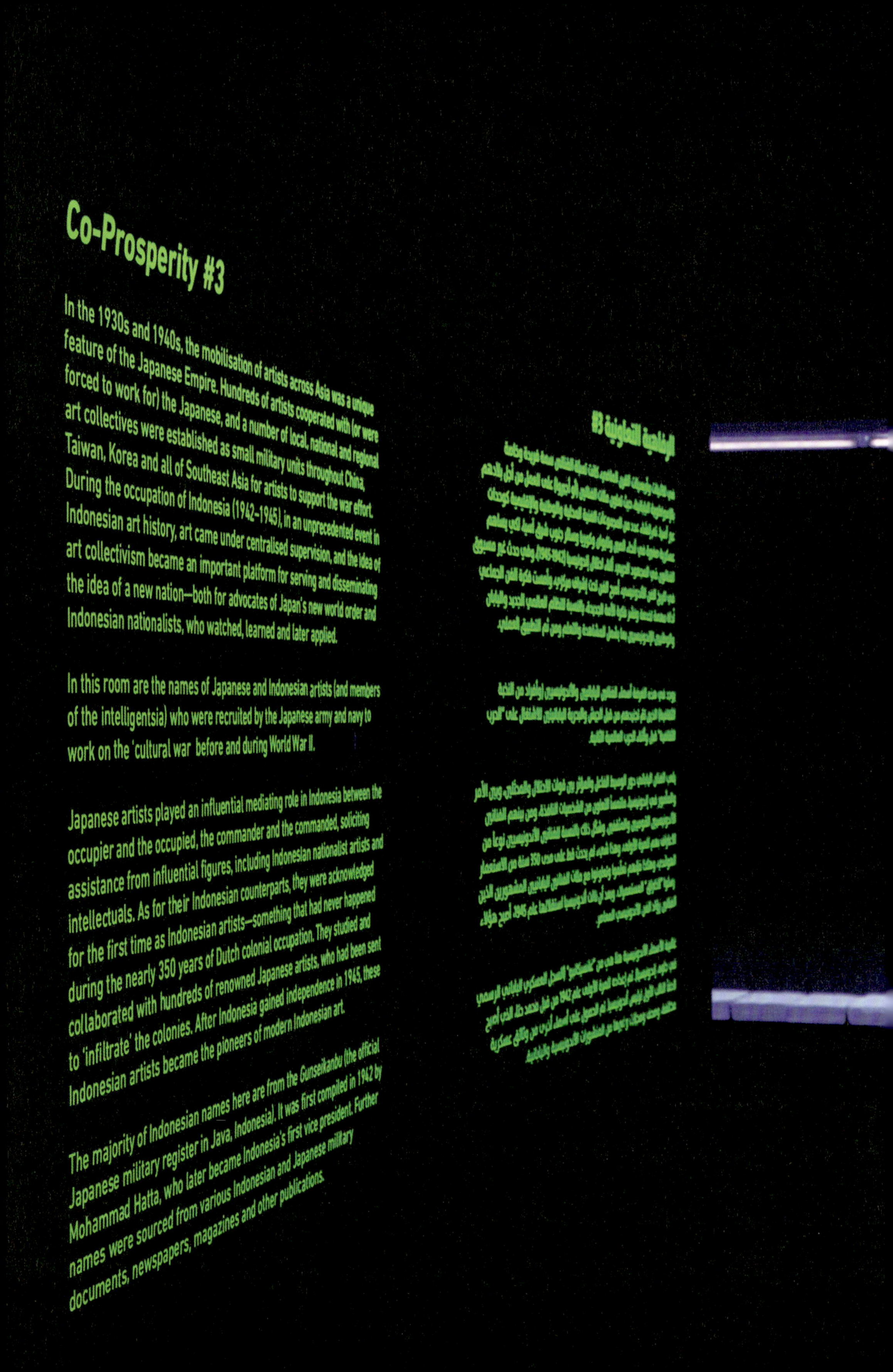

Co-Prosperity #3

In the 1930s and 1940s, the mobilisation of artists across Asia was a unique feature of the Japanese Empire. Hundreds of artists cooperated with (or were forced to work for) the Japanese, and a number of local, national and regional art collectives were established as small military units throughout China, Taiwan, Korea and all of Southeast Asia for artists to support the war effort. During the occupation of Indonesia (1942–1945), in an unprecedented event in Indonesian art history, art came under centralised supervision, and the idea of art collectivism became an important platform for serving and disseminating the idea of a new nation—both for advocates of Japan's new world order and Indonesian nationalists, who watched, learned and later applied.

In this room are the names of Japanese and Indonesian artists (and members of the intelligentsia) who were recruited by the Japanese army and navy to work on the 'cultural war before and during World War II.

Japanese artists played an influential mediating role in Indonesia between the occupier and the occupied, the commander and the commanded, soliciting assistance from influential figures, including Indonesian nationalist artists and intellectuals. As for their Indonesian counterparts, they were acknowledged for the first time as Indonesian artists—something that had never happened during the nearly 350 years of Dutch colonial occupation. They studied and collaborated with hundreds of renowned Japanese artists, who had been sent to 'infiltrate' the colonies. After Indonesia gained independence in 1945, these Indonesian artists became the pioneers of modern Indonesian art.

The majority of Indonesian names here are from the *Gunseikanbu* (the official Japanese military register in Java, Indonesia). It was first compiled in 1942 by Mohammad Hatta, who later became Indonesia's first vice president. Further names were sourced from various Indonesian and Japanese military documents, newspapers, magazines and other publications.

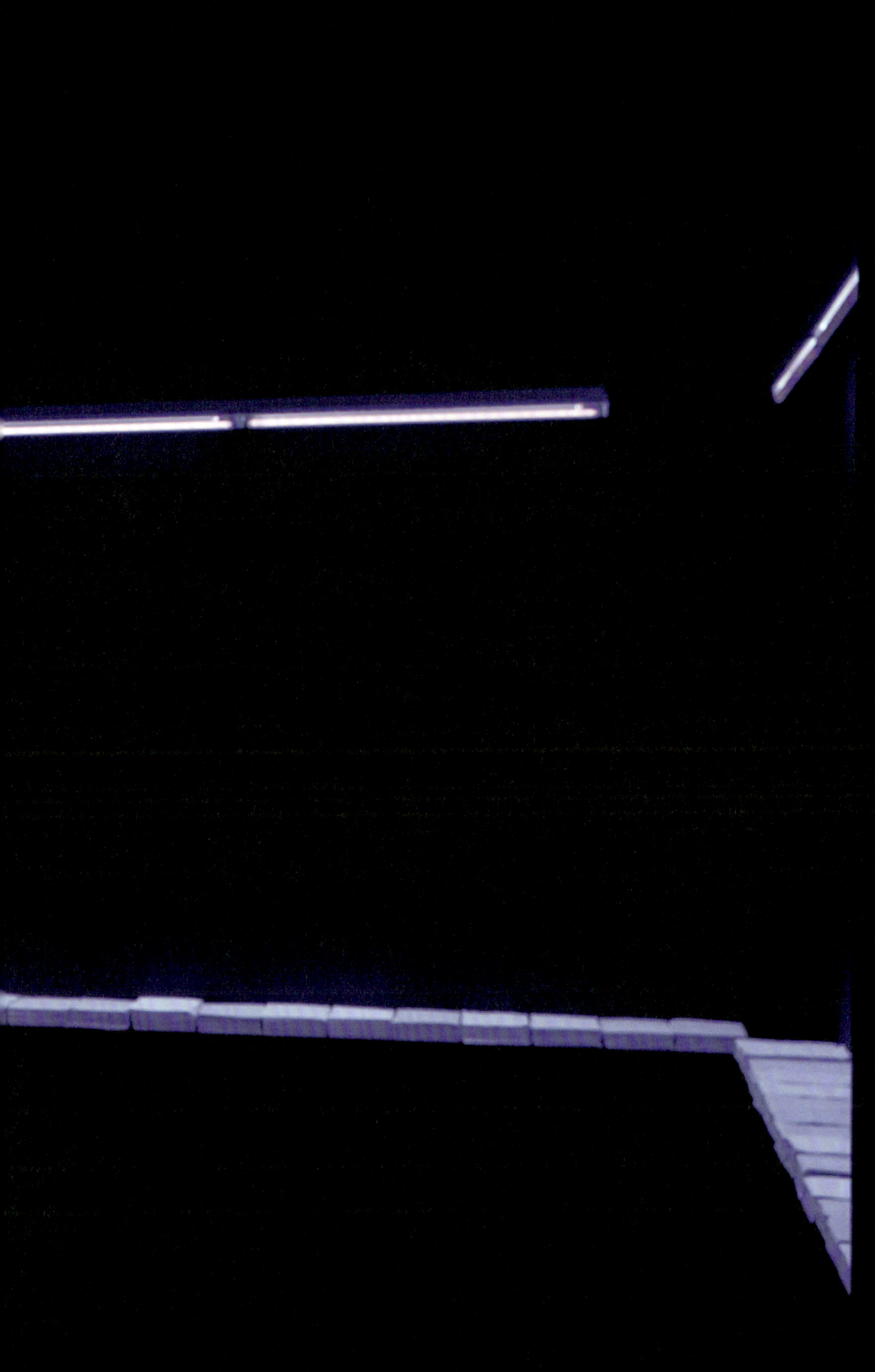

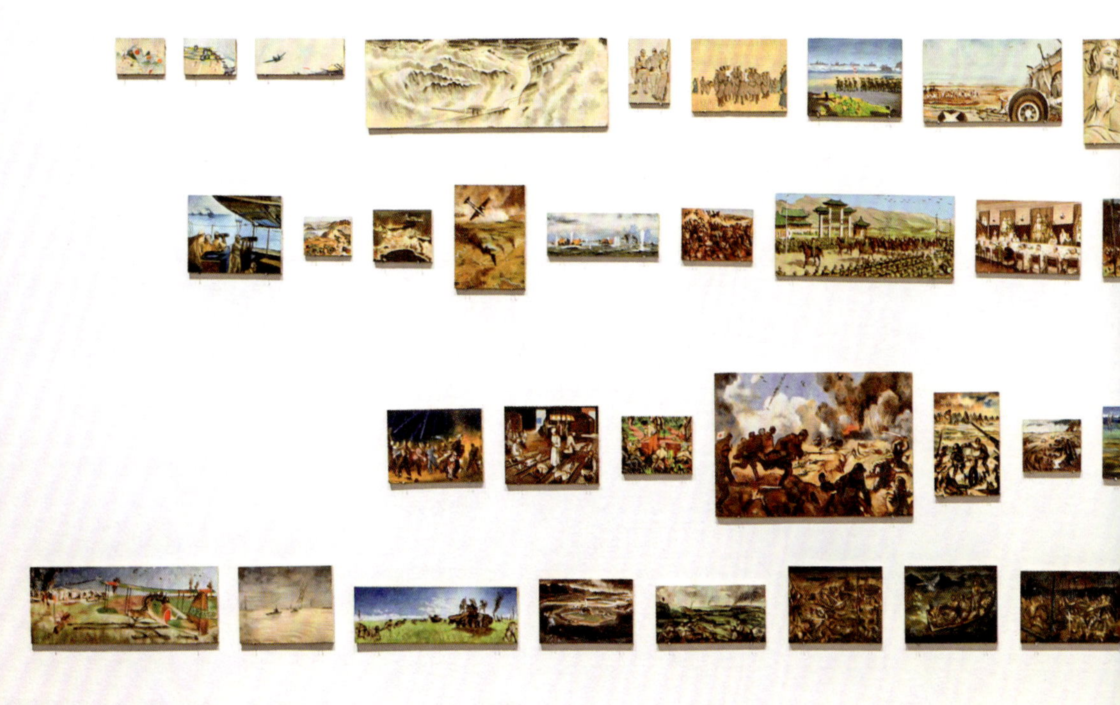

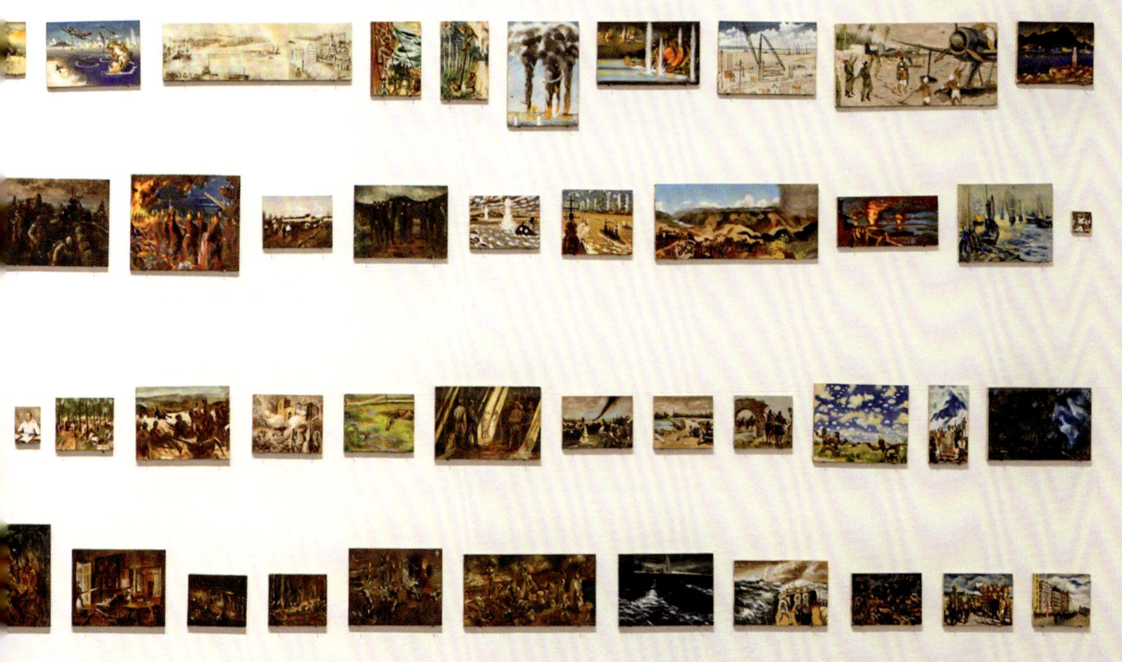

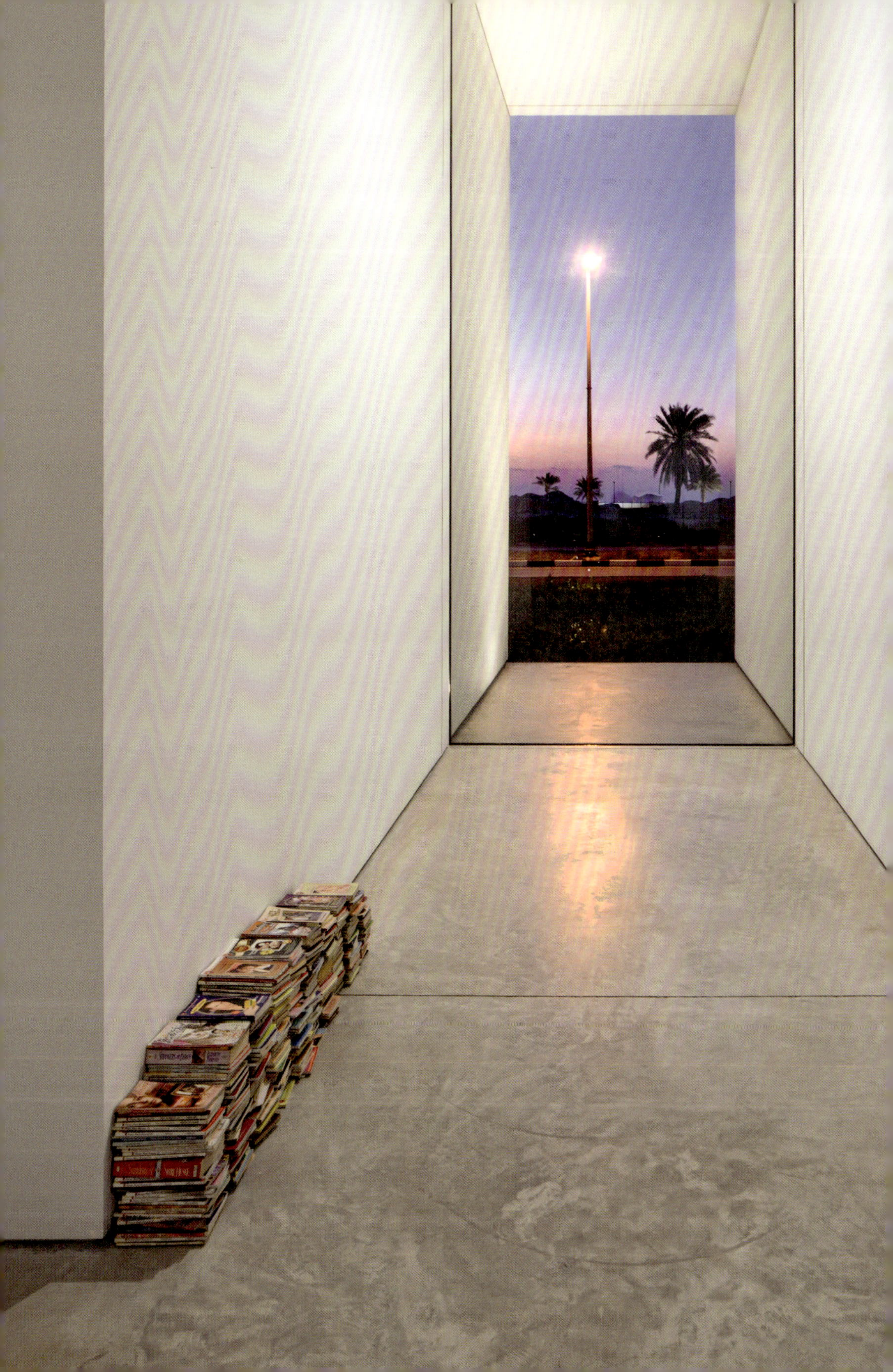

Migrant workers make up the majority of the resident population in the United Arab Emirates, with much of the domestic live-in maid services coming from the Philippines. 'Romance Section' is a collection of boot-legged, popular, short love stories written in Tagalog, their cheap print pages worn and torn, a reflection of the hearts and minds of the myriad women enduring semi-permanent removal from their loved-ones. The Philippines has systematised and institutionalised export labour as a national economy (in 2017, its net worth was estimated at more that USD31 billion). This immense mobile workforce is often culturally discriminated against, or physically and psychologically abused. This collection of print matter stands as a sculptural testament to these workers, whose days know not only duty and distance, but also love, lust and fiction.

Migrant workers make up the majority of the resident population in the United Arab Emirates, with much of the domestic live-in maid services coming from the Philippines. 'Romance Section' is a collection of boot-legged, popular, short love stories written in Tagalog, their cheap print pages worn and torn, a reflection of the hearts and minds of the myriad women enduring semi-permanent removal from their loved-ones. The Philippines has systematised and institutionalised export labour as a national economy (in 2017, its net worth was estimated at more than USD31 billion). This immense mobile workforce is often culturally discriminated against, or physically and psychologically abused. This collection of print matter stands as a sculptural testament to these workers, whose days know not only duty and distance, but also love, lust and fiction.

Lantian Xie

Romance Section, 2016

These are all of the books from the romance section at Book World, a second-hand bookstore in the Satwa neighbourhood of Dubai. In these glossy paperbacks are stories of encounters, intrigues, chances, intoxicants and ghosts.

Only a few of these books were widely distributed, so what you see here are materials that have occasioned traversals of various stakes to make their way to Dubai. Many of these works arrived with people in tow – people for whom Dubai is a temporary proposition, an extranational labour market; or those who have time to unload leftover print matter before going elsewhere.

Such matter, and its travels, render a certain force in its frequent comings and goings, splintering and scattering like confetti across suitcases and boxes and containers along the way. It seems determinedly mutable, as if evading index. Here, these books, purchased wholesale, are withdrawn from one circulation, one method of distribution, and entered into another (the art world). It's like reaching into a stream to pick out a fish, only to glimpse the world shimmer across its scales, and then catching it and letting it go into yet another stream. What is certain is that the world does not remain unmoved, even after the slightest of such shimmers.

Lantian Xie

Romance Section
2016–2019
All the books from the romance section at a used book shop
Dimensions variable
Partially produced by Sharjah Art Foundation
Courtesy of the artist and Grey Noise, Dubai

Page 216–217:
Photo: readsreads.info

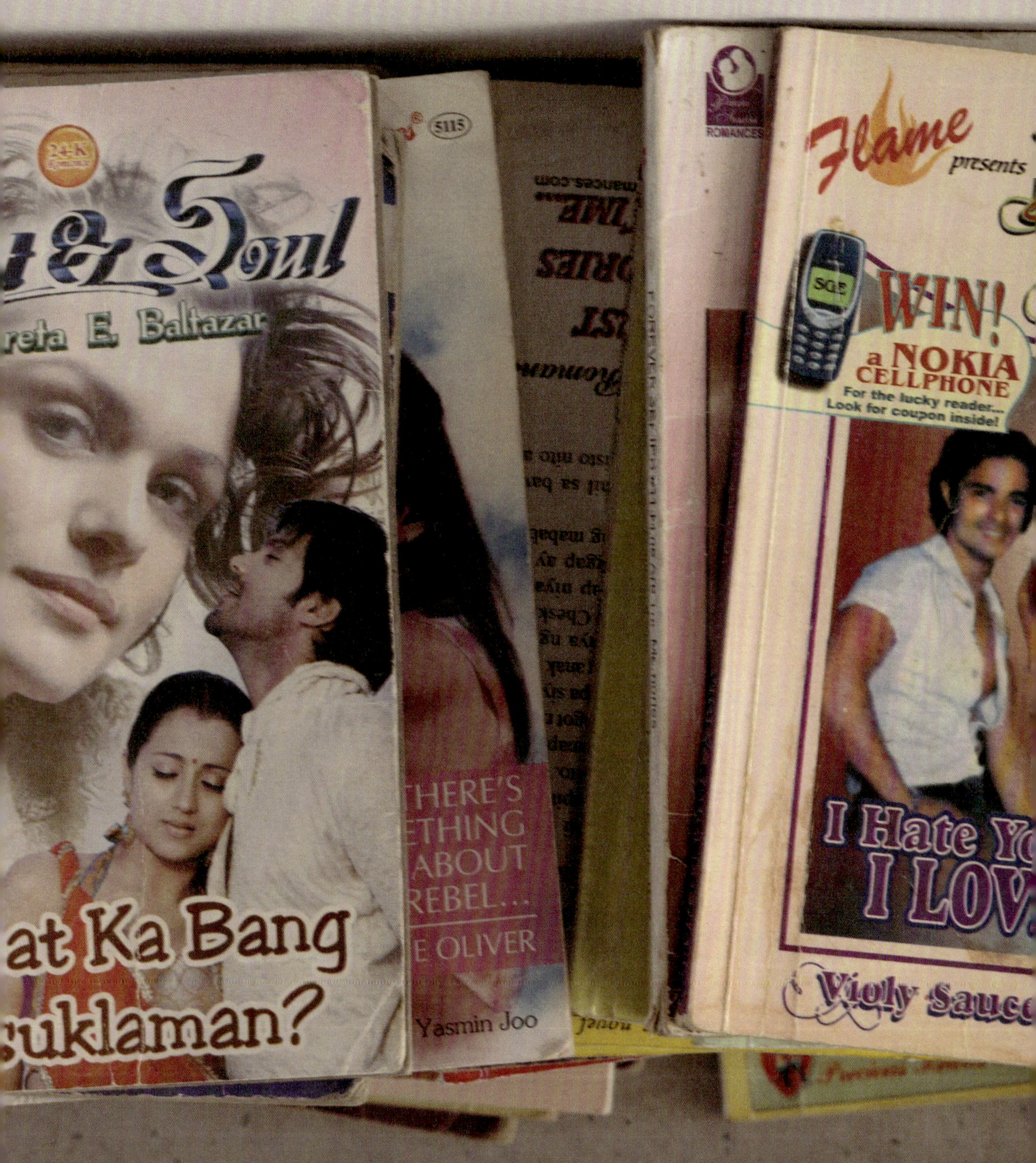

& Soul
E. Baltazar
at Ka Bang
uklaman?
5115
THERE'S
ETHING
ABOUT
REBEL...
E OLIVER
Yasmin Joo
ROMANCES
Flame
presents
WIN!
a NOKIA
CELLPHONE
For the lucky reader...
Look for coupon inside!
I Hate Yo
I LOV
Violy Sauce

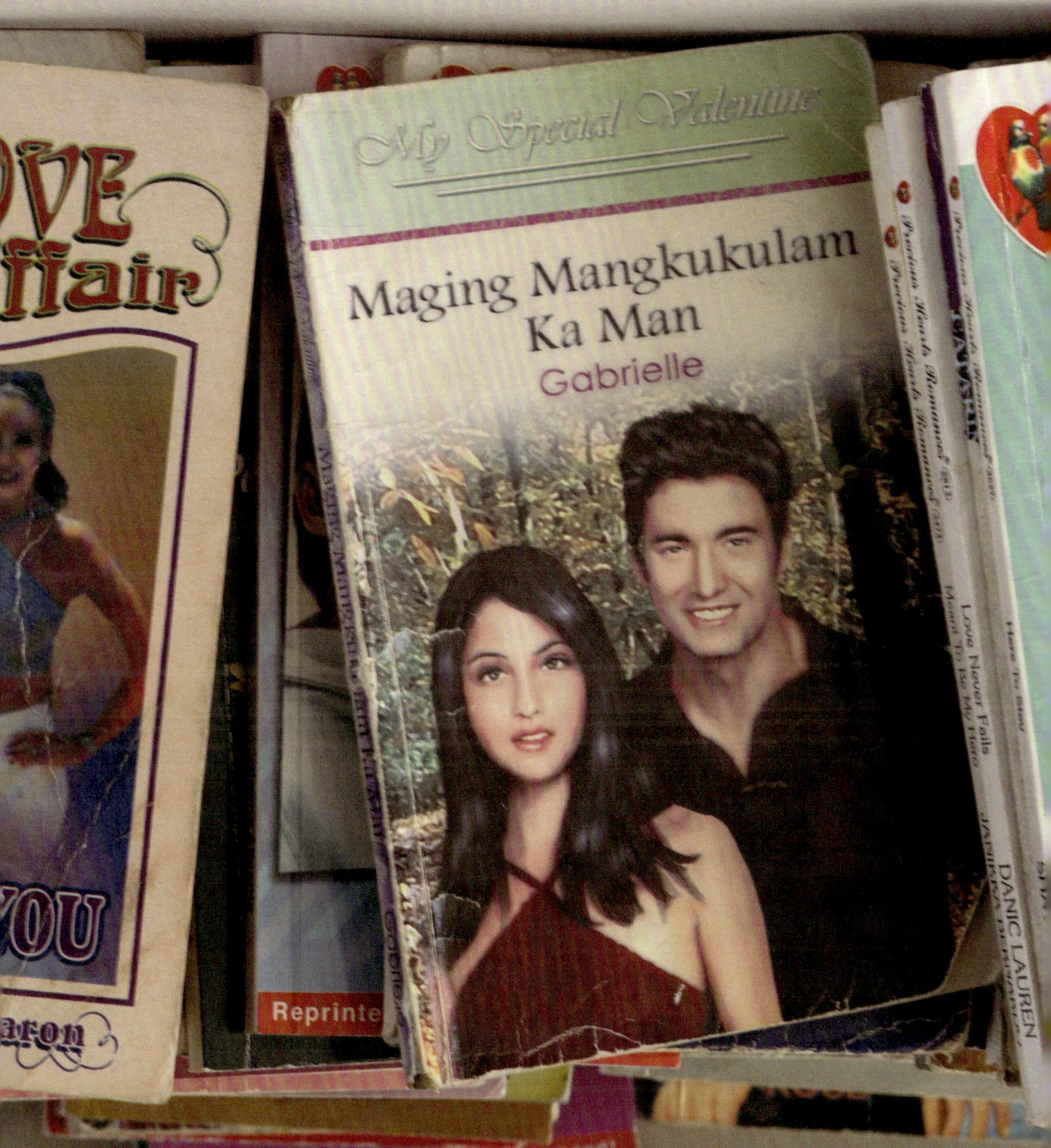
My Special Valentine
Maging Mangkukulam
Ka Man
Gabrielle
Reprinte
Reprinted due to insistent public demand!
Love Never Fails
DANIC LAUREN

Léuli Eshrāghi

tagatanu'u, 2017–ongoing

I am drawn to the embodied teachings that Indigenous histories call into being as realisations of ancestral Earth-centred ways of becoming and knowing. Beyond the performance of indigeneity or in deference to the contemporary art market, these markers are also for those outside the gallery or linked to all our relations beyond humanity. I am drawn to the kindness and critical care practices in writing/speaking/sensing encounters – through poetic expression, through ritualised actions in relational space – drawn to their ability to be more than the sum of reactionary, loveless warmongering and protectionist fever all around us.

In *tagatanu'u*, I create an alofisā (circular ceremonial space) dedicated to the ancestors of Samoan architecture and founded on vā (spatial, multidirectional relationships) with all kin, with sand from Sharjah's Al Hamriyah, in local recognition of the Great Ocean (Pacific Rim). In this performance, we enter the tala (history) of the eel named Tuna, who became the young coconut Niu, in order to provide for his human lover, Sina. I beckon ancestral time into the gallery space to question exoticised histories and the commodification of bodies, plants and medicine that have been simultaneously exploited and hidden by the missionary shaming of bodies, spirituality, sexuality – extracted as labour for plantations, tourism, military and security systems, nuclear testing. In speaking these lines in Gagana Samoa, 'ōlelo Hawai'i, Tałtan, Woi Wurrung, Secwépemc, French and English, I seek to assert multilingual futures beyond a consumptive Western gaze.

Léuli Eshrāghi

This work was developed with Rosanna Raymond, Paradise Cove collective, Ricky Tagaban, Bryan Kamaoli Kuwada, Peter Morin, Tania Willard, Sone Luna'i Eshrāghi, Yara El-Ghadban, Louis-Karl Sioui-Picard, Angela Tiatia, Tyson Campbell, Julia Packard, Doug Jarvis, France Trépanier, Lee Sum Yi, Qu Chang and Zoe Butt.

For Lēuli, Indigenous memory possesses ways and means of living and speaking, whereby the rituals of acknowledging cultural specificity and its movement across the Earth give recourse for collective remembering in defiance of capital and its zeal to conquer, possess and divide the globe. In this room, the artist invites you to sit, soften and lean in to read the various voices of Indigenous people, who have shaped a better understanding of their own diasporic journey and respect for their ancestors from Pārs, Samoa and Guangdong.

See the work of Kidlat Tahimik on pg. 146, who refers to 'kapwa', or his 'indio-genius' as his 'liberated interconnected indigenous spirit'.

For Léuli, Indigenous memory possesses ways and means of living and speaking, whereby the rituals of acknowledging cultural specificity and its movement across the Earth give recourse for collective remembering in defiance of capital and its zeal to conquer, possess and divide the globe. In this room, the artist invites you to sit, soften and lean in to read the various voices of Indigenous people, who have shaped a better understanding of their own diasporic journey and respect for their ancestors from Pārs, Samoa and Gwangdong.

See the work of Kidlat Tahimik on pg. 146, who refers to 'kapwa', or his 'indio-genius' as his 'liberated interconnected indigenous spirit'.

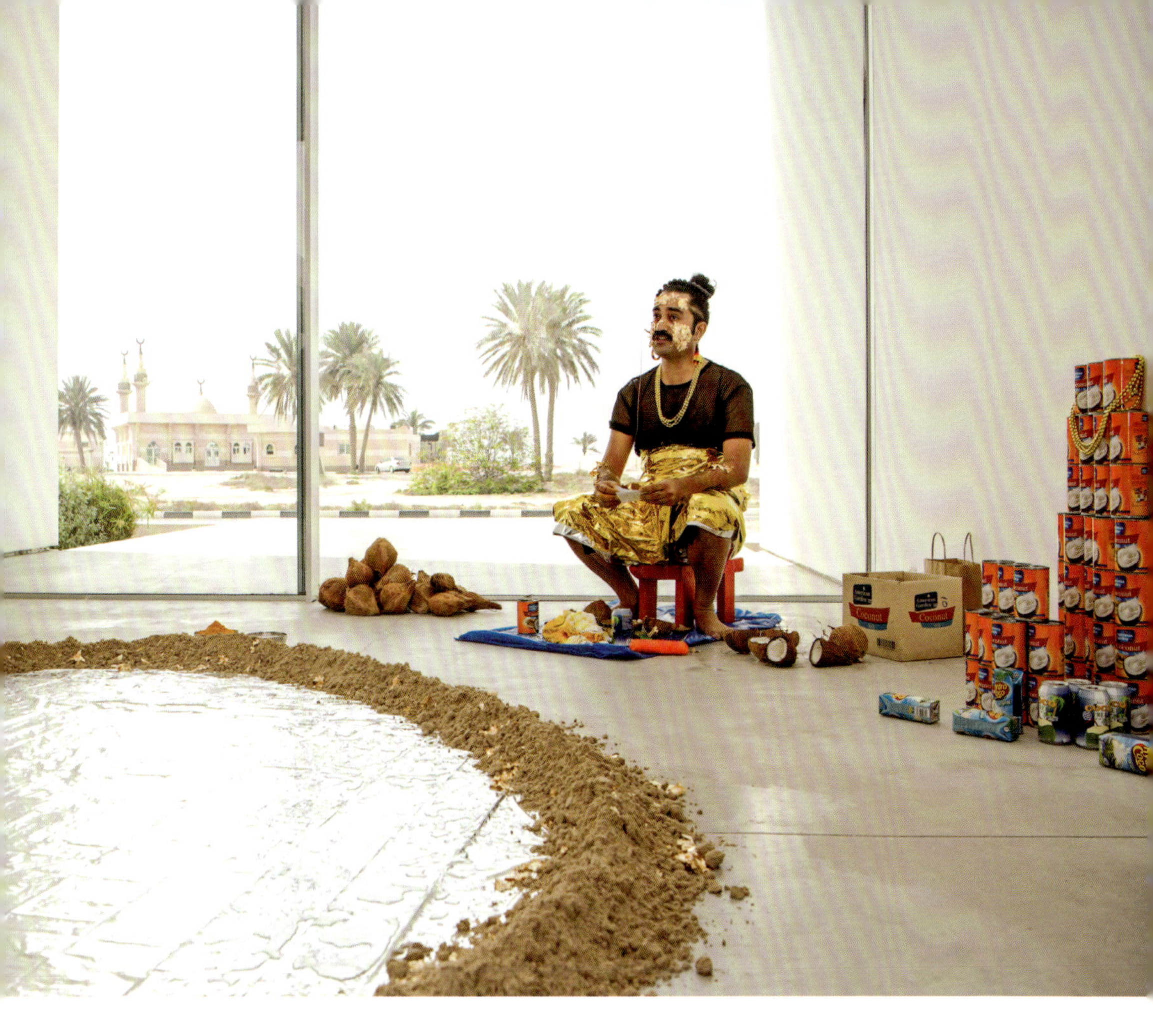

tagatanu'u
March 7, 2019
Performance with installation: sand, coconuts, coconut water, coconut milk, turmeric-infused water, charcoal, ochre, macadamia nuts, mylar emergency blankets, coconut scraping stool, metal bowls, books, digital images as slide presentation, cushions, rugs, plants
Dimensions variable
Commissioned by Sharjah Art Foundation
Courtesy of the artist

The opening-night performance began with the marking of the walls around the alofisā in two long lines of lega (turmeric), uliuli (charcoal) and sina (ochre) to honour the ancestors Tuna and Sina. Wrapped in emergency blankets, Léuli recited their texts, whilst scraping coconuts and pouring coconut water and milk into four brass bowls as processed macadamia nuts were handed out to the audience. Seeking to undo social taboos and to embody shame, Léuli handled water in various states – as salt sea water, electrolyte coconut water, thick coconut milk and ceremonial turmeric water – making overt sexual/political/military references to coded and non-English languages. The flowing waters of life were symbolically called upon to reframe decolonial attitudes towards ecological balance: to reconnect humanity in sincere genealogical terms with our eel–coconut tree ancestor, Tuna, and maker ancestor, Sina, who, in turn, is linked in Gagana Samoa to measina (fine weaving, literary works and the colour white) in ceremonial Samoan practice.

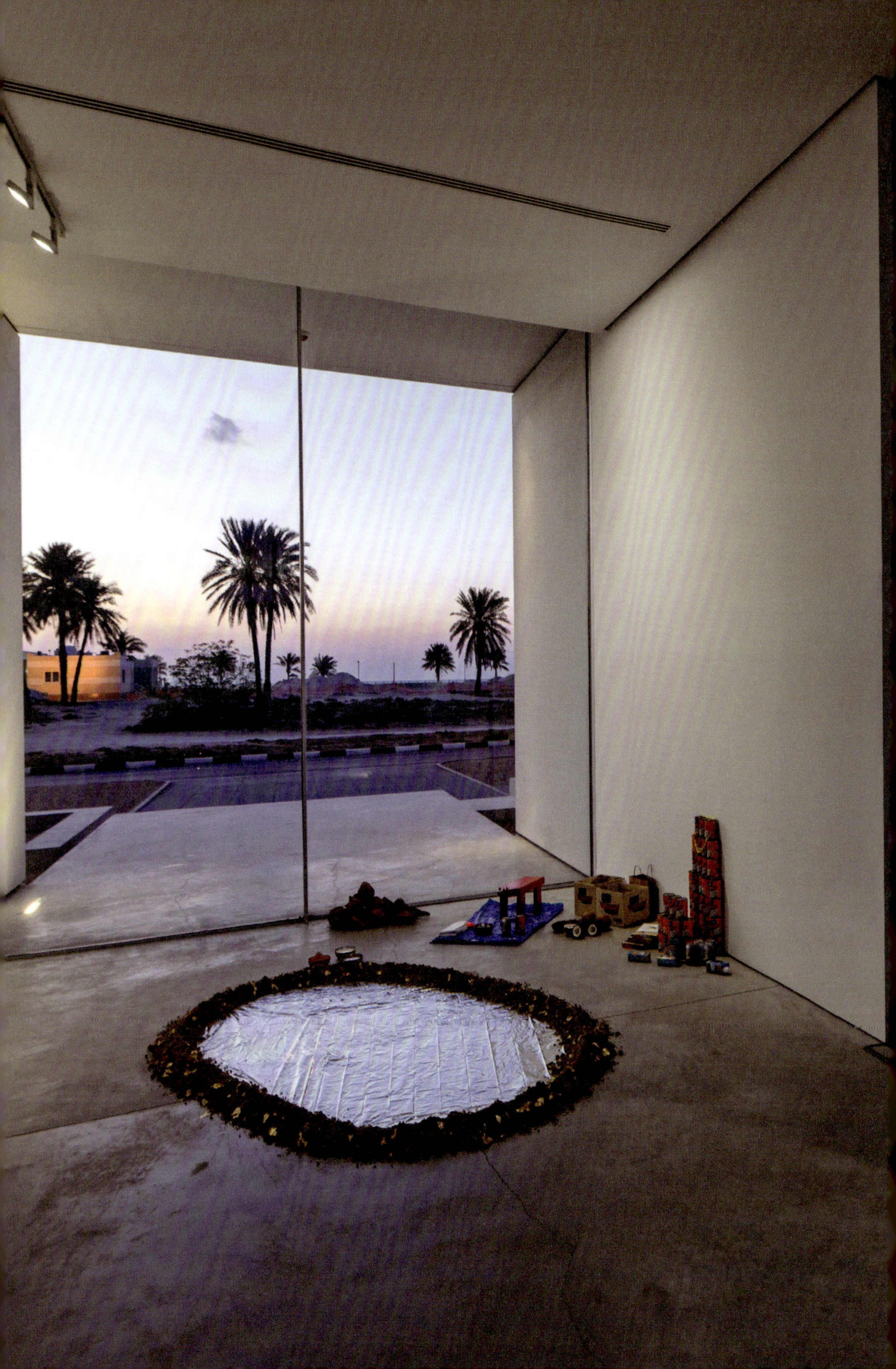

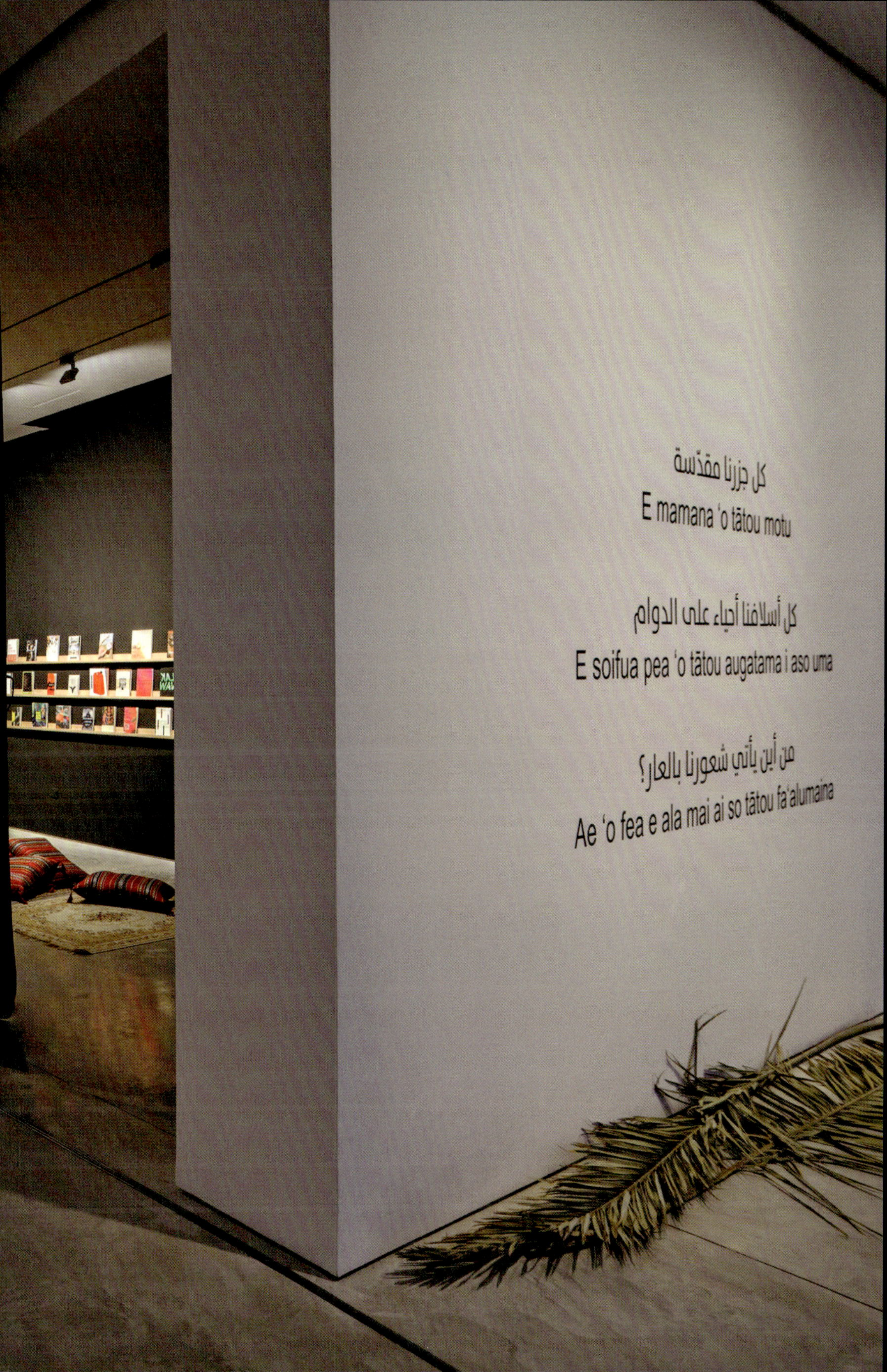

كل جزرنا مقدّسة
E mamana ʻo tātou motu
كل أسلافنا أحياء على الدوام
E soifua pea ʻo tātou augatama i aso uma
من أين يأتي شعورنا بالعار؟
Ae ʻo fea e ala mai ai so tātou faʻalumaina

Shiraz Bayjoo

Until the seventeenth century, Mauritius was an uninhabited island. Its people today can trace their roots almost exclusively to the exploits of European colonists. During French then British colonial rule, Mauritius was pivotal to the slave trade as a strategic trading port, attracting Chinese and Arab merchants, and trafficking slaves from India, East Africa and Madagascar.

The resulting differing ethnic communities of Mauritius (like so many postcolonial places) experience complex issues today in defining their place in the 'modern' world. Upon my own adult return to the country, I was taken aback by how racist I found the language – how market-stall workers, quite unapologetically, would use old, derogatory colonial terms to call out co-workers as '*matlo*' (deckhand) or '*malbar*' (nineteenth-century Hindu migrant). Indians who live on the islands surrounding the subcontinent seek a belonging through Hindu nationalism, and Muslims through the Arab World. In Mauritius, tracing one's ancestry empowers their local status, often burying the impact of colonial structures of power and its effect on their cultural identity – 'creole' or ex-slave communities are at once proud of descending from this community, whilst others remain inwardly ashamed.

The film *Île-de-France*, along with the accompanying paintings and photographs that expand this non-narrative film, focuses on objects, architecture and environments that recall historical encounters between Mauritius and its colonial past. These moving images refer to several 'ruins', from sugar plantations to the water mill of an early gunpowder factory, overrun with vines from banyan trees. Here, the tentacles of the Industrial Revolution reach out, as we start to unravel the ambitions of empire. My grandmother's fading wooden house in Port Louis, with its tropical garden, near-tamed in its pots, lies in poetic contrast to her interior world. Her creolity similarly sits 'contained' – framed, as decoration, deteriorating in domestic forgetfulness, its shadow moving across religious motifs and objects from Muslim and Indian traders who took possession of such former colonial mansions from the late nineteenth century onwards.

Shiraz Bayjoo

The moving images of 'Ile-de-France' (the French renaming of Mauritius) are eerily devoid of the human figure. Such conscious presence, however, is of undeniable imprint, as Shiraz's lens captures sound and image in poetic documentation of past and present colonial dominion. The passage of time – evidenced in the tropical overgrowth, the stylised wooden portraits of Mauritian Creole men and women, the pearl divers and their clunky metal suits that peek out of portholes, the myriad doorways whose locks are cracked and in need of oil – depicted in these images, moving or static, give presence to the repetition of History and the untamed wake it leaves behind.

The moving images of 'Ile-de-France' (the French renaming of Mauritius) are eerily devoid of the human figure. Such conscious presence, however, is of undeniable imprint, as Shiraz's lens captures sound and image in poetic documentation of past and present colonial dominion. The passage of time – evidenced in the tropical overgrowth, the stylised wooden portraits of Mauritian Creole men and women, the pearl divers and their clunky metal suits that peek out of portholes, the myriad doorways whose locks are crusted and in need of oil – depicted in these images, moving or static, gives presence to the repetition of History and the untamed wake it leaves behind.

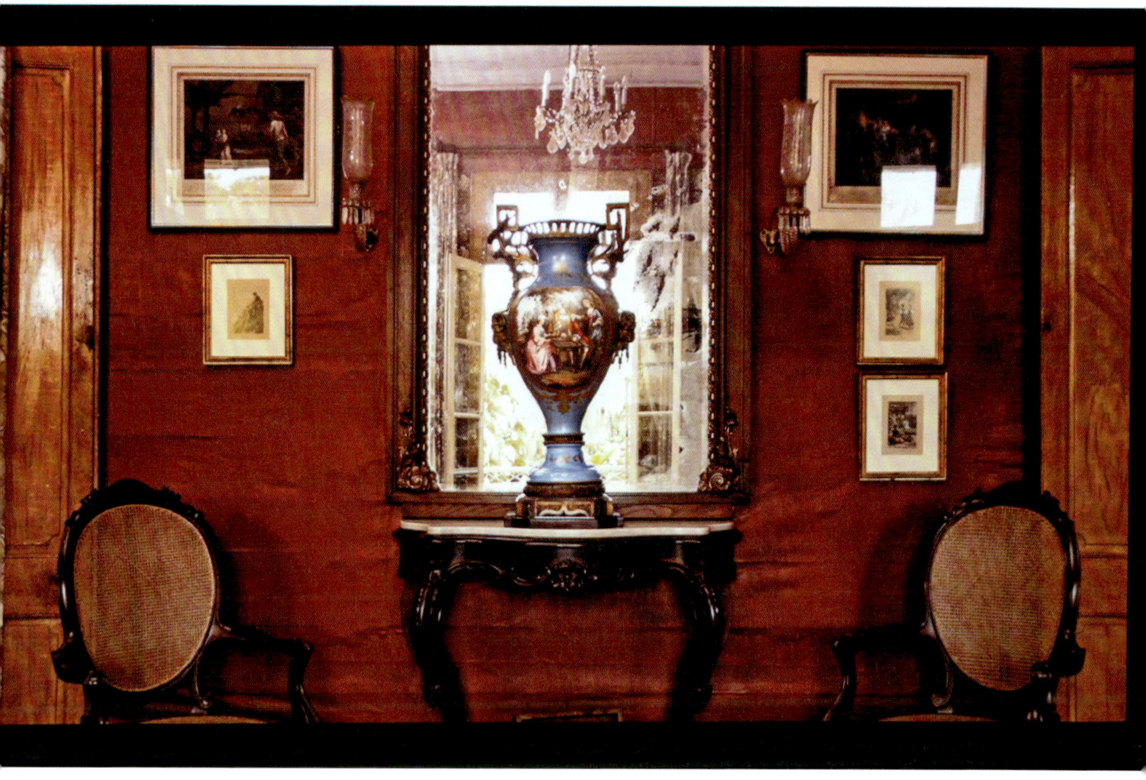

Page 224–225:
Ile de France
2015
Single-channel video:
HD Digital Super 16 mm,
colour, sound
31 minutes 18 seconds
Courtesy of the artist and
Ed Cross Fine Art, London

Page 224–225:
Various works
2012–2017
Acrylic and resin on wood,
acrylic, resin, reclaimed
furniture, HD Digital Super
16mm, stereo sound, acrylic
on board, metal, giclee
print on Hahnemühle,
acrylic and resin on board,
with reclaimed wooden
frame
Dimensions variable
Courtesy of Shiraz Bayjoo
and Ed Cross Fine Art

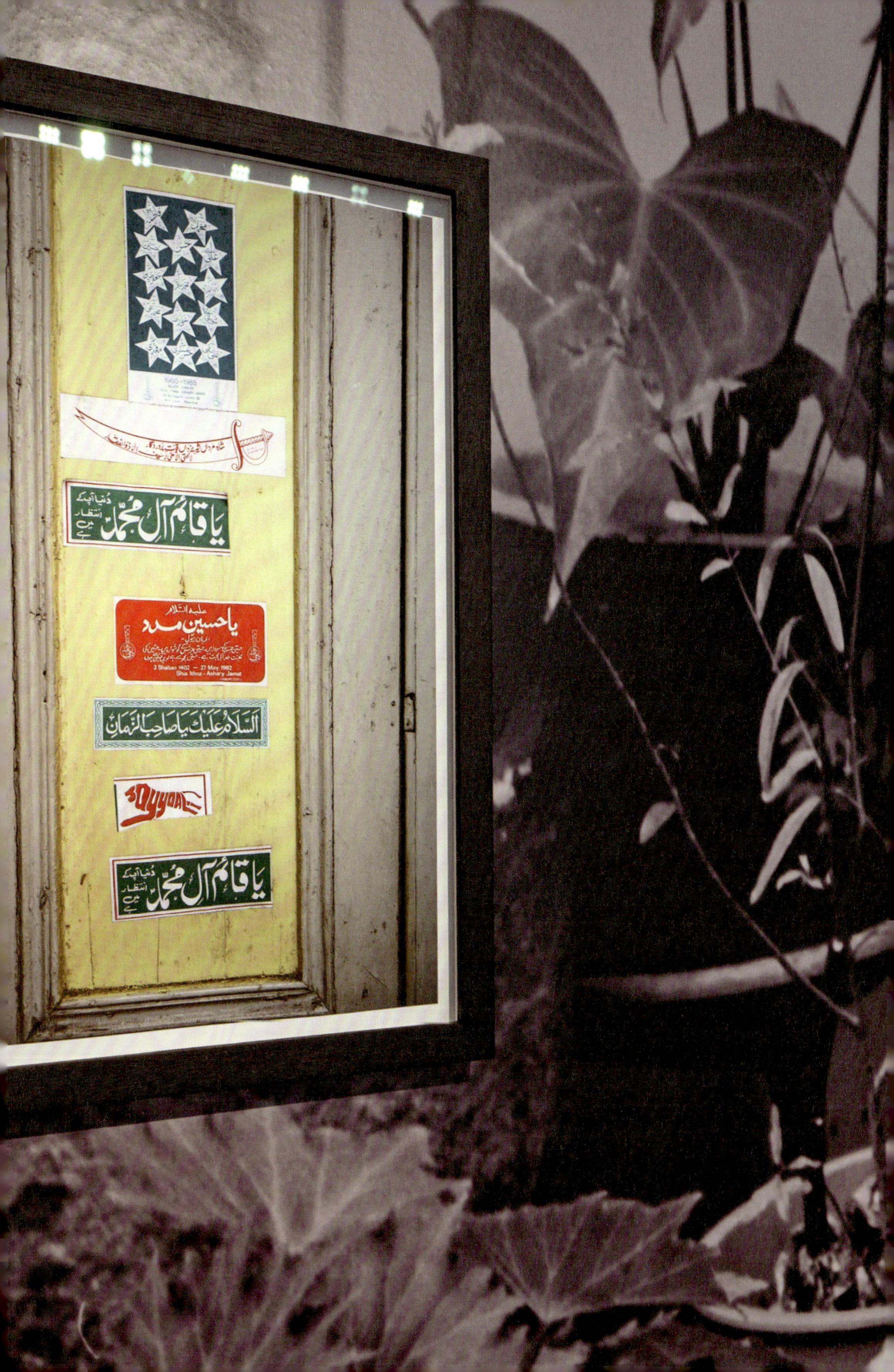
1960-1985
یا قائم آل محمد
دنیا آپ کے انتظار میں ہے
علیہ السلام
یاحسین مدد
3 Shaban 1402 — 27 May 1982
Shia Ithna - Ashary Jamat
السلام علیک یا صاحب الزمان
یا قائم آل محمد
دنیا آپ کے انتظار میں ہے

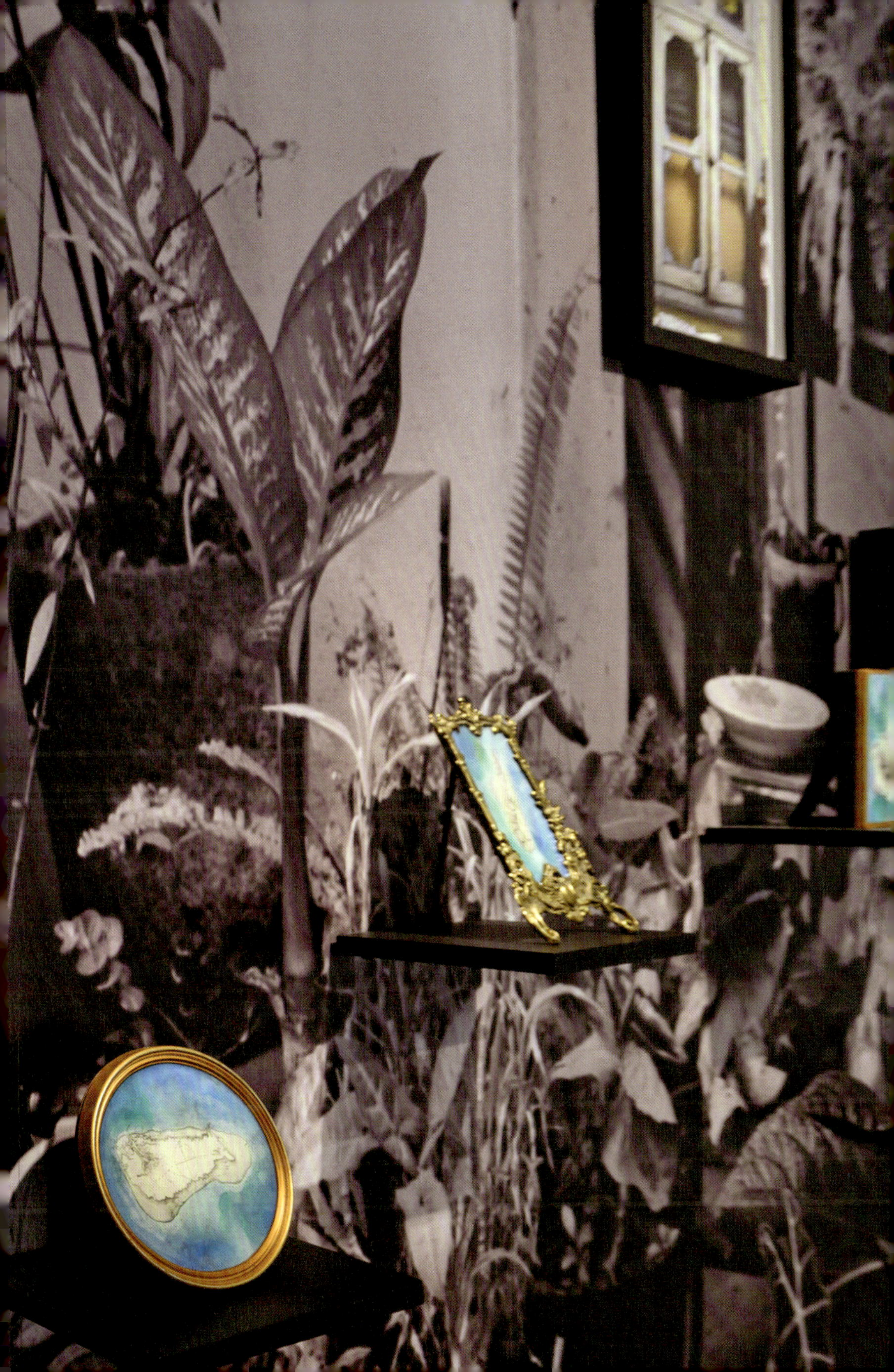

Ampannee Satoh

TUGU 1370: 1425, 2019

Ever since the reign of King Rama V (1853–1910) and his centralisation of power, many conflicts have arisen against Thai citizens with Malay ethnicity. King Rama V abolished the sultanate system in Thailand, increasing tensions between the dominant Buddhist society and the minority Muslims, with many Malay Muslims feeling discriminated against. An unmarked memorial in the former home of the Pattani kingdom in southern Thailand (where I was born) triggered my research into two particularly violent clashes between Buddhists and Malay Muslims.

In 1948, thousands of Malay Muslim Thais fled to Malaysia following the bloody 25 to 28 April confrontations in Dusun Nyor in Narathiwat province. Across the border, Malaysia was fighting for its independence from the British as well as battling the local communist insurgency. The direct cause and effect of the Dusun Nyor incident are still debated, but the series of fights that broke out between villagers, officials and insurgents ultimately led the Thai government to send three warships and one military airplane to the area. After the incident, an unmarked monument was erected (an oversized golden bullet); it is rumoured that the structure houses the bones of the Thai police who died there during the conflict.

Cycle forwards to 2004 in the same province: Prime Minister Thaksin Shinawatra's government is embroiled in a broad religious and political skirmish, with martial law initially being enforced following bomb blasts attributed to an illegal arms trade, rumoured to have been instigated by terrorist groups. The government deliberately chose the anniversary of Dusun Nyor as the date for extending martial law. Now referred as the Tak Bai incident, the clashes between the military, terrorist cells, Buddhists and Malay Muslims caused the deaths of nearly 100 people. Again, the Thai government failed to take responsibility for the actions of its military personnel during this atrocity.

The events in Dusun Nyor and Tak Bai occurred decades apart. But what is similar? I was born in Pattani and, as a Malay Muslim, am compelled to photograph the area's remaining memories; to leave an imprint; to create images as testament to these events – all in an attempt to make history matter.

Ampannee Satoh

Ampannee's film acknowledges these incidents by focusing on the tomb of twenty-eight people who died as a result of the Tak Bai conflict – a memorial built by local Muslims near the Taloh-Manoh Mosque in Narathiwat province. Here, Ampannee's eventual incantation of the Qur'an emerges with the ambient sound of nature – a prayer offered with respect and protection. It is to this latter point that we could recall another local memory of Dusun Nyor. It is said that upon final challenge by the police, the detained Malay Muslims appeared covered in coconut oil and armed with machetes, a stance rumoured to recall an ancient Malay ritual of defense. Regardless, both acts remind a militarised Buddhist ideology in Thailand that their 'truth' management could never erase their Malay roots as Islamic and Thai.

Amparnee's film acknowledges these incidents by focusing on the tomb of twenty-eight people who died as a result of the Tak Bai conflict — a memorial built by local Muslims near the Taloh-Manoh Mosque in Narathiwat province. Here, Amparnee's eventual incantation of the Qur'an emerges with the ambient sound of nature — a prayer offered with respect and protection. It is to this latter point that we could recall another local memory of Dusun Nyor. It is said that upon final challenge by the police, the detained Malay Muslims appeared covered in coconut oil and armed with machetes, a stance renowned to recall an ancient Malay ritual of defense. Regardless, both acts remind a militarised Buddhist ideology in Thailand that their 'truth' management could never erase their Malay roots as Islamic and Thai.

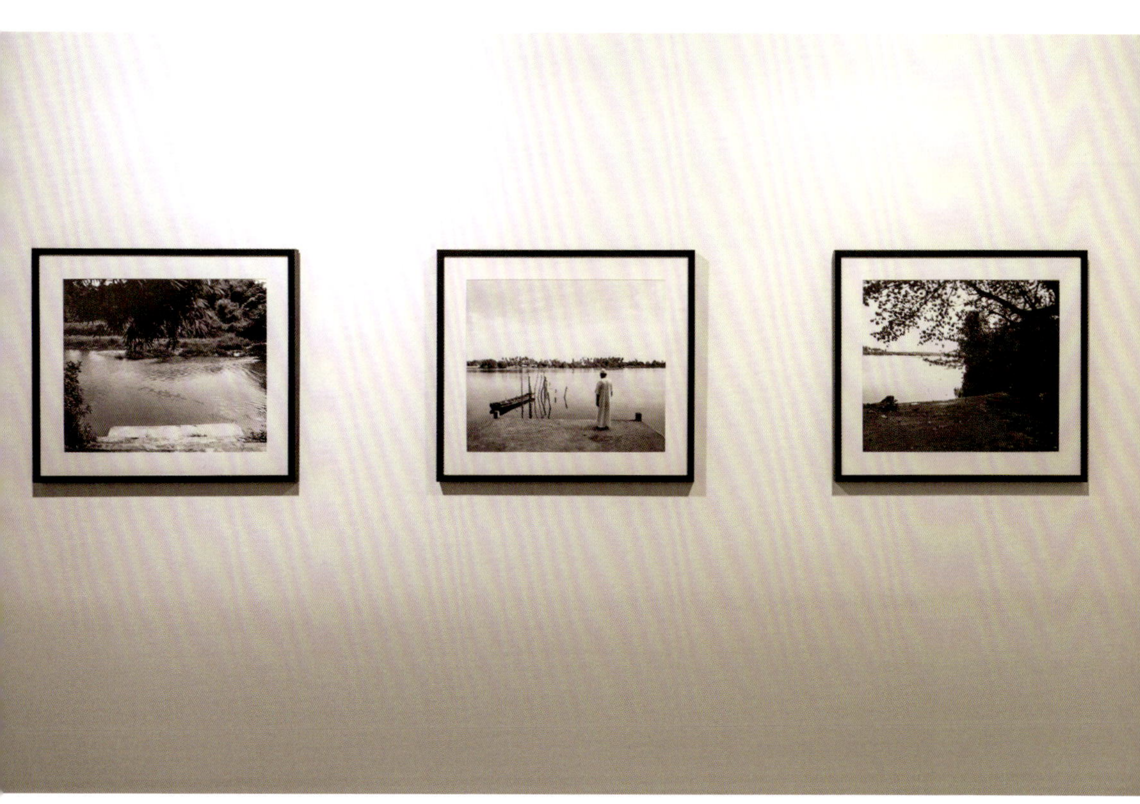

Untitled 3–5
2019
From 'TUGU 1370 : 1425'
Archival pigment ink
print on photo rag Baryta
Hahnemuhle
50.8 x 63.5 cm each
Commissioned by Sharjah
Art Foundation
Courtesy of the artist

Page 228–229:
Untitled 9
2019
From 'TUGU 1370 : 1425'
Single-channel video:
colour, sound
10 minutes
Commissioned by Sharjah
Art Foundation
Courtesy of the artist

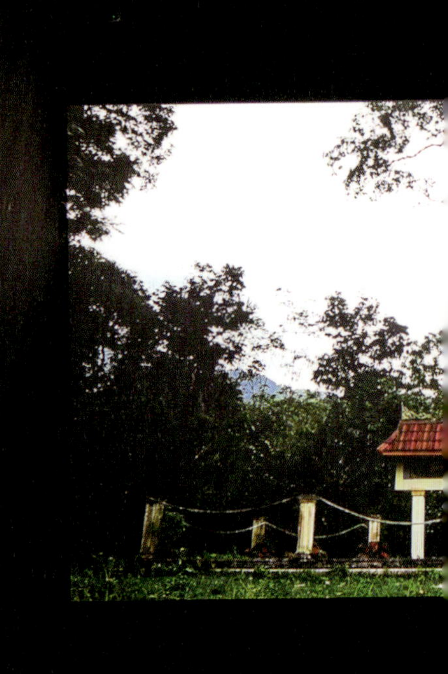

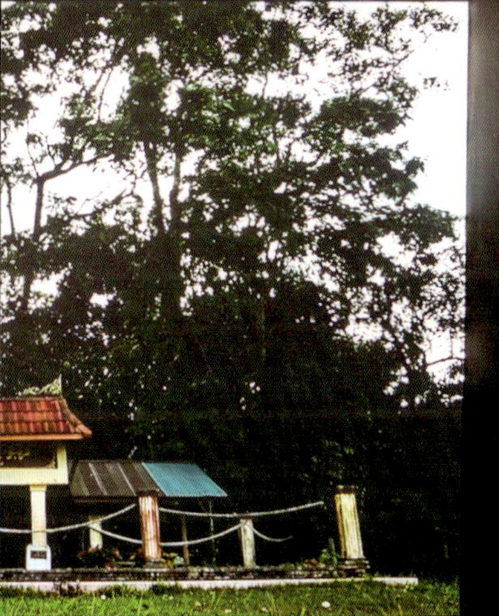

T. Shanaathanan

In the final moments of the Sri Lankan Civil War (1978–2009), thousands of people were killed in Mullivaikal, a narrow strip of land sorrowed by sea and military bombardment. Though the journeys and displacements of these individuals had been risky and painful, they had taken special care of their papers – a handful of certificates, deeds and other documents – believing that they would provide safety, security and a better future.

In our everyday lives, documents play a crucial role in forming one's location between place, self and other. They prove one's identity, ownership or relationships, thus becoming points of mediation, negotiation, resistance and agency. During the Sri Lankan Civil War, people were ruled by the terror of the government, militants, and local and foreign armed forces. In the context of bullets, bombs, barbed wire, economic embargoes, mass displacements, violence, riots, air raids and murder, many kinds of 'documents' were generated – at times, fictitiously so – or gained importance: travel permits, ration cards, various identity cards, police registration certificates, birth certificates, death certificates, certificates for the missing, land deeds, educational certificates, visas, photographs and so on. While certain documents became a sign of life in war zones linked to compensations, rations, migrations and identification, others, such as land deeds and loan contracts, faded in importance.

Drawers of war transactions attempts to map numerous kinds of documents, produced by state and non-state actors (e.g., the Liberation Tigers of Tamil Eelam, or LTTE) who negotiated histories of individuals on a daily basis. This collection of nearly eighty documents and the memories of their owners – in the form of testimonies and drawings – are exhibited in wooden cabinets. The cabinet, as a physical form and conceptual image, connects the colonial cabinet of curiosities that led to the development of museums and archives. By employing this particular method of collection and display, the work attempts to play with memory and indexing in relation to the everyday life of a war zone.

Check point I - VIII
2009/2019
From 'Check point'
Mixed media on paper
75 x 56 cm each
Courtesy of the artist

Prior to the arrival of the British in Ceylon (now Sri Lanka), the majority Sinhalese and minority Tamil communities coexisted with mutual respect. British colonial governance of divide and control, however, slowly mired these two communities in conflict. In 1956, with the passing of the controversial Sinhala Only Act, which declared English the national language, Tamil-speaking minorities became discriminated against; many lost employment, becoming deported, and subsequently, stateless. The Sri Lankan Civil War (one of the longest in modern South Asia) was a direct consequence of this act, with the LTTE seeking an independent Tamil state in the north and east of the island. This civil war ~~was~~ also had an undeniable religious dimension. The Sangha (Sinhala Buddhist monks) were not only against the sharing of power, but also opposed to key advocates of a military solution to the crisis. <u>This paradoxical influence is mirrored today in Myanmar, Cambodia and Thailand</u>, where Buddhist now defend the instrumentalisation of violence against Hindus and Muslims alike.

See the work of Ampannee Satoh on pg. 226 to read a Thai experience of this same reality

Prior to the arrival of the British in Ceylon (now Sri Lanka), the majority Sinhalese and minority Tamil communities coexisted with mutual respect. British colonial governance of divide and control, however, slowly mired these two communities in conflict. In 1956, with the passing of the controversial Sinhala Only Act, which declared English the national language, Tamil-speaking minorities became discriminated against; many lost employment, becoming deported, and subsequently, stateless. The Sri Lankan Civil War (one of the longest in modern South Asia) was a direct consequence of this act, with the LTTE seeking an independent Tamil state in the north and east of the island. This civil war ~~was~~ also had an undeniable religious dimension. The Sangha (Sinhala Buddhist monks) were not only against the sharing of power, but also opposed to key advocates of a military solution to the crisis. This paradoxical influence is mirrored today in Myanmar, Cambodia and Thailand, where Buddhist monks defend the instrumentalisation of violence against Hindus and Muslims alike.

See the work of Amporrnee Satoh on pg. 220 to read a Thai experience of this same reality

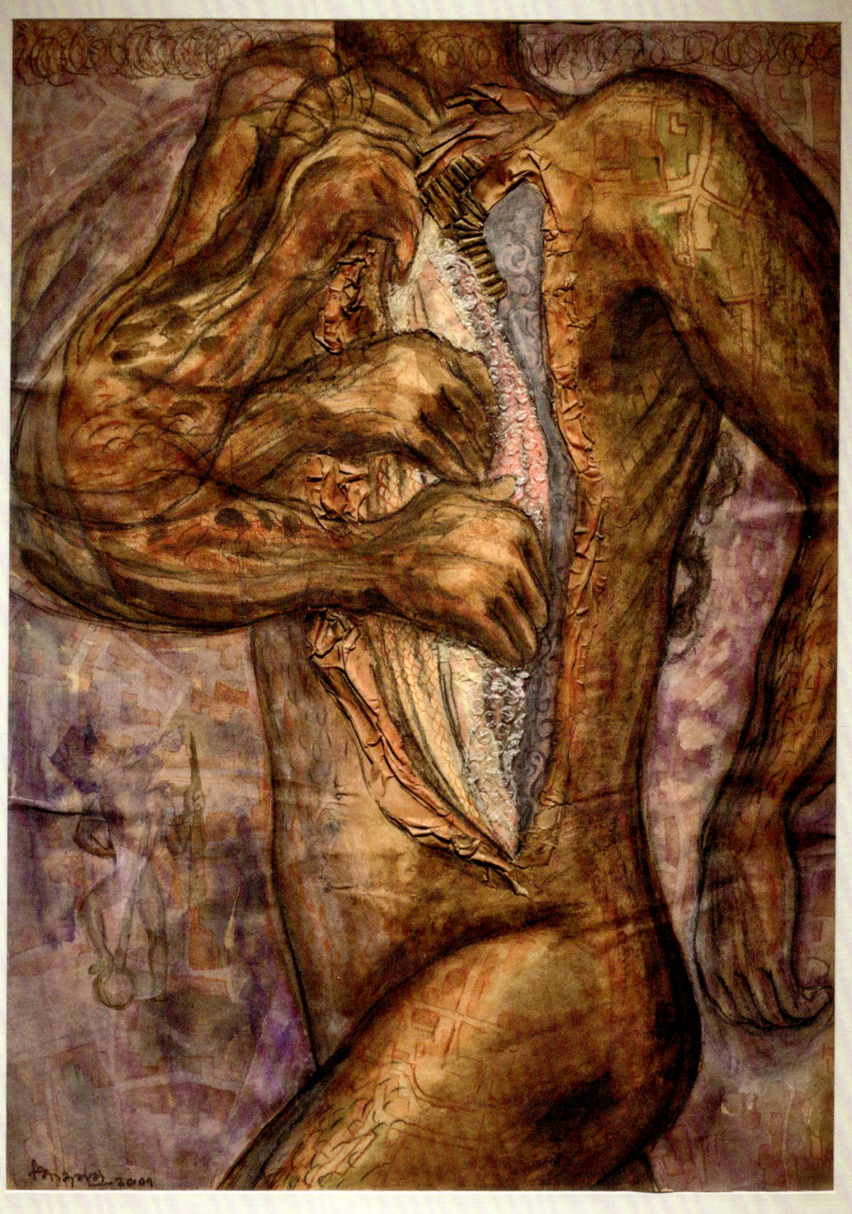

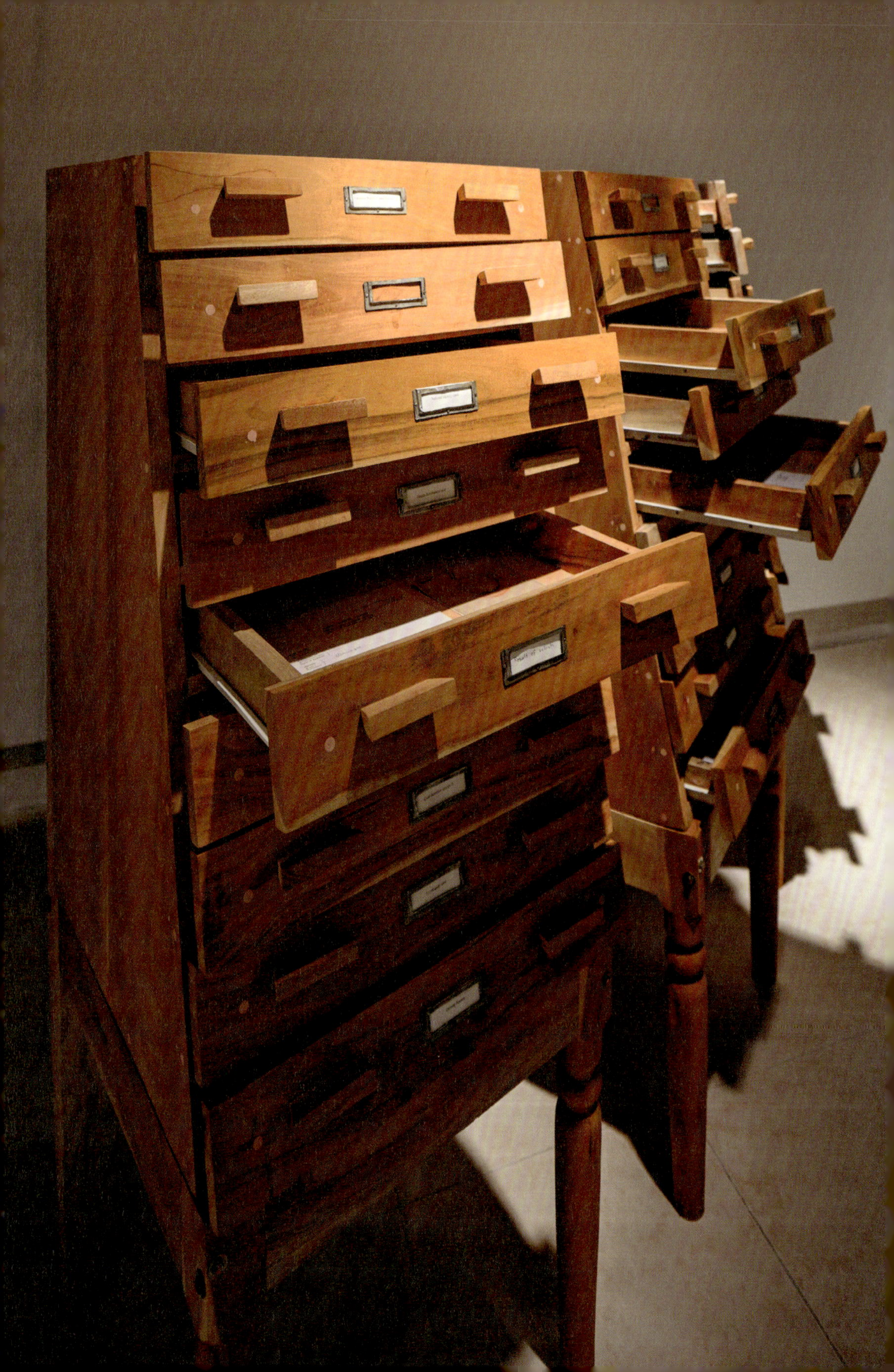

Nine paintings (*Check Point*) produced during the Sri Lankan Civil War depict the human body at checkpoints, a reference to the triangulation of document, site and body in generating/imposing/resisting dominant modes of power. Hence, such documents need performance and embodiment to be alive. These paintings also speak of how, in such zones of violence, the human body is used as a 'document', a transaction of power and control.

T. Shanaathanan

Drawers of War Transactions
2019
8 wooden chest of drawers, archival materials
150 x 60 x 56 cm each
Commissioned by Sharjah Art Foundation
Courtesy of the artist

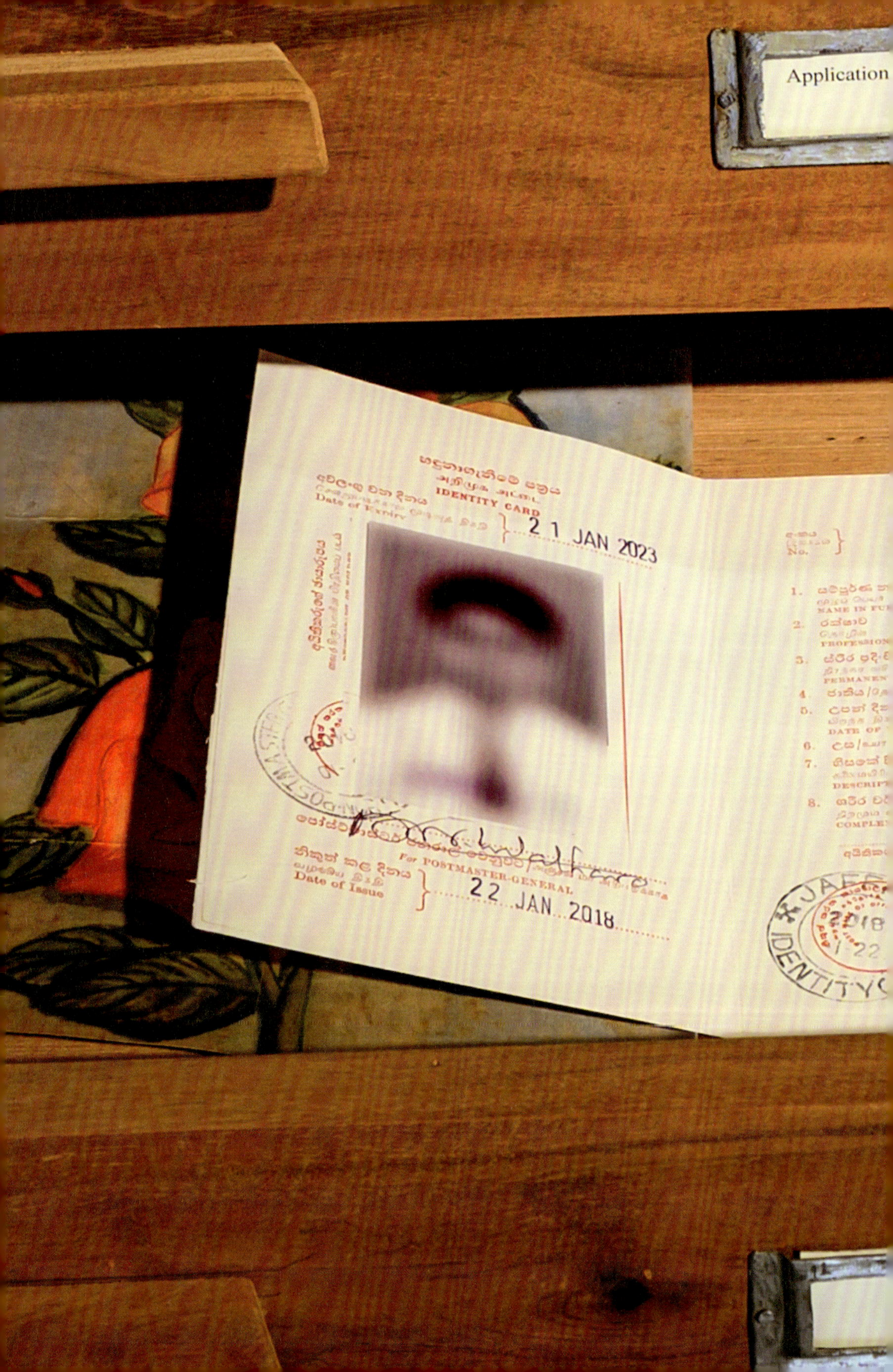
IDENTITY CARD
Date of Expiry
21 JAN 2023
No.
For POSTMASTER-GENERAL
Date of Issue
22 JAN 2018

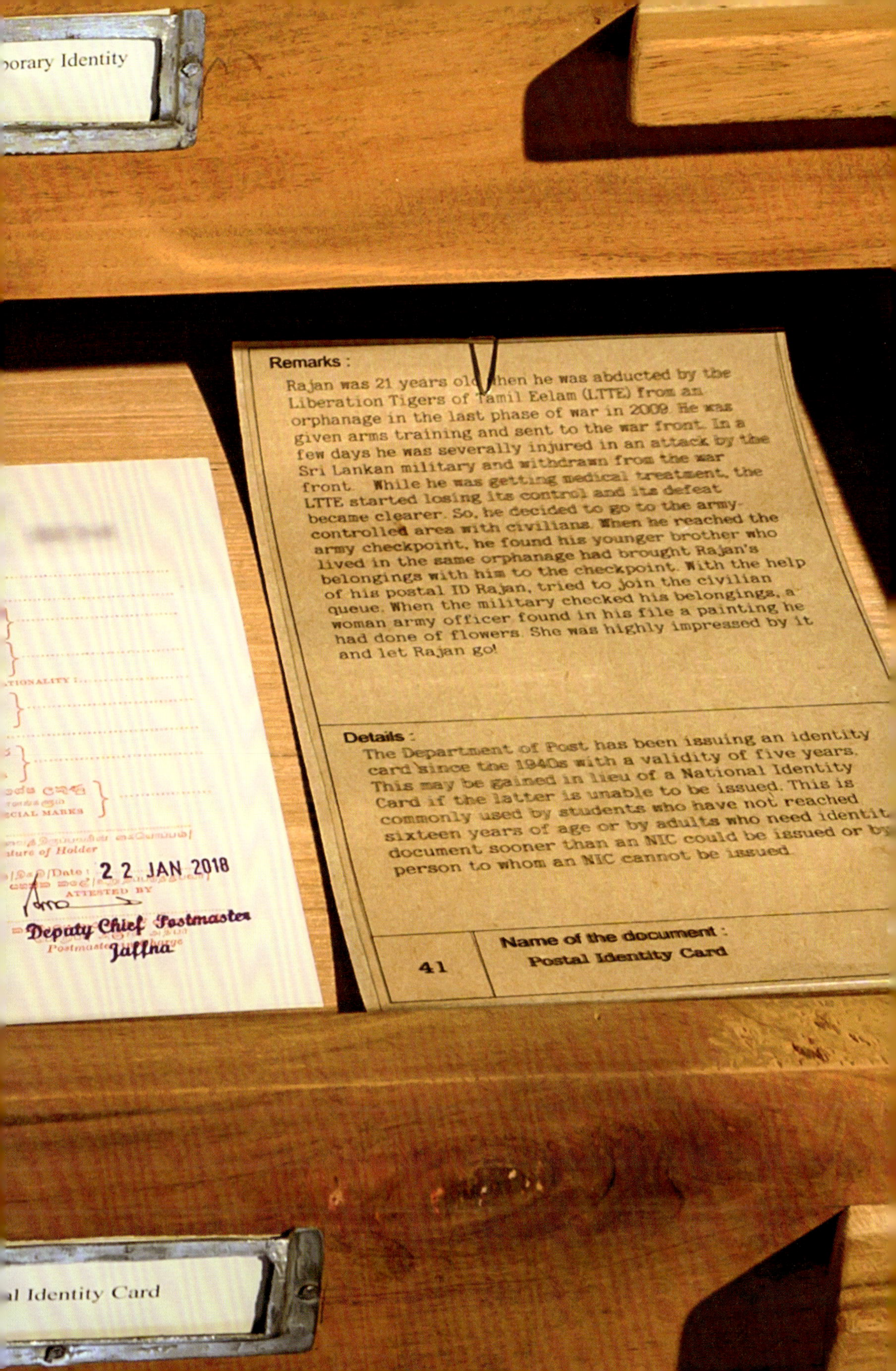

Remarks :

Rajan was 21 years old when he was abducted by the Liberation Tigers of Tamil Eelam (LTTE) from an orphanage in the last phase of war in 2009. He was given arms training and sent to the war front. In a few days he was severally injured in an attack by the Sri Lankan military and withdrawn from the war front. While he was getting medical treatment, the LTTE started losing its control and its defeat became clearer. So, he decided to go to the army-controlled area with civilians. When he reached the army checkpoint, he found his younger brother who lived in the same orphanage had brought Rajan's belongings with him to the checkpoint. With the help of his postal ID Rajan, tried to join the civilian queue. When the military checked his belongings, a woman army officer found in his file a painting he had done of flowers. She was highly impressed by it and let Rajan go!

Details :

The Department of Post has been issuing an identity card since the 1940s with a validity of five years. This may be gained in lieu of a National Identity Card if the latter is unable to be issued. This is commonly used by students who have not reached sixteen years of age or by adults who need identit[y] document sooner than an NIC could be issued or by person to whom an NIC cannot be issued.

41	**Name of the document :** Postal Identity Card

Identity Card

On a night when the lapwing
failed to call,
without electricity,
when all was invisible,
officers entered the village.

People gathered for prayer
along lines drawn,
as told by them,
expecting, at least now,
an answer for
their thousand years' petition.

People with nothing...

Sheets of rain fell and then ceased.
Somewhere,
sacks filled with shells and limpets
spill, scattering on the cement floor.

Everything finished in a
frivolous moment.

Holding pens that do not
miss their target and
and files with ink emptied,
the officers left in a haste.
Row after row,
upon the people who fell half-dead,
the identity card rests,
soaked in blood.

N. Athma
Aug 3, 2017

Translated from Tamil by Geetha Sukumaran

Shubigi Rao

Articulating the Archive: An Imprecise Index

The archive is accretion. Like the ever-expanding online universe, activated archives of physical materials are exponential. Under a briskly expanding accumulation of materials, both textual and digital, the urgent indexing of points and counterpoints, connotations and ramifications, beg to be cross-referenced and connected, where bookmarked sites are pages on our devices with a mountain of PDFs stagnating in unopened folders. Meanwhile, cartons of collected but uncatalogued newspaper clippings, articles and other textual materials gather guilt-laden dust. We think that digitising would solve this, but most scanning machines require flat, unbound pages, and so libraries have 'disbinded' books in order to preserve them. Libraries constantly shed 'obsolete' books, especially out-of-date encyclopedias. Digitising makes supreme the information that such materials hold, separate from the print on a page, and is thus impervious to the beauty of damage and decay. So, **the archive is also attrition**.

The archive is compressed. Disappearing content isn't limited to either the theft and appropriation of physical books and artefacts, or their decay and destruction. E-book licences are often short-lived, and disappear from libraries once they expire. Imagine the artwork vanishing from a book, because its licence was shorter than that of the text. Proprietary software, obsolete hardware (and software), redundant file formats and unreadable storage drives are more than the problems of obsolescence in technology. There is no agreement in file-sharing, licencing, archiving, sale and usage. Centralised repositories for online content and digital media exist, but are vulnerable to attack and loss, in much the same way as libraries have made easy targets throughout history. We are drowning in the digital deluge of images: every day, 3.2 billion more are taken. Our digital archives are like our brains – both greedy hoarders, but ultimately wasteful, disordered and unread. Our files fail, as do our memories. The velocity of obsolescence means that the technology that preserves and converts the archive may be what ultimately renders it unreadable.

The archive is archaeology. Our planet is the largest terrestrial archive, its indexical geological strata a natural record of chronological time, evolution and epoch, ecological trauma and radioactive fallout. The detritus of our civilisations, our waste, make new veins of plastics, aluminium cans and styrofoam. These are our artefacts, our future archaeologies. Our books rot, our words vanish, our girders twist and concrete crumbles, but our waste will be our legacy.

The archive is bated, like the Global Seed Vault; life in stasis, waiting for the apocalypse to blossom. Every archive is hushed, holds its breath. So do we, when we enter the archive, lose ourselves in its depths, revelling in being swept away by currents unknown, losing time, a delightful submergence.

The archive is fractured, perpetually partitioned; micro-fissures running along all the fault lines of human conceit and delusion. Always ideologically driven and abbreviated, the archive is easily co-opted for nationalist narratives and self-aggrandising imperialisms. Collections plundered from former colonies, still jealously guarded, rarely returned. Stripped of original context, artefacts are subject to an imposed taxonomy that erases original biomes and interrelational existences. Acts of naming expunge primary ownership, thus hiding the violence of the theft from their homes.

The archive is gravesite, a place of stillness, but charged with the corporeal, the immortal, the vanishing. Marcel Proust thought of the book as a vast cemetery, where for the most part, one can no longer read the faded names on the tombstones. So, too, the library mimics these headstones, keeping close their confidence. Steeped in human yearning to comprehend the unknowable, both sites are where the living commune with the dead, believing that they hold secrets we cannot know. Secrets to which we shall be privy, we hope, through frequent visitation of the archive, and eventual visitation of the grave.

The archive is reductive, like the racialist ethnographic and anthropologic device employed when speculating about the unfamiliar and the unknown. It is the forcible stratification of disorder and divergence to a solitary specific as representation of the native, the observed, the other. It is singular, too, in its stubborn peculiarity, in how no single archive is like another. It shares this conceit with every human ego, and so, it compensates (as we do) by striving for impossible individualism: whereas the unifying vision becomes the singular, filled with sullen promise, perhaps the archive is also the id.

The archive is inarticulate. Whose words tell our stories? The imbalance of gender, class, ethnicity and nationality (and all those hidden as displaced, stateless, incarcerated) is still acute. Archives and public libraries reflect that lack of parity: whereas to read the stories of the displaced, marginalised or indigenous, we have to default to reading 'primary source' texts written about them, often by colonisers. We must add to the archive, populate it with forms, genres and literary experiments that draw on our dissimilarities as much as they do on our shared legacies of trauma. But can oral histories create alternate archives? What epistemologies can be used without contamination? And is it possible, or even desirable, to build them in isolation? Perhaps it is in the vanished archive that we can apprehend the massive problem of articulating the silent – those ground under the wheel of cyclic history, where each spoke renders them mute.

J o u r n e y B e y o n d t h

e A r r o w J o u r n e y B e

y o n d t h e A r r o w J o u

r n e y B e y o n d t h e A r

r o w J o u r n e y B e y o n

d t h e A r r o w J o u r n e

y B e y o n d t h e A r r o w

J o u r n e y B e y o n d t h

e A r r o w J o u r n e y B e

y o n d t h e A r r o w J o u

r n e y B e y o n d t h e A r

r o w J o u r n e y B e y o n

d t h e A r r o w J o u r n e

y B e y o n d t h e A r r o w

J o u r n e y B e y o n d t h

For SB14, a toolkit is conceived as a set of artistic propositions that instructs an alternate methodology in the determination of Art. It critically engages the nature of 'intent' as a set of socially engaged motivations that have collective value and meaning. This conceiving is in homage to the agency of artists in their transmission of cultural knowledge – as provocative educators, cultural infrastructure builders, writers and archivists – as a critical element of their overall artistic practice. Such 'culture as resistance' is the creation of differing methods and processes for the collaborative and interdependent generation of historical consciousnesses, each contextually specific to their time and locale.

For SB14, a toolkit is conceived as a set of artistic propositions that instructs an alternate methodology in the determination of Art. It critically engages the nature of 'intent' as a set of socially engaged motivations that have collective value and meaning. This conceiving is in homage to the agency of artists in their transmission of cultural knowledge – as provocative educators, cultural infrastructure builders, writers and archivists – as a critical element of their overall artistic practice. Such 'culture as resistance' is the creation of differing methods and processes for the collaborative and interdependent generation of historical consciousnesses, each contextually specific to their time and locale.

e A r r o w J o u r n e y B e
y o n d t h e A r r o w J o u
r n e y B e y o n d t h e A r
r o w T o o l k i t s J o u r
n e y B e y o n d t h e A r r
o w J o u r n e y B e y o n d
t h e A r r o w J o u r n e y
B e y o n d t h e A r r o w J
o u r n e y B e y o n d t h e
A r r o w J o u r n e y B e y
o n d t h e A r r o w J o u r
n e y B e y o n d t h e A r r
o w J o u r n e y B e y o n d
t h e A r r o w J o u r n e y
J o u r n e y B e y o n d t h

31st Century Museum of Contemporary Spirit in Sharjah

Perception itself is action, 2019

We cannot exist beyond the realm of experience and time,
For we are nothing but their results,
We can merely perpetually observe things 'as they are',
Without judging whether they are good or evil, fair or unfair, right or wrong,
Until we attain a perfect understanding of the mind;
Only then can intention naturally manifest itself,
Into the intention that is free from any self-centred intention,
The realisation of that intention, itself, is also action

Today's world is replete with advanced knowledge, thanks to an extraordinary enhancement of humankind's technological abilities, which are often measured using the intelligence quotient (IQ). Unfortunately, material progress brings with it a loss of effective connections between people, as we only care about matters that concern personal interests. This results in low emotional quotient (EQ), which signifies the growing lack of empathy across our world today. In fact, an ideal society would be one that comprises both material development and inner peace. Still, the IQ and the EQ cannot fully exist without spiritual intelligence, or, as I like to refer to it, the 'love quotient (LQ)', which requires a true understanding of loving-kindness – our true nature, a virtue within all of us (though we might have forgotten it). Therefore, the question we need to address is: *Could it be that simply being aware of its presence is already an action taken?*

Perception Itself Is Action
2019
Photo of participants in workshop.
Commissioned by Sharjah Art Foundation

This project (workshop and ensuing exhibition) invites viewers to participate in creating a society in which one's LQ is acknowledged and treasured under the idea that we are each not just a part of society, but rather comprise the whole. ***Thus, we all share ownership of this project because the 31st Century Museum is, in fact, our collective body or life, our spiritual intelligence, our art.*** This collective ownership

I visited the 31st Century Museum of Contemporary Spirit in Chiang Mai, Thailand in 2016, and was moved by the text emblazoned on its external wall, 'Our Body, Our Museum.' The idea that a museum was something I carried with me every day was a kind of gift, as well as a responsibility, for I realised that it placed the onus on me – for how I perceive and categorise the world. Inside were the 'anecdotes' that Kamin had collected over the years; objects attached to stories of human empathy. A work by a man at a market, who painted in exchange for something 'useful' (not money); a sculpture of a woman who secretly cared for the well-being of a house rat; a photograph of two girls, holding up a sign to strangers in Chicago, reading, 'Have a good night!' These encounters touched Kamin as a form of 'spiritual intelligence', an art (an action) that reflected generosity and compassion, qualities of human production worth cultivating.

Check out the other toolkit of Gudskul on pg. 248

I visited the 21st Century Museum of Contemporary Spirit in Chiang Mai, Thailand in 2016, and was moved by the text emblazoned on its external wall, 'Our Body, Our Museum.' The idea that a museum was something I carried with me every day was a kind of gift, as well as a responsibility, for I realised that it placed the onus on me – for how I perceive and categorise the world. Inside were the 'anecdotes' that Kamin had collected over the years; objects attached to stories of human empathy. A work by a man at a market, who painted in exchange for something 'useful' (not money); a sculpture of a woman who sincerely cared for the well-being of a house rat; a photograph of two girls, holding up a sign to strangers in Chicago, reading, 'Have a good night!' These encounters touched Kamin as a form of 'spiritual intelligence', an art (an action) that reflected generosity and compassion, qualities of human production worth cultivating.

Check out the other tool kit of understand on pg. 248

can be achieved by sharing stories of everyday life as we come into contact with loving-kindness, through either first-hand experience with, or second-hand knowledge of, events. These anecdotes do not have to be grand stories, so long as they convey meaning and inspiration. In order to help the LQ take tangible form through the shared learning process, for SB14, the narratives of the participants, along with their visual accompaniments, is compiled in an e-book as a keepsake.

Kamin Lertchaiprasert

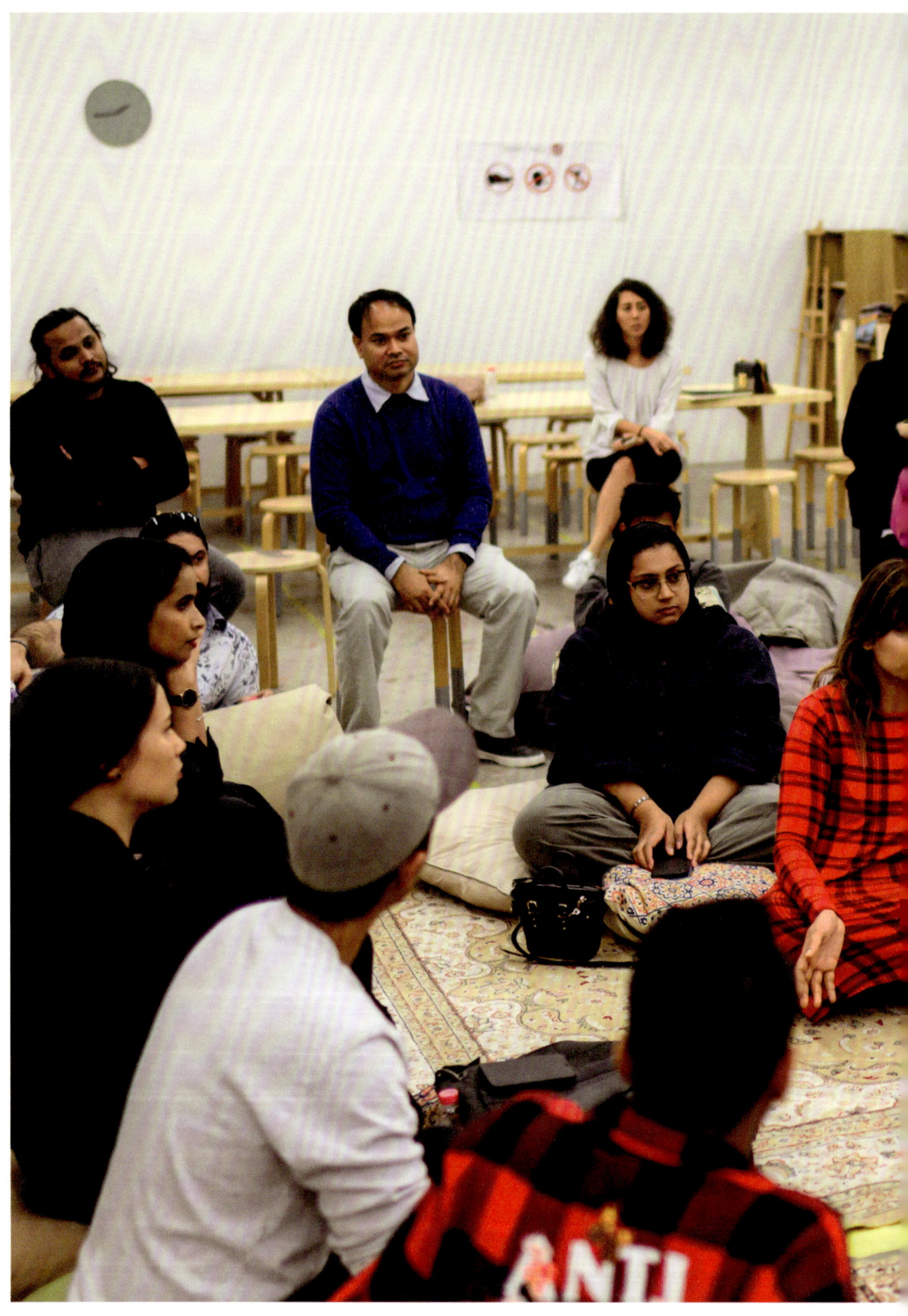
ANTI

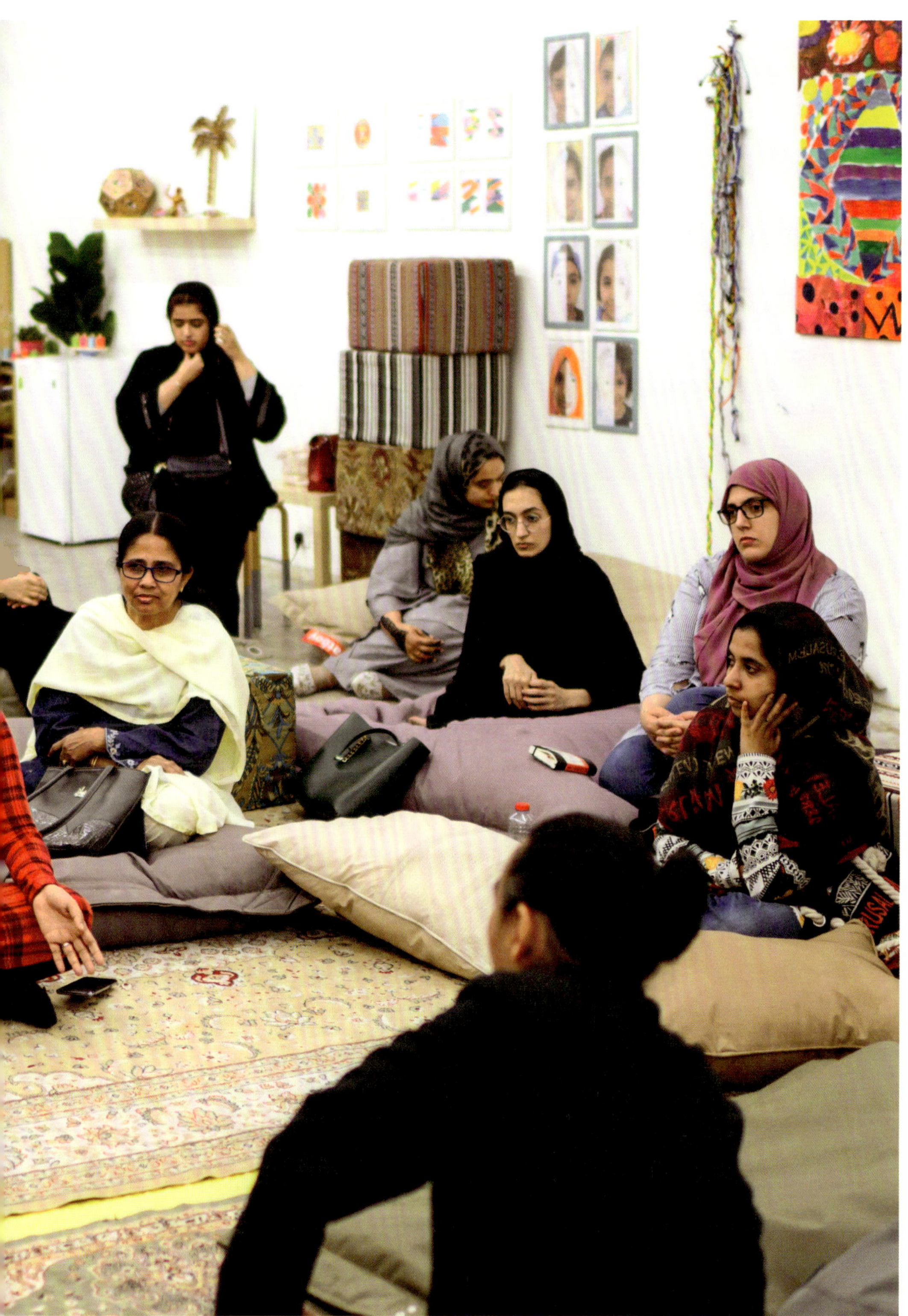

Gudskul

Speculative Collective, 2019

> *We can know more than we can tell.*
> —Michael Polanyi, *The Tacit Dimension* (1966)

Speculative Collective is the latest iteration of a knowledge-sharing and mapping module developed by Gudskul. It could be considered a collectivising tool, derived from what Gudskul is doing continuously in the context where we are based, in Jakarta, Indonesia. At the same time, the module's arrangement is extremely compressed, both spatially and temporally, in Sharjah.

In Sharjah, through a loosely defined process, strangers meet and share what they consider to be 'knowledge' by sequentially playing the role of both teacher and student, in a quick to and fro. The twist comes straight afterwards, when a newly formed pair couples with another pair, and is thus forced to form a temporary collective. Gudskul therefore designed a tool, through which participants could easily record this very process by themselves. Over time, these recordings on paper were then used to complete Gudskul's visual presentation for SB14. These recordings have also been collected in a small publication, which will be available before the closing of the biennial.

This 'forced collectivisation' tool originates from Gudskul's position of curiosity regarding the notion of the collective as a form of know-how, in which tacit knowing becomes clear and transferable through direct practice. Gudskul was founded by the artist collectives Grafis Huru Hara, Serrum and ruangrupa, to promote what they dub 'B-knowledge' – as in a B-movie or the B-side of a vinyl record. The aim is to decentralise assumptions of knowledge production as held and dictated by academic disciplines, catalogued by institutions and, thus, codified and cited within particular parameters. Different things ring differently under differing contexts and when held by various actors in society, not necessarily only in the hands of those who are assumed to be 'trained' and 'knowledgeable'.

Gudskul

Collective artistic action in Indonesia has been of critical fascination to much of Southeast Asia's contemporary art scene since the 1990s, with ruangrupa pioneering an interdisciplinary relationship between art education and its social meaning, and historical relevance. I have fond memories of visiting the collective's 'home'; smoke-filled lounge rooms alive with conversation, where questions were aired and literally answered from far-flung corners of the room; ethnomusicologists, anthropologists, linguists and more, sitting in their own worlds, within the nurturing, mentoring vibe of what has, today, grown to encompass GUDSKUL.

Collective artistic action in Indonesia has been of critical fascination to much of Southeast Asia's contemporary art scene since the 1990s, with ruangrupa pioneering an interdisciplinary relationship between art education and its social meaning, and historical relevance. I have fond memories of visiting the collective's 'home'; smoke-filled lounge rooms alive with conversation, where questions were aired and literally answered from far-flung corners of the room; ethnomusicologists, anthropologists, linguists and more, sitting in their own worlds, within the nurturing, mentoring vibe of what has, today, grown to encompass GUDSKUL.

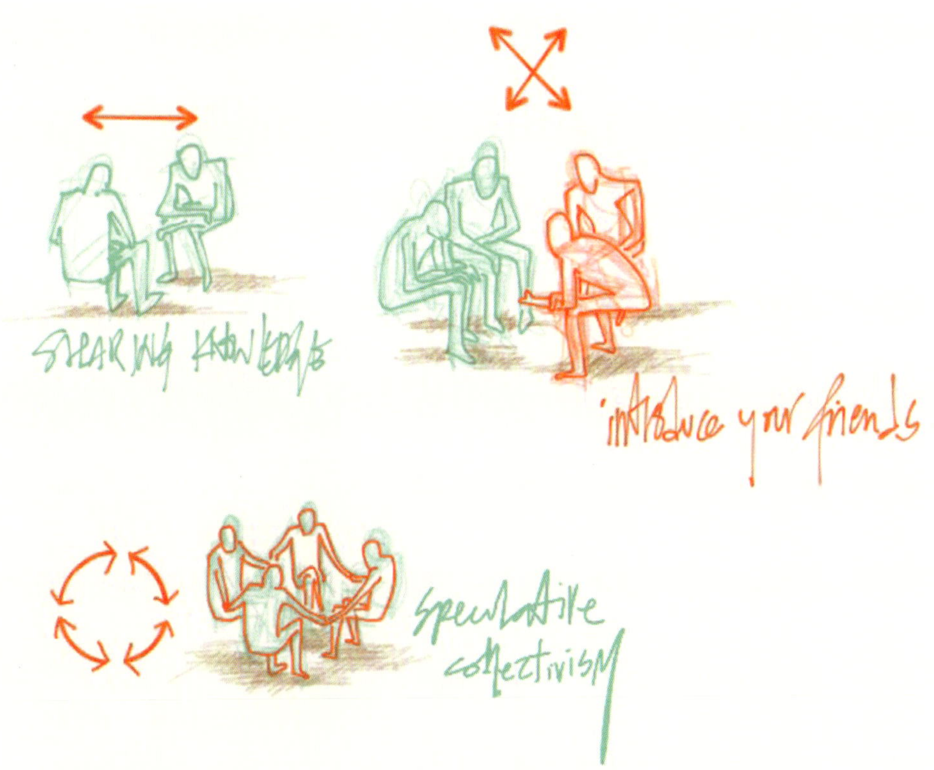

Knowledge Market: Speculative Collective
2019
Participatory activity drawings, mural, stickers, carpets
Dimensions variable
Commissioned by Sharjah Art Foundation
Courtesy of Gudskul

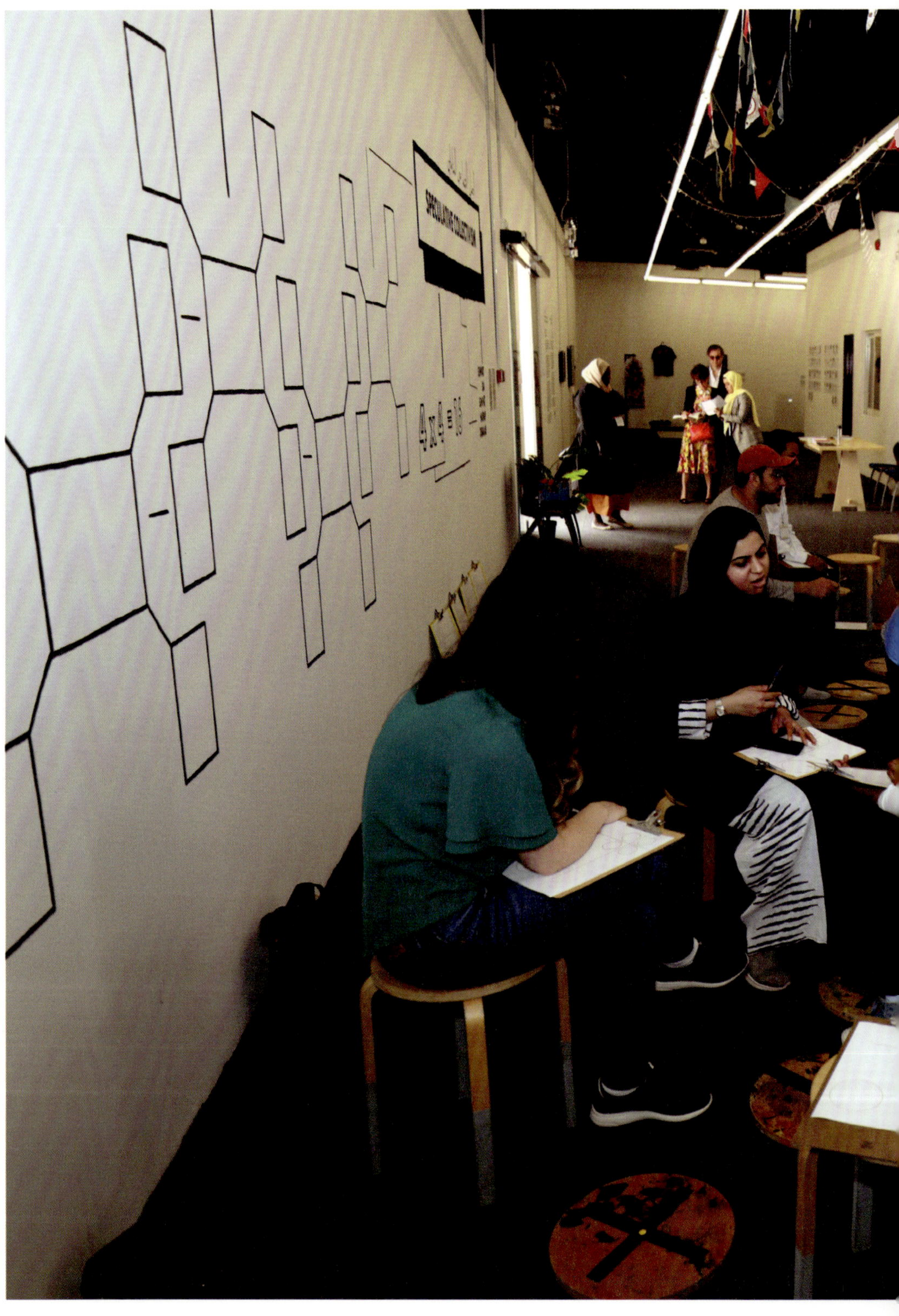
SPECULATIVE COLLECTIVISM
4 x 4 = 16

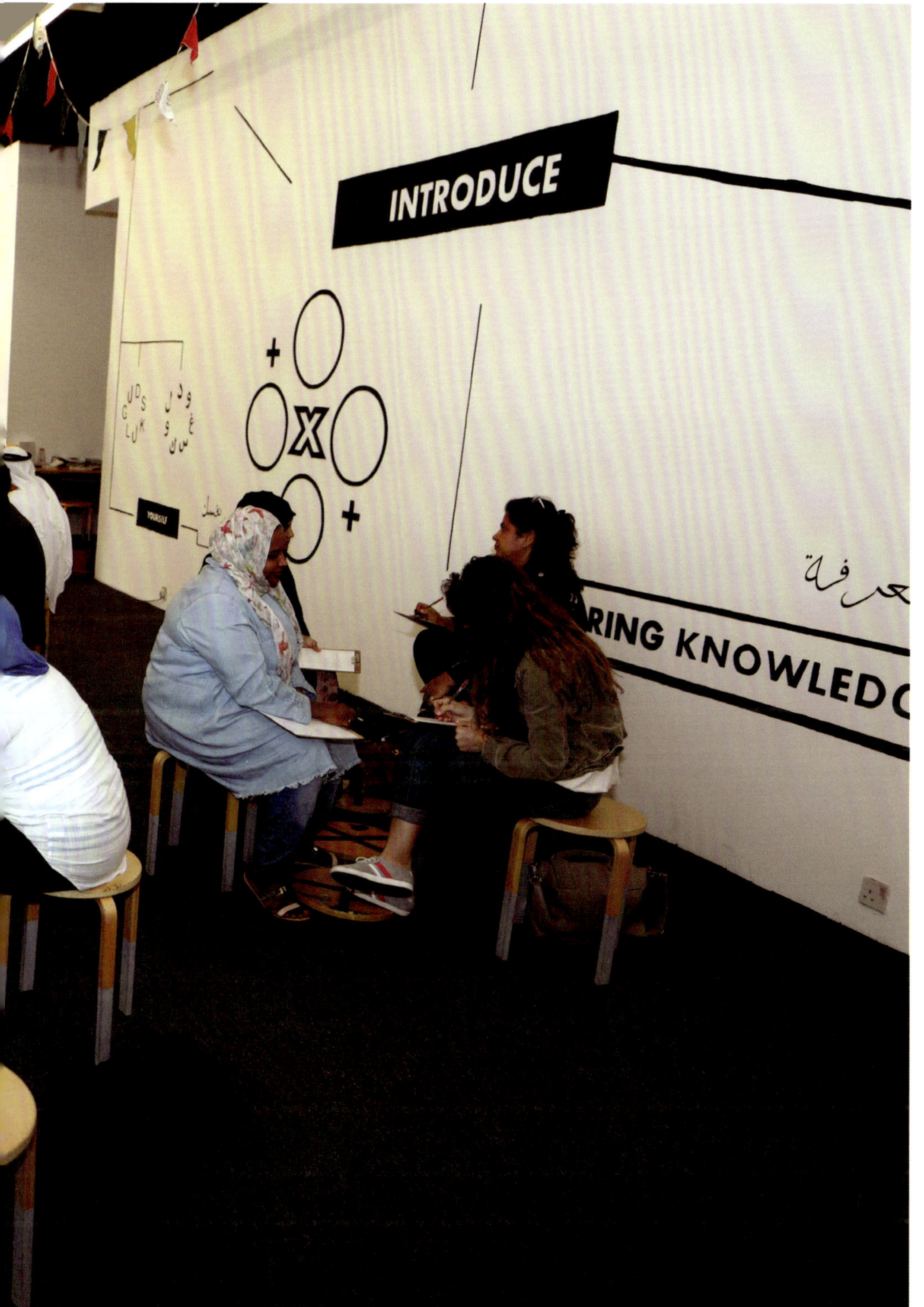
INTRODUCE
YOURSELF
RING KNOWLED

J o u r n e y B e y o n d t h
e A r r o w J o u r n e y B e
y o n d t h e A r r o w J o u
r n e y B e y o n d t h e A r
r o w J o u r n e y B e y o n
d t h e A r r o w J o u r n e
y B e y o n d t h e A r r o w
J o u r n e y B e y o n d t h
e A r r o w J o u r n e y B e
y o n d t h e A r r o w J o u
r n e y B e y o n d t h e A r
r o w J o u r n e y B e y o n
d t h e A r r o w J o u r n e
y B e y o n d t h e A r r o w
J o u r n e y B e y o n d t h

e A r r o w J o u r n e y B e

y o n d t h e A r r o w J o u

r n e y B e y o n d t h e A r

r o w L i s t o f w o r k s J

o u r n e y B e y o n d t h e

A r r o w J o u r n e y B e y

o n d t h e A r r o w J o u r

n e y B e y o n d t h e A r r

o w J o u r n e y B e y o n d

t h e A r r o w J o u r n e y

B e y o n d t h e A r r o w J

o u r n e y B e y o n d t h e

A r r o w J o u r n e y B e y

o n d t h e A r r o w J o u r

n e y B e y o n d t h e A r r

31st Century Museum of Contemporary Spirit in Sharjah
Perception Itself Is Action
2019
E-book
Commissioned by Sharjah Art Foundation

Documentation of *31st Century Museum of Contemporary Spirit in Bangkok - Land of Smiles*
2018
Single-channel video: colour, sound
14 minutes 21 seconds
Commissioned by Sharjah Art Foundation
Courtesy of Kamin Lertchaiprasert and Sound & Cloud, Bangkok

Itthipol Sakjaroanchaigul
The Hub Foundation
2018
Framed digital print on paper
36 x 51 cm
Collection of Kamin Lertchaiprasert

Kittikhun Munkit
Thank You
2018
Single-channel video: colour, sound
2 minutes 23 seconds
Collection of Kamin Lertchaiprasert

Kamin Lertchaiprasert
Panya Petchu
2018
2 coins
Dimensions variable
Courtesy of the artist

Treethep Silagailas
Uniform Shirt
2018
Acrylic paint on lab coat
Dimensions variable
Collection of Kamin Lertchaiprasert

Khadim Ali
In collaboration with Bamyan Art Space
Standing Flames
2019
From 'Flowers of Evil'
Acrylic, industrial paints, Dutch metal gold leaf on MDF
1785 x 539 cm
Commissioned by Sharjah Art Foundation
Courtesy of the artist

Khadim Ali
MoAB, Mother of All Bombs
2019
From 'Flowers of Evil'
Galvanised steel, hand woven rug, acrylic
780 x 210 cm (irregular)
Commissioned by Sharjah Art Foundation
Courtesy of the artist

Khadim Ali
In collaboration with Ali Baba Awrang
Metamorphoses
2019
From 'Flowers of Evil'
Paper gilded with copper leaf
Multiple components: dimensions variable
Commissioned by Sharjah Art Foundation
Courtesy of the artist

Khadim Ali
In collaboration with Mohammed Hadi Rahnaward and Aziz Hazara
I for Infidel, J for Jihad
Single-channel video: colour, sound; text book, posters, paper
16 minutes 13 seconds; dimensions variable
Commissioned by Sharjah Art Foundation
Courtesy of the artist

Khadim Ali
In case of emergency
2019
From 'Flowers of Evil'
Acrylic box, fabric, plywood, melamine oil paint and ink
Acrylic boxes: 90 x 70 cm each; Hammer 180 x 60 cm (irregular)
Commissioned by Sharjah Art Foundation
Courtesy of the artist

Khadim Ali
In collaboration with Sher Ali
Urbicide
2019
From 'Flowers of Evil'
11-channel sound: steel, metal, gold leaf; nylon thread on machine woven rug
Dimensions variable
Commissioned by Sharjah Art Foundation
Courtesy of the artist

Khadim Ali
Untitled 1
2019
From 'Flowers of Evil'
Gouache and ink on paper
90 x 139 cm
Commissioned by Sharjah Art Foundation
Courtesy of the artist

Khadim Ali
Untitled 2
2019
From 'Flowers of Evil'
Gouache and ink on paper
127.5 x 90 cm
Commissioned by Sharjah Art Foundation
Courtesy of the artist

Khadim Ali
Untitled 3
2019
From 'Flowers of Evil'
Gouache and ink on paper
86 x 134.5 cm
Commissioned by Sharjah Art Foundation
Courtesy of the artist

Khadim Ali
Untitled 4
2019
From 'Flowers of Evil'
Gouache and ink on wasli paper
55 x 71 cm
Commissioned by Sharjah Art Foundation
Courtesy of the artist

Khadim Ali
Untitled 5
2019
From 'Flowers of Evil'
Ink on gouache on paper
87 x 123 cm
Commissioned by Sharjah Art Foundation
Courtesy of the artist

Khadim Ali
Untitled 6
2019
From 'Flowers of Evil'
Gouache, ink and gold leaf on paper
100 x 70 cm
Commissioned by Sharjah Art Foundation
Courtesy of the artist

Khadim Ali
Untitled 7
2019
From 'Flowers of Evil'
Gouache, ink and gold leaf on paper
100 x 70 cm
Commissioned by Sharjah Art Foundation
Courtesy of the artist

Khadim Ali
Untitled 8
2019
From 'Flowers of Evil'
Gouache, ink and gold leaf on paper
100 x 70 cm
Commissioned by Sharjah Art Foundation
Courtesy of the artist

Khadim Ali
Untitled 9
2019
From 'Flowers of Evil'
Gouache, ink and gold leaf on wasli paper
55 x 71 cm
Commissioned by Sharjah Art Foundation
Courtesy of the artist

Khadim Ali
Untitled 10
2019
From 'Flowers of Evil'
Gouache, ink and gold leaf on wasli paper
55 x 71 cm
Commissioned by Sharjah Art Foundation
Courtesy of the artist

Khadim Ali
Untitled 11
2019
From 'Flowers of Evil'
Gouache, ink and gold leaf on wasli paper
70.4 x 55 cm
Commissioned by Sharjah Art Foundation
Courtesy of the artist

Khadim Ali
Untitled 12
2019
From 'Flowers of Evil'
Gouache, ink and gold leaf on paper
98.5 x 64 cm
Commissioned by Sharjah Art Foundation
Courtesy of the artist

Khadim Ali
Untitled 13
2019
From 'Flowers of Evil'
Hand and machine embroidery stitched on fabric and dye
662 x 153 cm
Commissioned by Sharjah Art Foundation
Courtesy of the artist

Khadim Ali
Untitled 14
2019
From 'Flowers of Evil'
Hand and machine embroidery stitched on fabric and dye
214 x 173 cm
Commissioned by Sharjah Art Foundation
Courtesy of the artist

Khadim Ali
Untitled 15
2019
From 'Flowers of Evil'
Hand and machine embroidery stitched on fabric and dye
203 x 142 cm
Commissioned by Sharjah Art Foundation
Courtesy of the artist

Khadim Ali
Untitled 16
2019
From 'Flowers of Evil'
Hand and machine embroidery stitched on fabric and dye
195 x 126 cm
Commissioned by Sharjah Art Foundation
Courtesy of the artist

Khadim Ali
Untitled 17
2019
From 'Flowers of Evil'
Hand and machine embroidery stitched on fabric and dye
194 x 167 cm
Commissioned by Sharjah Art Foundation
Courtesy of the artist

Khadim Ali
Untitled 18
2019
From 'Flowers of Evil'
Hand and machine embroidery stitched on fabric and dye
220 x 153 cm
Commissioned by Sharjah Art Foundation
Courtesy of the artist

Antariksa
Co-Prosperity #3
2019
Curated display of artwork and archival material
Commissioned by Sharjah Art Foundation

Featuring the following artists and works:

Makoto Murata
Petit Senso-ga
2016
153 miniature paintings: oil on board
Dimensions variable
Courtesy of Makoto Murata and SNOW Contemporary, Tokyo

Tsuyoshi Ozawa
'Painter F Song' from 'The Return of Painter F'
2015
Single channel video: colour, sound
12 minutes 13 seconds
Courtesy of Tsuyoshi Ozawa

Antariksa
Japanese collaborators
2019
110,000 copies of paper, printed in UV sensitive invisible ink
21 x 29 cm each
Commissioned by Sharjah Art Foundation
Courtesy of Antariksa

Japanese propaganda magazine archive #1–11
c. 1942
Paper, wooden frame with glass
Dimensions variable
Courtesy of Antariksa

Catalogue of The National Museum of Modern Art Tokyo Collection
Date unknown
Softcover book
23 x 30 cm
Courtesy of Antariksa

Book of Japanese War Record Paintings
1944
Hardcover/box set book
30 x 42 cm
Courtesy of Antariksa

Reproduction of a selection of works by Saseo Ono from *Koempoelan Gambar2 Dalam Mengikoeti Perang Di Djawa* [Collection of Drawings When He Joined the War in Java], published by Japanese Propaganda Division, Java #1–8
1944
Paper, wooden frame with glass
Dimensions variable
Courtesy of Antariksa

Japanese Propaganda Banners (based on Japanese propaganda posters in Indonesia)
c. 1942
8 banners
275 x 100 cm each
Courtesy of Antariksa

Surya Wirawan
Lutung Kasarung #1
2017
Linocut on paper, wooden frame with glass
62 x 45 cm
Courtesy of Antariksa

Surya Wirawan
Lutung Kasarung #2
2017
Rubber, wooden frame with glass
62 x 45 cm
Courtesy of Antariksa

Shiraz Bayjoo
En Famille 1–9
2015
From 'En Famille'
Acrylic and resin on wood
47.5 x 30.5 x 2 cm
UK Government Art Collection
Courtesy of artist and UK Government Art Collection

Shiraz Bayjoo
Ile de France
2015
Single-channel video: HD Digital Super 16 mm, colour, sound
31 minutes 18 seconds
Courtesy of the artist and Ed Cross Fine Art, London

Shiraz Bayjoo
Ile de France
2012
Acrylic, resin, reclaimed furniture
45 x 36 x 10 cm
Courtesy of the artist and Ed Cross Fine Art, London

Shiraz Bayjoo
Le grand L'Ile
2012
Acrylic, resin, reclaimed furniture
45 x 36 x 10 cm
Courtesy of the artist and Ed Cross Fine Art, London

Shiraz Bayjoo
Madagascar
2017
From 'Ocean Miniatures'
Acrylic on board, resin, metal
24 x 17 x 15.5 cm
Courtesy of the artist and Ed Cross Fine Art, London

Shiraz Bayjoo
Ma Coeur 2
2017
From 'Ocean Miniatures'
Acrylic on board, resin, metal
16.5 x 10.5 x 7 cm
Courtesy of the artist and Ed Cross Fine Art, London

Shiraz Bayjoo
Aldabra No.2
2016
From 'Ocean Miniatures'
Acrylic on board, resin, wood
22.5 x 17 x 2 cm
Courtesy of the artist and Ed Cross Fine Art, London

Shiraz Bayjoo
Fig. 7
2016
From 'Ocean Miniatures'
Acrylic on board, resin, wood
12 x 17 x 2.5 cm
Courtesy of the artist and Ed Cross Fine Art, London

Shiraz Bayjoo
My Old Place 1–12
2019
From 'My Old Place'
Giclée print on Hahnemühle
50 x 34.15 cm each
Courtesy of the artist and Ed Cross Fine Art, London

Shiraz Bayjoo
Port Hole (Triptych) Part 1, 2, 3
2017
Acrylic and resin on board with reclaimed wooden frame
35 x 50 x 3 cm each; irregular
Courtesy of the artist and Ed Cross Fine Art, London

Adriana Bustos
Playing History 2018
2019
From 'Vision Machine'
Watercolour on paper
50 x 40 cm
Courtesy of the artist

Adriana Bustos
Saigon Bunker 2018
2019
From 'Vision Machine'
Graphite, digital print on paper
50 x 40 cm
Courtesy of the artist

Adriana Bustos
Sojourner Truth 2018
2019
From 'Vision Machine'
Graphite, digital print on paper
55 x 45 cm
Courtesy of the artist

Adriana Bustos
Manhattan Project 2018
2019
From 'Vision Machine'
Graphite, watercolour paper
70 x 65 cm
Courtesy of the artist

Adriana Bustos
Machu Picchu 2018
2019
From 'Vision Machine'
Graphite, digital print on paper
60 x 55 cm
Courtesy of the artist

Adriana Bustos
Playboy Bed 2018
2019
From 'Vision Machine'
Watercolour on paper
75 x 50 cm
Courtesy of the artist

Adriana Bustos
Turner 2018
2019
From 'Vision Machine'
Watercolour on paper
55 x 45 cm
Courtesy of the artist

Adriana Bustos
How to use a gun 2018
From 'Vision Machine'
2019
Watercolour on paper
70 x 70 cm
Courtesy of the artist

Adriana Bustos
Massinger 2018
2019
From 'Vision Machine'
Graphite, digital print on paper
65 x 65 cm
Courtesy of the artist

Adriana Bustos
Kapeluz Indian 2018
2019
From 'Vision Machine'
Watercolour on paper
70 x 50 cm
Courtesy of the artist

Adriana Bustos
End of the World 2018
2019
From 'Vision Machine'
Watercolour on paper
75 x 60 cm
Courtesy of the artist

Adriana Bustos
Happy World 2018
2019
From 'Vision Machine'
Watercolour on paper
70 x 55 cm
Courtesy of the artist

Adriana Bustos
Ops room 2018
2019
From 'Vision Machine'
Watercolour on paper
70 x 40 cm
Courtesy of the artist

Adriana Bustos
Venus Planisphere 2018
2019
From 'Vision Machine'
Acrylic, graphite, silver leaf on canvas
180 x 180 cm
Courtesy of the artist and Nora Fisch Contemporary Art, Buenos Aires

Adriana Bustos
Official Territory 2018
2019
From 'Vision Machine'
Acrylic, graphite, silver leaf on canvas
180 x 180 cm
Courtesy of the artist and Nora Fisch Contemporary Art, Buenos Aires

Adriana Bustos
The sea and its multiple affluences 2017
2019
From 'Vision Machine'
Acrylic and graphite on canvas
45 x 600 cm
Courtesy of the artist

Adriana Bustos
Atlantic Complex 2017
2019
From 'Vision Machine'
90 watercolour on paper
20 cm diameter each
Courtesy of the artist

Rohini Devasher
Spheres
2017
Single-channel video projection: colour, sound; metallic paint, pan pastel, dry pastel, acrylic, charcoal, pencil, colour pencil on wall
22 minutes; dimensions variable
Courtesy of the artist and Project 88, Mumbai

Léuli Eshrāghi
tagatanu'u
March 7, 2019
Performance with installation: sand, coconuts, coconut water, coconut milk, turmeric-infused water, charcoal, ochre, macadamia nuts, mylar emergency blankets, coconut scraping stool, metal bowls, books, digital images as slide presentation, cushions, rugs, plants
Dimensions variable
Commissioned by Sharjah Art Foundation
Courtesy of the artist

Gudskul
Knowledge Market: Speculative Collective
2019
Participatory activity drawings, mural, stickers, carpets
Dimensions variable
Commissioned by Sharjah Art Foundation
Courtesy of Gudskul

Kawayan de Guia
Popular Extinctions
2019
35 mm celluloid film, metal, wood; single-channel video: colour
11 minutes; Dimensions variable
Commissioned by Sharjah Art Foundation
Courtesy of the artist

Anawana Haloba
A Dragon King in Sleepy Pride Rock
2019
Installation: synchronised animations with sound, postcards, prints, old televisions, train rail, dried maize cobs
Dimensions variable
Commissioned by Sharjah Art Foundation
Courtesy of the artist and Norsk Kulturråd, Oslo

Ho Tzu Nyen
R for Resonance
2019
From 'Critical Dictionary of South East Asia', 2012–ongoing
Installation with VR 360-degree video, ambisonic sound through headphones, single-channel HD video projection, 5-channel sound
Dimensions variable
Commissioned by Sharjah Art Foundation
Courtesy of the artist and Edouard Malingue Gallery, Hong Kong

Roslisham (ISE) Ismail
ChronoLOGICal
2015
Mixed media
Dimensions variable
Courtesy of the artist

Meiro Koizumi
The Angels of Testimony
2019
3-channel video installation: colour, sound; archival materials
47 minutes; dimensions variable
Commissioned by Sharjah Art Foundation
Courtesy of the artist, Annet Gelink Gallery, Amsterdam and MUJIN-TO Production, Tokyo

Jompet Kuswidananto
Keroncong Concordia
2019
Sculptural video installation: 3-channel video: colour, sound; glass, metal, light, carpets
15 minutes 33 seconds; dimensions variable
Commissioned by Sharjah Art Foundation
Courtesy of the artist

Nalini Malani
All We Imagine as Light
2017
11-panel reverse paintings on acrylic
187 x 106 cm each
Burger Collection, Hong Kong
Courtesy of the artist and Burger Collection, Hong Kong

Lee Mingwei
The Letter Writing Project
1998/2019
Mixed media interactive installation, 3 wooden booths, writing paper, envelopes
290 x 170 x 231 cm each
Produced by Sharjah Art Foundation
Courtesy of the artist

Neo Muyanga
house of MAKEdbA
2019
Interactive installation: 2 record players, sound, animated photograph, objects, furniture, lamps
Dimensions variable; 15 minutes loop
Commissioned by Sharjah Art Foundation
Courtesy of the artist

Tuấn Andrew Nguyễn
The Specter of Ancestors Becoming
2019
4-channel video installation: colour, 7.1 surround sound; inkjet on canvas, oil on canvas, graphite on paper, C-prints, sand
28 minutes; dimensions variable
Commissioned by Sharjah Art Foundation
Produced by Sharjah Art Foundation with additional production support from the San Francisco Museum of Modern Art
Courtesy of the artist and James Cohan, New York

Ahmad Fuad Osman
Enrique de Malacca Memorial Project
2016–ongoing
Mixed media installation: 73 objects; two single-channel videos: colour, sound; 33 interactive video interviews, archival materials
Dimensions variable
Partially commissioned by Sharjah Art Foundation
Courtesy of the artist

Phan Thảo Nguyên
Mute Grain
2019
From 'Mute Grain'
Three-channel video installation: colour, sound
15 minutes 45 seconds
Commissioned by Sharjah Art Foundation
Courtesy of the artist

Phan Thảo Nguyên
Dream of March and August
2019
From 'Mute Grain'
Watercolour on silk
14 diptychs, 1 triptych; dimensions variable
Commissioned by Sharjah Art Foundation
Courtesy of the artist

Qiu Zhijie
One Has to Wander through All the Outer Worlds to Reach the Innermost Shrine at the End
2016
16 colour prints
246 x 97.8 cm each
Courtesy of the artist

Qiu Zhijie
Map of Gods - God Never Rests
2016
Ink on paper
300 x 126 cm
Courtesy of the artist

Qiu Zhijie
Map of Travelers - Human Outpost
2015
Ink on paper
300 x 126 cm
Courtesy of the artist

Qiu Zhijie
Map of Social Science - The Skeptics' Society
2016
Ink on paper
300 x 126 cm
Courtesy of the artist

Qiu Zhijie
Map of Religion - Some People Always Tend to Believe
2015
Ink on paper
300 x 126 cm
Courtesy of the artist

Qiu Zhijie
Map of Tools - Labor-Saving Utensils Generating More Labor
2017
Ink on paper
300 x 126 cm
Courtesy of the artist

Qiu Zhijie
The Circulation of Revolution
2015
Ink on paper
300 x 126 cm
Courtesy of the artist

Qiu Zhijie
Map of Games - Used to Being a Loser
2015
Ink on paper
300 x 126 cm
Courtesy of the artist

Qiu Zhijie
Map of Natural Science - The Great Chain of Being
2016
Ink on paper
300 x 126 cm
Courtesy of the artist

Qiu Zhijie
Map of Human Emotions - Both Despair and Hope Are Extinct Volcano
2015
Ink on paper
300 x 126 cm
Courtesy of the artist

Qiu Zhijie
Map of Social Relationships - The Social Animal
2016
Ink on paper
300 x 126 cm
Courtesy of the artist

Qiu Zhijie
Map of Garments - The Clothed World
2017
Ink on paper
300 x 126 cm
Courtesy of the artist

Qiu Zhijie
Map of Art and Everyday Life - The Poets Even Been Driven Out of the Republic by Plato
2015
Ink on paper
300 x 126 cm
Courtesy of the artist

Qiu Zhijie
Map of Fate - Heaven's Movement Is Ever Vigorous
2016
Ink on paper
300 x 126 cm
Courtesy of the artist

Qiu Zhijie
Map of China-Arabs
2019
6 colour-print scrolls
246 x 97.8 cm
Commissioned by Sharjah Art Foundation
Courtesy of the artist

Lisa Reihana
Nomads of the Sea
2019
4-channel 3D UHD video: multi-channel audio, steel, lighting installation with sculptural components
19 minutes; dimensions variable
Co-commissioned by Sharjah Art Foundation and Creative New Zealand, Nga Aho Whakaari, Te Taura Whiri Maori Language Commission and Jan Warburton Charitable Trust. Co-produced by Artprojects and Reihanamations Ltd
Courtesy of the artist and Artprojects, New Zealand

Mark Salvatus
Notes from the New World
2015–2019
Multimedia installation with 2-channel video; assemblage and collage of magazine clippings; books; archival photographs from Lopez Museum & Library in Manila; drawings; found vinyl records; vinyl covers, vinyl players
12 minutes 24 seconds; dimensions variable
Partially commissioned by Sharjah Art Foundation
Courtesy of the artist and Salvage Projects

Ampannee Satoh
Untitled 1–6
2019
From 'TUGU 1370 : 1425'
Archival pigment ink print on photo rag Baryta Hahnemuhle
50.8 x 63.5 cm each
Commissioned by Sharjah Art Foundation
Courtesy of the artist

Ampannee Satoh
Untitled 7
2019
From 'TUGU 1370 : 1425'
Lamda print on sliver gelatin paper – Kodak Endura Professional Archival
120 x 180 cm
Commissioned by Sharjah Art Foundation
Courtesy of the artist

Ampannee Satoh
Untitled 8
2019
From 'TUGU 1370 : 1425'
Lamda print on sliver gelatin paper – Kodak Endura Professional Archival
8 x 10 cm
Commissioned by Sharjah Art Foundation
Courtesy of the artist

Ampannee Satoh
Untitled 9
2019
From 'TUGU 1370 : 1425'
Single-channel video: colour, sound
10 minutes
Commissioned by Sharjah Art Foundation
Courtesy of the artist

T. Shanaathanan
Check point I - VIII
2009/2019
From 'Check point'
Mixed media on paper
75 x 56 cm each
Courtesy of the artist

T. Shanaathanan
Drawers of War Transactions
2019
8 wooden chest of drawers, archival materials
150 x 60 x 56 cm each
Commissioned by Sharjah Art Foundation
Courtesy of the artist

Kidlat Tahimik
Ang Ma-bagyong Sabungan ng 2 Bathala ng Hangin, A Stormy Clash Between 2 Goddesses of the Winds (WW III – the Protracted Kultur *War)*
2019
Wooden carved icons, ritual objects, interwoven C-print photographs, projected images, audio, mosaic, rattan-basket figurines, back-strap bamboo loom, wrought-iron launch-pads, fibreglass, root sculptures, rotten fishing boats, sawdust, bamboo fences and runo-reed fauna
Dimensions variable
Commissioned by Sharjah Art Foundation
Courtesy of the artist

Kidlat Tahimik
Mababangong Bangungot [Perfumed Nightmare] (1977)
Director: Kidlat Tahimik
The Philippines
Narrative | 93 minutes
Tagalog with English and Arabic subtitles

Kidlat Tahimik
Balikbayan #1: Memories of Overdevelopment, Redux VI (1979–2015 and ongoing)
Director: Kidlat Tahimik
The Philippines
Narrative | 168 minutes
Tagalog with English and Arabic subtitles

Kidlat Tahimik
Turumba (1983)
Director: Kidlat Tahimik
The Philippines
Narrative | 90 minutes
Tagalog with English and Arabic subtitles

Kidlat Tahimik
Banal Kahoy - Holy Wood (1995)
Director: Kidlat Tahimik
The Philippines
Narrative | 44 minutes
English with Arabic subtitles

Kidlat Tahimik
Bakit Dilaw Ang Kulay ng Bahaghari [Why Is Yellow the Middle of the Rainbow? a.k.a. I am Furious... Yellow] (1980–1994)
Director: Kidlat Tahimik
The Philippines
Narrative | 175 minutes
English with Arabic subtitles

Kidlat Tahimik
Sinong Lumikha ng Yoyo? Sinong Lumikha ng Moon Buggy? [Who Invented the Yo-Yo? Who Invented the Moon Buggy?] (1978–1981)
Director: Kidlat Tahimik
The Philippines
Narrative | 95 minutes
English with Arabic subtitles

Lantian Xie
Romance Section
2016–2019
All the books from the romance section at a used book shop
Dimensions variable
Partially produced by Sharjah Art Foundation
Courtesy of the artist and Grey Noise, Dubai

Xu Zhen
The Starving of Sudan
2008
21 C-print on Dibond
120 x 80 cm each
Courtesy of the artist and Long March Space, Beijing

Xu Zhen
The Starving of Sudan
2008
Single-channel video: colour, sound
12 minutes 11 seconds
Courtesy of the artist and Long March Space, Beijing

n e y B e y o n d t h e A r r

o w J o u r n e y B e y o n d

t h e A r r o w J o u r n e y

B e y o n d t h e A r r o w J

o u r n e y B e y o n d t h e

A r r o w J o u r n e y B e y

o n d t h e A r r o w J o u r

n e y B e y o n d t h e A r r

o w J o u r n e y B e y o n d

t h e A r r o w J o u r n e y

B e y o n d t h e A r r o w J

o u r n e y B e y o n d t h e

A r r o w J o u r n e y B e y

o n d t h e A r r o w J o u r

n e y B e y o n d t h e A r r

J o u r n e y B e y o n d t h

e A r r o w J o u r n e y B e

y o n d t h e A r r o w J o u

r n e y B e y o n d B i b l i

o g r a p h y t h e A r r o w

J o u r n e y B e y o n d t h

e A r r o w J o u r n e y B e

y o n d h e A r r o w J o u r

n e y B e y o n d t h e A r r

o w J o u r n e y B e y o n d

t h e A r r o w J o u r n e y

B e y o n d t h e A r r o w J

o u r n e y B e y o n d t h e

A r r o w J o u r n e y B e y

o n d t h e A r r o w J o u r

31st Century Museum of Contemporary Spirit

Krishnamurti, Jiddu. *The Revolution from Within*. Prescott, AZ: Hohm Press, 2009.

Krishnamurti, Jiddu, and David Bohm, Dr. *The Ending of Time*. San Francisco, CA: HarperOne, 1985.

Bohm, David. *On Creativity*. Routledge Classics. Routledge, 2004.

Speech: Jack Ma on LQ

Adriana Bustos

Mbembe, Achille. *Critique De La Raison Nègre*. Paris: La Decouverte, 2013.

Mbembe, Achille. *Politiques De L'inimitié*. Paris: La Découverte, 2016.

Taussig, Michael. *Shamanism, Colonialism, and the Wild Man: A Study in Terror and Healing*. Chicago, IL: University of Chicago Press, 1987.

Taussig, Michael. *My Cocaine Museum*. Carpenter Lectures. Chicago, IL: University of Chicago Press, 2004.

Taussig, Michael. *The Magic of the State*. New York, NY: Routledge, 1997.

Blázquez, Gustavo. "Yuppies, Junkies, and Mules: Narcotic Subjectivities, Dialectical Images, and Contemporary Art in Córdoba (Argentina)." *Emisférica: #narcomachine* 8, no. 2 (2010). https://hemisphericinstitute.org/en/emisferica-82/blazquez.html#_edn1.

Ahmad Fuad Osman

Pigafetta, Antonio. *The Voyage of Magellan: The Journal of Antonio Pigafetta*. Translated by Paula Spurlin Paige. Prentice Hall, 1969. From the edition in the William L. Clements Library

Pigafetta, Antonio. *First Voyage Around the World by Magellan*. Printed for the Hakluyt Society, 1874.
"The Genoese Pilot's Account of Magellan's Voyage." ibid, 1-20.
"Narrative of the Anonymous Portuguese." ibid, 30-32.
"Pigafetta's Treatise of Navigation." ibid, 164-74.
"Names of the First Circumnavigators." ibid, 175 – 176
"Magellan's Order of the Day in the Straits." ibid, 177 – 178
"A Letter of Maximilianus Transylvanus (to the Most Reverend

Cardinal of Salzburg).” ibid, 179 - 210
“Log Book of Francisco Alvo or Alvaro.” ibid, 211 – 236
“Account of the ‘Trinity’ and her Crew.” ibid, 237 – 242
“Account of the Mutiny in Port St. Julian, and Gaspar Correa’s Account of the Voyage.” ibid, 243 – 256
“Cost of Magellan’s Fleet.” ibid, 257

Bergreen, Laurence. *Over the Edge of the World: Magellan’s Terrifying Circumnavigation of the Globe*. William Morrow and Company, 2003.

Boyle, David. *Voyages of Discovery*. Thames & Hudson, 2011. 66-83.

Brotton, Jerry. *A History of the World in Twelve Maps*. Penguin Books, 2012.

Pintado, Manuel J. *Portuguese Documents on Malacca, 1509-1511*. Kuala Lumpur: National Archives of Malaysia, 2012.

Pintado, Manuel J. *Malacca Historical Events and the Moves of Sultan Mohamude from 1512-1515 : Portuguese Printed Manuscripts and Their Translation into English*. 3 vols. Kuala Lumpur: National Archive of Malaysia, 2012/2015.

Pintado, Manuel J. *Malacca Historical Events and the Moves of Sultan Mohamude : Portuguese Printed Manuscripts and Their Translation into English. [Vol. 2] From 1516 to 1520*. Kuala Lumpur: National Archive of Malaysia, 2012.

Pires, Tomé. *The Suma Oriental of Tomé Pires: An Account of the East, from the Red Sea to Japan, Written in Malacca and India in 1512-1515, and the Book of Francisco Rodrigues, Rutter of a Voyage in the Red Sea, Nautical Rules, Almanack and Maps, Written and Drawn in the East before 1515*. Translated by Armando Cortesão. Vol. 1 and 2. London: Printed for the Hakluyt Society, 1944.

Alexander, Philip F. *The Earliest Voyages Round the World*, 1519-1617. Cambridge University Press, 1916. 1-84.

Hoffmann, Catherine, Helene Richard, and Emmanuelle Vagnon. *The Golden Age of Maritime Maps: When Europe Discovered the World*. Firefly Books, 2013.

Riffenburgh, Beau. *Mapping the World: The Story of Cartography*. Carlton Books, 2014.

Suárez, Thomas. *Early Mapping of Southeast Asia: The Epic Story of Seafarers, Adventurers, and Cartographers Who First Mapped the Regions between China and India*. Periplus Editions, 1999.

Turner, Jack. *Sejarah Rempah (Spice: The History of Temptation)*. Translated by Julia Absari. Jakarta: Komunitas Bambu, 2011. Originally published in English by Vintage Books, New York, 2005.

Sutarwala, Zahir, and Lucien De Guise. *Spice Journeys: Taste and Trade in the Islamic World*. Kuala Lumpur: Islamic Arts Museum Malaysia, 2006.

Burnet, Ian. *Spice Islands*. Rosenberg Publishing, 2011.

Loureiro, Rui Manuel. "Historical Notes on the Portuguese Fortress of Malacca (1511-1641)." *Revista De Cultura (International Edition) - Weapons, Forts and Military Strategies In East Asia - II*, July 2008, 78-96.

Abu Bakar, Yahaya. "Foreign Documents and the Descriptions of Melaka between A.D. 1505-1511." Proceedings of Malacca Seminar 1991. https://en.unesco.org/silkroad/knowledge-bank/religion-and-spirituality/foreign-documents-and-descriptions-melaka-between-ad-1505.

Fictions

Aminurrashid, Harun. *Panglima Awang*. Singapore: Pustaka Mĕlayu, 1958.

Talib, Abdul Latip. *Enrique Melaka*. PTS Publications, 2016.

Pacis, Carla M. *Enrique El Negro*. Cacho Publishing, 2003.

Yahya, Helmy, and Reinhard R. Tawas. *Enrique Maluku*. Jakarta: PT. Ufuk Publishing House, 2014.

Sah, Rosli Mohd. *Panglima Awang: Penguasa Lima Lautan*. Yamani Angle, 2014.

Cortés, Carlos. *Longitude: A Novel*. Philippine Writers Series. Quezon City: University of the Philippines Press, 1998.

Ampanee Satoh

Bungnag, P. (2004). Nayōbāi kān pokkhrǫng khǫng ratthabān Thai tǫ chāo Thai Mutsalim nai čhangwat chāidæn phāk tai Phǫ. Sǫ. (2475-2516) (Phim khrang thī 3) [The administrative policy of the government towards the Thai muslims in the southern provinces (1932-1973) (3nd ed.)]. Bangkok: Chulalongkorn University

Kobilin-Sing, W. (2005). Dusongyǫ sǫngphansīrǫikāosip'et thu'ng Tāk bai wipayōk (Phim khrang thī 3) [Dusun Nyor 1948 to Takbai tragic (3nd ed.)]. Bangkok: Ruam Duas Chuay Kan.

Nik Anuar Nik, Mahmud. (2006). Prawattisāt kāntǫsū 'ānāčhak Malāyū pāttānī 1785-1954 plæ dōi 'Apdunrǫya Pānæmālæ, Atthākorn Hayī'āwæ. (Phim khrang thī 1) [The History of the Malay Patani Struggle 1785-1954/ Translated by Abdulrahman Panamala, Atthakorn Hajiava. (1st ed.)]. Malaysia: Universiti Kebangsaan

Satha-anand, C. (2008). khwāmrunræng kap kānčhatkān khwām čhing pattānī nai rǫp ku'ng satawat (Phim khrang thī 1) [Violence and truth management, Pattani in the semi-century (1st ed.)]. Bangkok: Thammasat University

Anawana Haloba

Brautigam, Deborah. *The Dragon's Gift: The Real Story of China in Africa*. New York: Oxford University Press, 2009.

Brautigam, Deborah. *Will Africa Feed China?* New York, NY: Oxford University Press, 2015.

Moyo, Dambisa. *Winner Take All: China's Race for Resources and What It Means for the World*. New York, NY: Basic Books, 2012.

Moyo, Dambisa. *How the West Was Lost: Fifty Years of Economic Folly--and the Stark Choices Ahead*. Farrar, Straus and Giroux, 2011.

Center for International Private Enterprise (CIPE). "Proceedings of The New Great Game? China's Investment Model in the Developing World." YouTube video, 1:16:46. February 13, 2018. https://www.youtube.com/watch?v=TAQMzjMZl8M.

Ali, A. W. "China helps build TAZARA Railway to mark friendship." YouTube video, 2:41. March 27, 2013. https://www.youtube.com/watch?v=4nGFM1VFbKQ.

aaaricuny. “Living In Between: The Chinese in South Africa.” YouTube video, 1:18:34. March 20, 2012. https://www.youtube.com/watch?v=hqLW6XymO9k.

Mead, Nick Van. “China in Africa: Win-win Development, or a New Colonialism?” *The Guardian*, July 31, 2018. https://www.theguardian.com/cities/2018/jul/31/china-in-africa-win-win-development-or-a-new-colonialism.

“China’s Long History in Africa.” *New African*. March 11, 2015. https://newafricanmagazine.com/news-analysis/history/chinas-long-history-africa/.

Gadzala, Aleksandra W., ed. *Africa and China: How Africans and Their Governments Are Shaping Relations with China*. Rowman & Littlefield Publishers, 2015

Chutel, Lynsey. “No, China Is Not Taking over Zambia’s National Electricity Supplier. Not Yet, Anyway.” *Quartz Africa*. September 18, 2018. https://qz.com/africa/1391111/zambia-china-debt-crisis-tests-china-in-africa-relationship/.

Rotberg, Robert I. *China Into Africa: Trade, Aid, and Influence*. Brookings Institution Press, 2008.

Ya Salaam, Kalamu. “VISUAL ARTS: Africans In Chinese Communist Propaganda.” *Neo-Griot* (blog), January 10, 2014. http://kalamu.com/neogriot/2014/01/11/visual-arts-africans-in-chinese-communist-propaganda/.

Liyong, Taban Lo. *Another Nigger Dead: Poems*. Vol. 116. African Writers Series. Heinemann, 1972.

Liyong, Taban Lo. *Frantz Fanon’s Uneven Ribs*. Vol. 90. African Writers Series. Heinemann, 1971.

Antariska

Post, Peter, ed. *The Encyclopedia of Indonesia in the Pacific War*. Vol. 19. Handbook of Oriental Studies. Section 3 Southeast Asia. Leiden: Brill, 2009.

Ikeda, Asato, Aya Louisa McDonald, and Ming Tiampo, eds. *Art and War in Japan and Its Empire: 1931-1960*. Vol. 5. Japanese Visual Culture. Leiden: Brill, 2012.

Kaneko, Maki. *Mirroring the Japanese Empire: The Male Figure in Yōga*

Painting, 1930–1950. Vol. 14. Japanese Visual Culture. Leiden: Brill, 2016.

GUDSKUL

Simone, AbdouMaliq. *Jakarta: Drawing The City Near.* University of Minnesota Press, 2014.

Bey, Hakim. *T.A.Z.:The Temporary Autonomous Zone, Ontological Anarchy, Poetic Terrorism*. Autonomedia, 1991.

Freire, Paulo. *Pedagogy of the Oppressed*. 1968.

Rancière, Jacques. *The Ignorant Schoolmaster.* Stanford, CA: Stanford University Press, 1991.

Illich, Ivan. *Deschooling Society*. New York: Harper and Row, 1972.

Ho Tzu Nyen

Garland Encyclopedia of World Music (Book 4). 1st ed. Routledge, 1998.

Spiller, Henry. *Gamelan: The Traditional Sounds of Indonesia*. Santa Barbara, CA: ABC-CLIO, 2004.

Erlmann, Veit. *Reason and Resonance: A History of Modern Aurality*. Zone Books, 2010.

Kidlat Tahimik

Araneta, Gemma Cruz. "In Her Own Words." *Manila Bulletin*. August 30, 2018. https://news.mb.com.ph/2018/08/30/in-her-own-words/.

Acosta, Zofia. "4 Essential Works of Carmen Guerrero Nakpil." *Nolisoli.ph*. August 6, 2018. https://nolisoli.ph/47181/essential-works-carmen-guerrero-nakpil/.

Rufino, Marivic. "Historical Notes with Dynamite." *Business World Online*. June 18, 2012. http://www.bworldonline.com/content.php?section=Opinion&title=historical-notes-with-dynamite&id=53600

Rusling, James, General. "Interview with President William McKinley." *The Christian Advocate* (New York), January 22, 1903.

Wolff, Leon. *Little Brown Brother: How the United States Purchased and Pacified the Philippine Islands at the Century's Turn*. New York, NY: Doubleday, 1961.

Butterworth, Hezekiah. *The Story of Magellan and the Discovery of the Philippines*. New York, NY: D. Appleton and Company, 1899.

"Legend of Inhabian, Ifugao Goddess of Winds: Oral Transmission by Lopes Nauyac." Interview by Kidlat Tahimik. 1998.
Note: and subsequent taped talks with Mombaki Shamman Teofilo Gano and Mathhew Macadam.

Lantian Xie

Sarda, Shveta, and Azra Tabassum. *Trickster City: Writings from the Belly of the Metropolis*. Penguin Books India, 2010.

West, Kanye. The Life of Pablo. GOOD Music and Def Jam Recordings. February 14, 2016.

Yngrid, Heart. *Not Another Ghost Story*. 2012.

Lee Mingwei

Hyde, Lewis. *The Gift*. Vintage Books, 1983.

Koren, Leonard. *Wabi-Sabi for Artists, Designers, Poets & Philosophers*. Berkeley, CA: Stone Bridge Press, 1994.

Potts, Alex. *Allan Kaprow: Art as Life*. Los Angeles, CA: Getty Research Institute, 2008.

Léuli Eshrāghi

Teaiwa, Teresia. "Reading Gauguin's Noa Noa with Hau'ofa's Nederends: Militourism, Feminism and the 'Polynesian' Body." Edited by Stephen Muecke and Meaghan Morris. *UTS Review* 5, no. 1 (1993): 53-69.

Goodyear-Ka'ōpua, Noelani, and Bryan Kamaoli Kuwada. "Making 'Aha: Independent Hawaiian Pasts, Presents & Futures." *Daedalus* 147, no. 2 (Spring 2018): 49-59. doi:https://doi.org/10.1162/DAED_a_00489.

McMullin, Dan Taulapapa. "Fa'afafine Notes: On Tagaloa, Jesus, and Nafanua." Edited by Keith Camacho. *Amerasia Journal: Transoceanic Flows* 37, no. 3 (2011): 114-31.

Enomoto, Joy. "Where Will You Be? Why Black Lives Matter in the Hawaiian Kingdom." The Pōpolo Project. 2017. https://www.thepopoloproject.org/history-blog//where-will-you-be-why-black-lives-matter-in-the-hawaiian-kingdom.

Lisa Reihana

Maning, Frederick Edward. *Old New Zealand: A Tale of the Good Old Times by a Pakeha Maori*. Auckland: Robert J. Creighton & Alfred Scales, 1863.

Ormsby, Mary Louise. "Charlotte Badger." In *Dictionary of New Zealand Biography*, by Claudia Orange and W. H. Oliver. 1990. https://teara.govt.nz/en/biographies/1b1/badger-charlotte.

Black Sheep. "Pirate Mystery: The Story of Charlotte Badger." Radio New Zealand. March 19, 2018. https://www.radionz.co.nz/programmes/black-sheep/story/2018634264/pirate-mystery-the-story-of-charlotte-badger.

Mark Salvatus

Fermin, Jose D. *1904 World's Fair: The Filipino Experience*. Quezon City: University of the Philippines Press, 2004.

Yoder, Robert L. *In Performance: Walter Howard Loving and the Philippine Constabulary Band*. Manila: National Historical Commission of the Philippines, 2013.

Irving, D. R. M. *Colonial Counterpoint: Music in Early Modern Manila*. New York: Oxford University Press, 2010.

Meiro Koizumi

Grossman, Dave. *On Killing*. Boston, MA: Little, Brown and Company, 1995.

Van Der Kolk, Bessel. *The Body Keeps the Score: Brain, Mind, and Body in the Healing of Trauma*. New York, NY: Viking, 2014.

Utsumi, Aiko, Nobuhiro Kato, and Yoneko Ishida, eds. *The Two Battlefields of a Japanese Soldier—The Endless War of Hajime Kondo*. Tokyo: Shakaihyoronsha, 2005.

Nalini Malini

Das, Veena. "Language and Body: Transactions in the Construction of Pain." *Daedalus* 125, no. 1 (Winter 1996): 67-91.

Wolf, Christa. *Cassandra: A Novel and Four Essays*. New York, NY: Farrar, Straus and Giroux, 1984.

Devi, Mahasweta. *Breast Stories*. Translated by Gayatry Chakravorty Spivak. Kolkata: Seagull Books, 1997.

Faiz, Faiz Ahmed. "In Search of Vanished Blood." In *The Rebel's Silhouette: Selected Poems*, translated by Agha Shahid Ali. Amherst, MA: University of Massachusetts Press, 1995.

Ali, Agha Shahid. *The Country Without a Post Office*. New York, NY: W. W. Norton & Company, 1998.

Phan Thảo Nguyên

Archival Sources

Tao, Van, and Vietnam History Institute. *Oral Recordings of Vietnam Famine 1945 Witssesne.* from the archive of the Vietnam Revolution museum, Hanoi, Vietnam

Ninh, Vo An, *Photographs of Vietnam Famine 1954.* from the archive of the Vietnam Revolution museum, Hanoi, Vietnam

Published materials

Tao, Van, and Futura Moto. *The Vietnam Famine 1945, the Historical Records*. Tri Thuc Publishing House, 2013.

Hoai, To. *Dying of Hunger, from Old Stories of Hanoi*. Kim Dong Publishing House, 2003.

Mukherjee, Janam. Hungry Bengal War, Famine and the End of Empire. New York, NY: Oxford University Press, 2015.

Ali, Tariq Omar. *A Local History of Global Capital: Jute & Peasant Life in the Bengal Delta*. Princeton University Press, 2018.
Chattopadhyay, Bankim Chandra. *Anandamath*. E-book ed. 2016.

Hayashi, Fumiko. *Floating Clouds*. Columbia University Press, 2006.

Kawabata, Yasunari. *Palm of the Hand Stories*. FSG Classics, 2006.

Ishiguro, Kazuo. *An Artist of the Floating World*. Faber and Faber, 1986.

Akinari, Ueda. *Tales of Moonlight and Rain (Ugetsu Monogatari)*. Columbia University Press, 2007.

Du, Nguyen. *The Tale of Tu Thuc from Collection of Strange Tales (Truyen Ky Man Luc)*. Youth Publishing House, 2011.

Films

Floating Clouds. Directed by Mikio Naruse. Japan: Toho Co., Ltd., 1955.

Ugetsu. Directed by Kenji Mizoguchi. Japan: Daiei Film, 1953.

Akaler Shandhaney (In Search of Famine). Directed by Mrinal Sen. India: D. K. Films, 1981.

Ashani Sanket (Distant Thunder). Directed by Satyajit Ray. India: Balaka Movies, 1973.

Rohini Devasher

Clarke, Arthur C. *Rendezvous with Rama*. London: Victor Gollancz, 1973.

Indurkhya, Bipin. *Metaphor and Cognition*. James H Fetzer, Studies in Cognitive Systems ed. Dordrecht: Kluwer Academic Publishers, 1993.

Standish, David. *Hollow Earth: The Long and Curious History of Imagining Strange Lands, Fantastical Creatures, Advanced Civilizations, and Marvelous Machines Below the Earth's Surface*. Da Capo Press, 2006.

Lambert, Ladina Bezzola. *Imagining the Unimaginable: The Poetics of Early Modern Astronomy*. Rodopi, 2002.

Devasher, Rohini. "Strange-ing: Between Wonder and the Uncanny." *Technosphere Magazine*, June 2018. Sourced from https://technosphere-magazine.hkw.de/p/Strange-ing-Between-Wonder-and-the-Uncanny-d4vAUen6DpGSyhrMixkCa4

Shiraz Bayjoo

Vaughan, Megan. *Creating the Creole Island: Slavery in Eighteenth-Century Mauritius.* 2005.

Boswell, Rosabelle. *La Malaise Creole.* Berghahn Books, 2006.

Saint-Pierre, Bernardin De, and Jason Wilson. *Journey to Mauritius.* New York: Interlink Books, 2003. Originally published in 1775.

Demos, T. J. *Return To The Postcolony - Specters Of Colonialism In Contemporary Art.* Sternberg Press, 2013.

T. Shanaathanan

Jeganathan, Pradeep. "Checkpoint: Anthropology, Identity, and the State." In *Anthropology in the Margins of the State*, edited by Veena Das and Deborah Poole, 67-80. Santa Fe, NM: Santa Fe: School of American Research Press, 2004.

De Mel, Neloufer, and Chulani Kodikara. "The Limits of 'Doing' Justice: Compensation as Reparation in Post-War Sri Lanka." In *Violence and the Quest for Justice in South Asia*, edited by Deepak Mehta and Rahul Roy. Los Angeles, CA: SAGE Publications, 2018.

Shanaathanan, Thamotharampillai. "Commemorating Home: Art as Place Making, an Artist's Narration." *Journal of Material Culture* 20, no. 4 (2015): 415-28. doi:https://doi.org/10.1177/1359183515605858.

Tuấn Andrew Nguyễn

Saada, Emmanuelle. *Empire's Children: Race, Filiation, and Citizenship in the French Colonies.* University of Chicago Press, 2012.

Delanoë, Nelcya. *Poussières D'empires.* Presses Universitaires De France, 2002.

Ginio, Ruth. *The French Army and Its African Soldiers, The Years of Decolonization.* University of Nebraska Press, 2017.

J o u r n e y B e y o n d t h
e A r r o w J o u r n e y B e
y o n d t h e A r r o w J o u
r n e y B e y o n d t h e A r
r o w J o u r n e y B e y o n
d t h e A r r o w J o u r n e
y B e y o n d t h e A r r o w
J o u r n e y B e y o n d t h
e A r r o w J o u r n e y B e
y o n d t h e A r r o w J o u
r n e y B e y o n d t h e A r
r o w J o u r n e y B e y o n
d t h e A r r o w J o u r n e
y B e y o n d t h e A r r o w
J o u r n e y B e y o n d t h

e A r r o w J o u r n e y B e
y o n d t h e A r r o w J o u
r n e y B e y o n d t h e A r
r o w J o u r n e y B e y o n
d t h e A r r o w J o u r n e
y B e y o n d t h e A r r o w
C o n t r i b u t o r s J o u
r n e y B e y o n d t h e A r
r o w J o u r n e y B e y o n
d t h e A r r o w J o u r n e
y B e y o n d t h e A r r o w
J o u r n e y B e y o n d t h
e A r r o w J o u r n e y B e
y o n d t h e A r r o w J o u
r n e y B e y o n d t h e A r

Zoe Butt (Editor, Curator)
Zoe Butt is a curator and writer who lives in Vietnam. Her curatorial practice centres on building critically thinking and historically conscious artistic communities that foster dialogue amongst countries of the Global South. She is currently artistic director of the Factory Contemporary Arts Centre, Ho Chi Minh City, Vietnam's first purpose-built space for contemporary art. She formerly served as executive director and curator of Sàn Art, an independent contemporary art space in Ho Chi Minh City (2009–16); director of International Programs at Long March Project, Beijing (2007–09); and assistant curator of Contemporary Asian Art at the Queensland Art Gallery, Brisbane (2001–07). Her work has been published by Hatje Cantz; *ArtReview*; Independent Curators International; *ArtAsiaPacific*; Printed Project; Lalit Kala Akademi; JRP-Ringier; Routledge; Sternberg Press, amongst others. She is also a member of the Asian Art Council of the Solomon R. Guggenheim Museum in New York and, in 2015, was named a Young Global Leader of the World Economic Forum.

Lee Weng Choy (Associate Editor)
Lee Weng Choy is an independent art critic and consultant based in Kuala Lumpur. He is also the president of the Singapore section of the International Association of Art Critics. Previously, Lee was artistic co-director of The Substation in Singapore, and has taught at the School of the Art Institute of Chicago, the Chinese University of Hong Kong and Sotheby's Institute of Art – Singapore. He has done project work with various arts organisations, including Ilham Gallery and A+ Works of Art, both in Kuala Lumpur, as well as the NTU Centre for Contemporary Art Singapore and the National Gallery Singapore. Lee writes on contemporary art and culture in South East Asia, and his essays have appeared in journals, such as *Afterall*, and anthologies, including *Modern and Contemporary Southeast Asian Art*, *Over Here: International Perspectives on Art and Culture* and *Theory in Contemporary Art since 1985*.

Zakariya Amataya

A Thai poet with Malay roots in Southern Thailand, Zakariya Amataya is interested in global poetry. His translated work has been published regularly in international newspapers and journals. He founded thaipoetsociety.com and also ran poetry readings and events for many years. His first collection of free verse poems, *No Women in Poetry* (2010), was awarded the S.E.A. Write Award for Thailand in 2010. His second collection of poems was titled, *But in Us It Is Deep As The Sea* (2013). In 2011, he resided in Hawaii as part of the Doris Duke Foundation for Islamic Art's Artist in Residence Program. He also served as a judge for the *Phan-Wan-Fa* Thai Parliament Award Jury 2013 and the PEN International/New Voices Award Jury 2015. Since 2017, he has been the editor-in-chief of *The Melayu Review*. After a twenty-five-year hiatus in Bangkok and India, Zakariya moved back to his hometown of Narathiwat to write poems and collect stories and information about Thailand's complicated Deep South region. He plans to develop these narratives into novel form, as his daily routine ranges from attending lectures on literature to spending time amongst relevant regional and national educational institutes and organisations.

Anis Chouchene

Artist and poet Anis Chouchene is Tunisian by nationality, African by identity and human by belonging. Chouchene writes about and for humankind, telling stories emanating from his community to defend his existence and his generation. He calls for the embrace of peace as a common religion, dreams as a slogan, art as a weapon, the Earth as a home and difference as uniqueness. He affirms that 'the universe belongs to all of us'. Chouchene has been in charge of the cultural and artistic activities of the Manamty Society since 2014 and has participated in many arts performances and events related to his interests in poetry, music, dance, cinema and theatre. Chouchene has also been active in cultural activities and forums inside and outside Tunisia that are associated with human rights organisations and activists, including the Arab Institute for Human Rights, Amnesty International and Anna Lindh (2011–present).

Léuli Eshrāghi
Léuli Eshrāghi completed a PhD in Curatorial Practice at Monash University in 2018 and is the inaugural 2019 Horizon Postdoctoral Fellow with the Initiative for Indigenous Futures at Concordia University. He holds qualifications in indigenous arts management, francophone Great Ocean literature, indigenous studies and comparative cultural studies. Eshrāghi creates performances, installations, writing and curatorial projects centred on the body, ceremony, language renewal and hopeful futures. He exhibits and publishes regularly, and serves on the Aboriginal Curatorial Collective (Canada) board.

Sumit Mandal
Sumit Mandal is a historian at the University of Nottingham Malaysia who explores the connections that existed for centuries between societies separated by today's national boundaries. He focuses on the transregional histories of Muslim societies across the Indian Ocean, and is particularly interested in the place of the Malay world within those histories. In 2018, he published a book on the history and changing identities of Arabs in the Malay world titled *Becoming Arab: Creole Histories and Modern Identity in the Malay World*. He has also published articles on the cultural politics of Indonesia and Malaysia that have engaged the racialised politics of these nation states. In addition, Mandal has written on contemporary art and artists in both of these countries for academic publications as well as exhibition catalogues and magazines. His current research focuses on Muslim gravesite-shrines as historical inscriptions on the landscapes of the Malay world writ large (Indonesia, Malaysia and South Africa). He published an overview of the topic in 2012 in the journal *Modern Asian Studies*; a forthcoming article in *The Muslim World* relates the topic to transnational faith tourism in the Malay world.

Walter D. Mignolo

Walter D. Mignolo is the William Hane Wannamaker Professor of Romance Studies at the Trinity College of Arts and Sciences, a professor of Literature and the director of the Center for Global Studies and the Humanities at Duke University. He has been an associated researcher at Universidad Andina Simón Bolívar, Quito, since 2002, and an honorary research associate for CISA (Center for Indian Studies in South Africa), Wits University in Johannesburg. He is a senior advisor of the DOC (Dialogue of Civilizations) Research Institute, based in Berlin, and received a Doctor Honoris Causa Degree from the University National of Buenos Aires, Argentina (2016), and an Honoris Causa Degree from the University of London, Goldsmith (2018). Amongst his books related to the topic are: *The Darker Side of the Renaissance: Literacy, Territoriality and Colonization* (1995, translated into Chinese and Spanish); *Delinking: The Rhetoric of Modernity, the Logic of Coloniality and the Grammar of Decoloniality* (2007, translated into German, French, Swedish, Romanian and Spanish); *Local Histories/Global Designs: Coloniality, Subaltern Knowledges and Border Thinking* (2000, translated into Spanish, Portuguese and Korean); *The Idea of Latin America* (2006, translated into Spanish, Korean and Italian); and *The Darker Side of Western Modernity: Global Futures, Decolonial Options* (2011, translated into Korean), as well as *Estéticas y Opción Decolonial* (co-authored with Pedro Pablo Gómez, 2012); *On Decoloniality: Concepts, Analysis, Praxis* (co-authored with Catherine Walsh, 2018); and *Decolonial Politics: Colonial Differences and Border Thinking* (Duke Press, under contract).

Shubigi Rao

Singapore-based artist and writer Shubigi Rao makes layered installations of books, etchings, drawings, pseudo-scientific machines, metaphysical puzzles, video works, ideological board games and archives. These often immersive and tongue-in-cheek works demonstrate her diverse interest in subjects such as archaeology, neuroscience, libraries, archival systems, histories and lies, literature and violence, ecologies and natural history. Her current decade-long film, book and art project, *Pulp: A Short Biography of the Banished Book* (2016), is about the history of book destruction. The first portion of the project, *Written in the Margins*, won the Juror's Choice Award at the triennial APB Signature Art Prize 2018. Rao recently completed a residency at Künstlerhaus Bethanien, Berlin, and has presented solo exhibitions at Objectifs Centre for Photography and Film, Singapore; Künstlerhaus Bethanien; the National Museum of Singapore; Grey Projects, Singapore; and the Institute of Contemporary Arts Singapore.

Françoise Vergès

Françoise Vergès writes about the decolonisation of the arts, decolonial feminism, the racial Anthropocene, memories of slavery and colonisation. Since 2015, she has been curating the workshop L'Atelier with non-white artists in Paris and is also currently organising Decolonizing the Arts, a monthly seminar for her association's free university.

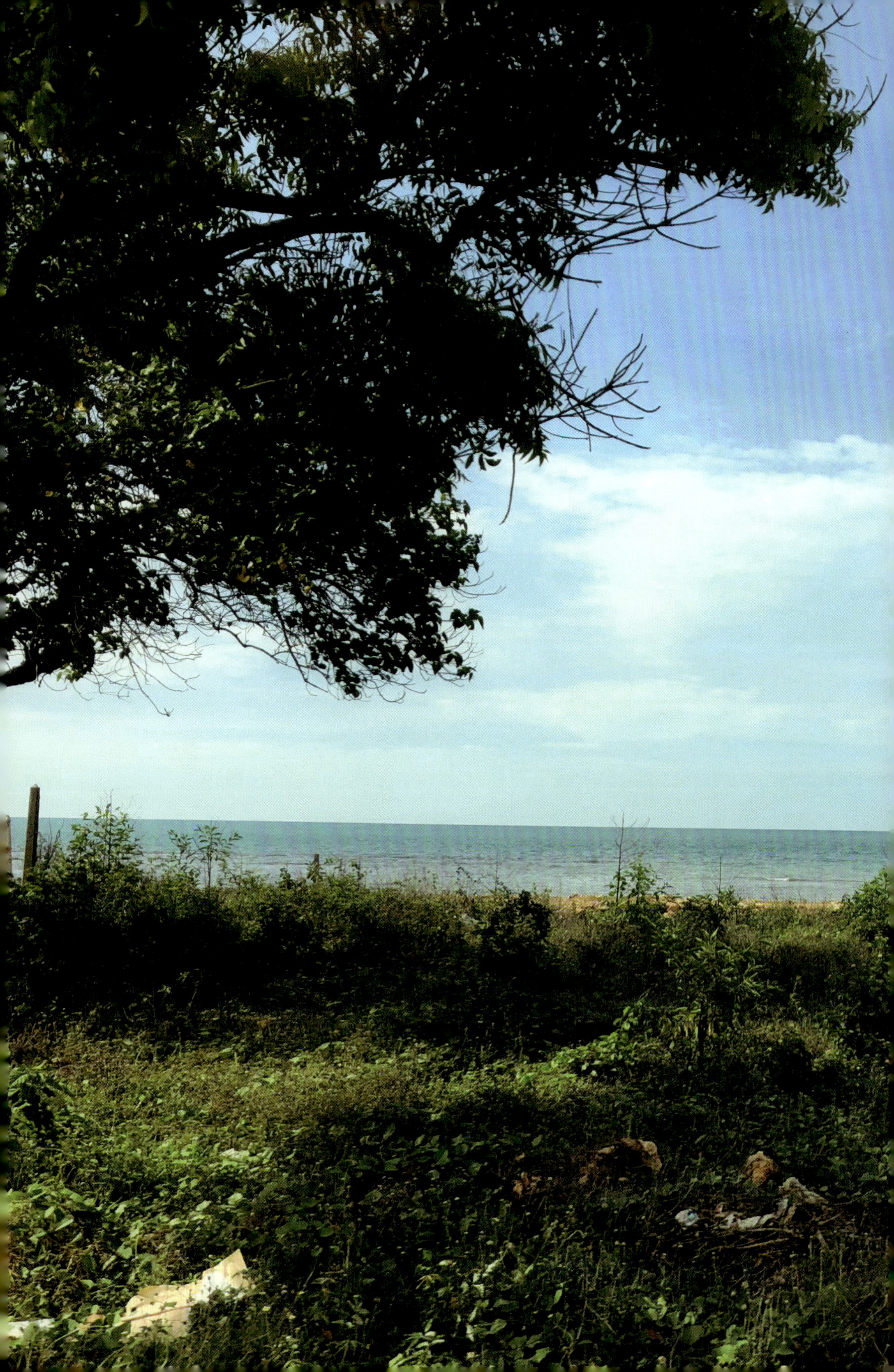

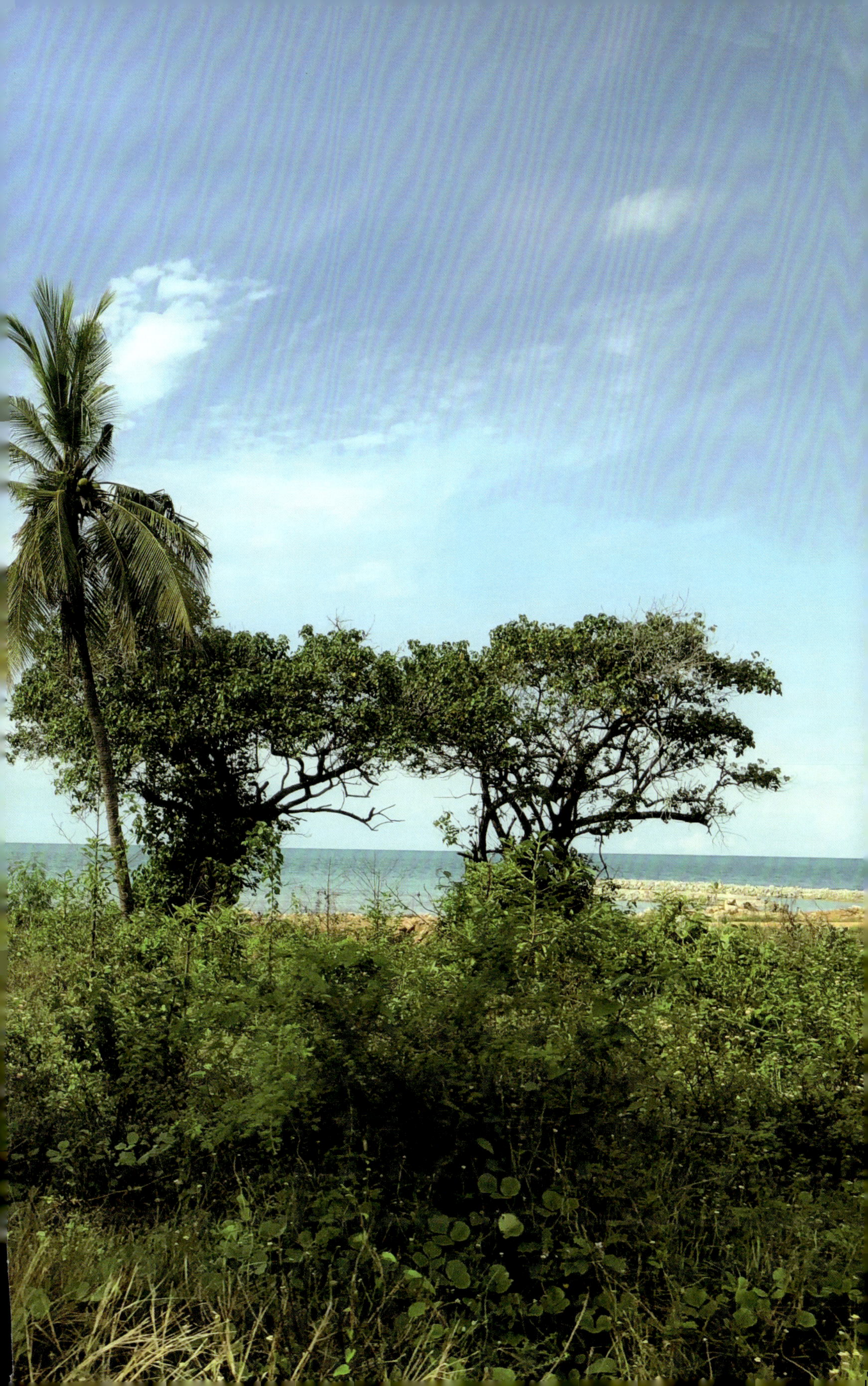

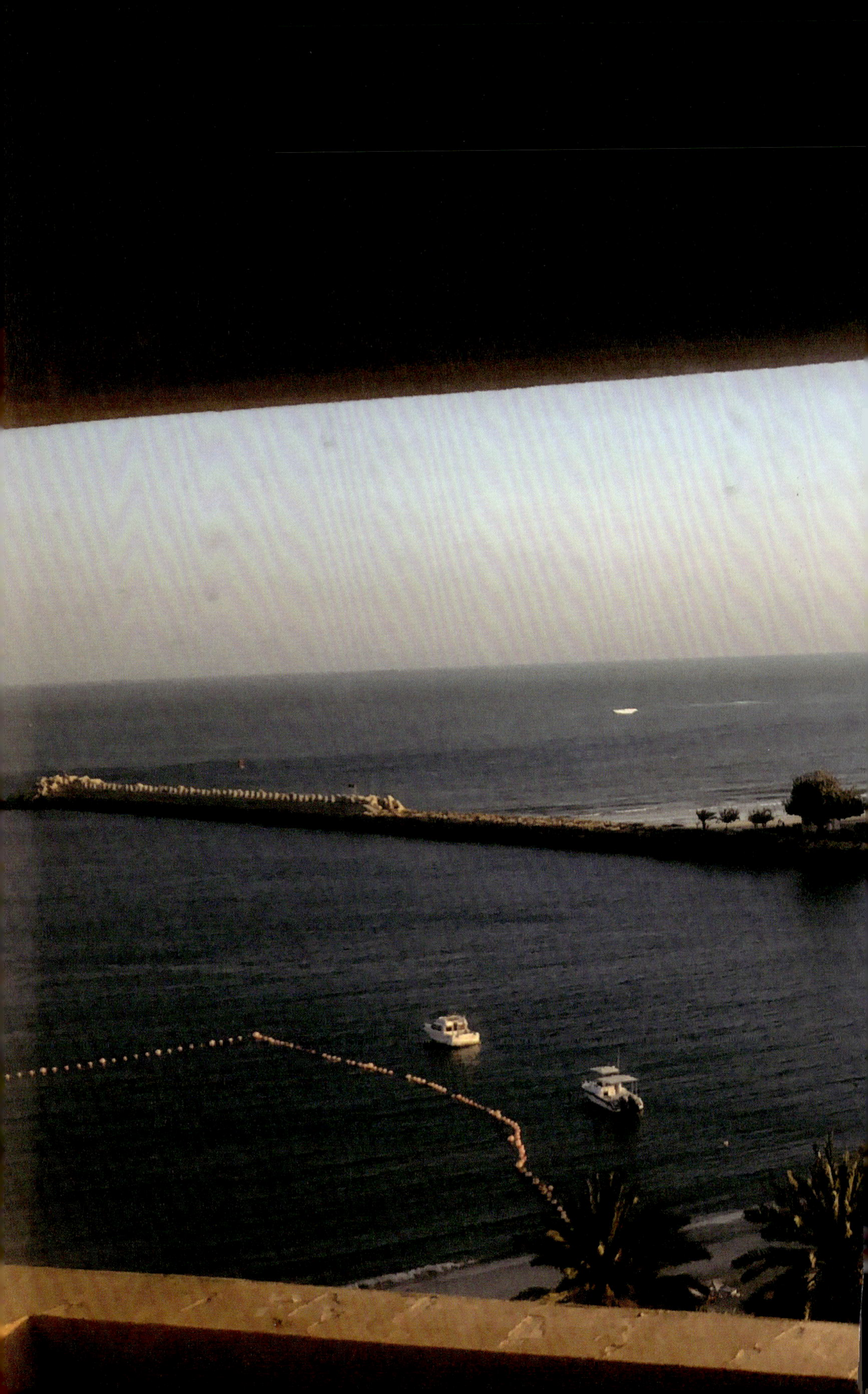

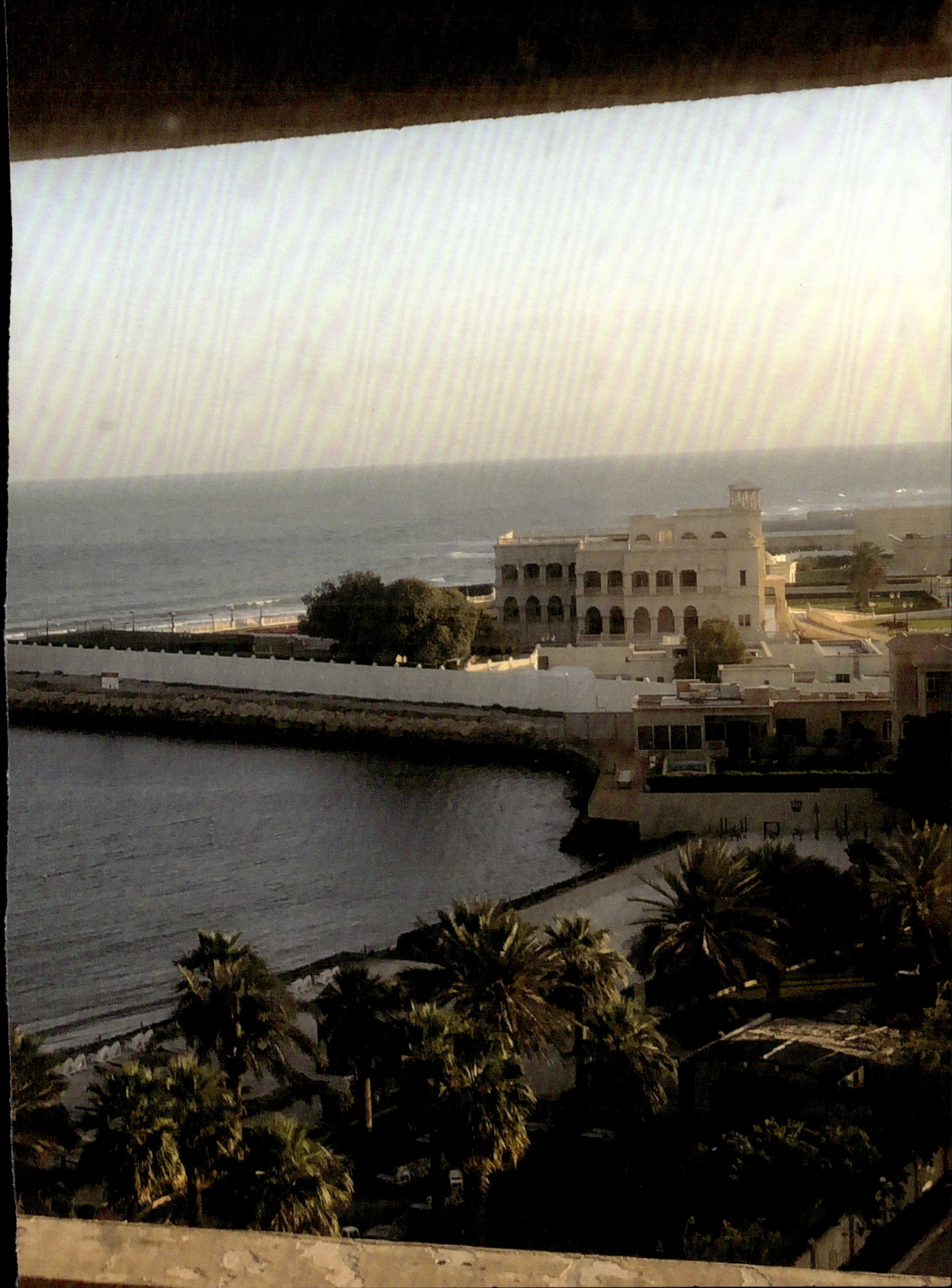